Work and the Family System

Work and the Family System

A Naturalistic Study of Working-Class and Lower-Middle-Class Families

Chaya S. Piotrkowski

THE FREE PRESS
A Division of Macmillan Publishing Co., Inc.
NEW YORK

Collier Macmillan Publishers
LONDON

For my parents,
Gabriel and Perla Piotrkowski

THE FREE PRESS
A Division of Macmillan Publishing Co., Inc.
866 Third Avenue, New York, N.Y.   10022

Collier Macmillan Canada, Ltd.

Library of Congress Catalog Card Number: 79-7478

Printed in the United States of America

printing number

1 2 3 4 5 6 7 8 9 10

Library of Congress Cataloging in Publication Data

Piotrkowski, Chaya S
    Work and the family system.

    Based on the author's thesis, University of Michigan.
    Bibliography: p.
    Includes index.
    1.   Family—United States.   2.   Labor and laboring
classes—United States.   3.   Middle classes—United
States.   4.   Work—Social aspects—United States.
5.   Housewives—Social aspects—United States.
I.   Title.
HQ536.P56   1979   301.42'0973   79-7478
ISBN 0-02-925340-5

Contents

List of Illustrations

Preface

In recent years there has been heightened interest among social scientists in the conjunction of work and family life, perhaps, as sociologist Rosabeth Moss Kanter (1977) has suggested, because of the increased employment of women outside the home, the new emphasis in psychology on the total life cycle, and a revival of interest in Marxian theory, all of which suggest connections between occupational experience and personal life.

My own interest in the quality of working life can be traced more easily. It stems from a view of the organization of productive life as important in understanding people's life experiences. As a graduate student in psychology, I investigated the literature on the relationships between work and mental health. My predisposition to consider occupational life as significant inclined me to ask about the possible interconnections between what usually are thought to be discrete phenomena. During this time, I also started working with emotionally troubled families in a mental health clinic. As I struggled to understand the complex processes I observed in these families, I began to wonder whether my clinical understanding could be enhanced by taking into consideration possible connections between psychologically significant familial processes and what occurred at family members' places of employment.

My experience as a teacher in a college program for working adults, most of whom were men employed in working-class and lower-middle-class occupations, further aroused my curiosity about the possibility that work and family life were meaningfully related. In our extended discussions, I noticed a curious duality in students' descriptions of their home and work lives. Although they asserted that their personal and occupational experiences were separate, the ways in which some of them described the day-to-day realities of their lives pointed to the existence of important interconnections. For example, they talked of lack of time with their wives and children as a result of their need to work overtime to maintain the family's standard of living and of their some-times frantic efforts to deal with familial concerns when they arrived home from work. They felt that their wives did not appreciate how hard they worked or the adverse conditions of their jobs; yet they reported that they rarely talked about their work at home. Though they sounded envious and angry as they described how they imagined women oc-cupied their days—watching television or spending their husbands' hard-earned money on shopping sprees—they had ambivalent feelings about their wives working outside the home. The physical separation of work and home seemed to create a gulf in understanding between hus-bands and wives and between fathers and children. These men some-times felt like "commodities" at home and at work.

Although these feelings were not shared by all, the themes emerged often enough to suggest that the separation of work and home that these men asserted might be "more myth than reality" (Aldous 1969). Com-mon sense also suggested to me the possible importance of work to a family's emotional life, for adults in our society spend most of their time in workplace and home settings. For example, examining employment statistics for one month in 1975, Hedges (1976) found that almost one-fourth of all full-time wage and salary workers spent more than forty hours per week at work at their principal jobs, excluding travel time. And Walker and Woods (1976) found that, in their sample, over half the nonemployed wives spent twenty-two to twenty-four hours at home. I wondered how "ordinary" families—in contrast to clinically troubled ones—fare in everyday life. I began to ask: what did we know about these relationships, and what did we have yet to learn?

The study reported here therefore describes my exploration of a deceivingly simple question: does work affect the quality of emotional life in families, and if so, how? In order to explore this issue, I inter-viewed at least one member of thirteen families, for a total of thirty men, women, and children. Two of these families also were observed in both their homes and places of employment. In most of these families, the husband-father was employed in a working-class or lower-middle-class occupation. Although my original question concerned paid work life, the concept of work soon came to include productive activities per-formed by the wife-mother in the home and without pay.

One might reasonably wonder to what extent my investigation was biased to perceive relationships where none existed. As long as the research procedure does not violate the integrity of the phenomena, the researcher's orientation is not necessarily harmful to the research en-deavor, for it can cause us to attend to relationships that had previously escaped notice. An important test of an approach that assumes that occupational experience has effects that range beyond the workplace is whether it helps us to uncover new data and articulate new situations for study, and whether it directs us to gaps in our knowledge (Sherman 1976). Though I assumed the importance of work life, I did not know whether it was indeed *meaningfully* related to what occurs within the family system, and I did not have concrete notions of what shape such meaningful interconnections might take. Moreover, I purposely included in my group of families some who saw no connections between their work and personal lives. Furthermore, findings were discussed with most research participants, who agreed that I had not done violence to their experience. (See Chapter 2 for a brief discussion of this collaborative procedure.)

In its emphasis on working-class families, this study can be viewed as part of an existing tradition (see, for example, Howell 1973; Komarovsky 1962; Lassen 1972; Rainwater, Coleman & Handel 1959; L. Rubin 1976; Sennett & Cobb 1972; Shostak & Gomberg 1964; and Terkel 1974). It departs from this tradition in that its scope is broader than studies focusing exclusively on work experience and narrower than studies attempting to describe family life or the marital relationship in general. The emphasis on the connections between work life and what occurs in the everyday emotional life of participating research families meant that a great many significant features of their lives only are touched upon or omitted altogether. Moreover, since my approach was unstructured and exploratory, in their interviews participants themselves determined, in part, the issues that were important.

I was not interested in marriage per se but rather in those aspects of the marital relationship that may be affected by work life. I do not deal directly with sex roles and the distribution of power in the marital relationship (see, for example, Safilios-Rothschild 1970), with socialization practices, with extended family networks (see Bott 1971), with the availability of community resources, or with the effects of unemployment (see, for example, Komarovsky 1940). Similarly, leisure is not treated as a substantive issue in its own right (see, for example, Meissner 1971). Although several dual-employee families are included in the research sample, the work experiences of employed women were not examined; similarly, single-parent, extended, and childless families were not included. The emphasis on two-parent families in which the wife-mother works within the home does not reflect an assumption that such families represent a desirable norm.[1] Rather, the decision to focus

[1]Over 50 percent of American families include two parents with children under 18 living at home (U.S. Bureau of the Census 1977). In 1975, 34 percent of husband–wife families conformed to the traditional model of breadwinner husband–homemaker wife. In 41 percent of such families both husbands and wives were in the labor force (Hayghe 1976).

on such families was made because of resource and time limitations and because of the need to simplify an already complex question about relationships between work and family life.

Our information about what occurs behind the doors of American homes is limited; researchers have studied families primarily in laboratory settings. This study is also part of a substantive and methodological tradition that utilizes naturalistic observation and in-depth interviewing of a small number of cases to enhance our understanding of how whole families function in everyday life (Bermann 1973; Golden 1975; Henry 1965; Hess & Handel 1957; Howell 1972; Kantor & Lehr 1975; Lewis 1959; Rapoport & Rapoport 1971). There are few such studies of whole families in situ and fewer still of clinically nontroubled ones. This study extends the growing body of substantive knowledge about ordinary families in their natural environment.

Unlike experimental research, qualitative research has no agreed-upon norms to guide the written presentation (Lofland 1974), for no neat dichotomy between findings and discussion exists. A problem in writing up these findings stemmed from the fact that the research focused on the connections between family and work systems. Systems imply interrelatedness; it is fitting that each theme should simultaneously touch on many others. Thus, themes did not emerge in a linear way, nor were "variables" connected in a simple one-to-one relationship. Writing, however, *is* linear, and so themes had to be treated one by one, as if they were independent, when in fact they are not.

Researching and writing about families are particularly perilous activities because the subject matter is emotionally compelling, for we have powerful conscious and unconscious feelings about them. This emotionalism is reflected in the current debate for and against the family as an institution. Whether or not present forms of the family will or should survive is a complex and difficult question that is beyond the purview of this book. My task was more modest: to understand and describe some of the forces that shape everyday emotional life in a few American families. In so doing, the study was meant to contribute to an understanding of families as related to other social institutions and to focus attention on a relationship between work and emotional life that is worthy of further study; to develop new hypotheses for further research; and to develop a conceptual framework that extends our understanding of work and family life. Despite the particular limitations of this study, I hope that what I uncovered in the investigation of a few families will prove relevant and thought-provoking to other mental health professionals, to those interested in work and mental health, and to those involved in formulating and evaluating social and organizational policies. Finally, I hope that what follows will be of interest and value to families themselves. Since the book is intended for the general reader as well as the interested professional, technical terms are explained when they are used.

The book is divided into four sections. Part I contains an overview of the relevant literature, a brief description of the goals of the study and the procedures followed, and a description of the research families. The interested reader is urged to consult the Methodological Appendix, in which the importance of qualitative and naturalistic research in the social sciences is detailed and the specific procedures of data collection and analysis are outlined. Part II presents the interview findings from a systematic perspective. Part III contains a case study of a single family—the Bernards—and explores the relationship between emotional and household life. In Part IV research findings are summarized and their implications are discussed.

Acknowledgments

Although they must remain anonymous, I am indebted to the research participants, whose openness and honesty made this project possible. My deepest gratitude goes to the Bernard family; I wish to thank them for their willingness to share their time and their lives with me. In his belief in the value of studying people in their natural settings, Eric Bermann served as a model and guide for me. Sheila Baler, Cary Cherniss, and Ann Hartman were supportive throughout the project. Joseph Pleck also provided valuable assistance.

This book is based in part on a doctoral dissertation undertaken at the University of Michigan. The study was partially supported by the H. Rackham School of Graduate Studies at the University of Michigan, which provided me with financial assistance in the form of a Rackham Predoctoral Dissertation Fellowship and a Rackham Dissertation Grant.

I would also like to thank Libby Slocum, Brian Tweedie, Jim Monroe, Maritza Cabrera, Paul Hench, and Nicholas Roomeliotis, who helped me with the often tedious tasks of coding data and transcribing tapes. My special thanks are extended to Gladys Topkis and Claude Conyers, of The Free Press. Their encouragement and forbearance saw me through the final stages of this project.

Finally, I am ever grateful to Sandy Orlow, who withstood the encroachment of the research project into our home life with remarkable equanimity. Not only did he do both his and my share of the cooking, cleaning, and shopping for several months, but he also typed endless drafts, made numerous and helpful suggestions, and proofread much of the manuscript. With great patience he managed the delicate task of knowing when to make suggestions, when to listen, and when to offer criticism. It was his friendship that enabled me to withstand those moments when the difficulties at hand seemed insurmountable.

PART I

Background
of the Study

Chapter 1 provides the background for this study of thirteen
families by introducing the reader to the topic of the relationship
of work and the family. Rather than presenting an exhaustive review of what has been written on the subject, the existing literature is examined from the point of view of the mental health
practioner and researcher interested in work and emotional well-
being and in the psychodynamics of family life. What emerges
from reviews of the research on work and mental health and of
clinical studies of families is that work and family life are viewed
as unrelated, separate spheres of human activity, particularly for
those in working-class occupations. This view is questioned and a
rationale is presented for using an exploratory, naturalistic research design for investigating the effects of work on the emotional life of families. The families who participated in the project
are described in Chapter 2, along with an overview of the
methods used for studying them.

Work and the Family

During the past twenty-five years, mental health professionals have become increasingly interested in the family—whether nuclear or extended—as the unit of treatment (Guerin 1976). An impressive clinical literature has emerged that attempts to understand the psychological life of people in terms of the transactions of whole families. The symptoms that individuals exhibit are understood as being intimately connected to the structure of interactions among family members (see, for example, Bateson 1960; Haley 1959a, 1959b; Jackson 1966; Minuchin 1974; Satir 1965; Wynne, Ryckoff, Day & Hirsch 1958). Moreover, this orientation assumes that current processes in the family can have profound impacts on the psychological well-being of its members.

The growing interest in families constitutes a movement away from a more traditional psychiatric orientation, an orientation that locates emotional difficulties in the individual patient; pathology is viewed as arising from early mother–infant interaction. The clinical spotlight on the mother–infant dyad has obscured the fact that they are part of a larger social field that may include not only the husband-father but also other family members. Rather than locate emotional difficulties only in very early development, the approach to the family as a whole attempts to illuminate the subtle interactions of ongoing family life that affect people in the present. Thus it is part of the emerging interest in life-cycle development.

To the study of whole families has been added the conceptualization of the family as a social system (see, for example, Hill 1974; Kantor & Lehr 1975). This approach implies that a family cannot be understood merely as a collection of individuals. Rather, it is a social group, continuous in time, composed of interdependent roles and people who interact according to implicit rules of psychological and social interaction. Individuals and interpersonal groupings, with their own histories and concerns, are subsystems within the larger system. A systems approach is useful because it forces us to look at what occurs among people as well as within them, and to search for coherent dynamic processes. Both the clinical research and theory on families have contributed to our understanding of the importance of microinteractional processes in families and the ways in which they facilitate or hinder the formation of personal identity and positive interpersonal relationships.

Opening Up the Family System

The difficulty with the concept of the family system as it is used by many mental health practioners is that the system implicitly is treated as closed and insular. Exclusive emphasis on the nuclear family unit implies that it is "suspended in time and isolated in space . . . outside of history" (Skolnick 1973, p. 44), following its own internal rules and unaffected by the world around it (Zaretsky 1976). One danger in this approach is that the family—instead of the patient or his or her mother—is viewed as the source of pathology, an orientation that may result in failures in therapeutic treatment (J. E. Bell 1970). In reality, families are relatively "open" systems; that is, they are embedded in a complex social structure and are connected to other social institutions in a variety of ways. Bell and Vogel (1960) have outlined some of the elaborate interchanges that occur between families and other social and cultural institutions.[1] Ecologically oriented therapists are beginning to turn their attention to the interconnections between families and other social systems (see, for example, Auerswald 1971; Culbert & Renshaw 1972; Hoffman & Long 1969; Mannino & Shore 1972).[2]

Work organizations are one type of social system to which families are connected. Despite the obvious importance of the job in people's lives—as judged by the amount of time spent working—mental health professionals have been remarkably oblivious to its possible effects. From her review of the literature, Golden concluded that "the clinical literature on families literally ignores the world of work, treating it as a dimension of life that has very little or no relevance to what happens in

1. Hill has described the family as a "'semi-closed system,' opening up *selectively* to transact business with other associations" (1974, p. 306). Speer (1970) has argued that the family should be thought of as internally open as well; that is, it also uses information from within the system as a basis for functioning and for changing its basic structure.

2. The ecological systems approach to family life focuses on the communications that occur in the interface regions between families and other social systems. Under this general rubric we might also include "network" therapies that include community and friendship networks in treatment (see, for example, Attneave 1976; Speck & Ruveni 1969).

4

the psycho-social interior of families" (1975, p. 19). Similarly, clinically oriented family researchers and theoreticians have neglected it, and suggestions for such research (J. E. Bell 1975; Riskin & Faunce 1972) generally have gone unheeded.

The research on work and mental health similarly treats families as unrelated to the world of work, although it has succeeded in making us aware that what people do for a living can affect them in psychologically significant ways (see, for example, Blauner 1964; Caplan, Cobb, French, Harrison & Pinneau 1975; Gurin, Veroff & Feld 1960; Kohn & Schooler 1973; Kornhauser 1965; Levinson 1969; Special Task Force 1973). It also suggests that those at the bottom of the occupational pyramid suffer the emotional effects of working in routine, monotonous, boring jobs. Those in the lower levels of the white-collar hierarchy—for example, clerical and sales workers—are also an especially strained group. Thus, people in such occupations constitute a particularly important focus for clinical research.[3]

Although traditionally oriented research does bridge the gap between personal life and work life, because its focus remains on the individual *within* the context of the job setting, it implicity considers work and family life to be distinct. Yet at the same time it hints at the importance of adopting a framework that considers the worker's family as part of the field of interest. For example, among Kornhauser's indices of the mental health of industrial workers was a measure of "hostility." Once we remember that "hostility" is an interpersonal construct, it becomes meaningful to ask in what ways feelings generated at the workplace can affect other family members and the processes of family life.[4] Even "self-esteem," an individual construct, can have interpersonal consequences. As Parsons (1955) has noted, the role of worker interpenetrates that of husband and father, for he occupies a "boundary role" between work and family spheres. In his recent review of the research on work and mental health, Kasl (1974) pointed to the need for studies of the relationship among life roles. One such study, by Mott, Mann, McLoughlin, and Warwick (1965), found that afternoon- and midnight-shift workers reported more difficulty in satisfactorily fulfilling their roles as husbands and fathers than did day-shift workers. The conceptualization of the family as a social system, which implies the interdependence of system parts, is useful here because it allows us to view

3. The research on work and mental health has been almost exclusively concerned with employed men; women have been "invisible" to sociologists of work (Oakley 1974a). The research on maternal employment was based on the fact of employment rather than its nature. (See Hoffman & Nye 1974.)

4. McKinley (1964), for example, tried to show that frustration generated in the occupational structure is related to the severity of a father's socialization practices toward his son.

5

the worker as intimately connected to others. Therefore, workplace stressors impinging on the worker may affect other family members.

The "Myth of Separate Worlds"

Despite the large amounts of time people spend in work and home settings, they themselves seem to conceive of these settings as unrelated. Most of the fathers interviewed by Aberle and Naegele (1952) reported no significant connections between their job situations and their behavior at home, and in her interviews with working-class couples Komarovsky (1962) found that most of the women rarely visited their husbands' places of work. Caplow (1954) has suggested that children often have only vague conceptions of their fathers' jobs because modern work is either highly abstract or fragmented. The world of work appears psychologically and physically remote from home life. Kanter has called this the "myth of separate worlds" and has described it as follows:

> In a modern industrial society work life and family life constitute two separate and non-overlapping worlds, with their own functions, territories, and behavioral rules. Each operates by its own laws and can be studied separately. If events or decisions in one world (such as wages awarded a worker) enter the other, they enter in the guise of external (and hence, often extraneous) variables but are not an intrinsic part of the operations of that world. They help shape a context, but little more [1977, p. 8].

(See also Zaretsky 1976; Rapoport & Rapoport 1965; Landes 1977-78.)

As participants in their culture, social scientists share in this segmented world view. Skolnick (1973) has described how the family has become idealized as the realm of affectivity, intimacy, and significant ascribed relations, in contradistinction to the public work world, which is impersonal, competitive, and characterized by the instrumental rather than the expressive.[5] In conceiving of work and family life as separate, mental health professionals are in good company. E. Pleck (1976) has chastized social historians for their lack of integration of labor and family historical research. Rainwater, in his preface to Young and Willmott's (1973) work on family life, has complained that "family sociologists and the sociology of work tend to proceed along their separate narrow ways barely acknowledging the existence of each other. . . . It often seems as if sociologists . . . observe an invisible boundary between them" (pp. xiv–xv).

In a recent collection of articles on work organizations, this seg-

---

5. This conception of the work world is, of course, limited. Rational evaluations of job performance are not used consistently; sponsorship and social networks also are powerful forces (Aldous 1969; Caplow 1954).

mented world view is stated explicitly. Families and work organizations are seen as separate but equal institutions. Their separation in time, space, and function allows the individual to "neatly compartmentalize" his or her life (Dubin 1976). Such sociological theory embodies the notion that not only are work and family institutions separate, but the separation is necessary for the smooth functioning of the social order.

Because such separation appears to be "natural" this viewpoint can too easily go unquestioned and unexamined. However, the apparent boundaries between work and life at home and their relegation to different fields of study are themselves socially determined. The "invisible" conceptual and psychological boundaries between work and family life have their counterpart in the physical separation of household and workplace that many historians locate in time around the emergence of industrial capitalism. Before people went to work in factories, work life and family life were much less segregated than they are today (Rapoport & Rapoport 1965).[6] Preindustrial agricultural societies involved families working and living together, with families providing not only their own food but also much else needed for survival (Ehrenreich & English 1975). For weavers and artisans, workplace and living quarters often were one, and "cottage industries" involved whole families in making cloth for market sale. In the initial stages of American capitalism families sometimes worked together in the textile mills, but this system gradually gave way to working with strangers. By the early twentieth century many of the productive functions that had been performed in American homes—the processing of food, the making of soap, clothing, and medicine—were located in industries outside it (Ehrenreich & English 1975).

In her speculations about the myth of separate worlds, Kanter (1977) has suggested that American capitalism saw family loyalties as threatening to the work discipline and the organizational loyalty it required. Families first were co-opted and controlled, and then the particularistic hold of families was broken. The worker was treated "as if" he or she had no other loyalties, and the emphasis on individual achievement made the family less important. Eventually, a newly mobile "isolated" nuclear family emerged, which was no longer dependent on familial ties for economic survival (Parsons 1955). The home gained in psychological importance as the center of "personal life," of subjectivity, privacy, and intimacy (Zaretsky 1976).[7] This assumption of separate worlds has come to pervade much of social science. The clinical

6. Compare E. Pleck (1976), which questions the comprehensiveness of this phenomenon.

7. Aronowitz (1973) has argued that the split between labor and private life is necessary because youths do not find pleasure in their jobs. In his view, the family realm constitutes a chance for adults to achieve mastery.

view that treats families as insular partakes of this tradition and reinforces it.

This brief overview of the changes in the relationship of work and family life brought about by industrial capitalism highlights the importance of considering our assumptions and our conceptualizations as historically and, to some extent, ideologically grounded. Work and family are static abstractions we use to conceptually organize dynamic patterns of human social relations. These relations and the interconnections among and between them have changed over time with changes in society and the nature of production. For example, it is thought that hunting and gathering societies had no word for "work" (Kranzberg & Gies 1975), indicating that for such peoples productive labor was coextensive with other life activities.

The significance of the social and ideological context is especially apparent in our notions of family. When we think of "the family," a particular image comes to mind. We imagine a married couple living with their children, responsible for their own support and managing the daily tasks of life together. When mental health professionals think of "the family," they implicitly are referring to the emotional relations of this co-residential kinship group. However, kinship groups, places of residence, and households have not always been coincidental, nor are they equivalent concepts (Skolnick 1973). In some societies, for example, fathers normally do not live in the same home as their children and wives. Households also can include nonkin. In fact, who is included in the kin system of the family also has varied over time and across cultures. Skolnick concluded, "The private, self-contained nuclear-family household is a modern life style that has occurred only within the twentieth century, and mainly in America" (1973, p. 19).

Household Work

Families and households, as Skolnick has observed, are conceptually distinct, historically changing constructs. Whereas the concept of the family refers to patterns of kinship and the relations among relatives, households are social systems[8] that organize material resources and labor for the social and physical maintenance and reproduction of people. Rapp (1978) has suggested that families are the normative way people are recruited into households. The fact that modern American residences not only contain kin but also are places where work is performed has been obscured by the conceptual confusion between families, homes, and households; by the emphasis on the modern industrial family as specializing in socioemotional functions (Parsons 1955) and as being a "consumption unit" (Young & Willmott 1973); and by our

---

8. The debate about whether household labor is productive in the Marxist sense is not addressed here.

8

notions of work as an activity performed for pay. The feminist movement and the recent attention to the sociology of housework (Ferree
1976; Gavron 1966; Glazer-Malbin 1976; Lopata 1971; Oakley 1974a,
1974b) remind us that although she does not receive wages, the housewife also works, turning wages into usable commodities that maintain
and reproduce human life (Women's Work Study Group 1976). Vanek
(1974) has estimated that urban married women not employed outside
the home[9] spend an average of fifty-five hours per week on housework,
family care, and related duties. Whether or not their wives are employed, husbands contribute one to two hours a day to household work
(J. Pleck 1977; Walker & Woods 1976). The limited research on working-
class women who work within the home indicates that they are a particularly alienated and depressed group, especially when they are removed from female kin (Ferree 1976; Gurin et al. 1960; Rainwater et al.
1959; Tallman 1969). This body of research reminds us that it is important to examine work both inside and outside the home, the interconnections between these activities, and the ways they touch the psychosocial
relations of family members.

An Alternative View

Although the predominant tradition in both clinical and social science theory and research has assumed the separation of work and family
life, an alternative perspective has pointed to the possible existence of
significant connections between them. Rainwater's criticism notwith-
standing, sociologists and others interested in group life have contributed to our conceptual understanding and empirical knowledge about
such relationships.

Rapoport and Rapoport (1965) have suggested that life-cycle factors
and the relative salience of work roles are important variables in understanding work and home interrelationships. They also have hypothesized that family and work life may be isomorphic, that is, that "similar-
ity of behavior patterning" may occur when modes of interaction at
work and in the family affect each other. They may be "complementary" and "heteromorphic" when activities at home compensate for
work life. Similarly, Parker (1967) has suggested that the relationships
between work and family spheres can be extensive (positive), neutral,
or oppositional. In the literature on the relationship of work to leisure
activities, three types of relationships have been posited: forms of work
activity may carry or spill over into leisure life, leisure activities may
compensate for lack of gratification in work, or the two types of activities may be independent of each other (Meissner 1971; Quinn 1974).

9. Throughout this book, "work" will be used to denote productive activities inside and outside the home. "Employment" will denote paid work. Although this distinction is not entirely satisfactory, it is useful for purposes of the discussion to follow.

Aldous (1969) has mentioned the carry-over of values and interpersonal styles from work to home life and has highlighted the importance of time factors, especially the "synchronization" of occupational and familial responsibilities. Kanter (1977) has suggested that we consider as important additional variables "emotional climate" and the relative "absorption" of family members by the requirements of occupational roles.

An empirically oriented sociological tradition has examined the relationships between social class or occupational status and structural family variables such as timing of first marriage, rates of fertility, and marital stability. Much of this literature is concerned with very poor families and has been ably reviewed (Aldous, Osmond & Hicks 1979; Furstenberg 1974; Rainwater 1974). Another research tradition examines the relationships of occupation to intrafamilial relationships, especially socialization practices (see, for example, Aberle & Naegele 1952; Gecas 1979; Gecas & Nye 1974; Kohn 1963, 1969; McKinley 1964; Miller & Swanson 1958) and marital integration (see, for example, Bernard 1966; Blood & Wolfe 1960; Bradburn & Caplovitz 1965; Gold & Slater 1958; Mott et al. 1965; Scanzoni 1970). This research hypothesizes that intervening variables such as occupational world view affect socialization values and that occupational power and prestige influence marital role relations. Again, there are comprehensive and recent reviews of this body of research (Aldous et al. 1979; Gecas 1979; Kanter 1977). Rather than attempt an exhaustive review of this research literature, I shall outline here some limitations of its use for the clinical study of whole families.

This body of research focuses primarily on the work of the employed male family member. In Scanzoni's (1970) theoretical model, for example, the key to marital satisfaction lies in the income, status, and prestige the wife derives from the husband's occupational role. The more positively a husband fulfills his instrumental duties, the more positively his wife will perform her instrumental household duties. The notion that household work (or a woman's paid work) may be an independent source of gratification or distress or may pose its own interface dilemmas is not considered.

The marital pair or the child-parent dyad is often implicitly used as synonymous with the whole family. Families and family members also are treated as dependent variables who are acted upon. For example, in the socialization literature, children are not viewed as actors in their own right. In contrast, a family-as-system approach enables us to consider families as functioning wholes and all family members as active agents. (See, for example, Golden 1975; Rapoport & Rapoport 1965.) With a dynamic formulation of the family as actor, we can ask how families negotiate the interface region between work and family systems. However, it is important not to overemphasize the "freedom" of family members to shape actively their own experience but to recognize the constraints on their ability to negotiate with other institutions.

Much of the sociological research utilizes "gross" variables such as social class or occupational status and deals with aggregates of people; the type of correlational knowledge generated by such research has been described as a "static snapshot" (Kanter 1977). We know little about how everyday life is lived out in individual families. While associations may be found between two variables that imply their causal connection, we are left guessing about the processes that underlie these found associations. For example, Kohn (1969) was unable to explain how it was that wives had socialization attitudes similar to those of their husbands, and W. G. Dyer (1956) could not explain the process whereby family members, including children, shared similar attitudes about the husband-father's job. We know that men who work afternoon shifts (during the late afternoon and evening) complain of difficulty in their roles as fathers of school-age children, but we do not know "what interactions take place between the worker and his wife and children which affect his psychological health" or "what sorts of interactions occur in the family which enable some of the workers to cope with these problems" (Mott et al. 1965, p. 315).

The use of gross variables obscures the concrete experiences of people, and static portrayals cannot take into account the dynamic processes in families that are of interest to the mental health professional. In considering the research on family stability and work status, Furstenberg criticized gross characterizations of work experience for restricting "the theoretical analysis of the relationship between work and family life. Since they capture so little of the quality of the work experience, they have relatively little to say about the way that experience impinges on family life" (1974, pp. 343–44). His criticism is equally applicable to the way family life is conceived. In her review, Kanter reached a similar conclusion.

> Despite the agreement that the family and the economy as institutions are linked in broad ways, the specific intersections and transactions between work and family, between occupations and families as connected organizers of experience and systems of social relations, are virtually ignored. There are only a handful of studies that consider the connections between forms of work and family life (as opposed to general social class and family variables). . . . And there is only a limited amount of research or theory that considers the behavior and experiences of people in both their work and family situations by looking at people in both contexts [1977, pp. 7–8].

In other words, existing research is limited in helping us to understand the concrete, microinteractional processes that connect the specifics of work life and psychological processes in families. Kanter concluded that the links between "working and loving" constitute a "social psychological frontier."[10] Because mental health professionals concern themselves precisely with the processes of loving in families and the ways that those processes can go awry, our clinical knowledge of family life can contribute to the understanding of this relationship.

Clinical Research

As Kanter has noted, the research literature that connects the specifics of work and family life is sparse. Research on work-related factors that influence the emotional dynamics of families is more limited still. However, researchers have begun to attend to this relationship.

Rapoport and Rapoport, anthropologists, have reported two studies (1965, 1971) of work and family interrelationships that are relevant to clinical research efforts. In their 1965 study, they used the normative life-cycle and life-crisis model of the preventative mental health movement as their frame of reference. They studied twelve couples who were going through simultaneous transitions in both work and family spheres. The males were young engineering students who were graduating from college and were recently married. The Rapoports viewed such status transitions as presenting a specific complex of "tasks" from which the subsequent pattern of work–family relatedness emerges. Their framework is noteworthy for its emphasis on the importance of life-cycle factors in both work and family spheres and for the view that families can act effectively to shape the patterns that result from the conjunction of work and family life.

In their later study the Rapoports reported research on five families in which they considered the husbands and wives "pioneers" because they both pursued active careers. Although they saw each family as unique, they also were interested in providing models for understanding the dilemmas (and resolutions to them) faced by those who have successfully evolved a dual career pattern. Thus, they were interested both in satisfactions and in stresses. They discovered satisfactions such as individual self-expression in work and self-reliant children; stresses included work overload, environmental disapproval for the dual career pattern, and difficulties in synchronizing work and family cycles.

Renshaw (1976) recently reported research conducted with managers of a large multinational corporation and some of their wives. Assuming, as did Rapoport and Rapoport, that the dynamics of the work–family connection would become more evident under conditions of stress, Renshaw interviewed couples in which husbands were undergoing international transfer and job changes and those in which the husband's job required a great deal of travel. Renshaw found that organiza-

---

10. Research such as Liebow's (1967) study of Negro street-corner men do provide such descriptions for some lower-class black families.

tional stresses would sometimes be blamed for family strain and vice versa, concluding that interface stress can be understood best as an interaction between organizational and familial stresses. The way a person coped with the stress was a function of his or her perception of having control over events, as well as of the objective events themselves.

In a recent unpublished study, Golden (1975) used the life-cycle orientation of Rapoport and Rapoport to examine the conjunction of work and family life. She conducted naturalistic observations of both home and workplace settings in the intensive study of two families with preschool children. Golden concluded that when families are young they need a great deal of psychic energy and time to function effectively. Yet at that point in their lives, their resources may be lowest. Husband-fathers are most involved in building their careers and spend much time away from the family, and there may be disruptive effects on both adults and children from the energic imbalances that occur. Father absence may be crucial for children between the ages of 3 and 6. Golden's innovation was in part methodological in that she observed family members across both settings.

Some Assumptions about Class

Although the research utilizing gross variables such as social class or occupational status includes studies of working-class and lower-middle-class families, the few studies that have attempted to illuminate the processes linking occupational life and the dynamics of family living have concentrated on families in which the husband-father is employed in a managerial or professional occupation.[11] This selective focus is not due merely to oversight or to the general lack of research in the field but reflects a bias that is self-reinforcing in that it precludes interest in such research.

Because the work life of managers and professionals is gratifying and "salient" for them, there is a tendency to assume that there is greater potential for conflict between work and family roles in these groups (Rapoport & Rapoport 1965; Young & Willmott 1973). Moreover, because these people bring their paperwork home, receive business phone calls at home, and think about business problems there, the "interference" is concrete and easily measured by the social scientist through self-report procedures. On the other hand, the well-documented lack of job-related ego involvement among many lower-level workers has led to assumptions about the relationship of work and family life among them that pass for social science "fact." On discovering that

11. In addition to the clinical studies cited above, it is noteworthy that the two articles about families appearing in Bryant's (1972) volume on the social aspects of work deal with ambassadors' wives and doctors' families.

work was not a central life interest among the industrial workers he studied, Dubin (1956) first suggested that they compensated by their involvement in other life roles. Since then, the assumption of compensatory "home centred" family life (Young & Willmott 1973) has been given much currency. [12] For example, Young and Willmott have asserted that the lack of job involvement of manual workers means that they have more energy to invest in wives and children.

A second assumption that passes for fact is the idea that noninvolvement in the job leads to a "natural" separation—or segmentation—of work and family life. Parker (1967) has proposed a "neutral" relationship between work and family life in occupations with regular hours and no "marked" physical and psychological effects on the jobholder. He has suggested that technical, routine, nonmanual occupations might show such a pattern. Such neutrality or segmentation is also assumed for "blue-collar" workers. For example, Blood and Wolfe have maintained that "generalizations about the separation of workplace and residence apply primarily to blue collar workers since they seldom have reason to be preoccupied with business problems in their spare time. The boss, however, doesn't have it so easy" (1960, p. 59). Kanter, following Dubin, has suggested that for "such workers work and family may indeed constitute highly separated, highly segregated worlds; each may operate on its own terms, with the other acting only as an externality (in the economic sense) or a boundary-setting condition" (1977, pp. 25–26). Once the assumption of such a separation is taken as factual, the need for study of interrelationships is precluded.

Goals of the Study

Just as work organizations are complex systems—with subsystems, organizational cultures, informal interpersonal networks, and instrumental aspects—so are families. In their households family members engage in instrumental work activities, they have their particular subcultures, they perform the tasks of socialization, and they bind people to society. Both work and family systems are "open" in that they are involved in elaborate interchanges with their social environments (Bell & Vogel 1960; Kahn, Wolfe, Quinn & Snoek 1964). Interfaces are those regions where the patterns of activity associated with such open systems touch or overlap. More specifically, the study described here explored

12. Compensatory leisure activities also have been touted as the prerogative of the working man. For example, Aronowitz has said that "leisure becomes a chance for the working man to locate himself as a significant actor in a private world" (1973, p. 91). However, the extent of such compensation is questionable. Rather, it appears that there is an "isomorphism" between work life and nonwork leisure activities (Meissner 1971; Young & Willmott 1973).

the dynamic processes linking work systems—including the household—and emotional life in families whose wage-earning members were employed primarily in working-class and lower-middle-class occupations.

The concept of a family's "emotional life" is difficult to define clearly, yet it is implicit in what mental health professionals mean when they refer to "the family." The working definition to be used here is that "emotional life" refers not only to family members' thoughts and feelings about themselves and each other, but also to their interpersonal relationships and the process whereby they achieve intimacy, meaning, and identity. When I discuss "families" and "family life" I shall be referring primarily to these aspects of the relations among kin. These relationships are rooted in the context of their day-to-day transactions about the business of living. The usefulness of a systems approach to families is that it forces us to examine the processes connecting people rather than seeing them as isolated individuals.

The focus on working-class and lower-middle-class families does not imply that the work–family nexus is unimportant for the families of businessmen, managers, or the very poor. Nor does it negate differences within classes or similarities between them. The decision to concentrate on working-class and lower-middle-class people was based on several considerations, including our knowledge from the available research on work and mental health that people in these occupational groups are especially stressed by their work. Yet for them in particular, work and family life are assumed to be segmented.

The participating families were of interest for themselves and for what they could suggest about the dimensions of the work–home relationship, both for the mental health professional working with families and for the researcher. The thrust of the study was to explore the ways in which work systems may affect the microinteractional processes that constitute families' emotional life. Families' impact on external work settings was not of concern here. Although individual families actively attempt to control and manage their lives, in the long run it is the institution of the family that has adapted—though not capitulated—to economic, political, and technological changes in society rather than vice versa (Nimkoff 1957; Vincent 1966). My questions were worker- and family-oriented, not based on the desire to determine how families could be made to interfere less with organizational functioning so that worker productivity could be increased. As a clinical psychologist I was concerned with the kinds of tasks families encounter in daily living. This clinical orientation also made me wonder about points of stress and dysfunction and about the ways in which families cope with the tasks of everyday life.

Given that we know little about how working-class and lower-middle-class family members fare as they move between work activities and intimate life, this study is exploratory in its inception and design. As we are at a frontier in our knowledge, it appeared premature to attempt to test elaborate hypotheses, "prove" causal connections, or present a fully elaborated theory. Instead the goal of the study was to find out what was there, develop further data, and suggest a framework for thinking about connections between work and home. One benefit of such an approach lies in its ability to generate debate and discussion while pointing to directions for further research. The theoretical notions provided by the literature—including concepts of time and energy, of isomorphism and segmentation—were used as sensitizing concepts and "working hypotheses" with which to approach the data. A more complete rationale for an exploratory, qualitative design is presented in the Methodological Appendix.

I have suggested that to treat work and family life as separate worlds is to impose on dynamic and interconnected social relations impermeable boundaries that may, in fact, not exist. At the same time, discussing the interface between work and personal life in families appears to give these spheres of activity discrete status, for they are treated as clearly bounded. This apparent contradiction ultimately must be transcended so that we can account, not only for the coherence to our historically founded notions of work and family as distinct systems of human activity, but also for their overlap and interconnection.

CHAPTER 2

The Research Families:
Interviews and Observations

Thirty members of thirteen families (including seven children) participated in this study. Data were collected in 1976 and 1977. Participants were drawn from two states: one in the Midwest and one in the Far West. Their areas of residence included major urban centers and their suburban surrounds, small cities, and semirural areas. Eighteen of the thirty participants were interviewed once; the others were interviewed on at least two separate occasions. Approximately 3.5 hours were spent in interviews with each family. Two of the families—the Turners and the Bernards[1]—were studied intensively. The Turner family was observed at home for one full day—from 6:00 A.M., when the family arose, until 10:30 P.M. Ezra Turner's work setting also was observed for an eight-hour day. Similarly, the Bernard home setting was formally observed for one full day and parts of several others, for approximately eighteen hours. An additional fifteen hours of more informal observing was done there. Richard Bernard was observed both at a part-time job and at his full-time job for a total of fourteen hours.

Participating Families: Who Are They?

Table 2-1 gives some of the demographic characteristics of the participating family members. Those who participated in this study were members of intact, nuclear families in which most of the women did not work outside the home at the time of the study. As we can see from Table 2-1, the participating families are racially and ethnically diverse.

1. Pseudonyms are used to protect the identity of the families who participated in this study. Minor details that might identify them also have been altered to protect their anonymity.

Table 2-1. Selected Characteristics of Participating Adults and Their Families

Characteristics	Men Interviewed N = 13	Women Interviewed N = 10	Families N = 13
Age			
Range	23–70	20–61	
Median	30	30	
Education			
Eight years or less	1	1	
Grades 9–11	0	0	
Grade 12	1	3	
Some college or special training	11	6	
Religion			
Protestant	8	7	
Catholic	4	2	
Other[a]	1	1	
Race			
Black	6	6	
White	7	4	
Currently Employed	12[b]	3[c]	
Dual-Employee Families			4[c]
Years Married			
Range			3–56
Median			7
Numbers of Children			
Range			1–5
Average			2.5
Life-Cycle Stage			
Preschool children			9
School-age children			2
Launching			1
No children at home			1

[a]One couple indicated that they were nondenominational.
[b]One research participant was retired at the time of the study.
[c]Although there were four dual-employee families, only three wives were interviewed.

The decision not to limit racial or ethnic diversity was made on theoretical grounds. Families were not to be compared on racial or ethnic bases. The assumption was made that class is at least as important as race and ethnicity in understanding family life. Although every family has its own culture, it was assumed that similar work situations would pose similar tasks for all of them

Most research families were classified as working-class or lower-middle-class. The notion of class always has posed problems for social scientists. Attempts at class categorizations are inherently difficult because "class" connotes the historical process of changing social relations rather than a static category (Thompson 1966). Fried has observed that the term "working-class" captures an "essential idea" that there exists a large mass of the labor force who "share many economic and occupational circumstances" (1973, p. 152). These shared circumstances include depending on their daily labor for their livelihood, so that economic recessions or ill health are serious threats. Their life chances remain largely limited by skills they can sell, and they are seen as relatively interchangeable in their occupations. The concept of class is important in helping us understand the roots of these shared circumstances and, therefore, people's differing experiences at the workplace. "Class" is used here to denote "groups of individuals who relate to the ownership and control of the means of production in similar ways" (Bowles & Gintis 1975, pp. 14–15). Those in working-class and lower-middle-class jobs are furthest from control over the means of production and are in jobs that are increasingly characterized by an erosion of skill and autonomy and by increasing atomization.

Following Levison (1974), occupations here classified as "working-class" include traditional blue-collar jobs and "hidden" ones such as service and police work. (Levison has estimated that over 60 percent of the male labor force is employed in such jobs.) Although it has been compellingly argued that the downgrading of many "white-collar" jobs makes it useful for us to consider them as "working-class,"[2] for purposes of continuity with existing literature the notation "lower-middle-class" will be used here for those holding low-level white-collar jobs.

Participants were employed in several different types of organizations. Of the men, four worked for public agencies, one for a small family-operated business, and the remainder for large corporations. If we include the retired participant, nine of the male participants worked in "blue-collar" jobs, including police work, service work, and unskilled and semiskilled factory work; two had technical "white-collar" jobs; and one was in a highly skilled clerical position. In addition, one participant—Ezra Turner—was a highly skilled technician and supervisor; the Turners were included as a contrast middle-class family. Of the three employed women interviewed, one worked on a production assembly line, one was a secretary, and one was a paraprofessional

2. Against the commonly accepted notion of a growing, skilled, white-collar labor force (Blauner 1964), Braverman (1975) and others have argued convincingly that, although more education might be formally required of the jobholder, automation has decreased, rather than increased, the skill level of white-collar workers and has made their jobs more routine, narrowing differences between them and traditional blue-collar workers.

counselor.[3] A fourth woman, not interviewed, also worked on a production assembly line.

Much of the research on the relationship between family life and occupational status has centered on the "lower class" and its "culture of poverty." This body of research has concerned itself with the impact of marginal and intermittent employment—and the ensuing poverty—on familial stability and role relations. As noted in Chapter 1, the research on work and family life among stable working families is sparse. The families who participated in this study were, by design, neither overwhelmingly poor nor "hard living" (see Howell 1972). Extreme poverty would have obscured the everyday relations of interest here. By and large, male participants can be described as stably employed. Their tenure with their most recent employers ranged from two weeks to thirty-eight years, with a median of nine years.

Annual incomes were difficult for many of the participants to determine because of layoffs, strikes, and variable overtime. I therefore estimated their base incomes as if they worked continuously at the rate of forty hours per week. Excluding one retired participant, the median base pay of the male participants was $12,500 per year; ten earned a base income under $15,000 annually. In eight families at least one employed member and often both were members of powerful unions; in another three families at least one employed member worked in a unionized industry. Of the twelve employed male participants, nine worked more than a total of forty hours per week,[4] including second jobs or overtime work. Of these nine, four worked more than fifty hours per week, thereby augmenting their base pay. In four families, income was increased by the full-time employment of wives. Thus, the estimates of *total* family income, including overtime, ranged from $12,000 to $35,000 per year. One research family earned their affluence by both husband and wife working a total of more than a hundred hours per week in a factory. Still, of the twelve research families in which the wage earners were not retired, nine earned total family incomes of between $12,000 and $16,000 per year, making them neither affluent nor poor.[5] The national median family income was $15,000 annually in 1976 dollars (U.S. Bureau of the Census 1977).

3. With more women becoming permanent members of the labor force, assigning a family to a particular class on the basis of the husband-father's occupation becomes a practice that must be reconsidered in the context of our notions of class (Oakley 1974a).

4. Hedges (1976) reported that 30 percent of men between the ages of 20 and 54 worked forty-one or more hours per week at their principal job.

5. Income is often used as a variable in determining class status. However, Goldthorpe and Lockwood (1963) have made an excellent case for the argument that sheer affluence is insufficient to raise a worker to the middle class; others have pointed out that the apparent life-style similarities among classes that come with affluence camouflage enduring class differences (Marciano 1974; Handel & Rainwater 1964).

The Research Families: Interviews and Observations

As a group, the male research participants were well educated. For the men the median educational level attained was two years of college, a figure slightly higher than the national median of 12.4 years of education (U.S. Bureau of the Census 1977). The median educational level was one year of college for the women. Although educational achievement often is included as a variable in determining socioeconomic status, L. B. Rubin (1976) has commented on the fallacy of considering all education as equivalent. The majority of participants went to local or community colleges with open-admissions practices. Some did not graduate from high school but obtained their high school equivalency diplomas in the armed services. For some, several years of college meant training in practical nursing or technical work. Of the men, eight were enrolled in school during the time of the research. However, this also must be understood in context: the college program they were enrolled in had no admissions requirements and was designed especially for working adults. Attending night school at a local college with open admissions has a different meaning from spending four years at an elite university. Their initial motivations in attending college also are illuminating. For most of them it was a way of earning money—a second job—as they received veterans' benefits. One participant enrolled both for the extra income and because he had been demoted during the recent recession, while fellow workers with college degrees were retained in their former positions. As they continued in school some became interested in learning and saw it as a potential opportunity for becoming occupationally mobile.[6]

The participating families were "inconspicuous"; that is, while they had their share of problems, they saw themselves as more or less "managing." Although they may have been perceived as "troubled" in the past and may seek assistance in the future, at the time of the study they neither defined themselves as being in difficulty nor were perceived as such by the social service, criminal, or educational systems. Such inconspicuous families were chosen for two reasons. First, if a family had an identified "patient" or "problem," attention would focus there, obscuring the ordinary and less apparent relationships that were my chief concern. Second, the existence of defined "problems" would contribute a tendency to overexplain work–home interactions in terms of family pathology.[7]

6. The group is unusual in that they chose to attend school. My impression is that this group of men was particularly industrious and had strong and supportive family situations so that they could go to school, even if on a part-time basis.

7. Originally, concepts such as "ordinary," "average," and "normal" were used in thinking about these participating families. These concepts proved problematic, for they have been used by mental health professionals to refer variously to conceptions of an ideal, to statistical averages, and to nonclinical populations (Bott 1971). Not only do we lack a

Because some variety was important for purposes of comparison, families at different stages of the life cycle were included. As Table 2-1 indicates, the participants as a group were relatively young. The youth of the sample is reflected in the fact that seven of the male participants worked a late shift. The model research family was thus a young Protestant family with two to three preschool-aged children. The husband-father was employed in a unionized working-class job, worked more than forty but fewer than fifty hours per week, and earned between $12,000 and $16,000 annually.

Capsule descriptions of the research families are provided in Table 2-2 to facilitate the discussion of findings in Part II.

The Data: Interviews and Observations

The research process began with interviews, which were analyzed thematically (see Methodological Appendix). The initial interviewing phase had several purposes: because this study focused on an interface region that is often obscured by being part of the "ground" of everyday life, the initial interviewing was aimed at sharpening my vision about what was important and at generating working hypotheses. The study of family life is particularly hampered because we are blinded by the familiar. Because only one of the families was studied in great depth, the interviews provided some comparative data by which the significance of patterns discovered in this family could be better judged. The rapport and working alliances developed in the interviews, as well as the information gathered, also were designed to facilitate gaining entrance into participants' homes for purposes of observation. The interviews also would enable them to evaluate me. My own class background, which is similar to that of the participants, facilitated my relationship with them; their homes were very familiar to me and I was able to settle in quickly and comfortably. Generally, I felt I was able to maintain what one participant called a "low profile."

Two families were observed in the course of their everyday lives. There were several rationales for using this research procedure in studying the interface of work and family life. Observations are particularly

---

clear conception of the "healthy" family, but the dangers described above are inherent in the application of any abstract ideal. The concept of statistical average fares no better, for we are left wondering, "Average in what way? How do we find the emotionally average family?" "Normal" sometimes is used to refer to those who have never been seen by mental health professionals for problems identified as emotional. The use of this normal–abnormal distinction not only stigmatizes but also is not very meaningful. Such normality certainly cannot be equated with mental health. More important, families seen in therapy represent a wide variety of adaptations, some more successful than others, and we are still unclear about whether and in what ways such families differ from nonclinical ones (Henry 1965). We also know that factors such as social class can make a difference in when and whether people utilize mental health facilities (Myers & Roberts 1959).

The Research Families: Interviews and Observations

Table 2-2. Brief Descriptions of Research Families

The Bernards (Observed)

Richard:	Aged 28. Police officer, midnight shift. Works between forty and fifty hours per week, including employment as a guard at a shopping center.
Alice:	Aged 28. Household worker.
Children:	Carrie, aged 5; James, aged 3; and Nicholas, aged 2.

The Colemans

Samuel:	Aged 32. Assembly-line worker, afternoon shift. Works between fifty and sixty hours per week, overtime.
LaVerne:	Aged 25. Assembly-line worker, afternoon shift. Household worker. Employed forty hours per week.
[Children:	Son, aged 3.]*

The Coopers

Eric:	Aged 30. Computer monitor, afternoon shift. Employed forty hours per week.
[Wife:	Aged 30. Household worker.]
[Children:	Son, aged 4; daughter, aged 4 months.]

The Doyles

Tom:	Aged 40. Traffic expediter, day shift. Works between forty and fifty hours per week, overtime.
Paula:	Aged 40. Secretary, day shift. Household worker. Employed forty hours per week.
[Children:	Jeff, aged 15; daughter, aged 14.]

The Ellisons

Ray:	Aged 32. Cook-supervisor, afternoon shift. Works between forty anf fifty hours per week, overtime.
Mary:	Aged 23. Household worker.
[Children:	Lucinda, aged 6; two other daughters aged 4 and 18 months.]

The Gateses

Ben:	Aged 29. Hospital attendant, day shift. Employed forty hours per week.
Pamela:	Aged 32. Paraprofessional counselor, day shift. Household worker. Employed forty hours per week.
Children:	Carletta, aged 11. [Four other daughters, aged 13, 9, and 2; two sons, aged 9 and 18 months.]

The Healys

Mike:	Aged 26. Machine operator, midnight shift. Works between forty and fifty hours per week, overtime.
Celia:	Aged 20. Household worker.
[Children:	Two daughters, aged 2 years and 3 weeks.]

The Johnsons (I)

Henry:	Aged 54. Dispatcher and deliveryman, day shift. Works between fifty and sixty hours per week, overtime.
Betty:	Aged 43. Household worker. Employed several hours per week in beauty salon.
Children:	Donna, aged 16; Sally, aged 19 (both at home); Tony, aged 23 (see below). [Another daughter, aged 21 (not living at home).]

Table 2-2. (*continued*)

The Johnsons (II)

Tony: Aged 23. Computer operator, day shift. Employed forty hours per week.
[Wife: Aged 23. Household worker.]
[Children: Tony Jr., aged 2.]

The Joneses

Jesse: Aged 28; Relief man on assembly line, afternoon shift. Works forty to fifty hours per week, overtime.
Sandra: Aged 22. Household worker.
[Children: Billy, aged 16 months.]

The Simpsons

Chuck: Aged 29. Forklift operator, afternoon shift. Works more than fifty hours per week, overtime.
[Kathy: Aged 27. Assembly-line worker, afternoon shift. Household worker. Employed forty hours per week.]
Children: Pete, aged 3. [Daughter, aged 9 months.]

The Turners (I)

John: Aged 70. Retired machine operator.
Josephine: Aged 64. Household worker.
Children: Ezra, aged 42 (see below). [Two other sons, aged 38 and 47.]

The Turners (II) (Observed)

Ezra: Aged 42. Supervisor-technician in a laboratory, day shift. Works more than sixty hours per week, including part-time work in upholstery cleaning business, on call for medical transplant society and part-time lab attendant.
Isabell: Aged 40. Household worker.
Children: Patsy, aged 6; Charles, aged 14. [Clarisse, aged 16.]

---

*Those who were neither interviewed nor observed appear in brackets. Names were not assigned to family members unless their name appears in Part II.

useful in detecting "latent" phenomena (McCall & Simmons 1969; Zelditch 1962), which include observable events to which the members of a system do not attend. For example, greeting behaviors are so ordinary that people do not think to comment on them. The events of interest to me were the everyday events that often go unremarked. The participants themselves were often blinded by their proximity to these events, which are so much a part of the fabric of everyday life that they pass unnoticed or are reported in cursory fashion. Families and individuals also have developed favored ways of explaining their lives, which may camouflage dynamics and sustain valued self-conceptions.[8] By augmenting the interview data, the observations would enable these dynamics to be "seen" and discussed.

8. Weller and Luchterhand (1969) reported important differences between conclusions based on interview data and those based on home observations.

Although both the Turner and Bernard families were observed formally, only the observations of the Bernard family were analyzed extensively. The observational data collected within the Bernard home and at Richard Bernard's work were thematically analyzed. In addition, the observational data collected within the Bernard home[9] were coded according to two a priori schemas, which are described briefly below and in greater detail in the Methodological Appendix.

Quality-of-Interaction Codes

Observations were coded for their psychosocial meaning. As used here, family interactions were analyzed into an interaction sequence with an initiation and response aspect. The initiations and responses were coded according to the categories summarized here. They could be coded into more than one category.

A. *Initiations toward Another*
   1. *Positive:* Cooperative–Affectional, Pleasure–Joy, Conversational
   2. *Neutral:* Objective
   3. *Mild Influencing*
   4. *Negative:* Strong Influencing, Disapproving, Blaming–Accusing, Antagonistic, and Unhappiness–Distress
B. *Responses to the Initiation*
   1. *Positive:* Positive–Direct, Positive–Cooperative, Overt Pleasure
   2. *Neutral:* Objective–Passive
   3. *Covert Negative:* Avoidant and Ignoring
   4. *Overt Negative:* Negative, Disapproving, Blaming–Accusing, Antagonistic, and Unhappiness–Distress

Content Codes

Observed interaction sequences also were coded for their manifest content. Again interactions could be coded into more than one category. The coding categories are summarized below.

1. *Domestic:* All household activity, including management of work and budgeting; nonphysical care of children and adults, such as chauffeuring to school; self-statements about a biological need
2. *Play*
3. *Social Interaction:* Can be positive or negative; can include greetings and statements about social behavior and relationships

9. Only verbal interactions, excluding the observer, were coded. In all, 15.25 hours of home observations were coded (2.4 hours were imperfectly recorded and, therefore, remained uncoded). For further details about the uncoded periods, see Chapter 7.

4. *All Other:* Includes references to the outside world, television, etc.

By subjecting the observational data to both thematic analysis and coding, complementary viewpoints on the data could emerge. In this way the biases inherent in any one approach to the data would be mitigated.

Collaboration

In the participants themselves, the researcher has allies. The assumption behind a collaborative design, as it was used here (see also Golden 1975; Rapoport & Rapoport 1971), is that people have knowledge of their own experience and can comment self-reflectively on it. They do not have to be highly educated to do so. When the participants are treated as equals, the usual researcher–subject distinction takes on a different meaning. Bakan commented on this distinction in describing the "mystery–mastery complex" in psychology:

> The scientist–subject distinction is a euphemism for the manipulator–manipulated in many research situations. Insofar as the methodological literature on this distinction allows for the existence of the psyche at all, it confounds the issue by presuming at least two different kinds of psyche. It ascribes autonomy, methodicalness, and rationality ... to the one, but rarely to the other [1969, p. 41].

The goal of the collaborative procedure, which involved participants in the interpretive process and what was written about them, is to enhance the researcher's rationality and understanding by allying with the participants. It helps guard against sociocultural bias (see Rodman 1964; Staples 1971; Ten Houten 1970) by buttressing the always fallible sensitivity and good will of the researcher. The collaborative process was used in some form with all participants, but because it was very time-consuming, it was elaborated only with the Bernard family.

The Bernards were given much of the observational data to read. In their struggle to come to grips with the data, they offered their own insights into family processes and their relationship to work. These interpretations and reactions were used as further research data and also were compared with the hypotheses emerging from my analysis.

The draft of the manuscript was discussed with most of the research families. Although it was costly, the benefits of such a collaboration for the research investigation cannot be overestimated. Sociocultural bias in interpretation becomes much less problematic, as does the danger of misunderstanding. Such a process also helps guide the course of research, and there is less chance of emerging with a description that is not grounded in the experience of those it purports to represent.

The Role of the Reader

For research to generate meaningful knowledge, it has to be understood by others than those immediately involved. In reading the analytic descriptions the reader might wonder how to evaluate their validity. Insofar as a description offers a way of structuring people's experiences and suggesting explanations for them, thinking solely in terms of veridical knowledge is misleading. The criteria for judging the final analysis must be whether it helps us understand what occurs in the lives of families, whether the interpretations maintain the integrity of the data, and whether the interpretations are "plausible." Plausibility can be determined by asking whether the descriptions are internally consistent and whether the data presented support the interpretations. Since the presentation of data is selective and the interpretations must be judged on the basis of the data, as much of the original data should be accessible to the reader as possible. In Part III, therefore, a full day's observation of both the Bernard home and Richard's work situation is presented, so that the reader will be able to come to his or her own conclusions about the data (see also Hess & Handel 1959).

The reader is therefore involved in an active process. Rather than absorbing "facts," she or he must actively digest the examples, analyses, and interpretations that I have offered. Readers can compare the data and ideas presented here with their experiences, thereby further enlarging the scope of the descriptions presented. While the reader may find himself or herself compelled to agree, on the assumption that multiple perspectives about family functioning are always present, it is more likely that differences of interpretation will arise. Ideally, this research will be part of an ongoing process of hypothesis testing and new discovery. Involving the reader in this dialectical process leads to the growth of further understanding.

Paid Work
and Families

As a member of both paid work and family settings, the wage earner traverses the region between them regularly. An examination of his experience provides a useful beginning in mapping the interface region between paid work and family systems of the participating families. The search for connections between the two systems traditionally has begun with this "boundary role." In Part II the interview data with twelve of the research families will be used to sketch some of the dimensions of this relationship and to develop our thinking about it. While the interview data allow us to map some of the boundary areas, they do not permit a detailed consideration of family systems. Such an analysis will be developed in Part III, where the experiences of one family—the Bernards—will be described in depth and the framework to be suggested here will be expanded to include the household work organization within the home.

In Chapters 3 and 4, interface patterns as they were uncovered in the interview data are described. These patterns are of two types: psychological and structural. In Chapter 5, three competing interpretations of the relationships between work and family are examined in light of the data. Considered are the segmentation and compensation hypotheses and an interpretation of the data that rests on personality as the explanatory construct. Finally, in Chapter 6 these relationships are considered from the point of view of children.

In Part II, the reader should keep in mind the exploratory goals stated at the outset. The interviews are useful primarily for suggesting pattern descriptions and sensitizing concepts that will be useful in further research on work and the family system.

CHAPTER 3

The Psychological Interface: Three Patterns

Kanter (1977) has observed that one reason connections between work and family have not been studied systematically is because of the underlying assumption in much of sociological role theory that people simply take on different roles in different settings and move easily between them. This point of view underlies the extreme segmentation position presented in Chapter 1. In psychology, extreme situationists similarly have argued that behaviors are context-specific in that human conduct is best understood as an immediate response to requirements of the setting (Bowers 1973; Harré & Secord 1973; Mischel 1969). If we accept these points of view, we no longer need ask about the ways people manage transitions between settings. It also is not necessary to consider the psychological links that may connect social systems through the individual who is a member of both. In the discussion that follows, the interview data will be utilized to illustrate the existence of psychological connections between participants' work experiences and their family lives. Since the breadwinner occupies a boundary role between external work organization and family system, the psychological link is mediated by his relationship to his work.

Three interface patterns were uncovered: positive carry-over, negative carry-over, and energy deficit. In the description of the first two patterns, the Turner and Johnson families will represent "ideal types." In discussing the third pattern we rely on interview data from a number of families. These patterns suggest some of the psychological dimensions connecting work and family life. They are not meant to be exhaustive. Those discovered were dependent on the participants studied, the nature of their work experiences and their family systems, and the researcher's orientation. Moreover, the patterns did not appear in unmixed form; many families exhibited several patterns simultaneously.

The Pattern of Positive Carry-over

The Turner family was included in the research sample as a contrast middle-class family. Ezra Turner and his wife, Isabel, have been married for twenty years. They have three children, aged 6 through 16, and have reached the "full plateau" stage of family life, the stage in which a family will not add new members but has not yet "launched" any children into adulthood. From my brief observations of their home life, I would characterize the Turners as an "open" type family (Kantor & Lehr 1975).[1]

When I first mentioned my study to him, Ezra was one of the few participants who was convinced that there "must be" some connection between what people do for a living and the quality of their relationships with family members. In our subsequent interview,[2] he elaborated this point of view:

ET: Like I always tell him [14-year-old Charles], "What would you want to do for a hobby? Once you establish what you want if you had all the money in the world and didn't have to work, what would you do?" Then if a person says, "Well, I'd like to do that," then, that's what a person should do to make his living. Then it's not like going to work. It's like your hobby and you're getting paid to do it.

R: Why do you think that's so important to people?

ET: [*Surprised*] I think a person should enjoy going to work!

R: I'm not disagreeing with you. I'm just wondering why you think that.

ET: I spend more time at [the hospital] than I do at any other place awake. I spend eight hours a day there. By the time I get home, a lot of times it's around ten o'clock or maybe six o'clock. I'm only going to be up another six hours, five hours at the most. So I'm spending all of my time on the job. I'm spending a third of my life on a job. I should enjoy that job. I should enjoy that third of my life. To me, that's really important. . . . You've got to do what you enjoy doing. . . . It's very important that a person has to do what they enjoy doing.

R: Otherwise what?

ET: Otherwise what? Well, you go to a job that you hate and it gets back to what we're talking about. You go to this job, these things are moving by, these things are banging down, people are yelling at you and then you come home and you've been in this mood all day. How can I relate to the

1. Kantor and Lehr have distinguished three types of families: the open, closed, and random family systems. The open family system is characterized by more variable family structures and mechanisms than the closed type. However, it is more stable than the random system. For example, during the day I observed the Turners, most family members ate dinner together, yet Clarisse's absence was readily accepted. In contrast, a closed family might expect all members to be present at a prescheduled dinner hour, whereas in a random type people might eat at separate times.

2. In the interview interchanges with participants, *R* denotes the researcher.

positive things—to my wife? How can I come home and say, "Oh, honey, how are you today?" Or wake up at three in the morning and say, "Wake up, wake up!" "What for?" "Because I love you." It's just—how can you—after you do something that you hate all the time. It just looks like you wouldn't be able to make the conversion back to being easygoing. . . .

R: Have you seen it happen?

ET: Yeah. . . . Half the people around that I know, they work on a job that they hate. They've got to get a couple of beers to calm them down. Then, tomorrow four beers and the next day, six. The next thing you know, they've conked out!

The Psychological Link: Job Gratification

Ezra considers himself to be unlike the people he described, for he loves his work, and among the research participants he spoke most positively about his job. For the past eight years he has been a technician-supervisor at an animal research laboratory in a hospital setting. Before that he was an orderly in the same setting, cleaning cages in the laboratory he now supervises.[3]

Ezra's feelings about his present position are reflected in the following interchange:

R: [To Isabel] When Ezra has had a bad day, now, can you tell?

IT: Not really.

R: Don't you have bad days?

ET: No. You know, a bad day now is when I go into a research meeting and I request $15,000 and I come out with $3,000. But that's not the same. That just means I got to go and do some more politicking and maneuver and that, you know. But it's just—no, I don't have any. [Pause] It's just a pleasant situation now. It's just altogether different.

R: The most pleasant work situation ever?

ET: I can't imagine—you know, like the program I'm in now, just to get a degree. I don't think I'd ever leave that job now that I'm on now! I really think—

IT: They'd have to shut the hospital down, I think.

ET: I can't imagine anything at the hospital that I'd rather do than what I'm doing now.

I had the opportunity to observe Ezra at the laboratory for a full day. Several aspects of his job situation impressed me. The physical environment was low-key, quiet, spacious, and clean; radios played softly, and there was little noise. Charles, his son, had described him as being

3. Isabel Turner had worked for many years as a practical nurse. After the birth of their last child she began to stay at home full time.

"on the run" all day, and I found this description accurate. We moved freely and energetically around the main building, to outlying buildings, and even drove to other hospitals during the day. In considering the physical aspects of his work environment I recalled his image about factory work:

> R: When we talked at the hospital . . . you said it was important for you never to work in a factory. You really have strong feelings about it.

> ET: Well, one reason why I wouldn't want to [work there] is 'cause I'd be confined to one little area. And there would be noise, and there would be moving things going by me.

Recently when he took a short-lived part-time job at an airport he became very sensitive to noise and was bothered by his eldest daughter's playing her phonograph. This sensitivity to noise was described by other research participants working in heavy industry. As he spoke of the noise at the airport, Ezra conveyed to me the impression that he felt assaulted by the environment there. In contrast, the physical space through which Ezra moved at work was very much "his" in that he exhibited a striking sense of security and control there. Consequently, I was not surprised when he told me he had helped to design the layout of the laboratory and the outlying buildings.

During the day I observed, Ezra made the rounds of the animals, took their temperatures, drew blood samples from a variety of animals— each task requiring somewhat different skills—ordered supplies, arranged for a conference, delivered oxygen tanks, calibrated technical instruments, and performed two operations. He had ordered the animals and after performing the operations will care for them and monitor their progress over the years. Thus, he will see the results of his efforts. Not only does he have the opportunity to do a variety of tasks that utilize his skills and allow him to learn new ones, but he also feels that through his work he is doing something useful in helping medical science. Feedback about one's job performance is important in reducing "role ambiguity" (Kahn et al. 1964) and the attendant strain. The work performed in Ezra's laboratory has been publicly recognized as "outstanding" by the hospital administration; thus, he can feel secure that he is doing his job well and that his work is esteemed and valued.

Nor was Ezra pressured by the work that had to be done, for he exerted control over his own schedule. Although he was so busy he took only five minutes for lunch, he stopped to chat with people in his wanderings around the hospital and took time to collect a piece of birthday cake that workers in another department had saved for him. The only time during the day that I was unable to talk to him was for fifteen minutes during one of the operations. The lack of pressure I perceived was confirmed by Ezra and by others in the setting. One lab technician volunteered that he liked his job because of the lack of pressure; in fact, he asserted that it was so pleasant there that a union was not needed.

When speaking of his previous job as an orderly at the same hospital, Ezra commented, "I always said that one day I'm going to be in a situation to make the work situation good and to make it where people don't mind going to work." Ezra feels that work in the laboratory is pleasant because of his efforts. For example, animal technicians do not ordinarily perform operations: this is a feature of the work role that he introduced. It is evident that Ezra has a great deal of organizational autonomy. Whereas supervisory personnel can sometimes find themselves in a stressful position between conflicting demands, Ezra rarely has contact with his superior, and he feels that he has excellent working relationships with those he supervises. The laboratory is his domain; when a new administrator threatened his autonomy several years earlier, it was legitimized once again by the head of the research unit. Most of the participants valued a certain amount of autonomy. Ezra was unique among them in that he had both autonomy and the power to effect desired changes. He summed up his position: "I pretty much have full control over the situation and it's just really, really a nice situation."

It has been suggested that one feature of what we call "play" is that pleasure is derived from the performance of the activity itself. Ezra is explicit in stating that, for him, working and playing are closely intermingled, and the sense of mastery he achieves doing his work is in itself self-enhancing. Not only is he validated in his position as provider for his family—a role he values—but he is confirmed as a masterful, competent person who maintains a sense of integrity by doing work he believes in. This confirmation comes not only from his personal sense of achievement about a job well done but also through the explicit recognition given him by the hospital administration. Erikson (1963) has suggested that "basic trust" is an attitude, gained early in life that our environment is safe and that we ourselves are reliable. This basic trust can be undermined or supported by later life experiences. Ezra's work experience seems to provide him with confidence about the world and about himself.[4] He is secure in his job, safe in his environment, and believes in his competence to handle the tasks at hand.

Availability, "Positive" Energy, and the Family System
At the end of the workday I observed, Ezra was in good spirits; he was working alone in his laboratory and just had successfully calibrated a machine. Ezra feels that the enjoyment and gratification he derives from his work extends into his relationship with his family. I had the

4. A sense of personal competence (White 1967) also can be enhanced by adult experience.

opportunity of observing a homecoming and an evening in the Turner home. The narrative of the forty-five minutes following Ezra's arrival illustrates the types of interactions occurring there.

"Reunion" (May 16)

It is a hot day in early spring. Isabel is sitting outside wondering whether she should wait dinner for Ezra. She asks 6-year-old Patsy whether she wants to eat or to wait for Daddy. Patsy would rather wait and goes off to play.

Ezra drives up and gleefully pretends to ride us down with his car. He parks and emerges wearing his green surgical shirt and cutoffs from which his undershorts are peeking. He is still dressed for the bicycle ride he took at lunchtime. He carries his briefcase and is beaming broadly as he walks up to us. Isabel smiles at his shorts and teases him: isn't he ashamed to have me see him "that way"? Ezra jokes back: I wouldn't have noticed if she hadn't mentioned it! He does not realize the extent to which his shorts are showing, and I tease back. As he sits down on the stoop he lets out a sigh. "What a day! Don't realize how much you need someone till he's gone." One of the lab technicians had left for vacation today. Ezra and Isabel discuss whether he will be putting fertilizer on the garden this evening. Ezra says he can't, as the rain will wash it off.

The children have heard him drive up, and Patsy rides up on her bike at the same time that Charles comes out of the house to greet his father. Ezra asks Patsy whether her gears are still slipping. She says, "No," not quite understanding him, and I remind her that I had had to fix her gears earlier. While they discuss Ezra's taking a look at her bicycle, Charles is trying to tell his father that he received a medal at school for outstanding performance at a track meet. Trying to make himself heard several times to no avail, he seems about to give up when Ezra looks up with interest and asks about it. Proudly and happily Charles explains about the medal and shows it off, telling him the circumstances of his receiving the award. Ezra is enthusiastic: "That's great!" Isabel adds, "That's your boy!" Charles is beaming, and he and his father discuss how long he can wear it. Isabel then tells Ezra that Charles said he didn't want to go to school tomorrow. His father asks him what that is about; Charles looks at his feet, mumbles something about "just kidding," and rushes off to join some friends in the backyard.

Meanwhile, Patsy has gone inside to put on a different sunsuit, as the one she is wearing won't stay fastened. She comes out and asks her mother to tie her suit and Ezra lovingly teases her about her "boobs" hanging out. Isabel admonishes him with a stern look. Ezra then turns his attention to Patsy's bike and says he'll need to fix the gear. They go into the garage to get some oil and then squat over the bike while he shows her where to oil it. Then they both hop on the bike to test it and ride off down the street. Isabel and I, still sitting in the driveway, see Ezra flying down the street on the bike, with Patsy in hot pursuit. They return and Patsy says knowledgeably, "Yup, that's what it needed—some oil." Ezra and Isabel smile at each other.

Isabel goes into the kitchen to put the remaining touches on the spaghetti dinner she is preparing, and Ezra and I remain outside to chat. Soon Patsy rides up on her bike, and as she gets off she hits her pubic bone, grimaces, and holds her groin. Ezra is very concerned and wants to know if she's all right. She doesn't answer him directly, though she nods and appears in pain. Finally, Ezra suggests that she have her mother take a look. He was obviously concerned but unsure about how to handle the matter. She goes inside and returns shortly. Ezra grabs her, pulls her onto his lap, and starts to nibble affectionately at her. She feigns protest but is delighted, and they discuss his animal bite and the scar on his arm.

Isabel calls them in for dinner and they sit down at the kitchen table. Clarisse, the eldest, is out with her friends. Ezra sighs. "What a day." Isabel asks about it, and Ezra tells her that Sid is on vacation and that having a new, inexperienced assistant on a difficult operation is not easy. Charles comes in and they say grace. Ezra asks him about the track meet as they prepare to eat, and Charles tells him the details as Isabel serves dinner. Ezra asks her whether she went to the insurance office today, and she answers that she tried but couldn't recall the forms he wanted. He describes them to her. As Isabel hands Ezra his plate, Patsy exhibits astonishment at the huge amount of spaghetti piled on it. Ezra tells her that he works and "burns up" a lot. They discuss the bread Isabel made and agree it is quite tasty. Then Isabel starts to tease Ezra by saying to him, "Your daddy said to stay out of his yard." Before he has a chance to respond, however, she asks whether he turned the water on in the garden before he left that morning. He did not. Patsy indicates that one of her cousins did it. They all discuss the fact that Isabel was minding Ezra's cousin's two children today while his mother went to the doctor. Ezra is sympathetic. "You must have had your hands full." "It wasn't too bad," she responds. Charles then enters the conversation and talks about his track meet at school.

Ezra then describes briefly what he learned at school[5] regarding the energy problem and gives his opinions about it. Isabel wonders what is to be done. Ezra thinks that rationing is inevitable, and they discuss how such rationing will be handled. The concern is with how much gas Ezra would need to get to and from work. Charles remarks, "If you don't go to work, you don't eat." They all suggest ways of dealing with the energy crisis. Then Ezra discusses his plans for being out of town. He announces that he's thirsty and, without being asked, Charles gets up and gets him an orange drink. (Ezra was sitting up against the wall at the table, and it would have been difficult for him to get up without disturbing others; the eating area is small.) Ezra asks about his eldest daughter's whereabouts, and then inquires into Charles's math test at school, but Charles hasn't received the results as yet. They discuss some people they know and talk further about the track meet at school and some of the young athletes there. Isabel asks Ezra if he wants some cake she made that afternoon—it's his favorite kind. He does, and Patsy brings the cake to the table. As the cake is served Patsy and Charles bicker slightly. Soon Charles and Ezra discuss their upcoming overnight canoe trip. They reminisce about their trip last year, the poker game they had, the weather, and the girlfriends some of the other boys missed. They laugh, recalling the events of last year.

Several connections between Ezra's work experiences and what I observed at home suggest themselves. Just as Ezra was physically active

---

5. Ezra is one of the participants who attend school part-time.

at work when I observed him, so was he equally vigorous at home. After finishing his dinner, he performed hard physical work in the family garden. His leisure pursuits are equally active: he skis, wrestles, and canoes. During the day the observations occurred, he had taken his bicycle to work in order to ride during the lunch period. Research suggests that people's leisure activities are similar in form to their work activities (see Meissner 1971). This relationship certainly holds for Ezra Turner. Moreover, the sense of security in his physical environment that I noted during the work observation was evident also in the home observation. Although I was startled when I saw him hurtle down the street on his 6-year-old daughter's bicycle, others remained nonchalant. Similarly, the lack of concern about Clarisse's whereabouts indicated a family sense that the world outside was trustworthy and under control.

At work, Ezra is a key figure in his laboratory, and he was the center of much of the interaction there when I observed the setting. Similarly, Ezra was at the center of an interactional network during the forty-five minutes reported above. He was involved in over 80 percent of all interactions and was the target of 31 percent of the initiations, more than any other family member.[6] Rapoport and Rapoport (1965) have used the term "isomorphism" to indicate similarities in behavior patterning in home and work settings. When we try to understand the sources of such possible isomorphisms, there is little theory to guide us. Since Ezra is a member of both settings, a psychological link suggests itself. The way Ezra feels about his work induces certain types of interactions within the family system. The broad smile on his face when he came home from work suggests that he was *emotionally available* and therefore *interpersonally available*, as indicated by his high degree of involvement in family interactions. As used here, emotional availability refers to a positive psychological state that leads to interpersonal availability, which refers to interpersonal behaviors. Such behavior has both an initiation and a response component. During the observation reported above, Ezra initiated more interactions than any other family member present. Of the total family interaction sequences, 45 percent were initiated by him.

Simple initiation rates are insufficient to describe what occurred during the observed period. When considering Ezra's interpersonal availability, the socioemotional quality of these interactions also becomes important. Coding for this component (see Methodological Appendix), we find that almost 74 percent of his initiations and responses were Positive, that is, affectionate, helpful, joyful, or conversational. The remainder were primarily Neutral. If Ezra had not responded so

6. Interactions in which I was involved were not coded. See the Methodological Appendix.

positively, other family members might have ceased their initiations toward him. Very few of these interactions were related specifically to his work. Yet we know that Ezra is gratified by what occurs there. We could suggest, then, that his work experience is brought into the family system through his emotional state and his consequent interpersonal availability to family members as evidenced by the number of Positive responses and approaches he makes in his interchanges with others.

The metaphor of energy interchanges is useful as a general way of characterizing this hypothesized connection between Ezra as an individual and the interactions that occurred at his homecoming. Working independently, Kantor and Lehr (1975) and Golden (1975) arrived at conceptualizations of energy dynamics in understanding family process.[7] To illustrate such energy dynamics, Kantor and Lehr contrasted two family activities:

> In one family, mealtime might be dull and unappealing, leaving its members bored and uninterested in what transpires. A second family may turn such a mealtime into an exciting occasion by having its hamburgers cooked over an open fire in the back yard. Both families could be acquiring the same amount of biochemical energy, yet one family could be experiencing social charge, while the other experiences an actual drain in social energy [1975, p. 91].

They described, further, such processes as fueling, tapping, charging, and discharging. Both Golden and Kantor and Lehr have suggested the importance of maintaining a balance between "positive" and "negative" energies in family systems.

Such conceptualizations of energy interchanges are still vague and necessarily problematic. To describe energy as positive or negative violates our usual conceptions of it, and what is high and what is low energy remain undefined. Also, the energy concept is applied sometimes to the individual and at other times to the social system. The greatest danger in using this concept is that one may reify what is essentially a metaphor and treat it as an explanatory construct rather than as a way of descriptively referring to a complex set of transactions. Despite these limitations in its use, such metaphors can be useful as *evocative* characterizations of the interface transactions that occur between individuals and their environments, whether those environments consist of other people or tools and machines.

Using energy metaphors, we could say that Ezra initiated a process of "positive" energy interchanges through his interpersonal availability to family members; he introduced laughter, joking, and personal energy for family activities. This energy interchange was mutually reinforcing.

7. While his concern was with instinctual energies, Fenichel also wrote of "mental energy exchange" and intake, consumption, and output (1945, p. 14).

He drove up in a way that invited Isabel to joke back, and in working on Patsy's bicycle with her, he helped her to feel important. His approving responses to Charles's achievement in the track meet helped to enhance his son's self-esteem. These interactions continued throughout the evening. Isabel, Patsy, and Ezra worked in the garden after dinner. While they expended much physical effort, they gained a sense of accomplishment working together, and they laughed over Isabel's timidity regarding a frog that they found. Still later, Ezra and Charles watched a television prize-fight together, keeping up a running dialogue about the relative merits of the fighters.

It should be noted that the energy cycle within a family can be mutually reinforcing. Other family members "charged" Ezra in return by showing him their love and appreciation. Patsy and Charles fueled the family system also through their achievements and development. Thus, "positive" energy was "created."[8] While Ezra's job takes him away from the family, I am suggesting that it returns "positive" energy to the family system through the translation of his feelings of well-being—his emotional availability—into interpersonal availability to others.

An implicit question, to be considered in Chapter 5, is to what extent the pattern described here can be explained solely in terms of Ezra's unique personality. Moreover, the portrait of the Turner family presented here implies a perfect integration of work and family life. However, in the discussion of the structural interface in Chapter 4, we will consider the dilemmas the work world posed for the Turner family and the solutions they devised.

The Pattern of Negative Carry-over

By focusing on the relationship Ezra Turner has to his work, I have suggested that the gratifications he derived from his work carried over into the family system through his emotional and interpersonal availability, creating a pattern of positive carry-over. Conversely, a negative pattern can occur when stressful feelings at work are carried into the family space. Moreover, these stresses can displace the potential for positive family interactions, while requiring family members to expend their personal resources in assisting the worker to manage strain. Again, an "ideal type" can illustrate this interface pattern.

The Psychological Link: Job Stress

Although I knew before I interviewed him that Ezra Turner perceived a positive dynamic between his work life and his family life, I had

8. Compare Raush's (1965) notion of behavioral reciprocity.

no idea where the Johnson family stood on this matter. The Johnsons were referred to me by their 23-year-old son, Tony.

Betty and Henry Johnson have been married for twenty-four years. They have four children, aged 16 to 23, but only the youngest two children are still at home. They are a family in the "launching stage" of the family life cycle. At the time of their first interview, Henry was working as a dispatcher and deliveryman for a small wholesale food distribution firm. Betty worked at home and also in a neighborhood beauty parlor for several hours each week.

It became apparent within the first five minutes of their joint interview that the Johnsons perceived Henry's relationship to his job as having a key impact on their life as a family.

R: How would you describe yourself?

HJ: Well, I worry about a lot of things that I probably shouldn't worry about. Well, more things about work than I should. And things that probably will never happen, I'm worrying—concerned about.

R: What kinds of things do you worry about at work that you think you worry about more than you should?

HJ: Well, like in one capacity there as a dispatcher—worrying about are my people going to show up to work the next day. Well, this is . . . normal that they would show. Well, I might wake up at two or three o'clock in the morning and worry, "Are they going to show up?" And then what's going to happen during the day. Are they going to be doing what's right? Just— you just normally worry about things, wonder about things that nine times out of ten never happen anyway.

R: Does that mean also you tend to worry sometimes about things you don't have control over, like whether somebody will show up?

HJ: Oh, yeah. Normally that would be what I would be concerned about. Is the day going to go right? Is the day going to go the way it should go? And, again, nine times out of ten, it does. But these are pretty much the things that I worry about there.

When I asked Betty about Henry's tendency to worry and wake up during the night, she confirmed what he had said:

BJ: Oh, yes. It happens a lot. He would wake up in the middle of the night, and then he'll wake up without even the alarm going off.

We know that people sometimes "worry" as a way of attempting to control their anxieties. Worry can become a way of rehearsing contingencies and therefore mastering potentially threatening situations. If one has considered all possibilities, then the situation is felt to be in hand. We might understand Henry Johnson's worrisomeness as a character trait and leave it at that. Other evidence indicates, however, that his tendency to worry is connected to his work. In other words, he does not worry about home life, and when on a vacation he reported that he only begins to worry a few days before returning to work. A more useful understanding of Henry's tendency to worry about work is one that considers the transactions between person and setting. We need to ask what there is about Henry's relationship to his job that provokes the excessive use of worry as a coping strategy.

Unlike Ezra Turner, Henry's work is a source of psychological strain. Kahn et al. (1964) have provided one key to understanding Henry's difficulties in their concept of a "boundary position." A person occupies a boundary position when his or her job duties require him or her to interact with people in more than one subsystem of an organization or with people in other organizations. Stress is created because people in these different systems all have differing expectations about how job duties are to be fulfilled. Boundary positions are a major battleground of organizational conflict. As a dispatcher and delivery-man, Henry occupied not one but two such boundary positions, and he absorbed the conflicts inherent in them.[9] As a dispatcher, he stood at a subsystem boundary, mediating between the deliverymen and the salesmen. When a deliveryman had a complaint about a salesman, he turned to Henry to manage the conflict.

> HJ: My driver would come back and complain, and then I would go and complain to the salesman. Well, that was—to me that was like talking to the wall. They don't care. I mean this is my impression. They don't care. They were making a sale.

In his job as dispatcher Henry had to ensure deliveries to the customers; yet, the salesmen made promises that the deliverymen could not carry out. Henry had no power in negotiating with the salesmen. He would become angry, and we know that anger is a difficult emotion for many people to manage because it threatens the loss of control. Moreover, when a deliveryman was absent, Henry sometimes substituted for him, and this additional work was also a source of stress, as well as something more to worry about. His drivers' absenteeism meant work overload, an overload made worse with age.

> R: Has that increased at all as you've gotten older, or has it gotten less? I mean, do you worry less?
>
> HJ: Well, I would think that it would probably increase more as I got older. I mean it's—it just feels to me that if there's three jobs to be done, if something should happen where the three jobs couldn't be done, I could

9. At the outset of the study, Henry was being moved from his assignment as a dispatcher to being a deliveryman. For a while, he performed both jobs. At the completion of the study, he worked only as a deliveryman.

42

> only take care of one of them. Where . . . if you're 20 or 30 or something like that, maybe you could handle all three of them. Now, I know I couldn't. . . . If you get down to it, there's nothing you can do about it anyway.

Henry also has a back ailment. Kahn et al. have pointed out that for a person to perform his or her assigned job role adequately, there needs to be a balance between the demands placed on him or her and the resources at hand. A significant and crucial feature of Ezra Taylor's work situation was the adequacy of resources to do the job. Henry, in contrast, described the inadequate time and—with age—diminishing strength to perform his job duties. Moreover, with the salesmen he lacked the power to effect changes that would ease the strain he experienced.

As a deliveryman, Henry now occupies another boundary position between these same salesmen and the customers outside the organization. Boundary positions are more stressful when a person is not the sole business contact with outside systems. Henry described this source of strain:

> HJ: The salesman says we'll have so many of these steaks, so many of those steaks. I'll sell you a side of beef. Well, obviously you take this and there's just so many parts in that thing. I don't care how you take it apart, that's the amount of parts you're going to get in it. Now, the salesman is going to tell them, "I'm going to give you these parts, plus I'm going to give you something else. I'll give you an extra handle or I'll give you this, or I'll give you instead of seven pebbles I'll give you ten." There's just so many parts in this thing; they know it as well as I do. And they know it as well as the butcher that's cutting it. But they're salesmen; they're prone to a little shoving and such things. These are the things that aggravate me. [As the tape ends he describes how this puts him in a difficult position with regard to the customers who expect him to deliver the goods. He is the one present when what they expect is not delivered.] And I just assumed that it was my job to make the deliveries and to make the customer happy, regardless of whether I delivered or my drivers delivered it. . . . Well, it had been explained to me that part of the driver's job is to cover up for mistakes made by other people.

Henry takes his work seriously. Doing his job well is an important source of self-esteem. However, in this boundary position he, again, is placed in a situation where he lacks the resources to satisfy customers while lacking power over the salesmen. Consequently, Henry often is angry at the customers and the salesmen.

Anger can be experienced as an overpowering emotion. Earlier I suggested that one of the ways Henry tries to manage his anxiety and gain control over his feelings is through worrying. Worrying also has the connotation of chewing things over until they become familiar and are finally mastered. Henry described this process:

HJ: I'll talk to myself a lot. I used to. Things just boil up inside. Sometimes it's easier to get it out and if I sit in there—they can be in their room doing their homework, and I'm in there talking to myself sometimes.

R: Does that make you feel better?

HJ: No, because I think I antagonize myself. It's like hitting your head against a wall. When you're through it feels so good. And it's something probably is not a good psychology or philosophy or whatever. But, not necessarily. Sometimes it makes me more aggravated.

R: Because you get all excited? . . .

HJ: I might have forgotten something that happened in the morning, but if I keep talking to myself long enough, I'll remember it. No, I don't think it ever did me any good. . . . If I can get around to the point where I maybe I can realize what the hell I am doing, then, if I can talk to myself the other way: "So what the hell is the difference? Sew it up!"

Henry's attempts to control his anger lead him in two directions. Sometimes, the feelings become intense and he relives them. At other times, he talks himself into a stance where the incident is less significant so that he attains some distance from it.

Unavailability, "Negative" Energy, and the Family System

Personal attempts to cope with work-related stress can affect other family members and the system as a whole. Although we lack observations of the Johnson family, we can look through Betty Johnson's eyes to gain perspective on how the family was affected by Henry's attempts to master strain.

R: How do you feel about your husband's worries?

HJ: I've probably bored them to death with my work.

BJ: It drives me crazy [stated definitely and tersely]. . . . I try to ignore it, but—he gets too involved. I mean, he brings work home too much.

R: You wish he were able to keep it at work?

BJ: [Indicates yes.]

R: Is that something that you've ever fought about?

BJ: Not in particular. But when he comes home like that it would bring up—I mean, it would cause tension.

R: When you say "like that," you mean—

BJ: Well, bringing all his work problems home, and he's involved in that. And then if he's mad or upset, then he's mad and upset all night and the next day. . . .

R: Do you think people should leave their work at their work?

BJ: Well, sometimes you can't. But I think you can get carried away with it. . . . If he had a fight with the driver or something, I mean, he was just very hard—I mean, he was just mad all night.

44

The Psychological Interface: Three Patterns

R: How did he act when he was in a bad mood? How did you know?

BJ: Well, he just walks in and lets everyone know he's had a bad day. . . . He walks in and says, "I'm tired." Or he comes in swearing about somebody or something. Then you can ask a question about—I don't care what question it was—and in one sentence it will immediately get back to what had made him [upset. *The tape ends as she describes how Henry cannot listen because he returns to the subject of what bothers him.*] Because this is not my husband's business. I mean, it's going to go on. So what? It bothers me that he gets so involved.

R: What do you do when he gets so involved and so upset?

BJ: There's really nothing—I read. There's really nothing I can do about it.

R: You tried to ignore it, then?

BJ: Yeah. I try. I learn to ignore a lot.

R: What did you do before you ignored it?

BJ: It would bother me. I'd get hurt.

R: You would get hurt?

BJ: Think it was me, or something. Or couldn't understand why he just couldn't forget it. When things would come up about the kids, I couldn't discuss it because sometimes it was just easier not to say something about what I had problems about because he was already so mad. But now I've learned to ignore it a little. . . .

R: Did [the children] react?

BJ: [*Nods*] To the point where they would come in, like maybe ask a question or something—the poor kids are noisy. Well, Henry didn't like the noise. Everything had to be quiet. . . . Well, it's like hard to keep them quiet. And it was hard to explain, "Dad's tired because he's worked all day."

R: It was your job to keep them quiet?

BJ: Yeah. As much as you can to keep four kids quiet.

Betty went on to comment, "Then there's someone like me, who's an outsider [to the job] but is involved, is really the one that suffers." Henry was present as Betty talked, and he seemed to concur in her description. He was sad as he commented:

HJ: My family hasn't had the greatest in the world as far as—rather, I haven't been as congenial, gay, and happy as I should.

R: It sounds like your temperament and the kind of work you do sometimes made things difficult at home for the family.

HJ: Well, I would say that was 90 percent of many of the problems we were having.

Henry's expression of anger about work while at home has several impacts on family members and interactions. The spatial separation of work and home obscured for Betty the source of Henry's anger and irritation. We might suppose that the slightest insecurity would cause her to experience his anger as directed at her. Eventually, she learned to cope by ignoring Henry. Such avoidance was designed to protect herself both from hurt and from her own anger, which was indicated in her comment, "I've learned to ignore it, so it's not that I holler and scream."

Betty's anger stemmed, in part, from Henry's interpersonal unavailability to her. She described Henry's inability to listen to her concerns because of his preoccupations with his feelings. Consequently, she did not talk over her everyday problems with him. We might suspect that such a process affected the pattern of closeness between them. Hess and Handel (1959) have noted that one of the most important dimensions of family psychosocial life is how family members work out patterns of separateness and closeness; Kantor and Lehr (1975) have described this process as "distance regulation." Betty's relationship with her children may have provided her with some of the intimacy she needed. Tony, their eldest son, talked of being particularly close to his mother. When he began to "act out" during adolescence, Henry was pulled abruptly into the center of the family to help deal with the crisis that was created. He sometimes left work during the day to deal with school officials and to attend to Betty and her deteriorating relationship with Tony. Betty reported that, during this period, Henry was available to her.

Insofar as Henry is taken up with coping with his anger, he is less able to tolerate environmental pressures. At times, he becomes visibly irritable with his children.

HJ: They [the children] would do the same thing.[10] Inwardly, it would possibly bother you as much if everything were fine. . . . But if you're aggravated, you have something else on your mind . . . you're a little quicker to say it. They can do the same thing and it would probably bother [me] almost as much. But if you're in a bad mood or down or tired or whatever it might be, you'd be a little quicker to come up with it.

The children learned to protect themselves from their father's bad moods by distancing themselves from him. Now, "I walk into the house at night," Henry said, "and these kids go to a back room and listen to records. I don't know if this is just a—" Betty interrupted him here to explain that it was due to their adolescence, but we are left wondering whether the pattern described above contributed to this gulf between Henry and his children. He was further removed from his children because Betty served as a gatekeeper of their father's moods, mediating between Henry and his children.

10. By this Henry meant that the children's behavior was more or less consistent from day to day, but his responses would vary with his mood.

BJ: Well, let's say for instance if something had come up with Tony and he wanted to talk to his dad— When I knew Tony was getting married . . . and then he said, "I'm going to tell Dad tomorrow." Now, this came out of the blue. So I called Henry at work to prepare him because not knowing what kind of mood he was going to be in, that this is serious and that Tony wants to talk to you.

Such a dynamic can establish long-term communication patterns that separate family members. In the pattern of positive carry-over, family members converged on Ezra Turner's arrival. Henry Johnson's very different experience at his workplace had the opposite effect of scattering them when he got home. We might say, additionally, that the carry-over of negative feelings into the family system established a series of "negative" energy interactions there. Observational data on home and work settings might have established similarities between the anger and tension Henry experiences at work and in the home sphere.

Home as Haven: Who Pays?　Henry needed the distance and space so created to recoup his personal resources and to manage his feelings in order for him to return to work the next day. When Betty commented on her efforts to keep the children quiet so that he would have such a space, she echoed a theme repeated in a number of other interviews. However, the creation of such a space meant that other family members had to adjust their needs and their activities. Thus, Henry's work experience intruded in the Johnson home space directly and immediately. The "home as haven" is a theme that recurs in the literature on work and on families (see Lasch 1977). The family is said to maintain and stabilize adult personality (McKinley 1964; Parsons 1955), to serve as an "oasis of replenishment" (N. B. Ryder 1974), and as a refuge against the brutality of the industrial world (Ehrenreich & English 1975). Ryder wrote that "the adequate functioning of individuals in the economic system, and thus of the system itself, requires effective maintenance of their emotional equilibrium" (1974, p. 712). In other words, both workers and work organizations are dependent on families to "replenish" the family member who must go out to work. That home is a "haven" for Henry is evident from the following comment he made in response to my question about why he lacks a sense of urgency at home in contrast to work.

HJ: Well, one thing I think is after it's all pretty much over with, at least here I'm home; I'm secure and I'm more or less, more relaxed than I am at work, or something like that. . . . So that's about it. I mean, a little more relaxed. It doesn't have to be done *now* and the world isn't going to end.

Whereas Ezra Turner had an expansive orientation to his environment and felt secure there, Henry contracts into his private space and rests there. He relinquishes some control and relaxes. Insofar as the home space serves as a haven for Henry and as a place where he can replenish himself, it helps to sustain him emotionally. But we need to consider its consequences for other family members. We noted that they sometimes had to give up their space to Henry. Moreover, Betty expended time and effort to create a quiet environment for him. Here we see her in the traditional female role of nurturer. As she spoke, her tone and her words suggested that she felt angry and bitter, as what she was receiving in return was not always clear to her. She had come to dislike housework more and more, and the paid work, which she enjoyed, occupied her for only a few hours a week. Her children were a source of deep gratification for her but also were sometimes a source of worry.

Golden (1975) has suggested that a family's reserve of "energy" is not endless, and that long-term energy "deficits" can be a strain. Using these notions we might say that in creating a haven for Henry, the family system paid a price in energy deficits that were expressed in dissatisfactions and estrangements. As we have seen, the home as haven may have its costs.

Variation on a Theme

The Healys are a young couple with two small children. Mike has worked in a factory for ten years, and recently he was given a different job that is extremely dirty and unpleasant. He is very dissatisfied with this change and is "bidding" on other jobs in the plant. In the Johnson family, Henry brought his negative feelings directly into the family space by talking about his work. A similar dynamic occurs in the Healy family, with an additional variant on the pattern of the negative carry-over, for Mike Healy also displaces angry feelings onto his wife, Celia.

R: Have you noticed any changes in the way Mike acts at home since he got this new job?

CH: [*Without hesitation and with much feeling*] He's a king crab! He goes to bed grouchy; he gets up grouchy!

R: How does he act?

CH: Real miserable! [*She giggles and sneaks a look at Mike.*]

R: Does he swear and get irritable?

CH: [*Acts delighted to have this talked about*] No—no. He just gets grumpy, like he was before you came. "Goddam this and blahblahblah!" And he's started. . . . He's crabby!

R: So he crabs at you and—

CH: Yeah!

R: —he crabs at Penny [young daughter]?

CH: No, not at Penny, just at Mommy? [*Laughs*] Just at Mommy.

MH: Don't yell at my kids.

48

The Psychological Interface: Three Patterns

CH: Don't yell at his kids. Just Mommy.

  R: Do you realize you're doing it?

MH: Yeah!

CH: Yeah. He thinks it's cute! . . . He comes home and says, you know, about his job, and I'm not even interested. But he gets so mad at work that he brings it home with him. He goes to bed grouchy and gets up grouchy.

  R: You're not really interested in hearing about it?

CH: No.

  R: Why not?

CH: Because it's the same old stuff. "I hate that job, I hate that job!" [Laughs] I'm so sick of hearing it! . . .

  R: When you start acting grouchy as Celia describes it, do you realize it's connected to your work?

MH: Yeah! . . .

  R: Do you think it's better to let it out?

MH: Sure, why should I hold it in?

  R: What happens if you hold it in?

MH? My ulcer would act up! . . .

  R: [To Celia] What do you think?

CH: I think he's wrong! I don't think I should be blamed for his job!

MH: Well, you shouldn't irritate me! You shouldn't say nothing to me! Then we won't argue. . . .

  R: Sounds like you've got a real bind here. You need to talk about your work or else your stomach acts up.

MH: Right.

  R: On the other hand, that creates a problem for you.

CH: Right.

  R: So what's the solution?

CH: Don't ask me. I wish I knew! [Laughs]

MH: Get a different job. . . .

  R: When you were on the job you had before, were you as grouchy?

MH: No!

CH: No! He was pleasant to live with! Now—forget it! He just jumps all over me! He just starts yelling at me, like he did tonight—you got up and he was real crabby. He just started yelling at me for no reason at all.

  R: So you're getting crabby because you know you have to get up and go to work. Is that right?

MH: Yeah. I guess so. Like I said, I just don't want to—when I don't want to be bothered, I don't want to be bothered. As far as my kids—I don't get crabby with my kids. . . .

R: So, even though you might be tired and grouchy, you have a lot of patience with them?

MH: For my kids, I got all the time in the world. . . . I love 'em. I mean, there's no doubt—I love both my kids. And I'd do anything in the world for them. I mean, I discipline them—don't get me wrong. I'm stern, but I can tolerate a lot off of them!

CH: Not off me!

MH: But you're not a kid!

CH: I know I'm not a kid! But you've gotta have patience with me too! I put up with these two [laughs] brats all day.

As with Henry Johnson, Mike's feelings about his work carry directly into the family system, and the theme of making space for the wage earner emerges once again. Moreover, in saying he does not want to be "bothered," Mike is telling Celia that he is not available to her when he is feeling upset.

Another variation of the pattern of negative carry-over lies in the dynamic by which Mike's anger about his work situation becomes displaced and transformed into hostile interactions with his wife. As an adult, Mike feels that Celia can take care of herself and he need not feel guilty about this process. In the interview he also expressed some resentment about having to work at a job he dislikes while she stays home. Celia manages the onslaught of her husband's moods differently than did Betty Johnson. Betty used to feel hurt and wondered if Henry were angry with her. Celia is straightforwardly angry and does not doubt herself. An important difference may be that she can see the connection between his work and his anger because of his recent job change. For Betty, this connection had been obscured. This difference also is important in helping us see that the nature of the family system and the other members within it can modify and temper the negative carry-over pattern.

McKinley (1964) also has suggested a form of such affective displacement when he hypothesized that men's status frustration in achieving occupational success would be translated into aggressive behaviors toward their sons. His findings were equivocal perhaps because his hypothesis was too broad. He did not foresee the variety of ways in which anger about work can carry over into the family system.

The Pattern of Energy Deficit

Participants rarely mentioned the extension of positive feelings from workplace into the family system. The carry-over of negative feelings was alluded to more frequently. Still more common were mentions of personal depletion and energy drain; yet this latter pattern was not recognized as an interface relationship. Whereas pleasant family processes and tension-filled ones are readily noted and reported, people tend to be unaware of what is *not* occurring between them. Yet, as we saw in the case of the Johnson family, what does *not* take place among family members can have significance equal to what does. Again, we can best suggest this pattern by turning to the words of the participants themselves.

The Psychological Link: Personal Depletion

Some reference to the wage earner's being tired or "physically and mentally beat" was made in ten of the thirteen families. One source of personal depletion is a strenuous and boring job, such as Samuel Coleman has on a machine-paced assembly line.

R: Is your work hard?

SC: It's not that hard, but it's a menial task. You know, it's more mental than it is physical with me.

R: You mean it's not physically hard, but it's mentally hard?

SC: It's a little of both, I'll put it that way. It's mentally and physically hard. It wears your body and your mind.

Eric Cooper, who was a computer operator and now monitors the information coming from a large computer, was adamant as he described the process of personal depletion arising from boredom with his job.

EC: I think a boring job, a job that doesn't take too much mentally from a person and doesn't take too much physically from a person, affects his home life also. I think he tends to become lazy. I do, personally. Before I got married I was a very energetic person. I was skinny; I'm overweight now, but I was skinny. I had a lot of energy. I was very sports-minded; I was always on the go. I had four or five hours of sleep at night; that was sufficient. I was never tired. The first couple years of marriage I was basically like that. I gained a lot of weight, though, but it was basically like that. But once I started getting into the job being boring, less mentally aware—I feel like I'm walking in a daze all the time. I mean, it's just something personal about me, but I just feel like I'm walking in a daze all the time. I don't feel like I'm mentally awake all the time. And I think a lot of that has to with the job because there is not much demand on my job or something like this. So I'm out of condition. I'm out of condition and I think I'm out of condition for doing anything. I get home from work and I'm just so *bored,* I don't feel that there is that much to keep me going at home, physically and so forth. So I think that has the tendency to make a person—me anyways—lazy. . . . But if I had a job that kept me going and kept me occupied at work or something to do instead of sitting around like I'm doing right now—it took more of my mental powers—this is one reason why I like school, because it gives me something to do—but it [work] has made me a lazy person.

When Eric started in computer work he felt a sense of challenge and mastery, for he performed many of the operations necessary for the functioning of the computer. He saw his job as "fun" and "interesting." A change in technology and finally a change in job assignment led to his present job monitoring a computer tape.

Boredom is tiring. Conversely, being presented with a challenge that tests our capabilities can be exciting. For example, Tony Johnson, another computer operator, described his excitement about trying his hand at writing a computer program on his own time.

> TJ: I was there two hours one night the other day—overtime, you know—getting this program to work. And I was a nut! I was going crazy. . . . I was "hyper." . . . If I've had a good day, like, I feel good. Like when I did my program, I walked home and called everyone in the world. . . . When I'm into things, I have all the energy in the world.

Psychologists lack an adequate language to describe the processes that Eric, Samuel, and Tony described. Often, enervation and boredom are viewed as indicators of inner conflict. Alternatively, we could examine the balance of costs and benefits in a worker's relationship to his or her job. Ezra Turner works hard but receives from his work a sense of self-worth and competence. Eric Cooper, on the other hand, trades his time and effort for a salary, but on a day-to-day basis he receives little gratification in return. Using energy metaphors, Kantor and Lehr would call these processes "charging" and "discharging."

While the concepts of charging and discharging may be useful metaphors for the phenomenon, they do not explain it. It is possible that the process of enervation goes deeper than a mere physical tiredness, for the men also were describing a mental fatigue. We may find some clue to the underlying dynamic in the recurring image of being "beat." As a colloquial term, it denotes being physically and mentally tired. However, the term also is used to signify being assaulted, suggesting that these men feel assaulted in their work lives. Mike Healy, for example comes home with burns and metal chips in his skin from the machine he tends. Samuel Coleman works on a machine-paced line that dictates the movements of his body. Losing control over one's body can be experienced as an assault on one's physical integrity. Tom Doyle described an attack on his personal integrity when he worked as a foreman and was required to carry out actions that he considered inhumane and unethical. He fought upper management constantly and subsequently developed a serious ulcer and began to drink, until he transferred to the clerical job he has at present. Being beat also carries the connotation of being defeated in an implicitly adversary relationship; we might say that Tom was defeated by his job.

Eric Cooper and Tony Johnson both used the symbol of death in connection with their concern that they lack job mobility and may have to remain in their particular positions. What such lack of mobility signifies is not failure to gain increased earnings but the loss of their "dream" and the potential for realizing their ideal selves. One's ideal self is merely an image and a potentiality until actualized, for it is through our actions that we become known to ourselves. Death of the opportunity for realizing this possibility can be experienced as the ultimate defeat.

TJ: Like I gave myself two years, so if I'm not out of there, I'm dead, really.

R: You say "dead." . . . It's as if you think of yourself as—

TJ: [*Interrupts*] Not dead, but I know damn well that if I'm not out in two years I'm going to lose the incentive to get out of that place, so in a sense it is dead. I mean, my dream is going to die.

Tony dreams of becoming a lawyer, and he fears being seduced by the financial inducements of his job. In going to work in a factory, Samuel Coleman also gave up a dream. We know that the threatened loss of one's ideal self can be depressing. Such a sense of depression emerged when Tony described his tiredness at the end of a workday.

TJ: It's a boring tired. It's like sleeping for twenty-four hours and you wake up and you're exhausted. You shouldn't be tired. . . . Maybe your brain is in idle so long that it's used to being in idle. . . . It's not a good tired, man. It's a shitty tired. It's just a lazy tired, man. You just don't give a damn and you're just not involved.

The boredom and lack of challenge Tony experiences at his work as a computer operator strikes at the heart of his ideal self. When he does work that is personally gratifying and confirms himself as a person who can meet challenges and succeed, he has "all the energy in the world."

Eric Cooper also described the threat to his ideal self that occurred when he became simply a "tape hanger." He became animated and angry as he talked.

EC: It took everything away from you, it really did. You were just a tape hanger. You were not a computer operator any more! You were much like you would be in a factory, like "bolt, bolt" as the machines went by. That's exactly what it was.

R: What did it take away?

EC: Before that, we would run the computers. . . . You felt more involved in your job; you felt more personal because the work that was coming out was work that you were doing personally. Whereas, when you went over to the [other] system, everything was taken away from you, basically. There was no opportunity to learn anything new. It was so monotonous. . . . There's no personal satisfaction in doing anything there. . . . You're not where you learn anything or where you really feel useful.

53

In becoming a tape hanger Eric Cooper felt alienated from his work and from the opportunity to become the person he wished to be—energetic, masterful, esteemed. He no longer felt connected to what he did and felt robbed of the opportunity to learn and to feel useful. Each day at work, therefore, may be felt as a personal defeat and loss. Sennett and Cobb have noted, "When you are just taking orders, you are not really alive..." (1972, p. 94).

Unavailability, Energy Deficit, and the Family System

We need to consider how personal depletion that originates in a person's work situation might affect family systems. Again the interview data give us some clues. Samuel Coleman commented:

SC: The work wears your body and just the thought—I don't know.... The assembly line has a way of just wearing you down by the end of a forty-hour week. You just be—mentally and physically beat! And you look forward to your two days off.... I think the guy that works in an office can come home and get more accomplished around the home than the guy working in the factory.

R: Really? How come?

SC: Because of the physical tiredness that the factory brings upon you.

R: You feel when you come home you're too worn out to do much?

SC: That's right. [Laughs] That's it. I am worn out!

Samuel imagines that the office worker can accomplish more at home than the production worker; that is, he has more physical energy available for his home life. Eric Cooper also thought that his depletion at work carried over into his personal life.

EC: My feeling is that if you're lazy at work, if you are not in demand at work, either mentally or physically, I think that it carries over into your family life. I imagine that with some people it doesn't. Some people, they would explode when they get home or something and become more energetic. But for me it works just the other way. Whereas if I'm not demanded at work and so, when I get home, it just carries over at home and I become more lazier at home.

Eric has suggested an isomorphism between what occurs at work and what happens when he comes home. Both Eric and Samuel make a point of never talking about their jobs at home, yet in the form of personal depletion their work experience nevertheless make themselves evident in the family system.

Like Henry Johnson, Eric wants his home space to be a haven.

EC: Where I got to go and put up eight hours or actually nine hours with the travel time and so forth, at work—with the hassles and tribulations that go on in work. With a boring job you have enough to go in there. Then you come home and you come home in a situation that your wife's in a bitchy mood or a bad mood. The kids are hassling everybody. You walk in; you not only have the hassles at work, which is different from the family, but you come home and you are walking into the middle of the furnace at home. This is where if the person is not too happy with the job that he is working with and comes home with this situation, that's where it could really affect the man.

The personal depletion Eric experiences at work makes it difficult for him to deal with the demands placed on him by the family system. At the time of the interview, the Coopers had recently had a second child. Golden (1975) has described the "high" energy needs of families with young infants; we know that parents often feel overwhelmed by the birth of a new child (LeMasters 1957). Eric's depletion makes it more difficult for him to meet the demands placed on him by his family. One solution the Coopers found to this difficulty was to place their older child in a day-care center, thereby easing some of the strain felt by his wife. Because he works an afternoon shift and his son is gone during the day, Eric rarely sees his little boy at a time of life when contact with his father may be particularly important.

Personal depletion and the need for space to "muster" (Kantor & Lehr 1975) personal energies may make a worker unavailable to family members. Tony Johnson described the interaction between his need to recoup his personal energies and his son's need for attention from Daddy. Before dinner he usually takes a short nap, but the rest is insufficient to deal with his son during the dinner hour, as the boy often refuses to eat.

TJ: I'm tired. I don't want to hear the kid screaming, stuff like that. . . . I don't think I'm spending enough time with him. . . . It's just that a lot of times when I get home from work, I'm tired and I just—the kid goes on all night.

R: He's very active?

TJ: Oh, yeah. He's all over the place . . . real "hyper" and stuff.

R: When you come home from work you're tired . . . and he's kind of hard for you to cope with? Is that what happens?

TJ: He's too loud sometimes or he wants to hit me in the head, and I don't feel like getting hit in the head because my head's tired. There's a lot of times when I have to shut him out for a while. And then there's the times when I can see him getting kind of bummed out, so then I'll play with him . . . he just looks at me and goes "Ahhh," you know . . . or he'll make sure that I know he's there, by kicking the window in or [laughs]. He doesn't kick windows in, but, you know what I mean, like making a scene.

When he is depleted from work, Tony has difficulty being interpersonally available to his child, both in finding it difficult to initiate positive interactions with him and to respond to him. Demands for attention are experienced as irritations. Tony tries to withdraw from his son, but his young son wants contact with his father. He cannot understand that his father is tired. Betty Johnson felt personally rejected and hurt by Henry's preoccupation; she did not understand the source of his anger. Little Tony cannot understand his father's indifference. He also may experience it as rejection, and his fussing may be his way of expressing hurt and anger as well as corralling Daddy's attention. Again, Tony Johnson rarely talks about his work while at home.

Jesse Jones, a relief man on an assembly line, described a similar pattern of unavailability to his young son.

> JJ: Like he would be crying sometimes or whining, and I would be trying to think about what I've got to do before I go to work. A lot of times it's running close to the time for me to go to work, and then he's pulling on me and she gets mad at me because I won't pay no attention to him and stuff like that. So sometimes I have to ignore him to think about other things.

Jesse sometimes has to "muster" his energies before going to work on a particularly unpleasant job. "I get me a couple hours more rest before I go in for something like that," he noted. Again the theme of a worker creating space for himself by withdrawing from his child, who wants contact with him, is repeated. Furthermore, this deficit pattern causes some tension between Jesse and his wife, Sandra. Jesse's personal energy becomes the battleground for systemic conflict about energy distribution, expressed in conflict and tension between himself and Sandra when he is unavailable to her.

> JJ: Even working a straight eight-hour day is kind of hard, because you get out of that factory, you is tired. . . . It's kind of hard for my wife to accept the fact that you're tired when you come home. Early the next morning, up on the floor [laughs], she's ready to go. She got something to do; she want me to take her. I have to get on up and take her. . . . Once you get out of that place you be relieved [laughs]. . . . If I work hard to get done in four hours, I have to really work hard. But you don't feel all that energy you used up until after you come home and lay down and relax. Then that's when it all hits you.
>
> R: And then how do you feel?
>
> JJ: Then you gotta rip and run; OK, say if my wife want to do something early in the day, we ripping and runnin' the streets, going to pay bills and stuff. By the time I get back I'll be rushing going to work and by the time you get to work you're really tired before you even sit down and start to work. But after you've started working for a while, you just get extra energy from somewhere and go on and get it dealt with. But that night it just builds right back up on you again. . . . If I had a job where I wouldn't be so tired, and I could work the shift that I wanted to work, there's a lot of different things we'd be doing—bowling, playing tennis, or something like that, maybe nothing but just riding bicycles!

Jesse is caught in a cycle of depletion. He tries to finish his work in four hours so that he can gain some rest at work, thereby easing some of the monotony that is also a source of personal depletion. Meeting his production requirement in four hours is particularly tiring. If he attempts to be interpersonally available to his son and wife as well, he becomes exhausted. But his and Sandra's social time together is limited because he works the afternoon shift. She feels lonely because she lives far from her female relatives, and she feels trapped in her house. Consequently, time spent with Jesse away from the house is important to her well-being. With the Joneses, as with a number of research families, there seem to be insufficient resources to meet everyone's needs. Thus, a pattern of energy deficit is created. Like most participants, Jesse considers himself a "family man" and would like to be able to do things with his wife and son that go beyond the essentials of shopping and daily chores. Bicycle riding is an activity that he imagines might be mutually "charging." Like Samuel Coleman, he fantasizes that a white-collar job would enable him to be more available to his family.

Insofar as personal depletion makes it difficult for workers to be available to other family members, it affects the patterns of closeness they establish. The work organization buys a worker's time and effort—his labor power—but his family also needs him. In the discussion of the Jones family, we see how these systemic conflicts are expressed through personal conflict between family members. This theme recurred throughout the interviews.

Negotiating at the Psychological Interface

In the descriptions of the three interface patterns, the crucial link between work and family systems was the psychological state generated by participants' relationships to their jobs. The patterns of negative carry-over and energy deficit were related to jobs that are stressful in some way. In contrast, the pattern of positive carry-over was related to job gratification and lack of stress. One way in which such patterns may be changed, therefore, is for an individual to alter the nature of his or her relationship to work to achieve better personal fit.

Ezra Turner was able to maximize the fit between his needs and his work by exploiting the opportunity offered by the hospital for horizontal and vertical movement. Though he started out as a cage cleaner and orderly, through his own initiative he used the available organizational latitude to seek and try a variety of jobs. By locating one that well suited him, he was able to maximize his choices and, ultimately, achieve job gratification. Because he has a great deal of power in his present supervisory position, he has been able to change the nature of that job so that he can learn new skills and optimize the potential for professional growth.

Powerlessness to Change Job Situations

For the most part, however, participants were relatively powerless, as individuals, to change undesirable features of their present job situations. Focusing on those in working-class and lower-middle-class occupations meant, for this study, that participants were near the bottom of their organizational hierarchies. Jesse Jones, for example, had ideas about how factory jobs could be improved through job rotation and better matching of workers to specific jobs, but he felt that such ideas would be discounted and that even the workers' knowledge of the machines they worked with was dismissed. He described himself as being only a "little ant" in the organizational scheme of things. After ten years on the job, Mike Healy was still "low man on the totem pole." Chuck Simpson, a fork-lift operator, did try to correct what he thought were inequities in his work load by asking his foreman to alter the work load. He met with no success because he was dependent on his supervisors to carry out his suggestions. Ultimately, he was powerless. The changes that workers could effect in their jobs were minor: they might work hard in order to lengthen their break time or team up so that they could alternate breaks. While such adjustments could reduce discomfort, they often had to be hidden from supervisors. On the other hand, major changes in the nature of jobs occurred to meet the needs of the work organizations rather than those of the workers and their families. For example, Eric Cooper felt a sense of mastery and achievement in his work with computers until new technology was introduced that turned him into a "tape hanger," a job he experienced as monotonous and demeaning. For Samuel Coleman, the community of friends at work made his assembler's job tolerable. When efficiency experts rearranged his job to increase production and profits, he felt that these changes destroyed the informal networks the workers had established. Gone was the "happy community" that was "full of life." In the interaction between work organizations and family systems, the more powerful system need not take into account the needs of the weaker. If the workers themselves are powerless as individuals to change features of their jobs at work, family members are even more distant witnesses of a process that, nevertheless, affects them.

"Locking-In"

In seeking to establish a more beneficial pattern that meets family and personal goals, an alternative to changing the structure of a given job is to search for a different one. The fewer such alternatives that exist for family members, the more constrained they are in negotiations at the interface. While his interest was primarily in the psychological relationship between a worker and his job, Quinn's concept of "locking-in" is useful here in helping us consider the structural variables that shape a family's options. Quinn defined "locking-in" as having three components:

> A low probability of the worker's securing another job as good as or better than his present job; little opportunity to modify a presently disliked employment situation by securing a change in job assignments; a low likelihood that the worker who did not like his job could take psychological refuge in the performance of roles not linked to the work situation. Each of these components equated locking-in with some type of limitation for the worker's chances of "escaping" either physically or psychologically from his present work situation. (1972, p. 56)

Constraints on Intraorganizational Mobility. One of the components of locking-in is a lack of opportunity to secure a change in job assignments, either through horizontal or vertical mobility. Quinn has suggested that such locking-in is particularly prevalent in organizations which are not expanding, in which hiring is done from without, and in which those at the lower hierarchical levels have little control over job assignments. These organizational features describe the automobile industry (Chinoy 1955), in which many of the research participants work. Again, when job assignments did change, they often occurred in accordance with the needs of the organization rather than the worker. For example, after ten years in the factory, Mike Healy was moved from a job in which he had some variety and felt some responsibility to a particularly dirty, wet, and boring one. Shift changes, too, had to await the careful seniority procedures initially instituted by the unions for the workers' own protection.

Chinoy has described the constraints on upward mobility in the automobile industry. When jobs are routine, it is difficult to display ability or initiative; thus, research participants felt that getting ahead was based on personal "pull" or worse. Moreover, executives and technicians increasingly are recruited from colleges and technical schools. The college program in which some of the participants are enrolled might help them achieve some mobility. However, it remains unclear how much the small-step mobility they could achieve would facilitate a better relationship between work and family systems. For example, Chuck Simpson became a foreman after the interviews had been completed. As someone new to the ranks of supervision, he was given an extremely difficult job that created entirely new interface dilemmas for his family, without the rewards yet being evident.[11]

Quinn also suggested that locking-in might be more prevalent in a

---

11. As an interesting follow-up note, Chuck eventually returned to his earlier job because of the strains his new job was creating in his family. He was shocked, for example, to find himself hitting his young son. The interface pattern had changed from one of modest deficit to negative carry-over.

small work organization because there are relatively few positions into which one can move. Thus, Henry Johnson's mobility was limited because the firm he worked for was a small family business and the highest positions were taken by the sons of the owner.

Constraints on Interorganizational Mobility. Another possible alternative for workers is to leave their present employing organization and look for other situations that might provide a more favorable relationship between their home and work lives. Some of the limitations on a search for extraorganizational alternatives include factors such as age, race, education, and the structure of the job market (Quinn 1972). Because the study took place during a time of high unemployment and many of the participants had limited skills, their job options were few. For example, when he was younger, Jesse Jones saw his alternatives as working in a factory or remaining in the armed services. The college education that some of the participants are striving for may increase their alternatives on the job market, but even a college education is becoming increasingly less valuable. For the nonwhite workers, discriminatory practices also affected their options. For older workers, any such alternatives were even more severely restricted. When, at the age of 39, Henry Johnson went to look for a job, he experienced age discrimination. When the organization in which he finally found employment began having financial difficulties, Henry felt fortunate to be kept on as a driver. Betty stated their position succinctly:

BJ: But let's face it. With this day and age, there could be that there was no place [for him]. So even though I worry about the type of work he does, I feel that he's damned lucky that there was a place, that there was something open.

Despite her dissatisfaction with the way Henry's work impinges on their lives, that job was preferable to no job at all. These larger structural constraints that are beyond any individual's control serve to limit the power of workers and their families to negotiate solutions to job-related stresses.

Summary and Conclusion

By focusing on the worker's relationship to his job as the psychological link between workplace and family spheres, three interface patterns were uncovered. The pattern of positive carry-over was evident in the Turner family. Ezra Turner derives a sense of esteem and identity from his work, and this personal gratification is made available to the family system through his ability to initiate warm and interested interactions and to respond positively to other family members. His availability "charges" family members, and he, in turn, is charged by them, thus establishing a "positive" cycle of interaction. He is a force for gathering family members together. Knowledge of this pattern is useful in giving us a sense of what is possible in the interchange between work and family systems.

Negative carry-over, a more common pattern among the research participants, was illustrated in the description of the Johnson family. Because of work overload and job role conflicts, Henry Johnson's job is a source of psychological strain that he tries to manage by "worrying." In this way, job-related stress is brought into the home space. We see here how personal attempts to manage work-related strain can cause tension within the family. Not only is Henry sometimes unavailable to respond to Betty's concerns, but at times he responds irritably to the children. Family members must expend their personal resources to create the space that Henry needs to recuperate and manage his feelings. One consequence of this process is that distance between family members is increased. A variation of this pattern was also mentioned briefly, using the Healy family as an example. In the variant pattern, negative feelings about work are displaced onto other family members.

The third pattern discovered was that of energy deficit. This pattern became evident when we considered what was not there. The research on work and mental health indicates that boredom, monotony, and underutilization of skills are also sources of psychological strain (Caplan et al. 1975; Kornhauser 1965). Such work is emotionally and physically draining without returning energy to the worker, who has traded time and effort for wages. I suggested that such jobs are also personally depleting, because they involve an assault on the self. In order to "muster" his energies, in this pattern a worker creates a psychological space for himself, thereby being interpersonally unavailable to other family members. The competition between systems for energy may be expressed in interpersonal conflict within the family. This pattern differs from that of negative carry-over in that feelings about work are not brought directly into the family system. In fact, these participants tend to adhere to the notion that their work and family lives are quite separate. In the discussion of the myth of separate worlds in Chapter 5, this latter phenomenon will be examined.

The interview data, thus, suggest that a job that is gratifying and meaningful, without being stressful and overly absorbing, may result in a worker being interpersonally available to his family. However, we cannot conclude that job gratification always leads to a pattern of positive carry-over. A pattern not described here, but mentioned in the literature on work and family life, is one exhibited in families where breadwinners are upper-echelon managers and professionals (Veroff & Feld 1970; Young & Willmott 1973). These men are gratified by and involved in their work, but their jobs are also stressful and preoccupying. Thus, they too are not interpersonally available to family members. What may be crucial in understanding Ezra Turner's situation is that his job is both salient and gratifying, while not being stressful and totally absorbing.

Work that is highly stressful, because of conflict or overload, can lead to attempts to cope with the resulting strain in the home space. A worker's need for personal space and the intrusion of job concerns may result in irritability, unavailability, and increased distance between family members. Finally, those jobs that are stressful by being boring and by underutilizing the worker's abilities may deplete the worker, resulting in his need for space and in his being unavailable to the family system. Insofar as workers and their families are relatively powerless in relation to work organizations while their alternatives are limited, attempts to alter negative patterns by changing job situations to increase person-job fit must be limited.

Pretheoretical Concepts

These patterns illustrate some pretheoretical concepts that may prove useful in future research measuring work and family links. The general notion of "carry-over" was found to be helpful in conveying the idea that there is a psychological relationship between what occurs at work and what occurs within the family. Other hypothesized carry-overs include the carry-over of values (Aberle & Naegele 1952; Kohn 1969). More specifically, the concepts of emotional and interpersonal availability were introduced to help us understand this carry-over process. Emotional availability was used to denote a worker's psychological state, resulting from his experience at work. This state, in turn, influenced his interactions with family members. Indicators of interpersonal availability were the frequency of a worker's initiations to others and the socioemotional quality of his initiations and responses.

Although the terms "isomorphism," "spillover," "generalization," and "carry-over" often are used interchangeably, I would suggest that the term "isomorphism" be reserved for the special case of carry-over in which some interactions at the workplace are carried over into some interactions in the family. The similarities need not encompass all aspects of interaction in work and family systems. For example, in the discussion of the Turner family, I suggested that there may be an isomorphic relation between Ezra's being at the hub of an interactional network both at work and at home. More complete data on the work settings of other participants might have provided other examples. For example, Henry Johnson and the salesmen at his place of employment may ignore and avoid each other, creating tension and anger in a pattern similar to that in the Johnson family. We might have found that the demands placed on

Henry at his job have a counterpart in the demands he places on family members. Careful observation may disclose other kinds of isomorphic relationships. The development of taxonomies of situations and human environments (see, for example, Fredericksen 1972; Moos 1973) may be helpful in identifying isomorphic relationships.

The psychological interface between work and family spheres cannot be understood without exploring the structural interface as well, for they are intimately connected. It is to an examination of the structural interface region that we now turn.

CHAPTER 4

The Structural Interface: Time and Space

Thus far, I have described patterns of relationships that are shaped by the psychological response of a worker to his job. His boundary position is central to understanding the psychological link between work setting and interactions within the family. However, in order for interactions to occur, time and space must be bridged, for interpersonal availability requires routes of access.

Both family and work systems utilize time and space in order to achieve their goals. Kantor and Lehr (1975) have described time and space as two "access" dimensions by which a family achieves its ends. Because work organizations buy the time of family members and take them out of the home space, they reach into a family's heart by affecting the regulation of distances among members. As was mentioned in the discussion of the Johnson family, the interaction patterns family members develop to negotiate closeness and separateness are central to their life together. People differ in their needs for contact and in their manner of arranging it. Insofar as these negotiations must occur in time and space, they can be affected by work organizations, for—in large part—they structure time and space for us. Time and space form the structural interface that connects our work and family lives. Several brief examples will help to illustrate this structural interface relationship.

Sandra Jones and her father were in conflict during her adolescence, and so she welcomed the long hours he worked, for it meant that dinner time would be less tense for her. In this case, the barrier of space and time served Sandra's need for distance from her father. Chuck Simpson and his wife, Kathy, used to work different shifts in the factory. During that period they separated, for Chuck "got into trouble" by spending too much time in bars without his wife. In an attempt to solve their problem, they arranged to work the same shift. Not only did they drive to and from work together, but they ate lunch together and took their work breaks together. This increased contact was uncomfortable for Chuck. Now he feels that he and Kathy have worked out a successful accommodation; they drive to and from work but take only one break together. The closeness Chuck found uncomfortable would have been ideal for the Ellisons, who dream of having a family restaurant so that they can spend more time together. Individual family needs and styles are, therefore, important when considering the nature of the interface relationship.

Time

Time is not a simple variable. Aldous (1969) and Kanter (1977) have suggested that three aspects of time are important to the work–family relationship: amount of time, daily timing, and life-cycle time. These three aspects of time emerged as central themes in the interviews.

Amount of Time

In the Johnson family, members' needs for separateness and closeness were not clarified. Betty wanted more time with Henry, but time and space compounded her difficulties in making contact with him. As a dispatcher and deliveryman, Henry worked long hours. He left the house at 7:15 A.M. and sometimes did not come home until 8:00 P.M., as he would wait for the trucks to return. Thus, he rarely ate either breakfast or dinner with his family. During most of the time the children were growing up, Henry worked Saturdays in his father's shop. The Johnsons talked to me about time primarily in terms of its impact on Henry's relationship with his children.

> BJ: For the first twelve years of our marriage, Henry worked six days a week. He worked Saturdays also. . . . Really, he had no time left to spend with his children. . . .
>
> R: Did you think you spent as much time with your children as you wanted to?
>
> HJ: Oh, no. I see it more here lately, more in the last ten or twelve years than I did before.
>
> R: How is it that you see it more lately?
>
> HJ: Well, we don't really have anything in common.

Sometimes it is difficult to notice a pattern of increased distance as it is being established, but it can have long-term consequences. Tony, the oldest Johnson child, recalled that he thought it normal that "everybody worked twelve hours a day." When Tony had difficulties at school during his adolescence, the arm of the family reached into the workplace and Henry was pulled into the family system, for he sometimes had to leave work in order to deal with a crisis situation. The Johnsons are still grateful to Henry's employer for lowering workplace boundaries. In the very act of giving permission, his employer remained the guardian of work time and space.

Betty, too, had feelings about Henry's long hours that went beyond their impact on his relationships with the children. She is bitter because she was not compensated for Henry's involvement. In discussing Henry's salary, I asked Betty what she thought about it.

> BJ: I don't think he was paid enough before for the responsibility and the hours that he put in there.
>
> R: Does that bother you?
>
> BJ: No, because I was used to it. He was never paid what he should have been paid, even before. It didn't bother me so much that I nagged about it. That was the way it was. But these hours and hours that he would work before with no extra money used to kind of irritate me because I didn't think he had to put in these hours, the extra hours that he put in with a lack of pay. . . .
>
> R: So you would have preferred fewer hours?
>
> BJ: Well, since the outcome was what it was.

It was not evident to me whether Betty had made her needs clear to Henry. What was apparent, however, was that she felt angry because money has been a constant source of worry for them and because she was not relieved of this problem by Henry's long hours at work.

While the quality of family interactions may be positively affected by Ezra Turner's feelings about his job, because of the hours he spends there, work threatened to interfere with the family's goals of intimacy and companionship. His job does not require a great deal of attention away from work, but it does require long hours. In fact, Ezra is sometimes away from home for two days at a time. Because he gives papers at conferences and meetings to enhance the knowledge about and status of his occupation, his job involves him in a great deal of travel. Culbert and Renshaw (1972) have described how work-related travel can be stressful to families. Moreover, like many other participants, Ezra has several part-time jobs. To earn extra income he is on call for the medical transplant society and has to go out at night several times a month. If an organ comes in late in the afternoon, Ezra may have to monitor it through the night until the operation the next day. He also has an upholstery-cleaning business with his brother that he attends to on weekends and is a part-time lab attendant. The extra money he earns in this way enables Ezra to send his children to private schools, where he and Isabel feel they will do better than in the public school system.

Still, the numbers of hours that Ezra works are not merely a function of economic necessity. He wonders whether he is a "workaholic" like his father, whom he admires a great deal. The elder Mr. Turner, whom I also interviewed, is retired from an automobile factory where he worked for almost forty years. His attendance record is unsurpassed there, he told me with pride. He is very active still and when I went to interview him was in the process of cleaning fish and making cheese. In working hard, Ezra is emulating his father. Several times during the interview Ezra mentioned his father with great pride and affection.

R: Your father worked in a factory.

ET: Yeah, he's the hardest-working man I ever seen in my life.

R: What do you mean?

ET: My father has always—when I was growing up I never knew him to get more than four hours sleep a night. He worked afternoons in the factory.

R. Starting about 4:00 P.M.?

ET: No, I think he started around 1:00 P.M. and then he would get off from the factory around 11:00, 12:00, something like that. Then he had a part-time job where he worked over at the golf course, like a night porter. And then he always had, you know, a little hog farm. He always had some kind of part-time job.

At the same time that Ezra values being a hard worker like his father, he also values family intimacy and time together. In fact, familial togetherness and companionship are a value shared explicitly by both Ezra and Isabel.

R: You keep stressing, throughout this whole interview, that keeping in contact . . . is really important to you.

ET: Right. Right. The whole thing of keeping in touch and the feeling that they, especially the children, that they know I'm there with them all the time. Any time they need me, they know I'm there.

Being interpersonally available to the children is repeated as a family value in what Isabel said as well. She told me how important it is for her to be home for the children.

IT: Like, now she [Patsy] comes in she's all bubbly about what happened in school and I'm *here*. If she's got a problem she's having in school, then I'm here to handle it. I'm here to hear it as soon as she comes in. And I think that's important, you know, that you can communicate with them.

Ezra and Isabel are aware of how time and space can serve as barriers, preventing access to the intimacy and communication they value. Ezra described his job as an orderly in the hospital:

ET: Man, you were just the low man on the totem pole. It was just a situation that I thought I didn't want to be in for all my life, that's for sure. Not only

67

that but especially at the city hospital. No matter how long you've been there, you still have to work all those odd-ball shifts. . . .

R: Were you on those kind of shifts too?

IT: I worked midnights most of the time. I rotated. Like on weekends, you would rotate with days. Well, with days, you would definitely rotate it.

R: How?

IT: Many days you would rotate every three or four months and then you'd work a double shift.

ET: She'd be on nights and I'd be on days and I didn't like that.

IT: We'd greet each other in passing. When I'd come home in the morning, he'd be gone. When he came home for an hour or so, I'd be laying down to get a nap before I go to work.

R: How do you think that . . . affects a relationship between a husband and wife?

ET: I would think that it would have to take something away from it. For me, it would. My idea of marriage is for companionship. If I'm not going to be home all evening, then there's no reason to be married.

The conflict is internalized in Ezra, for he values both time with his family and being a hard worker and provider, values he learned in his family of origin. Several years ago, when Ezra was trying to start yet another business, the threat from time and space became very real. Thus, the Turner family was faced with the dilemma of reconciling their familial goal of companionship with their economic needs and with Ezra's personal need to work hard.

Ezra Turner and Henry Johnson are unusual among the participants in the study in that they are highly involved in work from which they derive an important sense of personal identity. However, insufficient time with family members was mentioned spontaneously as a problem in all but one family studied.[1] Some viewed time at the job as the primary form of work intrusion into their family lives. In a recent study of employment, 42 percent of the men interviewed complained of some problem with their working hours (Quinn & Shepard 1974).

Daily Timing

It is not simply amount of time at work each day that can affect families. Daily timing also is important. The effect of timing on family dynamics is highlighted by shift work. Because so many of the research families were young, the seniority of the wage earners was insufficient to secure them the day shift. Consequently, many of those interviewed worked afternoon and midnight shifts. We have seen that Sandra Jones

1. Chuck Simpson did not mention insufficient time as a problem. His wife was not interviewed.

used work time as a way of avoiding conflict in her family of origin. Similarly, she reported that when she and Jesse were first married, their working different shifts kept them out of each other's way. Of the participants, only Mike Healy does not mind working the midnight shift; he prefers midnights to afternoons because the later shift will allow him more time with his children when they begin school. On the other hand, his wife, Celia, feels that the midnight shift deprives them of time together. Mott et al. (1965) have documented the "role conflict" experienced by men who work afternoon and midnight shifts, and, as Mike Healy understands, men working afternoons complained of insufficient time with their school-age children.

Among the families in which the wage earner worked an afternoon or midnight shift, only the Ellisons had school-age children. Lack of sufficient contact with his school-age daughter is an important issue for Ray and a source of sadness. He is disturbed when his children ask him, "Daddy, do you have to go to work today?" Family members are not simply passive objects to be acted upon. Six-year-old Lucinda Ellison was learning ways to increase her contact with her father, despite his hours. For example, Ray reported that in the week before the interview, she woke him up at 2:00 A.M. in order to show him her newly lost tooth and to ask about the tooth fairy. Several days earlier, she had awakened him to show him a picture she had drawn at school. Shift work can affect patterns of distance and closeness in families as family members actively try to meet their goals.

Mott et al. also reported that men working afternoon and midnight shifts felt they were unable to fulfill their protective function. With her husband working evenings, Mary Ellison said, "I feel like I'm the protector. While he's gone, I'm the protector. . . . I feel like I have to watch over us since he's not here." Fear of being alone at night was mentioned by wives in four of the seven families in which the breadwinner has worked a late shift. Again, when faced with dilemmas posed by time, families try to work out solutions. Sandra Jones described the various approaches she and Jesse have used to calm her night fear, which was triggered by hearing about a burglar in the apartment complex in which they lived. At the time, she was employed as a clerk while Jesse worked the midnight shift.

R: Do you ever become afraid in the evening?

SJ: Yes, when I first—when we first moved here, I was really afraid to stay here at night. I was so afraid that instead of coming home—my job was like fifteen minutes from the house, you know, a fifteen-minute drive—instead of coming home I went way on the other side of town to my girl-friend's house and I waited for Jesse to get off. . . . And he'd get there at about 4:15 [A.M.] to pick me up and I'd get home about 5:00, 5:30, take a bath, go to sleep for an hour or so, get up at 7:00 and go to work. Then finally, I just said that I was gonna have to go home, you know. I was just not getting enough rest. I just made up my mind that I was gonna have to come home every day. And so I started doing it, and you know, I'd always tell Jesse to leave a light on because you know, like in wintertime it would be dark by the time I got home and I would always tell him to leave a light on. And I got used to it. . . .

R: Did you talk about it sometimes?

SJ: Yeah, I talked to him about it the many nights he came home, when I first started coming home alone. It was a lot when he first came, you know he would come home and I, ah, would be sitting here crying. I just was scared to death, you know. And, ah, I really had to just think about going back South. I just really didn't like it up here. But after the guy [the burglar] turned himself in, I really got used to things. . . .

R: What did he do when he came home and found you crying?

SJ: He would come in, he would ask me what's wrong and I'd tell him, and he tried to reassure me that nobody would break in, and if they did, what I could do. Like I'm afraid of guns. . . . I'm afraid of guns and Jesse has two rifles and I just wouldn't allow them in the closet upstairs. And he took me out on New Year's, showed me how to shoot the gun and everything. He told me, you know, if I even thought I heard somebody trying to come in, then if I didn't want to shoot somebody, just shoot in the air, anything to make them think I was—he said it would at least scare them away. But he even talked about going, trying to go on days for good, but there is this lady who has more seniority than him, so she would easily bump him.

As one family, the Joneses would be no match for the highly structured and rule-governed seniority system that originally had been designed to protect workers. Thus, the Joneses searched for private and individual solutions to their dilemma. Sandra now sleeps with young Billy because she feels that he cannot fall asleep without her. Still, one wonders if it is not *she* who cannot sleep without *him*.[2] In the Bernard family, young Carrie began sleeping with Alice when Richard started to work the midnight shift because Alice did not want to sleep alone. These solutions introduce new patterns of contact within the family system. That these solutions to the problem of timing are only partial is reflected in the fact that all the nonemployed wives of shift workers whom I interviewed wanted their husbands to work the day shift.

Shift work highlights the importance of daily timing in the lives of families because it indicates how timing can cause stresses for family members and can affect the nature of their relationships. Shift work, however, is but a dramatic example of timing effects. As Kanter (1977) has indicated in her discussion of flextime, even shifting a work schedule by one hour can facilitate family goals and reduce strain. Some participants mentioned that they would prefer working a very early day

2. After reading this section, Sandra agreed with this interpretation and offered corroborating evidence, telling me she had nightmares during a night she slept alone.

shift so that much of the afternoon could be available for time with their young children, who go to sleep early in the evening. It may be that the basic nine-to-five schedule in effect in many work organizations is not optimal for the distance regulation needs of all families.

Life-Cycle Time

Time has different meanings at different stages in the life cycle of the family and its individual members. Two examples from the interview data illustrate the importance of the life-cycle dimension of time. Pamela Gates still remembers the fact that her father did not come to her high school graduation because he was working.

PG: You know, one of the things that hurt me most in my life—and I can't get it out of my mind, even now!—is when I graduated from high school. I wanted my father to be there *so* bad, because I graduated when I was 16 and I had shown him, "I told you, man, I was going to make it!" My father said, "I can't go, 'cause I got to work today." Oh, that hurt me more than anything! I just—at that particular day I hated him! That day I hated him and all the factories! . . . I just hated that. I never forgot it. . . .

R: Did you let him know how angry and hurt you were?

PG: No, I never told him. Even now he doesn't know.

R: Do you think it would have helped if he knew how important it was to you?

PG: No [*tired laugh*]. He still would have had to work!

R: Did you show your anger?

PG: Yes. I showed it. In a lot of ways that hurt me. Because after that I just—I don't know—I kind of lost [*pause*] I don't know if it was respect for him. I lost something. . . .

We can see that time spent with a family member is laden with complex meanings. Although Pamela is not certain why she "lost something" for her father, we can make some guesses about the meaning of this incident for her. Her father had encouraged her to go to high school, and her graduation was an important indicator of her success that she needed to share with him. She may have felt that, to him, work was more important than she, and she may have rejected him in turn. We might also hypothesize that in realizing that he had to work, her internal image of a powerful father was jeopardized. Her image of a powerful father was threatened again when she learned that he could not afford to send her to college as he had promised. It was with college in mind that she had gone on to graduate from high school. Although children may imagine their fathers to be powerful and good, in relation to their work and the resources necessary to meet family goals, working-class fathers may appear powerless instead. Pamela acted out her anger at her loss by turning to a group of peers who had not graduated from high school.

Pregnancy and the postpartum period were mentioned spontaneously in five families as a time when contact among family members was particularly important. Betty Johnson had been quietly ruminating while Henry and I were talking. Suddenly, she interrupted.

BJ: But when you talked about work, I can remember one time. . . . And that was the day when I brought Tony home from the hospital. And, first of all, I was lucky that my husband even got the time off to come get me at the right time. . . . This was the first baby. And, I mean, I sweated that he was going to be able to leave the shop to zip up. . . . You come home with a first baby, you know, and everything. Now, I think I'm going to cry because I really, really remember this. [*She begins to cry; her voice shakes.*] You're so happy, and you just want to be close, and, you know, he plops me and the kid and then he has to leave. Now, it wasn't his fault. But I'll just never forget that. I just felt, just awful. It's just something that I don't like to talk about. But that's how work—to me I just wanted to sit and be with him. I mean, I put the baby down, I mean, he was fine. And then, "Well, I gotta hurry now. I got to get to work." And it just really, really hurt. . . .

R: So you really wished that he would have stayed.

BJ: Uh-huh. And could have stayed home for a day or two. I mean, that's scary. You know, to be home, you know, with a baby and, you know, all the responsibilities.

LeMasters (1957) first alerted us to the fact that the first pregnancy may represent a crisis in the life cycle of young families. Golden (1975) has further described the "high" energy needs of families with young infants. Yet at this time, young husband-fathers often are deeply involved at the workplace. Young professionals are building their careers, while those in working-class or lower-middle-class occupations are working overtime to meet increased family expenditures. They are selling more of their time and effort when wife-mothers are most in need of it, and their low seniority and low power in the workplace make it difficult to adjust the work-time boundary to their needs. We need to begin identifying other life-cycle stages when the issue of time becomes especially significant for families.

Negotiating at the Structural Interface

When families and their members are attempting to maximize access to their goals and to regulate distances among each other, they are implicitly involved in negotiating at the interface between the work organization and the family system. Systems have boundaries. People must develop strategies for interacting where systems touch. In discussing the psychological interface, I suggested that these negotiations are constrained by the relative powerlessness of the individual worker to change jobs and, therefore, maximize gratification. The theme of relative powerlessness again arises when we consider time and space. How successful families are in meeting their goals depends, in part, on their power to structure time and space according to their needs. I noted that the Turner family was faced with a dilemma. Ezra works long hours, but the Turners also value contact and access to each other. Their solutions to this problem are instructive, for they sensitize us to the negotiations that occur in the structural interface region.

Bridging Space and Making Time

When I observed Ezra Turner at work, he received a card from Isabel that said, "I love you." Similarly, on the day I observed the family at home, Isabel mailed a card to Ezra. On the bulletin board in Ezra's office was a card from his daughter, Patsy, and a letter from her. Written in childish scrawl, the note read:

Dear Daddy,

This is a note to tell you how much I love you.
Please bring me some candy tomorrwo [sic].

Love,
Patsy

Ezra's small office provided a personal space in which he could keep the visible symbols of family relatedness.[3] The cards and letters may be thought of as condensed statements about family relationships. They are a way of renewing contact and reaffirming relationships. I have mentioned that the Turner family appeared to be an "open type" family. It may be that the independence family members exhibit depends on the existence of these routes of access.

The major bridge of access and contact that the Turners use is the telephone.

R: Do you call home when you're away overnight?

ET: Oh, yeah. Oh, they call me up all the time. That's one thing—when we're here, like we can call each other all the time.

R: [*To Isabel*] On what occasions would you call?

IT: Just if I'd feel like I want to talk to him. I just call him up and say—

ET: [*Interrupts*] Let me butt into that. She called me up today just as I was getting ready—and I was standing up with two of the surgeons and my hands was full of blood, and the phone rang and somebody answered. And she said, "I just want to tell you that I love you." And that's cool, you know. We just hung up and went back to work.

3. Dubin (1976) has pointed out that there is no research on the use of personal space in work organizations.

R: Ever an inconvenience?

ET: No.

R: Always enjoy it?

ET: Oh, yeah. The rule is if anybody calls, I'm busy, except Isabel. [*Laughs*] Or the kids call. The kids feel that anytime—well, she called and asked for a cookie because Isabel wouldn't give her a cookie. Or he'll call to tell me he made a nice tackle, or, you know. Communication. . . .

IT: Most of my calls on my phone bill—my long distance calls—is from Fort Louis. Usually, it runs anywhere from three to four or maybe five dollars a month.

ET: Can I say something else? It's important for me, too, for the kids to know that, even though that I'm not here, that they can get in touch with me anytime for any reason. You know, they don't have to say somebody got hit by a car before they can call. They can call me for *anything*, any time of day.

R: [*To Charles*] You call Dad anytime at work?

CT: Yeah.

R: When was the last time?

CT: I couldn't say.

R: What kinds of things do you like to call him about?

CT: I call him if I, like, got an A on a test. Like if I got a problem. If I want to talk it over with him, I call him up. If he's not home, I'll call him up.

IT: Most of the time I don't even know they done called him!

CT: Just sometimes, to talk to him. Just to say hi.

For the Turner family, communication means keeping the avenues of access to each other open. Ezra encourages the use of the telephone for all family contacts, however unimportant they may seem, and he makes a point of calling home every night when he is out of town. Perhaps the knowledge that they are there for each other when needed makes it more possible for them to be separate as well. Again, these telephone calls seem to be condensed statements about their affection for each other. Ezra felt that his part-time job at the airport the previous summer upset the family because he could not be reached by telephone.

The way the Turner family maximizes accessibility and contact by making workplace boundaries permeable to them is dramatized by Ezra's bringing his family to work with him. Just as he had power to give me access to the setting for purposes of observation, he arranges for family members to visit him at work.

R: What does your dad do all day?

CT: Well, sometimes I go to work with him, like when I'm not in school . . . and he runs all day [*laughs*]. He runs from one building to another and one place to another.... But he always seem to find some way, you know, make me enjoy myself when I'm up there with him.

R: Why do you go with him?

CT: I just like to.... I like the place, I like to see what he does, I like the people he works with.

R: That's unusual. Most people don't bring their children with them to work. How old were you when you started going? Do you remember?

CT: I was about, say, three or four when I first went there.... Sometimes, like a couple of summers ago, he'd take me up there like every day out of a couple of weeks. And I'd go up there and help him work and everything.

R: What kind of things do you do?

CT: Like sometimes I'd feed and water the animals. On a day he'd have an operation, I'd help him with the operation. And it's just like I'm an employee up there. I do like everything everybody else does....

ET: I like to have them with me.

R: Why?

ET: Because they're fun people.

R: So you want to spend time with your children and that's one way to do it?

ET: Oh yeah, oh yeah. By just keeping them with me.

R: And your work situation allows you to do that?

ET: Uh-huh.

R: How often do they do that?

ET: Generally in the summer time somebody'll have their kids there. We'll have at least, uh, somebody's kids there at least two or three times a month. But what we don't do is we don't—like if I bring my kids, then somebody else won't bring theirs.

R: Do you arrange it among you?

ET: It's sort of just like, you know, somebody'll say, "I'm going to bring my kid in tomorrow," then somebody'll know not to bring somebody else in. So ... if I'm going to bring the kids in, one of my boys in with me, and he'll bring one kid with him. And like I never take all of my kids. Now what we do do sometimes is, Isabel will bring the kids up, all three of the kids, and they'll spend a certain amount of time, spend a couple of hours, and then we'll go out to lunch and then fool around for awhile. And then I'll come back to work, and then they'll come back home.

R: Do you agree that that's important that your children go to see your husband where he's working?

IT: Yeah, I think it's important, you know, because, I think it's important that they spend as much time with him as they can, you know, because they get a chance to see him [laughs]. You know, 'cause he works, sometimes like he said, you know, he's on call, and he may have to be gone in the mornings, he may not be back again till real late....

R: That's unusual. Most people don't bring their children to work.

ET: [*Animated*] I could see it in a factory where in most situations most people just don't, and they never challenge management to the point where they would do it. Some of the other things that we're able to do there— like . . . we can all just shut down and go swimming. Or wife will bring lunch up and the whole crew will just have lunch outside . . . where work just does not have to a *sweatshop.*

The time spent together in this way consolidates the relationship between Ezra and his son. In working with his father, Charles has the opportunity to explore being an adult. His self-esteem is bolstered by being treated as a valuable contributing member of the research team. Stoke (1954) has suggested that identification is encouraged when the child and parent spend time together, when the parent's role is clear, and when the parent is treated as a powerful and respected person. The closeness of father and son was reflected in the interview situation. As we talked, Charles rested his head against Ezra, who had his arm around his son's shoulder. The time Charles spends at work with his father most likely consolidates this identification and allows Charles to experiment actively with a work identity at a time in his life when it is beginning to take concrete shape. By bringing his children to work, Ezra solves the dilemmas posed by time and space. Not only are they able to spend time together, but the time itself is extremely meaningful.

In considering the example of the Turner family, we must wonder to what extent the familial goals of communication and contact are sustained simply because they are able to be realized. The Turners were unusual in their ability to negotiate time and space with Ezra's work organization. Ezra is able to make the workplace boundary permeable for the families of those who work there because he has power in the setting. As an autonomous supervisor, he can establish norms that allow the entry of children. The ability of families to penetrate the boundary of the workplace by bridging space and time is dependent both on the nature of the work setting and the jobs in it and on the family member's location in the organizational hierarchy.

Among other research families, visits by family members were rare, a finding in keeping with Komarovksy's (1962) research on blue-collar families. Exceptions were the two families in which both the wife and husband worked in the same factory, and entry was gained on the basis of common employment rather than kinship. In the large industrial plants, these visits were carefully controlled by workplace gatekeepers and were limited to specially designated days when work did not go on as usual. For example, Celia Healy wants to take a tour through the factory where Mike works, but she has to wait until the door is opened again to family members.

CH: Like I said to him. I want to take a tour through his plant. I want to see what his job is like! I haven't yet.

MH: It hasn't been open!

R: Why would you like to?

CH: I want to see where he works!

MH: I would. I'd want to take her! I want to let her walk through there and hear all that fantastic noise. See, they think we got it made.

CH: No. I just want to see what kind of a place he works in! I've never been in an automobile factory, and I want to go in one. . . . I was pregnant the first time they had it open. The doctor didn't want me to go through and he didn't either.

R: Imagine what you're going to see there?

CH: No! That's just it. I don't have no idea what I'm going to see at all. A bunch of machinery, I know that much. But I don't have no idea. Like I went to my mom's factory when she used to work, but that's going to be completely different from his. I just seen these great big machines, and they just made elastic.

R: Do you think Celia will have a better understanding of you if she goes through?

MH: I doubt it. Because—well, they really doctor a lot of shit up when they got these tours. Let's face it, man. I mean . . . they got us scrubbing floors, painting floors, painting machinery.

Mike thinks that she will have a better understanding of why he is sensitive to high-pitched sounds if she visits the factory, but he despairs of her seeing his workplace as it really is. Possibly, the humane norms of the medical-research setting in which Ezra works facilitates the entry of family members, in contrast to the norms of the profit-oriented organizations for which most other participants work.

Workplace boundaries are not the same for everyone in an organization. For example, in order to bridge time and space through the mails, as the Turners do, workers must be able to receive mail with some regularity. Yet, very few of the participants I interviewed had a mailbox at their workplace. For the blue-collar workers such potential access routes are unnecessary for the adequate performance of their job duties. Moreover, personal space to keep familial symbols is also less available for the majority of people in working-class and lower-middle-class occupations. Ezra's office is small, but it is private.

The use of the telephone to penetrate the workplace boundaries was more frequent than the use of the mails. Everyone to whom I posed the question reported no difficulty in gaining access to a family member at the workplace. However, if we contrast the telephone use of the majority of participants with that of the Turner family, an important feature of the workplace–home boundary becomes clear. As a professional worker, Ezra has immediate access to a telephone; as a production worker, Jesse Jones finds access to the telephone more difficult.

R: Do you, during your time at work, talk to your wife at all?

JJ: Yes, I do. I call her.

R: You call her. During one of your breaks?

JJ: Right. Whenever I can get a break [*laughs*], you know, on the phone, when there ain't nobody lined up outside. Lotta guys get in the phone, you know, some regulars that be there every break, you know, get in and stay twenty, twenty-five minutes. . . .

R: How many phones do they have for you to use?

JJ: Oh, we got something like, we got three phones. And one of them, you just ain't got no hope of ever getting on, 'cause it's right next to this line right down in the corner. And somebody's on it all the time. And the other one is outside. You gotta walk a country mile to get to it. There's one that's closer to the break area, and usually if you're in the break area you've got to sit down on a bench and wait for whoever's in line, until it's your turn to go in.

Jesse's break time determines when he can reach out of the workplace, and other workers compete with him for the instrument of access.

As a supervisor in charge of his own work area, Ezra Turner has control over his telephone use. Mary Ellison, whose husband, a cook, has some supervisory power and autonomy, also uses the telephone frequently, and Ray Ellison insisted he would never take a job where his family could not have such access to him. With bitterness, Ray remembered being questioned about leaving his factory job to see his daughter during her major surgery. For those workers with little power, however, the telephone as an instrument for penetrating the workplace boundary is controlled by other gatekeepers. Consequently, distance regulation among family members is constrained. For example, when Celia Healy wishes to reach Mike, she has to telephone the security office, which contacts the area office, which then contacts his foreman, who relays the message to him. When Tony Johnson's wife called him at work because she was pregnant and fearful (he was working midnights at the time), he "got hassled at work for the phone calls. But, then, when they told me I could have no phone calls I told her to call more often because I was pissed."

Jesse Jones described these gatekeeping activities:

R: Does your wife ever call you at work?

JJ: She used to be able to call me. There used to be a number, but the foreman don't like to let you go to the phone, not unless it's an emergency or something like that.

R: So now, she can't call?

JJ: She can call. I can give her the number to a pay phone and have one of the guys transfer the information, and they'll come and let me know that she's on the phone, and they'll hold the phone for me. But you find a lot of guys that are getting ready to use the phone and the phone rings and they hang it up on her. Then they dial their own. She calls into the [personnel] office and somebody in the office comes down and says, "Go call you wife," and when you get ready to call her, they practically follow you there and they follow you back.

R: To make sure you're just—

JJ: Yes, and that's if they can't get nobody to relieve you. If they can get somebody to relieve you, they get somebody to relieve you and if you be gone too long, they'll go get the foreman and find out what happened to you.

Since Jesse is at the bottom of the organizational hierarchy, his use of the telephone is restricted by gatekeepers who guard the access point. Jesse's time at work is paid for; taking "time out" to make contact with a family member is taking time away the work organization and giving it to the family. The gatekeepers, therefore, "bind" the worker in while keeping the family out. Sandra recalled an occasion when she could not reach Jesse.

R: When Jesse calls you, what's the purpose of the phone call?

SJ: He usually just calls to see how my day was, what did me and Billy do. . . . Just to check and see how Billy is doing or what did we do during the day. . . . A lot of times I fix his lunch and sometimes he's not hungry at night, and when he calls, he usually lets me know if he wants me to go ahead and fix him something or either put the food up.

R: Has he done that since you were married or did [his calling] start at a certain time?

SJ: He used to do it when we first got married and then he quit doing it, because he never could. He said he was having a hassle with trying to get into a phone booth. After Billy was born—well, the closer it got to me going to the hospital, he started trying to call again. So it's been going on ever since.

R: Is that something you look forward to?

SJ: Yeah. I used to really look forward to it when we first got married. Then after he kind of slacked up calling me, when he called I knew he really wanted something, wanted me to come to the plant or he might have got something or sometimes he wanted to have for dinner, you know, want me to go out and buy something and I would come down and eat dinner with him. . . .

R: Do you ever have reason to call him at the plant?

SJ: He [Billy] gets sick or I have to rush him to the doctor or if I need something, that's the only reason I'd call.

R: Is it hard to get through to him?

SJ: It didn't used to be. I could get ahold of him right on the line and his foreman would answer the phone and get him right to the phone. But I called once and Billy was really sick and I had to take him to the doctor and I couldn't get through. The number had been changed. Jesse said that he was gonna get it and give it to me because what had happened, so many people were calling, and they were calling, and the phone was constantly ringing and they weren't getting any work done. So they changed the phone number one night. He said he'd get it and give it to me.

R: Were you upset the time that happened?

SJ: Really.... During the time, it was like during the winter months and it was cold, and Jesse had the car and I didn't have a way to get to the doctor.

We see here the ritual importance attached to the telephone calls between Jesse and Sandra. During her pregnancy, the ability to maintain contact was especially important, and his telephone calls to her signaled his care and love. Later, such telephone calls became part of their daily reunion ritual.

Sandra's comment that she would call Jesse's workplace if her son were sick indicates that family members seem to observe implicit rules about reaching into the workplace. Unlike Ezra Turner, who encourages his family to call him about "anything," telephone calls seemed to be reserved for emergencies and special occasions. To call more often might jeopardize the breadwinner's position at work. The less power participants have in the workplace, the more difficult it is for family members to reach through the workplace boundary. Participants' statements that they could call without difficulty should be understood in the context of these implicit rules and participants' relative powerlessness.

The Dilemmas of Selling Time

The position of workers in a capitalist society is characterized by the necessity for them to sell their time and labor to provide for their families' material well-being. The negotiations around time and space that I have been examining must ultimately be understood in this larger social context. Through Grønseth's notion of the "Husband–Economic-Provider Role," we can better understand the implications for families of the need to sell time. He has argued that with the processes of industrialization in both private and state capitalism, *"A historically new family structure was institutionalized in which one person, the husband-father, on the basis of his work alone, became chiefly responsible for the economic provision of his children and of their caretakers"* (1973, pp. 261–62; italics in original). In other words, in our society the survival of working-class and lower-middle-class family households is dependent primarily on the wages and salaries brought in from the external work setting. The worker mediates this dependency by serving as family provider and wage-earning employee. This dependency on an outside agency as the source of financial support poses a number of dilemmas in efforts to negotiate the time–space interface between work and home.

The Interlocking of Work and Family Systems. I have already introduced Quinn's notion of "locking-in" to describe how the individual worker may be unable to choose his work situation, occupation, or employer because of lack of power, opportunity, and mobility. Here I am concerned with the interlocking of the economic structure with the family system that forces people to remain on their jobs. The economic dependence on their jobs felt by participants was reflected in the repeated emphasis in all interviews on wages and "security."

Ray Ellison's interest in being a cook was predicated, in part, on the experience of factory work as too insecure because of layoffs, strikes, and changeovers. Ezra Turner left a high-paying construction job for reasons of security.

> ET: That [construction] was paying good money at the time, in '55. Well, we were making $114 a week and that was a lot of money. But then, soon as you finished a building, got near to finishing a building, you started wondering if we will be working tomorrow. So it came to me that—I don't know, some kind of—Daddy put it in mind that you've always got to work, that you've always got to take care of yourself. But then I got thinking—how can I be guaranteed—especially at that time, with the fact that people were getting laid off all the time. . . . So then I said, "There'll always be people who'll be sick. There'll always be sick people and people who need to eat." So I went to the hospital.

The interview with John Turner, Ezra's father, was permeated with the theme of security. He had grown up in a poor rural area; a steady factory job provided him with a form of security he had never before experienced. Ezra Turner learned his lesson well: people would always need medical care. Ray Ellison also kept in mind that people would always need to eat.

Insofar as they perceived limited opportunities in the job market, while at the same time being satisfied with their wages and benefits, participants were reluctant to consider a job change seriously. Their seniority cannot move with them. Locking-in becomes the dark side of security.

Dependent Children and Dependent Wives. The worker sells his or her time and effort to work systems, and regardless of the number of family members she or he must support, each worker receives a single wage. For unmarried individuals and childless couples, these provider roles may be less compelling. But the arrival of economically dependent children, at the same time that the wife may stop working for wages, binds the family provider to his job. Participants varied in how explicit they were in their feelings that family and children tied them to their jobs. To admit these feelings openly could threaten their sense of being loving parents. Nevertheless, despite the cultural sanctions one might expect against the open avowal of such feelings, they emerged with surprising frequency. For example, Mike Healy's dissatisfaction with his present job is expressed through his recurrent absenteeism. Mike had been saying that he would quit his job if Celia could get a job with the pay and benefits he makes. I asked him if he ever felt resentful about having to go to work.

MH: Yeah! I get pissed off. Some nights I'm watching a good movie and know I got to miss the last thirty, forty-five minutes because I got to go to work.

R: Who are you pissed off at?

MH: Myself!

CH: He does.

MH: It's my fault. I'm the one who wanted to get married. I'm the one who got married. I'm the one who had the kids, so—It's certainly not the kids' fault; it's not her fault. It's part of my doings. It's something I have to do. . . .

CH: Because if he didn't have us, he wouldn't have to do it. He wouldn't have to go.

Mike began with a joke but then became quite serious. He made it clear to me that he loves his children, but they are ultimately the ties that bind him.

Tony Johnson recalled the time he cried while at work:

TJ: Oh, just on graveyard was when I guess I was really depressed. First of all, because I was working that damn shift, and there were times when I just started crying. You know, I was blowing out. Like when she was pregnant, I was working graveyard. I was 21. . . . All of a sudden . . . I'm working this obscene shift for some obscene amount of money, and I got a wife at home that's pregnant with a kid and I just said, "What are you doing?"

The romantic ideology of family life and parenthood does not prepare young fathers (and mothers) for the economic realities of household and family life. Tony was unprepared for the panic he felt at suddenly being a provider. He now worries that he will give up his dream of becoming a lawyer, as he is beginning "to feel that trap."

Samuel Coleman did give up his dreams. He had wanted to go to college, but his mother was supporting a large family on her wages as a cleaning woman and, rather than college, Samuel ended up in the armed services. When he came out of the service, he undertook training as an aircraft mechanic, but his realization that he was the primary support for his new family forced him to give up that dream.

> SC: At that time I had got married and I guess my future was set. [*Laughs*] I had to work—I had to get a job quick. . . . After they phased out the airport out here, so, I had to give up that dream. I wanted to be an aircraft mechanic, you know, but that would have took two more years of school, and at the time I just couldn't afford it. I had to get a job. . . . After you get married you got to have a place to stay.

Samuel had learned that dreams are expensive. Earlier, he had tried factory work but hated it. He then went to work as a prison guard but experienced a sense of panic when his wife became pregnant.

> SC: She was expecting and I seen a mountain of bills. I don't know. I got, I guess, I got scared. I've got to go where I can make the money.

He turned to factory work once again.

> R: When you walked in the door the first time, did you think that this was a temporary job or did you know that you were going to be there for the next ten years?
>
> SC: I think that everyone that hires in, hires in with the fact that it's temporary. After you start working in the morning, you know you're not going to be there the rest of your life. Those were my feelings. . . .
>
> R: If you were a single man—
>
> SC: [*completes sentence*]—I wouldn't be there. I would not be there! I can support myself. I would never have left working for the prison, you know. I'd probably still been there.

Samuel now has seven years invested toward his retirement, years he could not take with him if he tried to find another job. Moreover, he is reluctant to give up the life style to which he has grown accustomed. He has exchanged his dreams for security and a new house.

Grønseth also has observed that the counterpart of the responsibility these men feel lies in the dependency their nonemployed wives experience. Thus, Celia Healy helps push Mike out the door to the job he hates.

> R: You're saying he doesn't want to go to work?
>
> MH: No!
>
> CH: No! I have to push him out that door at 10:30. Out! Out! He says, "I'm not going to work." He pulls that crap every night at 10:00. "I'm not going to work." [*Chuckles*]. . . .
>
> R: What if he didn't go to work?
>
> CH: I'd kill him! [*Giggles*]. . . . They told him the next time he's absent again, it's three days off and we can't afford that. . . . That's why I have to keep pushing him out that door, so he don't lose that job.

R: You're really dependent on that job.

CH: [*Laughing*] Well, if he gets fired, then this house goes and everything in it!

Celia laughed as she talked, but despite her giggles we sense the deadly seriousness of what she is saying. The Healys just have begun to manage financially and they have a new baby. Mike hates to go to work and is irritable and difficult with Celia when he comes home; nevertheless, she forces him to go. He has few options open to him, although he is bidding on another job. Even with ten years of seniority, he feels that he is "low man on the totem pole."

Betty Johnson is older than Celia and has lived with her economic dependence for some time. At the time of the interview, the fear accompanying her feelings of being dependent began to surface, as Henry had just returned from the hospital.

BJ: I could never support myself. I don't know what the hell I'd do. . . . I mean, I was never even a salesgirl, you know. Now, when you're over 40. . . . I don't even know how to type.

R: That's a very frightening feeling.

BJ: It is. Scares the hell out of me.

Now Betty is encouraging her daughters to gain some skills in order to have something to "fall back on."

For most of the participants, the combination of being economically dependent and structurally locked into a job can mean that household financial considerations are given priority over other needs of the family system and its members. This is reflected in the decision made by the Jones family to stay in the city where Jesse's job is located. Although both Jesse and Sandra would prefer to live near their respective families of origin, they live hundreds of miles away because Jesse would have difficulty supporting their family in their parents' community. Sandra Jones talked about feeling lonely and depressed living away from her mother and sister,[4] but Jesse would have to give up nine years of seniority at the factory if they left. Sandra attributed her initial decision to live "up north" to the ideology that says that a woman must follow her man.

SJ: I just feel that a woman should follow her husband. He's the breadwinner and when I'm not working, we still make it; whereas I feel if it was just me, it would be hard on me without him. And I just feel that I should follow him wherever his work is. I don't necessarily have to work and I can go home when we have the money and the spare time. Then I can go, where it would be hard for him to come back here.

4. Tallman (1969) has described the depression of working-class women who move away from their social networks. Bernard (1976) has linked the decrease in "homosociality" with female depression.

Alongside the ideology lies the economic reality of her dependence on Jesse and their mutual dependence on his well-paying job. In order to maintain their family, she subordinates her personal needs to economic realities. However, she and her family may be paying a price in her recurrent feelings of sadness and loss. For the most part, Jesse remains unaware of Sandra's quiet despair and the source of her bad moods. Sometimes when she begins thinking about "home," she wishes he could remain with her instead of going to work. But she reported that she lets him know about her need for his presence only when he can take off his "personal days" and not lose pay. More important, Sandra does not want to bother Jesse with her feelings.[5]

> SJ: I wouldn't want him to go to work with it on his mind that I'm for some reason unhappy today.... I found out that with working and having problems, something on your mind, it's hard to stay at work—hard to work. It seems like it makes the day longer. I wouldn't want his day harder for him thinking that I wanted him at home.

Instead of talking to Jesse about her sadness, she finds something around the house to occupy her. To lighten his load, Sandra is protecting Jesse in his role as breadwinner, even if it means becoming more depressed herself. She is now considering an alternative solution: by returning to paid work, she hopes to dwell less on her loneliness. However, in order to arrange child care for young Billy, she thinks they will have to work different shifts. Thus, the interlocking of family and occupational systems, reflected in Jesse being tied to his particular job, has created a dilemma for the Jones family that still awaits an adequate solution.

The Dilemma of Overtime. Time to be intimate with the family competes with time to be sold for a living. This dilemma, evident during an ordinary work week, is accentuated during "overtime." For several reasons, the participants' attitudes toward overtime was one of ambivalence. Overtime was seen as time stolen from the family. But working overtime was also the only way many of the participants could achieve a comfortable standard of living.[6] Eric Cooper desires overtime income that is not available to him as a white-collar worker. The choice is not his. In contrast, for participants who have production jobs in the auto plants, overtime is only partly voluntary. Consequently, many of them work

5. Lopata found that many of her working-class respondents saw their role in regard to their husband's job as providing a "happy home" and "as maintaining a good atmosphere just before the husband leaves home for work in the morning" (1971, p. 102).

6. Sennett and Cobb also have commented on the "balancing act" of overtime. A worker wants to be with his family, but the only way to provide decently for them and "give his life some greater meaning" is through longer hours at work (1972, p. 125).

nine-hour days and six-day weeks, resenting the forced overtime but wanting to avoid being deprived of it when they need the money. In these latter cases, the family's economic needs combine with the enforced demands of the work organization to deprive family members of emotionally necessary time together.

Summary

Family members use time and space to negotiate the patterns of closeness and distance among them. Because work and home settings are separated in space and because employers buy the time of family members, the way a work organization structures time and space is one key to the family's process of distance regulation. Without sources of independent wealth or means to self-employment, people are entirely dependent on wages gained from selling their labor in the marketplace. These conditions are a source of strain for the families interviewed and limit their ability to maximize access to family goals.

The number of hours a family member works, the timing of these hours, and the life-cycle stage of the family and its individual members were each considered important features of the structural interface. The ability to decrease distance by bridging space was also a way in which families attempted to establish contact. However, workplace boundaries are not equally permeable to all workers and their families. The power of the worker in the organizational setting was reflected in the ease with which he could reach out of the workplace and into the home. Similarly, family members were reluctant to reach into the work setting for fear of jeopardizing the worker's position there. In the negotiations that occur over space and time, the participating families are relatively powerless with regard to the work organization. Stierlin (1959) has noted that in the relationship between a powerful person and a weaker one, the more powerful one need not take into account the needs of the other. This principle seems to apply in the boundary negotiations between relatively powerless individual families and the external work organizations to which they are connected.

CHAPTER **5**

Evaluating
Alternative Interpretations

In the discussion of the psychological interface, I presented a view of how work experiences can carry over into the familial space. In the analysis of the structural interface, I argued that through time and space and the phenomenon of locking-in, work intrudes on family life in ways that are beyond the control of the individual worker and his or her family. We are now in a position to compare this perspective with three competing interpretations of the work–family relationship.

The "Myth of Separate Worlds"

The extreme segmentation hypothesis, presented in Chapter 1, assumes that life is divided into several parts, each of which is lived out independently of the others. In this view, people take on different roles in different settings and move easily between them. It follows that transitions between settings are not at issue because life spheres are neatly compartmentalized. In fact, Dubin (1976) has suggested that the separation of workplace and home in time, space, and function facilitates this compartmentalization. However, the interview data indicated that a number of participants found that transitions between settings posed problems. They required psychological and physical space to move from the role of worker to that of husband–father. These data provide evidence that the compartmentalization is not complete, and the transitions are not smooth.

A less extreme position is that work and family life are separate for those people for whom work is not a central life interest. This view has been applied, in particular, to those in working-class and lower-middle-class occupations, which generally do not allow for personal involvement. What emerges is a portrait of uninvolved workers who easily shuttle from workplace to home, assuming different roles as they move between the two realms. Since work roles are not "salient" for them, lack of involvement in their jobs leads, in this view, to a natural separation of work and family life. This position was described in Chapter 1 as part of the "myth of separate worlds."

Participants themselves subscribed to this viewpoint. Ezra Turner and Henry Johnson were unusual in their explicit acknowledgment of the connections between their work experiences and emotional life in their families. The majority of participants claimed, as did the men interviewed by Aberle and Naegele (1952), that for them work and family worlds were psychologically distinct.

(SAMUEL COLEMAN, assembler)

SC: Once I punch out, I forgot that day in the factory. . . .

R: If you've had a bad day at work, how do you act? . . .

SC: I don't take it out on the family. [Chuckles]

R: What do you do?

SC: I usually just keep it to myself and hash it out with myself. But I don't bring it home, no.

(TONY JOHNSON, computer operator)

R: Do you think your work life affects your home life?

TJ: I don't think so.

R: Do you think they're separate?

TJ: They're definitely separate.

(ERIC COOPER, computer monitor)

EC: So I just pretty much leave my job where it's at. Then I pick it up the next day when I come in.

R: That means you don't think about it at all after you walk out the door?

EC: Usually not; I don't think about it.

R: How long does it take you to drive from your job?

EC: Just going home. That's all. I just think about other things. My job doesn't enter into my conversation at home or what I think about.

(TOM DOYLE, traffic expediter)

TD: My family life is my family life. It's entirely away from everything else. It has nothing to do with anything else I do.

This apparent separation of spheres was evident in participants' reports that they neither thought nor talked about work at home. Refraining from talking about work, in some cases, may have been actively reinforced by wives. For example, Tony Johnson noted that when he tried to talk to his wife about his work life she changed the subject.

Evaluating Alternative Interpretations

Eric Cooper commented sardonically, "I don't really think that most wives really, really care about what goes on at work with their husbands." This sentiment was echoed by several men. If we rely solely on the participants' own descriptions, we would have to accept that, for them, the "myth" is reality. How, then, are we to reconcile these assertions with the psychological and structural interface dilemmas described in the preceding chapters?

Since the same participants who asserted the separation of work and family life also mentioned in their interviews the experiences and events I have described in the interface patterns, we might conclude that these relationships were obscured for them. Although participants often mentioned insufficient time with family members, they did not see lack of time as a way in which work shaped their family life. (Samuel Coleman was unusual in specifying the role of work time in his family life.) Since time and space relationships comprise the background of everyday experience, the existing order is taken as natural and given. People also have difficulty in recognizing the larger structural constraints on their lives because we commonly think in terms of individual explanations. Consequently, the phenomenon of locking-in also was not recognized as an important interface relationship. In other words, the structural interface relationships were obscured in everyday life.

Participants also did not seem to perceive clearly the patterns of psychological relationships between their work and family lives. The energy deficit pattern contrasts interestingly with the reported incidents of positive carry-over. Participants connected coming home singing and smiling with a good day at work. On the other hand, the effects of personal depletion were not recognized. It may be that this pattern represents enough of a norm so that only deviations from it are perceived. Moreover, as I have suggested before, what is *not* there too easily goes unnoticed.

Another possible reason that the psychological interface is obscured is that separation of home and work may be a widely held value, grounded in the desirability of protecting both breadwinner and family from work-related stresses over which they have no control. This value may be inferred from statements by participants who directly reported negative carry-over in their lives. Celia Healy explicitly stated that Mike should not bring his work problems home. Betty Johnson wished Henry would leave his job at the workplace. Henry Johnson, too, wished he could separate work and family life in order to save himself and his family distress.

HJ: I wish that I wouldn't be as conscientious at work that I bring it home. I'd rather be able to go down like a lot of people that I work with. They work there eight hours and that's it. . . . I'd like to leave it. I'd like to not bring that home. What we have home, I'd like to have that here. . . . You work,

> you work period. You've got to work or you don't eat and nobody else eats. So you've got to do that. Do something that's maybe enjoyable, or at least be able to leave it there.

Valuing the separation of spheres also may explain why participants were reluctant to describe negative carry-over when it did occur. Open discussion of negative carry-over by participants may have been hindered by the notion that work and family life *should* be separate and by the social desirability of such an attitude. Such a value, as Kanter (1977) has noted, makes it difficult to ask people directly about the separation of life spheres. Participant responses to direct queries on this topic were sometimes at variance with the themes that emerged in their interviews.

Active Psychological Disengagement

There is yet another way in which we can understand participants' assertions about the separation of spheres. Kahn et al. (1964) have described "psychological disengagement" as a way of dealing with some job-related stresses.[1] The concept of psychological disengagement suggests an active coping process whereby workers and their families try to maintain boundaries between work and family by not talking, consciously thinking, or caring about work. In contrast, the segmentationist view assumes that for those who are not involved in their work, such a separation is a natural consequence of noninvolvement. This latter assumption implies that a worker and his or her family are passive objects of a natural process. However, the words of the participants themselves suggest that they actively attempt to separate work and family life in order to deal with work-related stresses.

Eric Cooper explained why he attempts to separate his work life from his family:

> EC: Since I am associated with both worlds—my work world and my home world—I separate those two because to me they are two separate things. That's why . . . when I leave my work at work, I don't want to spend time at home working on work. You know what I mean? I have my home life and I have my work life and I want to keep those two separate because they are two important things. I don't want to mix them up because if something should go wrong at one place, it can have serious effects on the

---

1. Kasl (1974) has suggested that the process of disengagement described in the social gerontology literature may be similar to the process of "retrenchment of goals and aspirations" (p. 185) in older workers, making them more satisfied with their jobs than are younger workers. However, Cumming and Henry's (1961) theory of disengagement as a natural process and as a successful adjustment to aging has been criticized. For example, Crawford (1971) found that disengagement from life activities was experienced as undesirable and stressful by an elderly sample.

other place because they are so intermixed. I want to keep them separate, so if something goes wrong in one place, I don't have to worry about that in my other place.

Eric seemed to contradict himself when he described both the "intermix" of the two systems and their separation. This apparent contradiction is resolved when we understand that he actively tries to maintain their separation by not talking about work while at home and trying not to think about it. He feels that his wife is uninterested in his work and if we could observe the process between them, we might see that she helps maintain the boundary between work and home through the manner in which she communicates the disinterest he reported.

Additional evidence of participants' active attempts to maintain such a boundary is provided in the following interview segment with Samuel Coleman. He recalled the advice he gave his wife when she began working in the automobile factory:

R: If you've had a bad day . . . you don't talk about it when you come home at all? Do you ever tell your wife about it?

SC: No, I quit that and I advised her to do the same. Leave work at work!

R: Quit that? Does that mean you used to do it?

SC: I used to. I seen it wasn't no—nothing really she could do about me complaining to her. She probably had the same kind of day. I told her: just leave her job at her job and I'll leave mine at mine. . . . The best is to forget about it. Take it for what it is.

R: You mean people insulate themselves, then don't feel it—

SC: [Interrupts] Right. Because you don't get any justification out of it. You just torture yourself with it. Just forget about it and—

R: How do you learn to forget about it? . . .

SC: Put it in the back of your mind. You can do it!

Samuel hinted that the process of disengagement was learned over time as a way of protecting both himself and his wife from the anger and frustration he sometimes felt with his foreman and his job. We can hypothesize several steps in this process. He entered the factory with the assumption that this job would be temporary, and this assumption enabled him to manage anger and frustration. However, once he realized he would most likely be in the factory for the rest of his working life, he had to find other ways to cope with the feelings. Learning to "put it in the back of [his] mind" was one such mechanism. Had we been present, over time we might have seen the psychological interface pattern change from one of negative carry-over to one of depletion and deficit. Interestingly, when he worked as a prison guard he found it difficult to forget the problems of the prisoners, just as Ezra Turner could not forget the suffering of hospital patients when he worked as an orderly. Disengagement may be especially difficult for those in human-service occupations.

The theme of learning not to care over time was stated more explicitly by Tom Doyle, a traffic expediter for a large corporation.

> TD: There is no such thing as common courtesy. There is no such thing as courtesy, period. It's a "dog-eat-dog" operation. . . . Only I can turn it off now.
>
> R: How?
>
> TD: [*Quickly*] I just turn 'em off. . . .
>
> R: How do you turn it off?
>
> TD: I turn 'em off just like I could go like that— [*snaps fingers*]. Completely put them out of my mind.
>
> R: Did it take you a while to learn to do that?
>
> TD: Yeah. . . . My boss used to just be miserable to me. [*Chuckles*] Because that's the way he is. [*Laughs*] He's changing. We're changing him. But that's the way he is. It used to keep me on edge all the time. And now I don't argue with him; I don't say anything to him. I just ignore him. And if he were to come up . . . and start in on me, I'd just look him in the eye and I'd think, "You're an ignorant individual, and you don't know any better. And I have done my job. And it is right. You don't know what you're talking about, but I'll sit here"—I'm thinking all this while he's yakking!—And I used to get upset and I don't anymore. If that place burned down, I'd get up and get my coat and walk out. I'm completely divorced from it. . . .
>
> R: How did you learn to do that?
>
> TD: As a matter of survival. In other words, if you can't stop all of this, you can't let it kill you. So the only other thing to do is just cut it out.

Again, we can infer a sequence of increasing disengagement. When he first joined the corporation, Tom Doyle was in management training. However, the personnel practices so angered him and so violated his sense of personal integrity that he became physically ill. Slowly, he began to give up his dreams and ambitions, and now he is awaiting retirement. He still becomes infuriated by the "dog-eat-dog" operation, but he has learned to "divorce" himself. Fairbairn (1954) has called the "plate glass feeling" that Tom described a form of defense.[2]

---

2. Schizoid defenses, which include depersonalization and derealization, may be understood as a withdrawal from interactions that threaten the integrity of the self. By seeming to withdraw the "real" self from interaction, this type of defense gives the illusion of personal control and autonomy. Sennett and Cobb have noted a similar process in their study of workers. They described the "protective alienation" of the "real person" from the "performing self" (1972, p. 194). (See also Guntrip 1969.)

Evaluating Alternative Interpretations

Disengagement and the Threat to Self.   I have suggested that the effort to maintain a separation between work and family life stems from a desire to protect the breadwinner and his family from work-related stresses. The process of trying not to think, talk, or care about work is part of this active disengagement, which contributes to the myth of separate worlds. That this disengagement process is a means of personal defense is reflected in the powerful images used by Samuel Coleman and Tom Doyle. Henry Johnson, too, had talked about the futility of hitting his head against a wall. These are images of death, of torture and survival. They imply that these men feel they may be destroyed or maimed if they are unable to protect themselves from what occurs at the workplace. In the discussion of personal depletion, I suggested that people can feel assaulted by being robbed of the opportunity to actualize themselves in their work. Powerless and locked into their jobs, workers also can feel endangered by the rage and frustration that ensue. Even Mike Healy, who reported being satisfied with his job, harbored powerful feelings.

MH: I like my job! I don't mind working for [the] company! I mean, it's been good to me. I've been there ten years. I feel I've got a lot to show for what I've—Sure, I don't make as much as the man who works out on the street, but if you break it down to all my benefits, I make more—as much or more. . . . You figure, we're catching up to these people that work for themselves, slowly but surely. We don't pay no Blue Cross, we don't pay no dentist; we don't pay none of that. That's all paid for!

R: One of the reasons I got the impression you weren't so crazy about your job was from some of the things I used to hear you say. But maybe I'm wrong about that.

MH: It's like this. I feel there's got to be a better life than working a machine all your life. That's one reason why I'm going to school. I mean, I told her: I can't see me pounding a machine for thirty years. I just feel like I can better myself. I wouldn't mind even going on salary, or anything, being a clerk, just to get out and get away from the machine.

R: What is there about the machine that—

MH: Get's old! I mean, you know. You've got to make so many parts every night, you know. And it gets monotonous after a while. It gets old. . . . You can train a monkey to do this! I mean, you know, I can bring my goddam *kid* in there!

R: How does it make you feel to be working at a job that requires little training?

MH: It irritates me! I mean, it does. I mean . . . you get jobs like that—they're boring. . . . "Why can't I take this home? My kid would enjoy doing this! It's a fascinator, you know!" Hell, I could be laying in bed sleeping, telling him, "This is what I want you to do. . . . When you get tired, walk

> away and play with your toys, but make sure they're all done when I get up."
>
> R: What effect do you think it has on people when they work on boring jobs like that year after year?
>
> MH: It depresses them. Well, some people, I guess, tolerate it. You know? Other people—the other people, I guess, just get so depressed.
>
> R: What do you mean "depressed"? . . .
>
> MH: I don't know. To me, it's depressing. You got a job that's just boring as hell.

When Mike first entered the factory he had few concrete goals for himself. Currently, he has only vague notions of what he would like to achieve in his work, but he is certain that "there's got to be a better life." Participants' sense that life has more to offer was reflected in their hopes that their children will have more than they do (see also Chinoy 1955; Sennett & Cobb 1972).

One could argue that these feelings were elicited by the interview situation; however, this caveat does not mean that these feelings were invented. Rather, the interviews momentarily disturbed an accommodation process whereby participants have learned to manage their feelings by disengaging from their work roles, rendering the work itself less salient. I have suggested that their integrity is assaulted by the workplace; the hierarchical social relations there are also a source of tension for some of them. Insofar as such feelings are sources of stress, they are normally managed by participants in order to protect themselves and their families. "Apathy" is the term commonly used for this defensive maneuver. It may be an aspect of the process by which people try to maintain a boundary between work and personal life. This active disengagement process appeared to be especially bitter for those white-collar participants who had had hopes that they could actualize their ideal self-images through interesting work.

Is Disengagement Successful? Not all people can distance themselves from their jobs. For Henry Johnson, in a boundary position between two work systems, disengagement is difficult. As Kahn et al. (1964) have noted, psychological withdrawal, as a technique for dealing with work-related strain, is limited by the amount of necessary communications a person at the boundary has with those "role senders" who are the sources of distress. But Henry's difficulty in disengaging comes not only from his boundary position; he also risks losing the gratification he derives from his involvement. The envy he expressed toward young, "apathetic" workers barely hid his disdain, for he derives his sense of worth from being the type of worker who "does something, plus." For example, when there is a security problem at night, he is called. Being an involved, responsible, hardworking employee makes him feel valuable and needed.

R: Perhaps your father once tried to give you the message that things couldn't go on without you [at work]. . . .

HJ: I think I've certainly got the idea that they won't survive without me and obviously would pine away. It's hard to believe, though.

R: Well, maybe it also . . . makes you feel important? . . .

HJ: Well, at 30 it might be the greatest thing in the world to feel that you're indispensable. But after a little while and you get a little older, you begin to realize that they got along various times when I was down there without me. Quite obviously they do it. Someday, it's going to sink in. . . . Someday it might. I'll get around to believing it. We had a couple of presidents who died and the country got along without them. . . .

R: That doesn't mean people are replaceable. It's just that you know things do go on [without you].

HJ: It's nice to think, like you say, that you feel a certain importance or something like that. I think it's sort of nice to figure that way. Maybe they can get along, but it's going to be a little tougher for them.

Although Henry claimed that age should teach him that the business would survive without him, we can imagine that, as he grows older, the experience of being invaluable would be even more crucial to his sense of personal worth. Ezra Turner is fortunate in having a job that is both nonstressful and personally rewarding.

Others who have succeeded in not talking about work may also be paying a price for their attempted solution. Several participants worried about not having enough to share with their spouses. If they cannot share their work experiences, then the lives of spouses grow further apart and this, perhaps, compounds difficulties in communications. For professionals, such communication may be facilitated because their work is intrinsically interesting. But as Eric Cooper commented, wives "have enough of their own boredom at home to hear about my boredom at work." The combination of little understanding, past experiences of powerlessness to help their husbands, and fear of negative carry-over effects may discourage wives from listening. We must wonder about the consequences for marriages when large segments of couples' separate experiences are not available to each other.[3]

Moreover, even when people think they are keeping work concerns out of the home by not talking about them, they may be communicating them in subtle ways. We know from clinical experience that people

3. Bernard (1972) also has suggested that husbands and wives may become alienated from one another because of their differing work experiences. Blood and Wolfe (1960) and Komarovksy (1962) have discussed the issue of the husband's talking (or not) about his occupational experiences. This subject requires further research.

express their distress in a variety of ways that are not always consciously controlled. For example, industrial work can be dangerous, but when I asked Jesse Jones, relief man on an assembly line, whether he ever worried about being injured on the job, he laughed at my question. In the second interview his concerns about working under potentially dangerous conditions surfaced spontaneously.

R: How do you feel about your surroundings [at the plant]?

JJ: Well, when I first started working down there, it more or less sort of scared me. Here I am thinking I'm in a place where I might could lose a leg or hand, a forklift might kill me, or something like this, you know. But after working on all of them so long, you know, you just get used to them.

R: So you are afraid that you might lose a part of your body?

JJ: Yeah.

R: It does happen to people, I guess, doesn't it?

JJ: Right, and every time something like that happens, you know, you can hear a silence seem like all through the whole plant. . . .

R: You're afraid of the [forklift] drivers. Why? . . .

JJ: They'd be flying up and down the aisles, the parts would fall off and stuff like that. I've seen cases where parts almost fell on me.

R: How do you feel after that happens?

JJ: It just scares the devil out of you, but after it's over, you just forget about it. . . . Seems like you're working and trying to survive at the same time.

When an accident occurs at the plant, Jesse's first action is to discover who is at fault. Thinking it was a worker's own carelessness seems to make the fear more manageable because the accident is preventable through one's own efforts. A faulty machine or another worker's carelessness, however, is frightening. Jesse said that he tries to forget about these incidents. Certainly, such worry might be incapacitating. I then asked him if Sandra knew about the dangers at the plant.

JJ: I don't think so, because at times she comes down to the plant when we get off the line and everything had been shut down for the day. We had stopped working.

R: So she doesn't have a sense of how dangerous it is?

JJ: No, no.

R: Would it bother her if she thought about it?

JJ: Maybe so, maybe so.

R: Is that something you talk about a lot?

JJ: Never a word.

With this last response to my query, Jesse indicated his conscious silence about his concern. Yet when I interviewed Sandra separately she told me, unhesitatingly, that she did worry about his being hurt.

Evaluating Alternative Interpretations

R: Do you ever worry about Jesse getting hurt?

SJ: [*Indicates yes*] I worry mostly about the job . . . because I went down to the plant over Christmas and they had, like, a party down there, and I cooked a cake for the party, and I went down there and Jesse showed me the different jobs and stuff. I—a lot of them are very dangerous. I've known women and men, too, that get their fingers cut off the hand. You have to be really careful and watch what you're doing. You have to be on your p's and q's too much.

R: Is that something that's in your mind a lot or—

SJ: Yeah, I think about it quite a bit.

R: What do you think about, exactly?

SJ: Just, you know, what would happen if he gets hurt and just the idea of something like that happening to him.

R: It almost sounds as if you were rehearsing it because you expect it might happen.

SJ: Ah hah. [*Laughs*] Yeah. . . .

R: Did you start worrying after you saw [the machines] or from people you knew previously who were injured? . . .

SJ: Just from knowing people. . . . No, just people that Jesse worked with or something, and he came home and told me about.

R: Does he know you worry?

SJ: No.

R: Do you talk about it with anybody?

SJ: No, it's just something there that I think about once in a while.

R: What triggers it?

SJ: Yeah, something like he'll tell me or—I don't know. Sometimes I just get—at night I can just be laying in bed and if he's late coming home from work, then my mind goes to that—what could be happening, you know. . . .

R: Do you know how he feels?

SJ: No.

Jesse thinks he is keeping his fear of injury from Sandra by not talking about it explicitly. Nevertheless, in his story telling and attempts to master his fear, he communicates his own dread to her indirectly. A solution for the Joneses might be for Jesse never to mention incidents from work. However, he told me he wants to share his work with her so they will have more in common. It is a way of making contact. Here we see the dilemma that work stress poses for families. To be successful in keeping work concerns out of the home by not talking can mean the creation of even greater gulfs in understanding between husbands and wives.

Despite their efforts, participants cannot maintain impermeable boundaries between work and home by disengaging, not talking, and not caring. In the discussion of psychological and structural interface patterns, I have suggested that these efforts cannot be entirely successful. The myth of separate worlds can be upheld as long as the connections between spheres remain obscured. But for most participants, maintaining a solid boundary between workplace and home is beyond their individual control.

Compensation

The hypothesis of compensatory gratification, outlined in Chapter 1, asserts that when workers are unable to achieve gratification from their work roles, they achieve alternative gratification in roles outside of work. The alternative gratification of interest to us here relates noninvolvement in work roles to increased involvement in family roles, or what has been called becoming "home centred".

Aldous has combined the idea of compensatory gratification with that of the home-as-haven to suggest that men in blue-collar and quasiprofessional jobs, "far from seeking to carry over job-related behaviors to the family, often look to their homes as havens from job monotonies and as sources of satisfaction lacking in the occupational sphere" (1969, p. 172). This notion can be evaluated in light of the data presented here.

Men Do Not Seek to Carry Over Work Concerns. In discussing the myth of separate worlds I suggested that, indeed, men actively try to keep their work-related concerns from intruding on the home space. They try to accomplish this task by not thinking or talking about work and by withdrawing from involvement with their work roles. However, a distinction must be made between what they value and seek to accomplish and what actually occurs. In the previous discussion, we saw that these efforts are not always successful. Henry Johnson cannot always disengage, and despite the belief that he does not talk about his fears to his wife, Jesse Jones's concerns are nevertheless communicated. The displacement of work-related anger onto family members also is sometimes beyond personal control and comprehension. Finally, as we have seen, carry-over can be obscured and structural interfaces can go unrecognized.

Men Look to Their Homes as Havens. Again, the interview data support the notion that some men look to their homes as havens. This haven has different meanings for different individuals. Eric Cooper does not want to walk into a "furnace" when arriving home. We can infer that, to him, the home as haven means that the family system is free from trouble and conflict. Henry Johnson explicitly sees his home as a place to relax and implicitly as a place to work out his worries about his job. Tony Johnson and Jesse Jones described the process of carving out physical and psychological spaces for themselves. Again we need to contrast the real with the ideal. While Eric may need his home to be a haven, such a conflict-free realm is not possible for him. And for those who do manage to carve out some space, we saw that the family system may pay a price for being an "oasis of replenishment" in that other family members have to give up their space and their activities. Finally, the decreased emotional and interpersonal availability of the worker creates interpersonal tension. As suggested in the discussion of the Johnsons, the home as haven has its costs.

Men Look to Their Families as Sources of Satisfaction Lacking in the Occupational Sphere. Of the thirteen male workers interviewed, six spontaneously mentioned that they are family men or that their families "come first." The role of father-husband is more "salient" to them than their work role and they receive more satisfaction from it than from their jobs. Again, however, we must distinguish between an expressed devotion to a role committment and the real context in which such committment is carried out. To assert the value of family involvement is different from being able to realize it. The frequent complaints about insufficient time with family members—children in particular—indicate that involvement in this role, and therefore the ability to obtain satisfaction from it, is limited by the time constraints of the work setting. Jesse Jones, for example, imagined the bicycle trips his family would take together if they had more time. While they take pride in their ability to provide well for their children, participants lack the time to be as involved with them as they wish.

Insufficient personal energy also can interfere with the ability to make real the commitment to a role. Young and Willmott (1973) have assumed that a manual worker's lack of involvement at work means increased energy to invest in wives and children. Beneath this assertion lie two assumptions: (1) people have a given amount of energy that is distributed in one sphere or another and (2) complete disengagement from the work role is achieved. Such a formulation is insufficiently dynamic because it does not account for the transactions I have been describing, for such jobs can be enervating, depleting, and upsetting. As a result, emotional availability to initiate interactions and to respond may be limited. I would not argue that workers do not find satisfaction from their involvement with wives and children. In fact, many of the men I interviewed are particularly interested in their families. I would simply point out that the time and energy demands of the work setting impose constraints on their ability to be as actively involved with family

99

members as they would like. This theme emerged repeatedly in the interviews. In contrast, it appears that when work is involving and gratifying—as in Ezra Turner's case—then active, emotional involvement with family members is possible. The irony may be that those who most want greater involvement with their families may be among those least able to achieve it.

Some Thoughts on Leisure

More commonly, the compensation hypothesis has been applied to leisure rather than to family activities. The hypothesis states that people compensate in their leisure activities for gratifications not achieved at work. The data collected here do not address the question of leisure in any depth, so no extensive attempt to deal with this question will be made. However, they do suggest some ways we might think about the issue.

As mentioned in Chapter 1, the research on leisure points to the conclusion that one's work activities are similar in form to one's leisure activities (Meissner 1971). Thus, Eric Cooper reported that his boredom and enervation make it difficult for him to devote effort to his great love, golf. Ezra Turner, as the research on leisure might predict, is the most active of the participants—he canoes, wrestles, camps, skis, and hikes. Chuck Simpson, a forklift operator, seems to present an enigmatic case as the other participant who is very active. He skis, motorbikes, and snowmobiles. Yet, if we consider his work experience more closely, we see that he also is among the most mobile and autonomous of workers—he is active driving his forklift, takes his breaks when he chooses, and organizes his own activity. More important, Kathy Simpson's grandmother lives with them and cares for their home and two small children, so Chuck is free from many of the demands of everyday household life. After the data were collected, Chuck was promoted to a supervisory position and, in adjusting to his new job, he reported being too tired to participate in his usual leisure activities.

Some of the leisure activities participants described seem to be a way of escaping from bound time and the pressures of their roles. For example, Henry Johnson loves to fish, for fishing means a reprieve from responsibility. Listening to music was frequently reported as a way of relaxing. What is important for our purposes is that when leisure activities become another way of making psychological space, such activities can further serve to "block out" family members. Such leisure, while being essential to help maintain the worker, may contribute to the process of energy deficit in the family. The research on leisure and work life might fruitfully look into what purposes leisure activities serve and which family members are excluded from or involved in them.

Personality and Setting

For the most part, sociologists have taken up the questions of segmentation and compensation because their concern is with how social structure affects people. From a psychological orientation, we can ask a very different question about the interface patterns I have described. An alternative viewpoint, not yet considered, is that these patterns are a function of disposition and personality traits. This viewpoint, in contrast to the situationist position, would suggest that enduring personal traits and coping styles—formed early in life and rooted in an individual's personal history—are responsible both for the way he or she interacts with family members and for the manner in which he or she relates to work. For example, we could say that Ezra Turner is a warm, outgoing person and that his personality characteristics independently shape the way he relates to both his family and his job. In an analogous way, we could argue that Henry Johnson is a tense, nervous man and that these personality traits explain interpersonal relationships within the Johnson family that are independent of his work experiences.

To test the effects of personality on the behavioral patterns discussed requires longitudinal data that would follow people through job changes. Although such data are not available, the interviews provide some data bearing on the question, for participants mentioned changes in the psychological interface patterns with job changes. In the excerpt from the Healys' interview, reported in Chapter 3, Celia complained that Mike had become a "king crab" with the change in job assignment. If personality alone could explain the way these men related to their families, we would expect their behavior to remain fairly constant over time, since it is assumed that adult personality is relatively fixed. All told, such explicit changes in the psychological interface patterns were mentioned in five of the research families.

In the interview with the Turner family, there was evidence that Ezra was not always interpersonally available when he came home from work. As he described his former job as an orderly in the same hospital, such an alternative pattern emerged.

ET: You know one thing. When I started at [the hospital], I worked on the nursing service on the wards, and I have really had to really take a lot of shit. Just really take a lot of it.

R: What kind of shit?

ET: Just shit. A lot of times the nurses would come in and they would be mad and maybe they would be cranky and they would really be nasty. You were always referred to as "you boys do this; you boys do that." It was just crap. And I always said that one day I'm going to be in a position to make the work situation good. . . . A lot of times I'd come home and be really uptight.

IT: But then sometimes, he'd be, yeah, he'd be very uptight, kind of crabby sometimes. I could spot it immediately and I would just kind of, just leave him alone.

ET: They'd all start running, that's all.

IT: [*Laughs*]

ET: The thing that bothered me is the, ah, my sense of helplessness, you know, as far as the patients themselves. There was just nothing I could do to help out, to make them well. I wanted to make people well and I couldn't make them well because I wasn't a doctor, and the doctor wasn't making them well. And I knew I had to get out of there because I was getting heavy.

R: You went to . . .?

ET: Went to research. Because it was a combination of the crap and the helplessness and just a whole conglomeration of things. I'm surprised that you stayed with me, honey, but aren't you glad?

IT: Aren't *you* glad? [*Laughs*]

R: Do you think that caused stress at home?

IT: No, I don't think it really caused stress because, like I say, I would recognize when he's had a bad day, so we would just kind of leave him to himself and wouldn't really pressure him. In other words, we just wouldn't bother him. Just more or less let him, in other words, let it wear off.

R: So you created a space around him where he could sort of "defuse"?

IT: Yeah.

ET: Uhum. Yeah. What I usually would do is I'd come in, go upstairs, and lie around.

R: How long would you stay there?

ET: Oh, five minutes. But then, the kids were smaller and I don't think that they really knew anything. You know, Isabel would just say, "Daddy's tired."

IT: Uhum.

The Turners described what has been termed a pattern of energy deficit, in which Ezra was less available to family members. Although the Turners, like other families interviewed, were hesitant to discuss this pattern, in his comments about being "uptight" and "heavy" and his joke about Isabel's not leaving him, Ezra hinted that this job may have created strains for him and his family. Isabel minimized the strain, as did Betty Johnson, by evaluating her husband's mood and creating the physical and psychological space necessary for him to recuperate.

Betty Johnson also remembered a time when Henry was in a less stressful job situation. We had been talking about Henry's dislike for his job.

> BJ: The only time when I could say he was happy working is when he left the shop; he started working for where he is now. They didn't know if it was going to be permanent and they put him in the warehouse where he had absolutely no responsibilities. He went in at 8:30; he got out at 5:30, and it lasted for about three months and it was the most wonderful three months of our marriage. . . . He was a different person. You could talk to him; he was relaxed; he was interested in things. He was just relaxed. Then, he decided it was going to be permanent; then, they started giving him responsibility.

Betty described a pattern in which Henry was emotionally and interpersonally available to her and the children—he could listen to them. Although Henry did not remember the specific time Betty referred to, he did remember a time in their marriage when things were going well. Betty was adamant in attributing this change in Henry to his work circumstances. Henry's job has changed once more. He is no longer a dispatcher, and he now comes home less upset but exhausted from lifting heavy weights. The pattern may be shifting to one of energy deficit. However, patterns of relating developed over time do not change readily. Henry still does not eat with Betty and the children.

Tom Doyle recalled the time he was a foreman and was "hard to live with." He experienced this job as an assault on his integrity because he was required to carry out management practices he felt were immoral. In fighting management he developed an ulcer and even found himself drinking. His wife, Paula, also talked about this earlier period in their lives in her interview.

> R: That seemed to be quite a difficult time for him.
>
> PD: It was. Yes. But I felt at the time—and I still do—why should I. . . . When we were first married, when the children were younger, I used to meet him at the door with, "Guess what Jeff did today? Guess what Jane did today? Guess what happened?"—this and that. I don't know what happened, whether I read something somewhere or what, but I try not to do that. . . . This particular time when it was so bad for him and he was miserable, why should I tell him that I'm not sleeping or that I'm worried. . . .
>
> R: Were the blow-ups more often then?
>
> PD: Yeah. . . . He'd be home on the weekends and it seems that every weekend was nothing but one big fight. The children and I would be glad to see Monday come. When they'd be going to school, he'd be going. . . . In fact, it was bad because the three of us were building a life without him.

R: And you think it was directly connected with the type of work he did?

PD: Oh, no question in my mind, no question at all. It made him a miserable son of a bitch. That's the only words I can use to describe—just completely, horribly miserable.

R: He had mentioned he was an SOB. He didn't give me the details on it.

PD: We looked forward to seeing him go to work—to be out of the house and out of our life. We were tense even when he was asleep, we were tense. . . .

R: Did things change when he got his present job?

PD: Well, he got his present job because working on the floor made him so ill he had to leave. He couldn't take it physically anymore. It took time, but gradually it just evolved and revolved and he just became a different person.

R: How? How did he become a "different person"?

PD: Well, he became more involved with us, and his attitude changed . . . and he gradually worked his way back into the position that he had before. But he took a year. Almost a year.

R: Did the relationship between him and the children change then?

PD: It did, but I still think a lot of it remains, especially with Jeff. There are times when he can't seem to make any connection with Jeff and other times they seem extremely close. . . . There was a time when Tom said I talked for them. Like he would ask them something and maybe I would interject and answer, fearing maybe that they would give the wrong answer and get him angry. So I would answer for them. I would answer for them. So if they wanted something. . . . But again, I think this goes back to when he was so miserable that they couldn't talk to him, or felt they couldn't as little children 'cause they didn't know what kind of answer they'd get. So I would do the talking. And they would say, "I want to do this and that. Would you ask Dad?" So there was a time there when I would do all the asking.

R: Was this when he was—

PD: Yes.

R: —working supervision.

PD: Yes. And so now we've done a reversal of that within the last couple of years. I've made a conscious effort.

Paula Doyle has described a number of processes and patterns that are by now familiar. She talked of Tom's unavailability and the negative carry-over of angry feelings into the family system. Communication patterns in the family were affected and, as in the Johnson family, Paula served as a mediator between husband and children, thereby establishing a long-term pattern that they consciously tried to change. The Doyles now consider themselves a close-knit family, even though, in

Tom's relationship to his children, they still see some of the effects of that time in their lives.

Summary and Conclusions

The portrait of the noninvolved worker for whom work and family life are naturally separated, i.e., segmented, must be reconsidered. Rather than something that happens to them, noninvolvement appears to be part of the active process whereby workers try to manage feelings of anger, frustration, and powerlessness generated by their work experiences. Once we understand the attempted separation of spheres as an active stance that is learned over time, we can begin to resolve the apparent contradiction between the interface patterns described and the participants' belief in the myth of separate worlds.

When considering people's responses to the question of whether work affects their family life, we must distinguish between the reported attitude and its underlying meaning. When someone tells us that his work life is divorced from his family life, he may be making a statement about a value, a wish, or a struggle. To the extent that they can only conceive of harmful effects of the carry-over from work to home space, participants valued the separation of spheres and were reluctant to describe negative interface patterns. To admit that their work concerns do extend into the family might imply a failure in their responsibility to their families. Thus, they asserted the separation and actively attempted to disengage. We know from clinical experience that people use such schizoidlike defenses to manage threats to themselves. What we call worker "apathy" may be one such defense.

But to conclude that participants try to disengage and maintain boundaries between work and family life is not to imply that they are entirely successful. The same participants who asserted the separation also described insufficient time and contact with their families and personal depletion and its effect on family relations. In fact, we may find that the pattern of energy deficit in particular is associated with disengagement as a coping mechanism, and that this pattern appears to be what has been called segmentation.

Kanter (1977) has suggested that corporate capitalism treats the worker at the workplace "as if" she or he had no family. Similarly, the interviews suggest that workers and family members may have reason to act "as if" there were no workplace. Such a stance maintains the illusion of autonomy and personal control. A danger for families in maintaining the myth of separate worlds is that the strains created by interface dilemmas will be understood as private and personal, leading to ineffectual searches within or outside the family system for personal or interpersonal ways to ease those strains. As long as the interface connections remain obscured, failures in coping can result in family members blaming each other.[4]

The notion that noninvolvement leads to compensatory gratification through involvement in family roles also must be rethought. Rather than supporting this hypothesis, the interview data suggest that the proposition must be rejected as it now stands. As the Turner family illustrated, a nonstressful and gratifying job allows for high levels of family involvement. Conversely, those who feel assaulted, depleted, and uninvolved in their work may have little personal energy to invest in their families despite the fact that such involvement is valued and desired. Finally, we must conclude that we cannot measure the extent to which family members are home-centered by asking people how much time they spend at home, nor can we be satisfied with measuring role salience simply by asking them whether work or family roles are more important to them.

Finally, we considered the notion that "person variables" account for the types of behaviors described by participants. Behavior is a highly complex phenomenon. Without question, personality variables affect the way in which a person relates both to his work and to his family. We know that the way a person copes with stresses generated by the structure of the work organization and the requirements of work roles is partly a function of personality factors (Kahn et al. 1964). For example, we have seen that Ezra Turner managed his exhaustion by making space for himself and, ultimately, by obtaining another job. In contrast, Henry Johnson is a worrier. Tom Doyle and Mike Healy have a "short fuse," which affect the particular form the interface patterns take. The personal history and style of other family members also influence the interface patterns that develop and their meaning for family members. For example, Celia Healy is openly angry at Mike for his unavailability, whereas Betty Johnson attempted to ignore Henry while she blamed herself.

Still, the data about job changes do not support the notion that the behavior reported by the participants is entirely a function of the enduring traits a person "has." Other evidence also suggests that what we consider to be stable personality traits may themselves be subject to change as a result of a person's work experiences (Kohn & Schooler 1973). The process of disengagement as a way of coping with job-related distress may involve extensive changes in self-perception, values, and defensive styles. As Mischel (1977) has noted, settings may differ in the extent to which they influence behavior and, we might add, feelings and personality traits. Because work environments tend to be structured,

4. Feldberg and Kohen (1976) similarly have argued that family members interpret as private and personal their failures to meet one another's emotional needs, a failure that stems from pressures placed on families by the capitalist corporate order. Divorce, and the search for fulfillment in new families, is one attempt to find private solutions.

especially for those at the lower levels of organizational hierarchies, people's experiences at work and the ways they respond to stress are remarkably similar in given job situations; personality factors seem insufficient to explain them (Kornhauser 1965; Mott et al. 1965).

I have also suggested that social setting variables can affect the kinds of solutions people devise for dealing with emotional strain and the dilemmas posed them by work situations. For example, limits to inter- and intraorganizational mobility, to telephone calls and other routes of access, were setting variables that had to be taken into account when attempting to understand interface relations and the ways in which participants manage them.

The relationship of all family members to their social environments also can affect the work–family relationship. Possibly Isabel Turner could manage Ezra's depletion when he worked as an orderly because she had independent sources of esteem and sustenance through her own work as a practical nurse (she worked outside the home at the time) and her involvement in her church. The nature of the family and household systems also must be taken into account. For the Coopers, Eric's depletion may be especially troublesome because they have a new baby in the family and his wife needs a great deal of support and contact herself.[5] This complex set of transactions will be considered more fully in Part III.

We also have seen that the extreme situationist position is not supported by the data indicating difficulties in transitions between settings. The debate over whether personality or setting characteristics best account for human behavior has moved toward an interactionist position (see Lewin 1935; Magnusson & Endler 1977). The most viable theoretical position, implicit in this study, is one that takes into account the complex *transactions* among work organizations, household and family systems, and individual history and personality. Transactionalism is implicit in a systems perspective, for—as Pervin (1968) has noted—the transactional view assumes reciprocal, rather than cause-effect relationships and the interdependence of parts, rather than the independence of variables. The transactional concept is dynamic, for it attempts to move beyond conceptions of linear interactions between static, closed, and unchanging units, whether such units be persons or families. Overton (1973) has noted that such a dynamic, as opposed to mechanistic, view requires a paradigm shift in psychology. (See also Spiegel [1971] for a transactional view.)

5. Maddison (1974) has provided anecdotal evidence from his clinical practice that doctors who feel "depleted" by their work want to be "mothered" by their wives but, instead, encounter more demands from wife and children.

CHAPTER 6

From a Child's Perspective

Unfortunately, research on work and families has tended to ignore the perspectives of children, treating them as dependent variables upon which adults act. In this study too, interviews were conducted primarily with adult members of families. Consequently, the analyses presented in the previous chapters examined the interface relationships from the adults' points of view. There is only minimal research directed toward children's understanding of social institutions (Furth, Baur & Smith 1976), including work organizations and their attendant roles. Yet we know that children have attitudes about the paid work of their parents (W. G. Dyer 1956). Research by Furth et al. and the theoretical framework proposed by Kohlberg (1969) suggest that children's attitudes toward and understanding of work organizations and roles are related to their age, that is, their level of cognitive development.

Of the twenty-seven children living at home in the research families, over half were under the age of four. Attempts to interview children were difficult, both because of their youth and because many of the teenagers were reluctant to be interviewed. Consequently, only seven children were interviewed. No systematic attempt was made to relate the children's level of cognitive development with their experiences of the work–family relationship. Although the data on the children are scant, given the exploratory nature of the research project, they still can be utilized to suggest research questions about the meanings of the interface relationships for children and to highlight the need for further research in this area.

That even young children may be sensitive to financial and security considerations is shown in the interviews with 5-year-old Carrie Bernard and 11-year-old Carletta Gates. When I asked Carrie about her father's job as a police officer, she was clear that her father works for money and that her mother likes his job because it pays for food and clothing.[1] Thus, connections between work and family spheres may be learned early in life. For Carletta, wages and security were being integrated into her plans for the future.

R: Ever thought about what you'd like to be when you grow up?

CG: [*Without hesitation*] A teacher . . . because I like children.

R: What kind of teacher?

CG: I'd like to be a teacher for about the sixth or seventh grade. . . .

R: What do your parents think about the idea?

CG: My father doesn't like it that much because he says there's a lot of teachers going on strike, and—but I'd still like to teach.

R: What does he mean that there are a lot of teachers going on strike?

CG: Because they're losing jobs and they don't get paid enough.

She told me later that she might become a secretary instead.

The Psychological Interface

Just as the psychological interface patterns posed dilemmas for adults, they also confront children with problems with which they must cope. In the discussion of the energy depletion pattern, I mentioned a remark by Tony Johnson that he sometimes has to "shut out" 2-year-old Tony Jr. because he is tired from work. He reported that his son reacts either by looking unhappy or by making a fuss. We can assume that Tony Jr. is unable to understand why his father is withdrawing from him because he does not see the connection between his father's behavior and his work. This situation can readily result in self-blame and anger toward the rejecting parent. Tony's report of his son's reactions suggests that Tony Jr. is both angry at his father and blames himself for his father's withdrawal. Young Tony is still sufficiently egocentric to believe that he causes his father to reject him, but we saw that even adults may blame themselves because the psychological and physical separation of workplace and home obscures their interconnection. If such a father-son relationship were to continue, the anger and feelings of rejection ultimately might cause a rift between them. Paula Doyle suggested such a problem between her husband and her son due to the carry-over and displacement of negative feelings when Tom worked as a foreman. Paula thinks that it will take much time for the relationship to fully heal.

In contrast, Carletta Gates clearly connects her father's bad moods to his work as an attendant in a hospital.

1. Kohlberg (1969) has proposed that only at the concrete operational stage of cognitive development (ages 6 to 8) do children exhibit an understanding of the work-for-salary exchange, the scarcity of money, and therefore the importance of the (father's) work role.

R: Can you tell when he's had a good day at work or a bad day, just by looking at him?

CG: Uhum. When he has a good day at work he plays with us and he's [*pause*] happy. But when he's had a bad day at work or something like that he comes in stormy—something like that.

R: Does he get irritable at people?

CG: Yeah. Especially at my mother.

R: They start having a—

CG: —fuss. . . .

R: Do you think he knows he has these different moods?

CG: I think he cares about them, but I don't think he knows they're that irritable. . . .

R: What do you do when this happens?

CG: I tell my mother sometimes, and she tells him that the kids don't like the way he's acting. Sometimes he says he can't help the way he acts because if he's had a hard day, and he doesn't want people bugging him, and my mother says, "Well, you don't have to blame them—the kids— just because it happened at work," or something like that.

R: That happens in a lot of families and it's hard for everyone. What do you think you could do to make him feel better?

CG: Maybe stay out of his way more when he doesn't feel good.

R: What happens when you get in his way when he doesn't feel good?

CG: He storms and hollers.

Carletta described the variant of the direct carry-over of negative feelings. Rather than actually talking about work-related problems, Ben Gates displaces his distress by "storming" at the children and his wife. Carletta contrasts the positive interactions that occur when he is feeling particularly good to their opposite—Father's storminess and moodiness. She feels that the most helpful course of action at these times is to create psychological and physical space for him.

The differences we infer between Tony Jr. and Carletta may be a function of their ages and their different understandings. However, we also saw that Betty Johnson blamed herself for her husband's behavior after work. Developmental maturity may be a necessary but insufficient condition in understanding that a husband-father's behavior at home may be connected to his daily experiences at work. A crucial factor in Carletta's not feeling personally rejected may be her perception of just such a connection. From her experience, she also prefers that her father work rather than be unemployed. In the Gates family, the interface relationship is made clear to Carletta when her mother admonishes her father not to take his upset out on the children. We might hypothesize, then, that when the myth of separate worlds is maintained, it would be more difficult for children not to feel rejected, and then depressed and angered, by their parents' carrying over negative feelings from work. Such situations are difficult enough for an adult to manage; they are especially difficult for children, who are concerned with their personal worthiness.

Locating the source of her own father's moods was also a theme in the interview with Carletta's mother, Pamela.

R: Have you ever worked in a factory?

PG: No. I worked in a factory one time two days. I could never work in a factory.... My dad's worked in a factory ever since before I was born. He's still working in a factory.... When I was growing up he worked on a production line. [*Shakes head*] I don't [*sighs*]. ...

R: You shake your head and sigh?

PG: I just couldn't see how people worked in a factory?

R: How did you get that idea, that it's not a good place to work?

PG: Because my father used to come home so tired all the time when I was little. When I was a little girl I used to say, "Not me." [*Sighs*] He never— you know, as soon as he got home he ate and conked out. That's all he ever did. My grandfather was the same way. ...

R: I'm interested in why you didn't want to work there. What did your father have to say about factory work, or did he?

PG: Yeah. Yeah. I used to hear hear him talk about it. [*Laughs*] He used to say, "Go to school, get an education, *never* have to do like I did and that's work in a factory all your life." That's one of the things he always told us ... and I got three brothers and they will just definitely won't work in a factory.

R: Did he say any other specific things about why it was so terrible?

PG: [*Laughs*] No. He didn't really say why it was so terrible. It's just that—the fact that he came home and conked out every night was enough! He was always too tired to do this with us and too tired to do that! ... My father usually worked weekends, unless they were on strike or something. Then he slept all weekend [*laughs*] to try and catch up on the rest he didn't have.

Pamela also perceived the source of her father's mood to be his work, a connection facilitated by the fact that her father pointed out the interface relationship to her. Thus, she did not conclude—as she might have— that her father was avoiding her or was not interested in her. Pamela Gates still hates the black lunch pails that symbolize to her her father's and grandfather's jobs.

Space, Time, and Separations

The structural interface relationship that takes family members out of the home also has implications for children. There are hints in the data that the spatial separation of work and home may pose learning tasks for young children who are, as yet, anxious about separations from parents and who—depending on their age—lack a sense of time that can tide them over such separations. Among participating families, some young children seemed to develop rituals for managing the comings and goings of the father. For example, while interviewing Sandra Jones, I noticed that 16-month-old Billy stood waving out the door when his father left for work on his motorcycle. When I asked about this "bye-bye" sequence, Sandra told me that this ritual was a recent development. Previously Billy would cry and make a fuss when Jesse left, and sometimes it took her half an hour to calm him. Similarly, Ray Ellison's youngest daughter, aged 18 months, used to cry when her father left for work but now she receives a happy kiss instead, while his 4-year-old instructs Ray to tell the friend who picks him up that "he has a pretty car." Pamela Gates remembers greeting her grandfather at the bus stop everyday when he came home from work as part of their reunion ritual.

Rituals such as these may help ease separations; their very regularity can be comforting. Similarly, reunion rituals may help ease reintegration into the family. We know that many societies use rituals to help deal with major transitions and discontinuities. Although rituals are more obvious in children, adults also seem to utilize them, and perhaps these daily rituals serve similar purposes for children and for adults. For example, some of Jesse Jones's calls to Sandra from work served such a purpose.

Insofar as ritualistic behaviors require regularity of time, we must wonder what occurs for young children whose parents work rotating shifts or changeable hours. Would separations be more difficult for them to manage? It would be helpful in future research to be able to compare children of different ages whose parents work an irregular shift with those whose parents work constant hours to determine whether they show differences in anxiety around separation or differences in ritualistic behaviors. How the parents handle such separations might also be a crucial factor. To what extent are the ways we learn to deal with daily work separations and reunions in our families of origin carried over into our adult lives?

Separation anxiety may be activated when we cannot see someone and know she or he is safe. A number of participants worried about the husband-father's being injured at work. For example, Henry Johnson's children reported worrying about their father's safety when he is on his delivery route. Similarly, Carletta Gates worries about her father's physical safety. Recently, Ben Gates started a job as an attendant in a hospital for the mentally ill. We can surmise that, without previous experience with such hospitalized patients, he has to master his own fears about working there. Thus, he tells stories to his family, and Carletta worries about him.

R: What do you think about his working there?

CG: I don't like it because he might get hurt. You know, one of the patients might go "bad" or something. . . . When something happens at home or at school, and then I think about it. . . . When somebody gets hurt or something. The other day the principal told us not to throw snowballs, and they had a snowball fight and the boy got hit in the eye, and his eye was bleeding.

When her father was moved to another floor, Carletta told me, "That helped out." Carletta may be learning that the work world is dangerous. Not being able to see that her father is well must necessarily intensify her fantasies.

The theme of work-related injury as a concern emerged in three of the seven interviews with children. In the following excerpt, 3-year-old Pete Simpson illustrates the fact that even very young children can be sensitive to this issue. Recently his father had been injured on the job.

R: What does your daddy do at work?

PS: Work.

R: Do you know what he does?

PS: Yeah.

R: What?

PS: Carries.

R: He carries?

PS: Yeah! He gots a hilo [forklift truck], too, like mine.

R: What does he do with the hilo?

PS: Puts stuff on it. Whole bunch of stuff on it, and he went on the railroad track and he falled off it and he put the thing right down like that. And he falled right off!! And he couldn't keep up! Keep coming down.

Both 11-year-old Carletta and little Pete were able to articulate their feelings, and therefore we might conclude that they were coping well. What of children with a family member in a highly dangerous occupation, such as mining? How do they manage their fears? Are the fears talked about openly by families or does the subject remain closed and "taboo"? The frequency with which this theme arose in this small sample indicates the usefulness of further research on this subject.

Identification. "Identification" is a term sometimes used for the complex process whereby children internalize parental attitudes, behaviors, and roles, so that they form part of an integrated identity structure. Stoke (1954) has suggested that the process of identification is in part dependent on the child's "degree of acquaintance" with the person with whom an identification is attempted. If we understand "degree of acquaintance" as familiarity and time spent with the person, we need to wonder about how the separation of work and home affects this process. Not only are fathers gone much of the time, but because only part of their life activity is visible and known to the child, fathers are only partially familiar. Would the identification process be hindered when fathers work the afternoon shift or are cross-country haulers? Or is the father image idealized, as Bach (1954) has suggested, in the case of father absence? Stoke also mentioned the perceived power of the father as an element facilitating identification. What happens when a child suddenly comes to see his or her idealized, powerful father as relatively powerless with respect to the world of work? I suggested this dynamic in discussing Pamela Gates's disappointment and loss when her father went to work on the night of her graduation. The process of identification was at issue for at least four women in the study who mentioned that they wanted their sons to be able to spend time with their fathers and to have a "male image." I suggested that in the case of Ezra Turner and his son, Charles, the resulting identification was strengthened because of the special times they spend together at Ezra's workplace.

The concept of identification implies content as well as process. Although we know little about children's socialization and/or learning about work roles (Moore 1969), we can assume that attitudes toward work roles are internalized in some way. Stoke mentioned that the visibility of the role can affect the identification process. From the perspective of cognitive development, Kohlberg (1969) has suggested that the concrete, physicalistic nature of a young child's thought processes and interests leads him or her to define social roles in terms of physical characteristics and differences. Caplow (1954) has noted that work in modern industrial societies can be so fragmented or abstract that children have trouble conceptualizing the work role and what it entails. In other words, abstract or fragmented work would be difficult for the young child, who thinks concretely, to comprehend. This difficulty seemed to be reflected in 3-year-old Pete Simpson's comments about his father's and mother's respective jobs. He had been taken to see his parents at work and eagerly told me about his father's forklift truck, noting that he, too, had a little "hilo." However, when I asked him what his mother did at work, he appeared to be stymied. He found it difficult to talk about and, we might infer, comprehend her work as an assembler of carburator parts.

R: Have you ever seen [your father] at work?
PS: Yeah! On his hilo I seen him!

From a Child's Perspective

R: When did you see him? Do you remember?

PS: My mom took me there. Yeah.

R: She took you there for a visit?

PS: No. They had *nothing* there for me to eat.

R: There was nothing there to eat?

PS: No!

R: So, you didn't enjoy it too much?

PS: Yeah, it was so cold out there! Yes. Freeze my butt off! Fly away!

R: Do you want to drive a hilo too?

PS: Yeah, but I can't when I'm little.

R: What do you want to do when you're big? Do you know?

PS: I'm going to work!

R: What kind of work are you going to do?

PS: Work, and run 'em.

R: Do you know what kind of work you're going to do?

PS: Yup. Drive a hilo!

R: Just like your daddy?

PS: Yeah. I got a little one. . . .

R: What does your mom do?

PS: Work too. . . . At another one [i.e., building].

R: At another one!

PS: Yeah, by my dad.

R: And what does she do over there?

PS: Work.

R: What kind of work? Do you know?

PS: Yeah. Her runs—[*pause*]. I can't—ain't coming on yet.

R: It's hard to explain, isn't it?

PS: It won't come on. . . . Well, I won't go!

For Pete, his father's work involved more easily comprehensible activity than did his mother's. What might be some of the consequences for children when work roles are either invisible to them or enigmatic? To the extent that such roles remain vague and indistinct, we might imagine that children would find it difficult to try on the work role in their fantasy life, as Pete Simpson was able to do by playing with his forklift truck. Yet, at some point most children will be workers. The pressures for little girls to become housewives may be compounded by the general invisibility to them of work roles outside it.

In bringing his children to work, Ezra Turner makes a point of exposing them to a variety of work roles.

ET: I just don't want them to think that they're limited to any particular thing to do. Well like, you know, I've gotta be a factory worker, I've gotta be a doctor or a lawyer, I've gotta be. . . . They can be anything, as long as they get some ideal [sic] once they go through these jobs.

R: Do other people bring their children too?

ET: Yeah. The ones that want to. Like Bob, you met him. He brings his boys in. And I think that's very important.

R: Why?

ET: Well, it's very important, especially from a black's point of view. I think when I grew up we were more or less—you just thought that the only place to work was in a factory or in a store. And not only do I show them what I do, I try to expose them to every job within the hospital so that they can get an idea. You know, they talk to the doctors and, on a level that, you know—not asking questions all the time, but just talk to them. And they see the different jobs they're doing and they see the jobs being done up in the administrative offices and the research offices and the laundry and in the housekeeping department, the yard. So they'll get—exposure is the word. So they're exposed to every kind of job that there is, as much as I can expose them to it. So they have a better variety of choices.

On the other hand, Tom Doyle wants to protect his son from working in a plant and, therefore, does not want him to see his place of work.

R: Have your children ever been to your office?

TD: No. I wouldn't take them. [Pause]. . . . I never want him to go into a plant. Never. Not in ten thousand years. . . . I don't think he'd be happy.

It has been argued that work identity begins to crystallize in latency (Neff 1968) and adolescence (Erikson 1963). We can assume that learning about the external work role begins very early, because even 3-year-old Pete Simpson was interested in and played at his father's work. Are occupational possibilities more varied for those young people who have been exposed to a variety of work roles before and during adolescence? The invisibility of parental paid work experiences and their lack of knowledge of other work roles may be special handicaps for working-class children, whose occupational choices already are limited by socialization (Kohn 1969), the school system (Bowles & Gintis 1976), and the class structure (Fried 1973). Mike Healy told me he had had no work-related goals; only now, after he is already locked into a factory job, is he beginning to wonder what else he might do. While most participants mentioned wanting their children to have white-collar jobs, they were very vague about what such a job would entail. This vagueness would make it difficult for their children to consider these work roles concretely. Psychologists have studied occupational choice in terms of personal dynamics (see, for example, Bordin 1943; Roe 1964). It would be of interest to study attitudes toward work in terms of the visibility of such roles to the child, and in terms of the extent to which and manner in which parents talk about their own work.[2]

Learning about Interfaces

It is not sufficient to consider how children learn the content of work and family roles, for they also are learning about the relationship between them. When children reach adulthood they, too, must cope with the dilemmas posed by their work and family life. The interviews with Carletta and Pamela Gates suggest that people begin to learn about interface patterns early in their lives. Not only do children learn what their parents want them to learn, but they also learn by observing, listening, and responding. Carletta is learning to cope with her father's moods by creating space for him. She thinks that "maybe staying out of his way more when he doesn't feel good" might serve as a solution to the problem of her father's stormy moods. In other words, she is learning to adjust her needs to give him psychological and physical space. We have seen that this maneuver is a common procedure by which participants try to manage the patterns of energy depletion and negative carry-over. We may assume that at some point in her adult life Carletta will be faced with a similar problem, either for herself or other family members. At that time the learning that occurred with respect to her father may be used in coping with work-related strain.

The interview with Pamela Gates also indicated early learning about work and about interface patterns. She was aware, as a child, that her father's and grandfather's personal depletion affected the way she could relate to them. In Pamela's family of origin the interface pattern was labeled and acknowledged so that she could make some concrete decisions about it. Consequently, in her adult life she tried to protect herself from the energy deficit pattern by attempting to assure herself of work she would find satisfying. Her effort was reinforced by her father, who told her, "Go to school, get an education, *never* have to do like I did and that's work in a factory all your life." Pamela rejected the pattern by rejecting the factory, as did her brothers. Now, when she sees her husband falling asleep after work, she gets upset because she is reminded of the pattern she struggled against.

Ezra Turner rejected working in a factory, a job his father had for almost forty years. Still, he learned from his father the solution of taking his children to work when time and space create barriers to family intimacy. When I asked Ezra where he got the notion of taking his children to work, he was unable to remember. But as we talked about his father,

---

2. Exploratory research on this subject is being conducted.

his memory was stirred, and he recalled that he sometimes went to "work" with his own father.

> ET: And I guess, now that we're talking about it, I guess that's where I got the idea of taking my children to work! Because he couldn't take us to the plant, but he would always take us to the farm and to the golf course. Then one time we were farming some other land . . . and he always took us there. [*Recalls his father taking them to the park and zoo once.*] That's the only time he ever took us out anywhere. But he always took us to work with him. We would do things like—he made work fun! Like we had to cut down trees for a bridge or something, you know. Well he'd cut the tree just about all the way down, and then he'd allow us to climb the tree, and then he'd fell the tree.

Ezra remembers these times warmly; they represented an opportunity to be close to his father. His mother remembers encouraging her husband to take the boys with him so they would have time together with their father, who sometimes worked a sixteen-hour day. John Turner reported that he wanted his boys to understand the world, and that was why he took them along. To each family member the events had a slightly different meaning. Ezra's son, Charles, is also learning a way of solving dilemmas posed for families by time and space. He, too, has warm feelings about going to work with his father. What remains to be seen, of course, is whether Charles will work in an organization that allows such a solution.

Henry Johnson also rejected his father's work, but he seems to have incorporated his father's attitudes toward the relationship of work and family. As his father did, he works long hours and remains, in some ways peripheral to the family system. As his father did, he feels that he is fulfilling family obligations by providing for them. Even though he worked with his father, he never felt close to him, and Henry now complains of lack of closeness to his own children. In the past few years, he has established a more positive relationship with his son, Tony. Both the Johnsons now say it is important to have work that one likes.

It may also be that Henry's intense involvement in the small family-run business where he works and from which he has difficulty disengaging is related to the fact that he worked in his father's electrical repair shop for over twenty years. Although he hated the business and did not continue it after his father's death, he was treated by his father as if he were indispensable to the functioning of the shop. Just as his father needed him, he now feels indispensable at work, and the feeling of being valuable is an important source of satisfaction for him. His son, Tony, on the other hand, is hoping to have a career he enjoys. Moreover, rather than repeating his father's carry-over of negative feelings into the home, Tony is one of the participants who does not talk about work at home. Chuck Simpson also perceived a pattern of negative

118

carry-over in his own family of origin and has tried to develop a different relationship to his work and his own family.

We do not know why some children accept aspects of their parents and identify with them, nor why other aspects are rejected. Similarly, it is not clear why certain ways of coping with work stresses are internalized while others are not. From Pamela Gates's case, we can hypothesize that when the interface pattern is made explicit and recognized by the family, children may experience more choice in the matter of what they will emulate and what they will reject.

Conclusion

The ways in which the psychological and structural interface relationships affect children of different ages is an open research question. Similarly, the factors influencing children's learning of work roles and interface patterns are necessarily complex and require systematic investigation. I have suggested that what is learned in the family of origin can affect adult experiences in the interface region. Thus, when considering the complex transactions among personality, work setting, and family life, such personal history must ultimately be included. Longitudinal research may help unravel these complexities.

As children develop into adults, most enter into new family arrangements. Each adult then brings past experience with interface relationships to his or her new family. We might predict, then, that conflict may occur as couples negotiate the management of the relations between work and home. Mike Healy, for example, thinks it is acceptable to express his job-related frustration with Celia but not with his children. Celia disagrees. How will their children integrate their parents' differing viewpoints? Perhaps Ben Gates learned that when he is feeling strain from work it is acceptable to yell and scream a bit or to lie down and "conk out." This solution, however, is not satisfactory to his wife, Pamela. Sandra Jones commented that during the first year of her marriage to Jesse they saw each other infrequently because they worked different shifts. She appeared to be satisfied with this arrangement because, she noted, it helped to prevent conflict between them. I have described how her father's long hours at work helped her to avoid conflict between them. Now Sandra is considering working a different shift from Jesse in order to facilitate child-care arrangements for Billy. Yet, when I talked with Jesse, he thought that if Sandra were employed again he might have to accept a lower job classification and therefore less money so that he could work the day shift. To him, being together as a whole family is particularly important because, in some ways, he had never had such a family. Thus, the Joneses differ in their conceptions of the way time and space should be arranged in relation to their work and their family life. At the time of the interviews, they had not talked over this matter; they seemed to assume agreement. This analysis suggests that we conduct research to determine not only what happens across generations of families, but also what negotiations about the interface occur in the formation of new ones.

PART III

Case Study:
The Bernard Family

We turn now to an investigation of the interface of work and family life in one family—the Bernards. The sensitizing concepts and mode of analysis introduced in Part II will be utilized in an attempt to understand these relationships. The decision to focus in-depth attention on the Bernards was due, in large part, to the fact that they were one of the two research families in which the husband-father's workplace was readily accessible to me for observation (see Methodological Appendix). Of these two families, the Bernards were more demographically typical of other research families than were the Turners, who were included in the sample as a contrast middle-class family. Although the Bernards may appear to represent an atypical case study because Richard Bernard is a police officer and hence has a "dramatic" job, the stresses facing them did not appear to be qualitatively different from those confronting the other research families.

Part III begins with an introduction to the Bernard family (Chapter 7), and the complete transcripts of one day of observation in both home and work settings are presented. The relationship between Richard Bernard's work experience and his transactions within the family are examined next in Chapters 8 and 9. However, this analysis remains incomplete until Alice Bernard's work experience in the household is examined (Chapters 10 and 11). In this latter discussion, the traditional orientation, which looks only at the interface between paid work settings and family life, is expanded to include a conceptualization of the home as a work setting. Finally, both Alice's and Richard's work are considered simultaneously for their effect on the emotional life of the Bernard family (Chapter 12).

Introducing the Bernards: A Day in Their Lives

Alice and Richard Bernard, both in their late twenties, have been married for seven years. Their small rented home, next to a busy highway, stands on several acres of land, on which Richard tends some chickens and cows.[1] They have lived in this area for over a year; before that they lived in Carlton City, the large metropolitan area in which they both grew up. Richard has worked as a policeman for six years—first in Carlton City and now in Centerville, near which they live. He also has two part-time jobs: he works as a security guard in a shopping center two nights a week and, like other participants, attends school one evening per week to receive veteran's benefits. Richard's single motivation in going to school is financial. Even with these two part-time jobs, the Bernards feel that they barely make ends meet. During the course of the research, and before the observations began, Richard's work shift was changed from the day to the midnight shift. Alice works in the home, caring for it and their three children. Carrie, aged 5, looks much like Richard, with his dark hair and features. Three afternoons a week she goes to nursery school. Tow-haired James, aged 3, and 2-year-old Nicholas spend most of their time at home with Alice.

When first encountered, Alice is a bit shy. She described herself as someone who likes to "check things out" before committing herself. Once at ease she becomes a lively young woman with an easy laugh, a woman who talks readily and is taken to making faces to complement the expression of her feelings. This latter trait is engaging; she seems comfortable and familiar—like an old high school friend—and often uses her humor to manage her anxiety. Richard is the quieter of the two; he

---

1. The beef he sells helps to defray the cost of the farm and provides fresh meat for the family. He also sells fresh eggs to friends and family.

agreed that he is most comfortable in the outdoor world of "doing." He likes nothing better than to look over the fields, which symbolize peace to him and help calm the inner turmoil he sometimes experiences. His tendency toward reticence has given others the impression that he is somber, an image he dislikes. Yet, with those close to him he is light and teasing, a quality he considers a personal fault, for he realizes that others do not always understand his intent. It is precisely such ambiguity that permits him to express his feelings—whether of anger or affection.

Alice and Richard share a similar background. They are both third-generation descendants of Catholic immigrant families. Richard's grandparents came from Europe and—to reflect their assimilation into the predominant culture—took an American surname, an action Richard regrets. His paternal grandfather was a laborer, and his father is an engineering technician in a large industrial firm. Richard's mother was trained as a nurse and was sometimes employed when he was growing up. Alice's grandparents emigrated from the British Isles. Her paternal grandfather also was a laborer, her father is a master electrician, and her mother worked in the home during the time Alice was growing up. Both Bernards come from upwardly mobile immigrant families who wanted their children to live out the American dream more fully. As the oldest children in their respective families, Alice and Richard represent "sounding boards" to their parents. As in many of the other families interviewed, contact with parents by telephone or visit is frequent. They live approximately thirty miles from their parents.

As a result of their similar backgrounds, Alice and Richard hold a common set of values. While not deeply devout, they attend church regularly and are serious about their beliefs. Both are very conservative politically and value respectability and stability in the community. Having assimilated well into the predominant American culture, they are disdainful about those groups that have not. Their outlook is reflected in some of the values they hold for their children: obedience, honesty, and sincerity. Just as their parents wanted them to do better than they did, Alice and Richard want their children to have more security and opportunity than they have had. This means moving into professional, white-collar occupations. They would like Carrie to be a nurse and James and Nicholas lawyers or even senators. Like some of the other men interviewed, Richard also harbors the wish that at least one of his sons will become a successful athlete. Athletics is a masculine pursuit and offers the opportunity to "make it big." For the most part, Richard and Alice have given up the dream of making it big themselves.

Alice and Richard met at a summer job while in their last year of high school and dated briefly.[2] They corresponded occasionally when

2. Table 7-1 outlines the important life events for the Bernards.

Richard enlisted in the armed forces in order to fight in Vietnam. Their stories of this initial courtship differ, for Richard saw her as more serious than he. During Richard's stay overseas Alice spent two years at a small college for women. Her parents had expected her to become a nun, a possibility she never considered seriously. College attendance also was something she felt was expected of her, but she soon realized that at that time a college education was not a goal she aspired to. Alice left school and took a job in a travel agency, where the only training she felt she received was how to be cordial to the public. The job offered her little opportunity for reward or for attaining a sense of accomplishment; she worked for low pay and disliked the job intensely.

Alice was working at the agency when Richard came out of the service and their courtship began in earnest. At the time, Richard, like many young veterans, was feeling embittered and angry. He had seen hard service in the war, having killed and been shot at for his country, but he felt that people did not care, understand, or appreciate what he had done. For months Richard was listless and depressed. The vigilance he had developed fighting in the jungles of Vietnam had no real place in civilian life, and he described himself as becoming very suspicious of people. Alice was someone he could talk to. Recalling that time, Richard noted, "I needed someone just to hold on to, just to talk to and just to be with." Alice also seemed to Richard to be a "family" person, for Richard wanted to have a family and "settle down." For her part, Alice saw Richard as strong and aggressive, an image that appealed to her. More than that, he made her feel "needed" and he appreciated who she was. She recalled, "He really wanted to know *me*. . . . I could see that he saw that there was value in me . . . worth to me."

By the time they were married, Richard was working as a shipping and receiving clerk in a large department store. Within the year he was promoted to assistant manager because, he said, "the manager liked me."[3] Alice was still working in the travel agency, but quit her job when she became pregnant with Carrie. Richard then left his job with the department store—which paid very little—and went into the police academy in Carlton City. Police work was the closest he could come to a military occupation in civilian life. He liked the order, the sense that he knew what was expected of him, and the clarity about right and wrong. Alice and Richard had "great expectations" about this job. The vigilance he had learned in the military was turned to a useful purpose.

James's birth, two years after Carrie's, made Richard and Alice feel "smug"; they had a perfect little family—one child of each sex.

3. Sennett and Cobb (1972) have commented on the difficulty many working-class people have in taking personal responsibility for upward mobility in the occupational hierarchy.

Table 7-1. Chronology of Important Life Events for the Bernards

Year	Richard	Alice	Age
1967	Meet		17
1968	Begins military service	Begins college	18
1969	Leaves military Job at department store	Leaves college Job at travel agency	19
1970	Marry		20
1971	Enters police academy	Leaves travel job	21
1972	Carrie is born Carleton City Police Department		22
1974	Applies for Centerville job James is born		24
1975	Nicholas is born Begins Centerville job Threat of layoff Move to Centerville		25

Nicholas's birth was unplanned and, on the heels of James's, created much hardship for Alice. She had never enjoyed midnight feedings, and now she had three children under the age of 3. Moreover, like other young women I interviewed, she was becoming disillusioned with being a full-time household worker, a job she had taken on with enthusiasm when she first married. The period after Nicholas's birth was especially trying for her, and she prefers to keep that time of her life "on a shelf."

When they describe their marriage now they talk of the "good years" and the "bad ones." Like other couples, they have had their ups and downs, but their basic respect and affection have endured. Richard accepts Alice's newly emerging assertions of independence and identity, even though they threaten his power in the family system, because he loves her. His marital model is based on his parents' marriage. Richard perceived his mother as doing exactly what his father wanted; she asked his permission "for everything." But Richard also knows that his mother was not very happy in this submissive position. While such a marital relationship might serve his needs, Richard concedes that if Alice were "like a robot" it would not serve hers. In front of Alice he still uses the language of paternalism, telling me that he "lets" her go out when she wants to, language familiar to me from my other interviews. Privately, however, he told me sadly that Alice no longer asks his permission—she simply tells him where she is going.

Introducing the Bernards: A Day in their Lives

Alice realizes that Richard is changing, as she is, and she understands his support of her moves toward independence as a sign of his love. Yet their caring for each other is not always expressed openly and directly. When direct expressions of affection emerged in their joint interviews, Alice became aware of how generally indirect were her appreciations of Richard. Rather than express her loving feelings explicitly, she regales him with negative stories about other husbands, implying that he is different. Richard's affection also is not shared directly but is expressed as teasing. And just as love is not always expressed directly, so sadness is not shared. Sometimes Richard has difficulty listening to Alice's fears and concerns because her being upset hurts him. Alice worries that Richard does not share his fears and worries with her, but when Richard does talk of his troubles, she is concerned that the strength she depends on will evaporate (see also Bernard 1972).

When Alice and Richard argue it is primarily about money.[4] While they agree on how to spend money for their children—good clothing, quality medical care, dancing lessons for Carrie—conflict occurs when Alice wants money for herself or for social activities. When, during the course of the research, Richard abandoned his desire to own their home in the immediate future, these conflicts diminished, and Richard handed over to Alice many of their budgetary decisions.

Alice and Richard describe themselves as growing closer again during the past two years. Until that time they felt they had "fallen into a rut," taking each other for granted and losing a sense of meaning in their relationship. They attribute the recent change to the fact that they had moved away from their previous support networks and were forced to rely on each other more. Alice thinks that if they had stayed in the city, Richard would have grown closer to his occupational cronies instead, while she would have been part of the wives' social network (see also Bott 1971).

When I first interviewed the Bernards, Richard did not appear to be dissatisfied with his job and, like many participants, felt that he kept work and family separate. Alice was more visibly discontented with her job as a household worker and, in her expressions of dissatisfaction, was more vocal than the other women interviewed. However, many of the feelings she expressed so clearly were echoed by other household workers. As the research progressed, the sources of stress and discontent in both their work situations emerged more clearly. During the course of the research, Alice and Richard Bernard considered a move to another

---

4. Blood and Wolfe (1960) have found that money is a major source of conflict between husbands and wives. Finances were a source of concern for a number of the families interviewed.

state where Richard might find more satisfying work. They are a family searching both for a solution to the dilemmas posed them by their work experiences and for meaning in their lives.

All told, I spent over seventy hours with the Bernard family, talking with them, observing their daily life, and talking with them again about what I had seen and heard. We have discussed what preceded and what will follow. In some ways their story is unique. However, in their struggle to accommodate their personal and family needs to each of their work lives, they are like the other families interviewed, even though their attempted solutions may be unique to them.

Observations of Home and Paid Work Settings

The scientific enterprise, which aims at explaining phenomena, requires that the raw data from everyday life be rearranged and analyzed. The end result embodies the biases of the researcher. Even when the goal is description, the researcher is in the position of a documentary film editor choosing what material to present and when. The audience can be left wondering what was omitted. Why did a particular scene receive special attention? In order to respect the integrity of the everyday life experience of the Bernard family and to present the reader with an independent basis for judging the subsequent analysis, the field notes from two observational periods will be presented in their entirety. This presentation will also serve to flesh out the account of the Bernard family so that the reader will come to know them as full-dimensional people.

The processes of entry into and observation of the settings are described in the Methodological Appendix. Some limitations on the completeness of the data include the fact that not all family groupings could be observed simultaneously, that I could not carry a field notebook into Richard's work setting, and that my mental acuity was reduced during the night of observation (see Methodological Appendix). In addition, because of the exhaustion of observing and my subsequent participation in family interactions, the home visit on the Base Day described here is imperfectly recorded between 4:00 and 5:10 P.M., 8:45 and 9:30 P.M., and 11:00 and 11:30 P.M. Consequently, these periods, totalling 2.4 hours, were not coded. In all, 10.5 hours of home observations on the Base Day were coded, as were 4.75 hours on other days, for a total of 15.25 hours of coded home observations. Although these gaps in the available data introduce undesirable distortion into the quantitative analysis, the latter is only meant to be suggestive and is supplemented by qualitative analysis.

Despite these imperfections in the data, both Richard and Alice read over the observational notes and agreed that they accurately portrayed their family life as they experience it. Following a previous agreement, the Bernards deleted or changed minor details that they thought might identify them. Interactions among family members, however, remained unaltered.

A Night on Patrol with Richard

This Sunday evening (April 24) began with one of Richard's part-time jobs as a security guard for a local shopping center. Alice and the children had gone to visit her mother for the day and did not return home until late evening. From the shopping center we moved on to the police station. It should be noted that when cars were stopped at traffic checks, I was asked to remain in the police car.

5:50 P.M.

When I arrive at the house, it is beginning to drizzle. Alice and the children had gone off to her mother's house. Richard is in his uniform, polishing his belts and brass trim. We chat briefly.

Before we leave for the shopping center, Richard hides his gun, for he worries that someone might break into the house. He and Alice are concerned also about James's interest in his guns. Once, when James was little, Richard playfully shot at an animal; James wanted to shoot the gun too. Now he has become particularly interested in guns. We finally leave. Richard has his portable radio in hand.

We use my car, as his truck cab is dirty. We take the back-roads approach to the shopping center through some farmland: Richard wants to show me the largest dairy farm in the area. As he talks I remark on how much his heart is in farming, and I ask him if he thinks he'll ever have his own farm. He feels this is an unlikely possibility as he could not raise the initial capital needed to buy land and machines. I ask him where he acquired all his knowledge about farming and animals, unusual in a city person. He explains that when he worked days on his patrol route, he spent a lot of time talking to the farmers in the area. They loved seeing him—feeling they were "getting their protection"—and they also loved talking about what was important in their lives—their farms. He chuckles as he tells me that secretly he was getting information from *them*. I don't ask why he was so secretive about it, and he does not volunteer a reason.

We drive to the police station, which is now closed and empty. Inside it is unpleasant and Spartan. There is nothing pleasing about this work space—it is barren, institutional, and depressing. The main room has some wooden desks, a table with a phone and typewriter, a bulletin board with wanted notices and police business, a gray filing cabinet, gray lockers where the police keep their clothes, an area for processing suspects, and a counter. Richard looks into his file and finds a notice indicating that he has to be in court in two days. He becomes irritated and his face takes on a clouded

129

look, for this will interfere with his sleep. We go into the office to look for the release form that the sergeant was supposed to leave for me to sign; it's not there. Richard hunts one up. He then takes a shotgun from the cabinet and explains that Alice is nervous about his having a shotgun in the house. Richard's locker is sparse. Some of the men have a cartoon or saying on their locker. Richard's locker has on it the reminder of a court notice.

Richard selects a car to take to the shopping center. It's close to 7:00 P.M. and already getting dark. We leave and stop at a local store, where he buys a newspaper and some gum. As we are about to drive out of the parking lot, he notices a young man walking out of the store. "I know that guy with the funny face and I think he recognizes me," he tells me. He explains that he can't be "too careful." He's glad he always carries a gun because there are plenty of people "doing time" at the state prison who would love to catch up with him. I'm beginning to get a sense of Richard's constant vigilance.

7:00 P.M.

We arrive at the shopping center. Richard parks the police car at the back of the rear parking lot where he can see the back of the buildings and the entire lot. He feels he acts mainly as a deterrent. Before police were hired to patrol the lot, the windows of shopper's cars were often broken and the tanks of cars filled with sand.

Richard unfolds the newspaper and starts to read the ads for farms and livestock. He turns on music and offers me some gum. It begins to drizzle more heavily now. He tells me about a man who lives in a house near the side of the parking lot who's "out to get" the policemen in the area, "so if you hear shooting, duck." I ask him if he's joking; he becomes serious and tells me he's not. He also shows me how to use the radio and tells me his code number "just in case" anything happens that night and I have to call in for help.

I ask him about the feeling of being a "target." He tells me he's used to it; he's been a target since he got out of high school and enlisted in the armed forces. Later, we talk more about this experience.

A car stops in the driveway. Richard's job is to keep the driveway clear, so we drive over to the car and he asks the woman to park elsewhere. Once during the evening we use the bathroom in the store, and Richard drives around the lot once to make a tour of it. Occasionally, Richard has to get the key and turn on the lights in the parking lot. Tonight, someone else has done it. Several times each half hour he turns on the police radio to find out if anything is happening that he might help with. It's now beginning to rain steadily and Richard tells me there's "not much action" when it's raining. He doesn't even like to stop cars because he doesn't want to get wet.

The evening is uneventful. It's quiet and boring as we watch the parking lot. I comment on how boring sitting and waiting can be. I ask if he resists coming. Richard laughs. "That's why I always come . . . late." Richard tells me he's thinking of quitting security if he can make some money on the beef he sells. "I'd rather stay home with the kids," he notes; "I'm not that money hungry." Richard says that when it gets dark there are lots of comings and goings in the lot and he becomes more attentive. However, on occasion, he has fallen asleep.

10:45 P.M.

We drive to the building to pick up the stores' money for deposit. Richard waits until the last car leaves and goes into the building, coming out after several minutes with a money bag. We drive by the bank and he deposits the money in the depository, to which he has a key. It's too late to go home now, so he will call home from the station. Sometimes when they let him out earlier he goes home briefly before starting his shift. We drive to the police station.

11:00 P.M.

We go inside and he comments, "Now we'll sit around and wait for the other players to show up." His shift doesn't start until 11:45 P.M. He makes two telephone calls while we're there. He calls Alice, who has just arrived home from her visit to her mother's. They discuss the possibility of her having a party for her cousin in the summer, to which he is agreeable. He also mentions to her that he's going to be getting another calf. When he gets off the telephone he tells me about an aunt of hers who died of cancer and how sad it was to go to the funeral because she had so many children. He also calls the man who owns the calf, and they agree about the price.

At about 11:40 P.M. people start arriving from the end of the afternoon shift. Richard is sitting at the desk and says hello to people, but he is generally not a participant in their discussions. By 11:45 most of the night-shift contingent—including his partner, George—have arrived. I'm surprised to see some female police officers. There is a lot of "ribbing" among the men, in which Richard does not participate a great deal. However, he does talk to some of the men. When they have a private story to tell, they take each other into another room. Richard telephones someone to ask him about the events of the day and notes them down on paper. He tells the person that he has an observer and assures him the observer has received clearance from his superior officer.

11:50 P.M.

Richard goes outside and chooses the Ford tonight, indicating that it's a good car to sleep in. I settle in the back seat while Richard goes back inside briefly. When he returns he tells me they have a "run." A union hall has been vandalized. He and his partner put their gear—shotguns, helmets, and the like—into the car and Richard drives us quickly to the scene.

CASE STUDY: THE BERNARD FAMILY

When we get there, George goes inside to talk with the people, while Richard walks around the building, seeking clues to the vandals. He is very observant, noticing markings that I found difficult to see. He looks for footprints, squatting close to the ground, and then walks next door. He knocks on the door and tells me to stand aside for safety reasons—someone could be inside with a shotgun. A woman answers the door and Richard politely asks her if she heard any noises in the last several hours. She tells him that she heard dogs barking about an hour earlier. We then walk back toward the union hall, and Richard finds some footprints on the ground. Everyone comes out to look at them. Richard tells George what the woman reported. He then notices another nearby house that people are looking out of, and wonders if they may have noticed anything. We walk leisurely out of the parking lot, across the street, and around the corner. Richard tells me he likes walking, despite the cold, because he doesn't like sitting for eight hours. We talk to the people at the house, who report that they heard nothing. The man he talks to is very polite and friendly. He tells Richard about a time when some youngsters vandalized his car. On the way back, Richard tells me that "this used to be a nice neighborhood." I am cold and get in the car with George while Richard is still outside talking to the union officials. Richard then gets into the car and George begins to write up the report. George asks Richard who I am, and Richard explains that I am doing a study of families and their work. I add that I have known Richard for a while, and George remarks, "That explains it." Normally, he says, when observers are present everyone behaves strictly and is "up-tight"; instead, Richard has been relaxed and acting his usual self tonight.

1:40 A.M.

Richard pulls in at a drive-in restaurant for a snack. We order our food; then Richard drives across the street where he sees another patrol car. He parks parallel to it, so that the drivers can converse through the windows. The car is parked in such a way that George is between Richard and the other driver. George and the other driver do most of the talking. In a while, another car drives up and parks next to Richard's car on Richard's side. Again, George does most of the talking, though Richard does participate in some of the banter. Each car seems to have a talkative partner and a quiet partner. They talk about other policemen, officers, and in particular about their supervisors. They also talk about amusing incidents that happened the night before. There is a great deal of kidding about each other and what they are planning to do to certain supervisors they don't like. One had called Richard on the carpet to discuss his "attitude." There is a lot of hostility toward these supervisors, expressed through joking behavior. They also talk about needing to "look productive," and how ridiculous it is to stop cars just to have it on one's work sheet. Richard mentions that in another city he heard that officers used to go into graveyards and do "birth checks" just to have it on their activity sheets. They would also stop cars with more than one

132

occupant so they could list a lot of names on their sheets. While Richard participates in the banter less than the other officers, he is listening and laughs at their tales. One of the cars is called on a "run" and leaves immediately.

2:30 A.M.

Soon we leave too, and as we drive along, Richard asks George about stopping a car he spots. It has no hood and wired-on plates; George agrees. Richard tells me he has a "seventh sense" about people in "funky-looking" cars such as this one, as they are often up to no good. He puts on his flashing lights and the car pulls over to the side of the road. It is dark and drizzling. Richard and his partner get out of the car to ask the driver for identification; each has one hand on his gun. They bring the driver's licenses back to the car to check on whether there are warrants on the two men they've stopped and to check the registration on the vehicle to determine if it was stolen. They discuss whether they should give them a ticket, and Richard suggests that they simply issue a warning. Richard drives up alongside the other car and hands their licenses back through the windows. Richard and George ask the men when they are going to get their car fixed. The driver says they have a hood for the car but just haven't gotten it on yet. They let them go with a warning.

George then notices another police car stopped about a quarter mile up the road. They both chuckle when they hear over the radio that some other police officers have made some "traffic checks." Richard and George are amused by the game they are all playing—stopping cars in competition in order to appear productive. George asks Richard to flash his lights at the car up the road, but the other car doesn't notice. Richard drives up alongside the police car, and the occupant says, "See, we can do it too." Throughout the night there is intermittent chuckling as "private" jokes that I do not understand come over the radio.

Richard and George then begin their patrol of a major business route, driving in and out of parking lots, checking the stores and offices. In one shopping center parking lot Richard sees several parked cars and remarks that if they're there again tomorrow he will check to see if they're stolen. It is pointless to check now since he doesn't know if they were there yesterday. At another business establishment, George notices a parked car with some people in it. (I am amazed at Richard's and George's ability to notice detail.) Richard drives up behind the car. The manager of the establishment is in the car with a young woman. Richard drives off and jokes that the manager must have promised to make her the head cashier.

3:30 A.M.

We stop at a coffee shop for coffee and donuts. Here the woman on duty gives Richard a bag of day-old donuts for his animals. Earlier we had discussed the fact that his uniform brings him such minor privileges. I am about to sit facing the counter, but Richard tells me they always face outward so they can keep an eye on the patrol car, which contains expensive equipment. He has his small radio with him. It's also an expensive piece of equipment, but he claims it doesn't work too well. George notices mud marks on the large front windows of the shop and speculates that some "kids" who were leaving the store as we entered may have smeared them. George goes to the restroom, and shortly thereafter a car drives up whose driver waves at Richard. Richard becomes suspicious and uneasy, but when George returns he tells Richard it is a fellow officer and goes out to speak with him. George returns shortly and tells Richard about a confrontation he once had with the driver of the car.

We leave the coffee shop and Richard and George begin their patrol of the business area again. Richard asks George about a wedding he had gone to. George notices a man with a crowbar standing next to a building. Richard drives by and we find two men there, who say they're painters and have just finished painting the store. They have paint on them. Richard and George chat with them about the weather and then leave.

A call comes through on the radio about a suspicious vehicle parked on a residential street. Richard and George discuss the location of the street. Richard suggests they turn right; George thinks they should turn left. Richard turns right, goes one block, and then he turns around. Richard and George finally notice a pickup truck with three men asleep in it. Richard drives up next to the cab and shines a light at them. Richard and George get out and knock on the window to awaken the men. Richard asks for identification, but initially the men do not understand. They are still half asleep. Richard repeats his request several times. Finally, several pieces of identification emerge. Richard returns to the car to examine them while George pokes around the back of the truck. The men claim they're out of gas. Richard asks them about this for a while, and then asks if they have any money for gas. One man tells him that his brother-in-law lives nearby and that they did try to awaken some people to call him. Richard comments that this is probably what prompted the call to the police station.

Richard indicates to George that he'd like to give them a ride to a gas station. George is agreeable. Richard calls in to the police station and asks if there are any nearby gas stations open. He learns that there is one not far away. Richard jokes about taking one of the men "in," and then he tells them he'll take one of them to a gas station. One of the men gets in the back seat with me and we drive to the gas station. There is some kidding about taking him to jail, but we drive to the gas station. At the station George notices a woman in a car and makes comments about her appearance. Richard asks if he'd like to take a look at her, and he lights up her car with a spotlight. The man from the pickup gets his gas. There is some joking in the car. We drive back, drop him off, and Richard and George wish him luck. The man thanks them.

I find that it's a struggle to stay awake. We get a call for a back-up vehicle at about 4:00 A.M. and set out for the location where a break-in is thought to have occurred. Richard realizes one road is blocked, turns around, and finally gets there. A vehicle drives by quickly, and Richard immediately turns around and begins to follow it, eventually putting on his blinking lights. Richard and George discuss the possibility that this car is involved in the break-in. The car stops and pulls over. Richard is right behind. He and George get out of the car. It is cold and raining lightly. Richard approaches the driver's side, George the passenger side. They ask the occupants to get out of the car and Richard makes the driver walk a straight line. Meanwhile, George finds two opened beer cans and an unopened six-pack of beer in the car. He empties the opened cans and puts the package on our hood. Richard and George return to the car with the suspects' identification, which they check on the radio. One of the men walks over to Richard's side of the window and protests that they aren't drunk. George warns him that if he wants to make any more trouble, he'll end up in jail. Richard says little. The driver protests to Richard that he hasn't done anything; Richard calmly and firmly tells him to go back to his car and wait. George is more threatening than Richard, who is very matter-of-fact and firm. George suspects that there is a warrant on one of the men but a check reveals that, instead, his brother is wanted. The driver approaches again. Richard tells him to take the beer—which is still on the hood—leave, and drive very carefully and slowly. The man appears very grateful; he thanks Richard profusely and shakes his hand. He assures Richard that he'll be careful and that he'll drive straight home. Finally they leave.

We patrol the roads for a while. Richard asks George, "Did you hear Nicholas won a bat at Bim's?" He chuckles. "It's bigger than he is." He then tells George he may have problems getting Alice and the children to the airport for her visit to her sister. He may have to take time off. After some time we near Richard's house. He shines a light on the house and then drives further down the road to point out to George the goose and little ducks that have settled in a pond formed by the recent rain. Richard and George chat about another pond with some ducks.

We leave this area, and Richard tells me he will show me the communications center. He drives to the main station and the communications center. George goes into the communications room to talk to the others, teasing and joking with the men. Here, Richard takes me into another room and introduces me to one of the sergeants. Richard takes out a map and indicates where his church is, and the location of the farm where he owes some work. (Richard sometimes trades his labor for farm help and items he cannot afford to buy.) We remain there for twenty to thirty minutes.

5:00 A.M.

When we leave George takes the wheel. On our way out of the driveway, we pass another officer standing by one of the gas tanks. The officer complains vociferously about another officer and then we drive on. George drives around in the open country. Everything now is very still. Nothing is coming over the radio. I am very tired. We talk about how difficult it is to stay awake when nothing is going on. They say the only things that happen at this time are traffic accidents.

I am exhausted. While George is driving, Richard falls asleep and, taking his cue, so do I. At one point I wake up briefly and notice that we are parked and that George is also asleep.

6:30 A.M.

We wake up. The sun is coming up, and there is some traffic on the road. George drives around some more and then we head back to the station. We arrive at 7:00 A.M. and wait outside for several minutes. Finally Richard goes inside. He spends the time left on his shift labeling some photographs with a fellow officer, as Richard will be taking them to court tomorrow. They discuss how to arrange them and what labels should be used on them. There is a great deal of kidding and rowdiness at the station, some of it antagonistic and hostile. A fellow citizen is there and he looks at me bemusedly as the officers gripe and kid. They're complaining about each other's not being able to do things "right." Richard finishes up and puts his pictures in an envelope and into his file. We leave at 8:00 A.M. I am just beginning to get a brief second wind.

The Base Day: At Home with the Family

By a previous agreement with Alice, I was to arrive at 7:30 A.M. when she and the children usually arise. I stayed until Alice prepared to go to sleep that night. During most of the Base Day (March 21), I sat in a chair in the dinette area where most household activity was centered. (Figure 7-1 gives a floor plan of the Bernard home.) When Alice and the children went out I accompanied them.

7:40 A.M.

I arrive ten minutes later than the time Alice and I had agreed upon. It's a cold spring morning; an early spring snowfall covers the ground. Alice had heard my car drive up and she greets me, still sleepy, in her bathrobe. She is still waking up as I put my things away and find a chair in the kitchen to locate myself.

7:45 A.M.

Three-year-old James is the first of the children up. He also has sleep in his eyes. Alice asks what he wants for breakfast and he goes to the cupboard and pulls out a cereal box, chatting to Alice while he does so. Meanwhile Alice is preparing frozen waffles for the other two children.

136

Figure 7-1. Floor Plan of the Bernard Home[a]

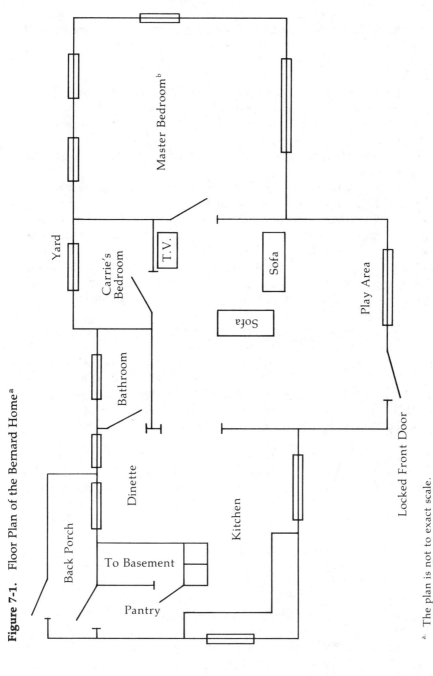

a. The plan is not to exact scale.
b. The boys shared this bedroom with Alice and Richard. Richard had meant to complete an attic room for them, but at the time of the study, this project was not completed.

Soon Nicholas, aged 2, wanders in. After walking into the bathroom he sits at the table, watching me silently. He says nothing, seeming not quite awake. Alice places the children's plates in front of them, and they slowly begin to eat.

8:00 A.M.

Alice goes into the bedroom to wake up Carrie, her oldest child. Carrie had been sleeping with her, as Richard is working the midnight shift. Carrie was up late watching television. She sits down at the table but is barely awake, taking no notice of me. She sits in front of her plate, slumped in her chair. The general energy level of all the children is low—they are still sleepy and don't say much.

Alice goes downstairs to the basement to turn on the washing machine. Then she comes up and works in the kitchen area.

At 8:10 A.M. Richard, in full uniform, comes home. Alice hears him first and James, grinning, announces, "Daddy is home," an announcement that is echoed by Nicholas. Richard walks through the kitchen and playfully pulls James's ear, who is pleased and giggles. Richard says hello to Carrie but she seems oblivious to his presence and doesn't respond. James worries out loud that Carrie is not eating her breakfast. Richard walks through the kitchen into the living room.

Alice goes into the bedroom to change the sheets. She complains to me that with the bed being slept in for sixteen hours each day, she has to change them more often. She piles the sheets in the corner of the kitchen near the living room archway, and the two boys, now awake, jump on them. Then they follow Richard into the bedroom where he has gone to change his clothes. Carrie is still at the table, but now she is showing some interest in her food and is beginning to eat.

8:15 A.M.

I can hear the boys chatting to their father as they watch him change his clothes. Alice tells me that this is a daily ritual. I hear Richard's deep voice answering them. They come out of the bedroom together. Richard, now in his farm clothes, goes to the small pantry in the back of the kitchen. The boys begin to play in the sheets again. Alice follows him to the pantry, and I hear them talking about their budget and how much money is left. Alice tells Richard she needs to pick up some clothes from layaway and needs some money.

Alice then goes into the living room to vacuum. She tells me she has to get her vacuuming done when Richard is not sleeping. Richard comes into the kitchen and begins to get out juice for the children, but Alice tells him they've had theirs. Richard then goes into the bathroom, which is just off the kitchen. The boys seem concerned that he has closed the door, and they try to open it. Later I learn that the norm in the house is not to close doors; he is doing so because of my presence. I move into the living room temporarily to give him privacy.

While Alice is vacuuming in the living room, the boys are running around the kitchen. James drapes himself over a chair, and Nicholas lies on the pile of sheets; then they reverse positions. Carrie is still at the table with her juice. She is eating her breakfast very slowly.

Alice comes to the archway of the kitchen and says, "Come on boys, let's watch 'Captain.'" The boys run into the living room. She then says to Carrie, "Come on Carrie, finish up." James turns on the television set. Richard is in the pantry behind the kitchen preparing food for his animals. Alice is cleaning up in the kitchen.

Momentarily, Nicholas comes in to say that "Captain" is over. Alice sends him back to the living room, where Nicholas starts to look for his teddy bear and his blanket. Alice has gone into the bedroom to vacuum and helps Nicholas by finding his blanket for him. The boys now move between the television set in the living room and the bedroom, where Alice is vacuuming. They are interacting with her. Carrie is still quietly languishing at the kitchen table. Finally, the television show catches the boys' full attention; they watch raptly, thumbs in their mouths, holding onto their blankets and teddy bears.

Alice comes out of the bedroom, goes into the kitchen, and talks to Richard. Does he realize his name tag is off his uniform? She had noticed it. I cannot hear the details of his response, but it is short and matter of fact.

8:30 A.M.

For the second time Alice urges Carrie to finish eating. Her patience seems to be wearing thin. She warns her to be finished by the time she has finished changing the sheets on the bed. It is quiet now that the boys are watching television; Alice is now in the bedroom changing the sheets, and noises can be heard from Richard, who is still in the back pantry preparing his animals' food. Quietly, Carrie asks Richard for some more juice; no one hears her. Listlessly and without much energy she repeats her request.

In the living room, James begins to look at his cutout book and interacts with his teddy bear. He's sitting on the sofa. Nicholas is on the floor, and occasionally I can hear him talking to the television characters.

Alice now prepares to dress the children. She takes their clothes out of a dresser in the main bedroom and lays them on the sofa. As she moves through the living room to the kitchen, she asks James curtly to take off his pajamas. She enters the kitchen, where Carrie is still sitting over her breakfast, and irritatedly admonishes her to finish up, as the bed is done. This is Alice's third request to Carrie, who has been sitting over her breakfast, slouching in her chair and playing with her food since 8:00 A.M.

Once again, Alice asks James to take off his pajamas, but he protests that he is not finished "reading." More sternly now, she repeats her request, but he continues to look at his coloring book. Then he wanders over to me to show me his teddy bear. He is using obvious stalling tactics—to him there are more interesting things to do than dressing. Carrie also is still at the kitchen table, passively resisting her mother's admonishments.

Finally, focusing on James, Alice picks him up and starts to undress him, but he protests that he can do it himself. With this show of force, James begins his job. Alice then turns her attention to Nicholas and begins to undress him. As soon as her attention shifts to Nicholas, James asks for help with his shirt. While Alice is dressing Nicholas he continues to watch television, seemingly oblivious to the fact that his mother is clothing him. He repeats sentences he hears around him.

To no one in particular, since her mother is in the living room and her father is busying himself heating up his animals' food, Carrie asks for some more juice. She repeats herself quietly. Being the only adult in the room, I pour some for her.

Alice tells me that "Captain Kangaroo" and "Sesame Street" really quiet the children down. Without them, she says, "I don't know what I'd do!" While Alice is dressing Nicholas, James asks her for something. Alice is now annoyed and in a quick, irritated voice tells him, "Wait till I finish." James then concerns himself with his Snoopy socks, which he shows me. Nicholas starts to occupy himself with his coloring book.

Alice turns her attention to Carrie, telling her to get dressed. Carrie is still sitting at the table and is making no move to finish. Alice gets a washcloth and brusquely wipes Carrie's mouth.

Alice then moves into the living room to change Nicholas's diaper. Clearly, this is an event he does not like and he begins to protest loudly. In the meantime, Carrie has begun to move. She tells me she'll be 6 soon and takes off her pajamas. In an irritated voice, Alice tells her to dress herself. Carrie and Nicholas discuss their Snoopy items with me. Nicholas is particularly interested in the cap of my pen, to which he points. James is in the living room "reading." The television set momentarily distracts Nicholas and Carrie. Nicholas continues talking with me about my pen. He obviously is interested in my notetaking and my writing. Meanwhile, Alice has gone into the basement to do another load of laundry.

8:45 A.M.

I can hear Alice in the basement putting clothes into the dryer. Richard has gone outside to feed his animals. The children are now in the living room. Carrie and James are watching television; Nicholas is playing near the rocking chair on which his father has draped his uniform.

Alice comes up from the basement and goes into the bedroom to vacuum, warning Nicholas to stay out of "Dad's pockets." I have moved to the living room. Nicholas trips over my feet trying to move toward the television set. He approaches Alice and tells her he hurt his head; she is at the door between bedroom and living room. She gently kisses his head and he seems satisfied.

Alice continues vacuuming in the bedroom. Carrie is dressing while watching television, and Nicholas hovers at the bedroom–living room doorway until Alice emerges with the vacuum cleaner. On the way to the kitchen with the vacuum, she admonishes James to stop sucking his thumb.

Alice begins to vacuum in the kitchen dinette. When she turns on the vacuum cleaner, Carrie turns up the volume on the television set. Carrie and James are watching television; Nicholas is occupying himself in the play area behind the sofa. Carrie and Nicholas are sitting on the sofas, sucking their thumbs and holding their blankets. Alice announces from the kitchen that they will have to clean up the play area after "Captain" is finished.

Nicholas brings his blocks into the living-room television area. James asks Nicholas if he can "help." Nicholas has already made two trips gathering blocks from the play area and taking them into the living room. (This is after Alice has given them notice that they will have to clean up soon.) Alice notices the block-carrying activity and twice insists that they put them away. James, who has just begun to help Nicholas carry the blocks into the television area, gets admonished as well. Once again, Alice insists to Nicholas that he play in the play area. Nicholas's solution to his dilemma is to play at the boundary between the living-room and the play areas. He carries the blocks to the end table marking this boundary and begins to pile the blocks on it, soon incorporating the lamp into his play. James helps him. Alice does not notice this new, forbidden activity.

While the boys are playing with the blocks on the end table, Alice briefly talks to Richard, who has come in from outside and is in the back pantry—at the boundary between outside and inside. Alice has started the dishes in the kitchen. She does dishes only once a day, she tells me. She then starts to vacuum again, which causes Carrie to turn up the volume on the television again. Alice occasionally stops, throwing a block she has found in the kitchen into the play area. She appears not to notice the block-building activity on the end table. She tells Carrie to bring her the hairbrush so that she can brush Carrie's hair. I get the sense that Alice gives Carrie her instructions before she is actually ready to brush Carrie's hair because getting the brush will take some time. Carrie rises from the sofa at her mother's request but becomes distracted by the television program and then increases the volume when Alice begins vacuuming again. Carrie is now standing motionless in front of the set. Once again Alice tells her to get her hairbrush; Alice sounds tried and irritated now. To deal with Carrie's unwillingness to move, Alice bargains with her by telling her to wait until "the Captain" has finished his explanation and then to get the hairbrush. Meanwhile, the boys have thrown a number of the blocks off the table. Alice goes into the living room, gets the hairbrush herself, turns the volume on the television down, and begins brushing Carrie's hair. Carrie remains in front of the set, captivated by it.

Alice now notices that the table is being used for play and warns James and Nicholas sternly against this forbidden activity. They ignore her. She goes into the kitchen and puts water on to boil. Again she comes to the living-room–kitchen archway and warns Nicholas to clear off the table. James starts to help Nicholas, but she tells him to stop, as she asked Nicholas to do it. Nicholas begins to comply.

Alice goes into the living room and gets her *Reader's Digest* from under the television set. She will try to get some reading done while eating breakfast. As if by signal, James follows her into the kitchen and asks her what she is doing. Alice explains that she hasn't eaten yet. Nicholas gets his blanket from the living room and comes into the kitchen dragging it behind him. In a tired voice, Alice tells him not to drag it on the floor, which isn't clean. The children momentarily return to the living room and "Captain Kangaroo."

9:00 A.M.

The children are in the living room watching "Captain Kangaroo." Alice finally begins to finish preparing her own breakfast—a cup of tea and an instant waffle. She tells me that she and Richard had once thought of a legal separation in order to get welfare because of their financial difficulties. Richard comes in from the yard—he can be heard in the back pantry. Immediately Nicholas comes into the kitchen, followed by Carrie and then James, although they don't overtly acknowledge their father's presence. Alice asks James to put the margarine in the refrigerator, which he does, and then she asks Nicholas to get his shoes. He toddles off to the living room. Carrie starts to play with the vacuum cleaner, which is now in the kitchen. Alice tells her to stop. She is irritated and already tired, it seems. She tells the children the play area has to be picked up, but they make no moves in that direction. Alice does not follow it up, though I am beginning to visualize her as a foreman trying to get stubborn and resistant workers to do their job.

Finally, Alice sits down at the kitchen table with her waffle, tea, and *Reader's Digest*. Immediately, Nicholas and James, who had gone back to the living room, return to the kitchen and hover near her. Carrie again begins to toy with the vacuum cleaner. This time Alice says nothing. Alice puts on Nicholas's shoes, which he had brought to her, and then James starts playing with the vacuum cleaner. Alice tells them to go into the play area. Clearly, she is trying to create some personal space for herself in which to read. Richard comes in, washes up at the sink, and tells Alice he is going to bed. She asks whether he wants to be awakened for lunch. He indicates that he does if the weather's "OK." Richard seems tired; Alice seems tired. Very little passes between them. Carrie and Nicholas have gone into the living room and James announces that they'll be busy, and then he wanders into the play area.

For a moment Alice has quiet, but immediately James returns to complain that Carrie isn't helping to clean up. From the kitchen, Alice admonishes Carrie roughly to help clean up. It almost seems as if there is a conspiracy to prevent Alice from sitting down and resting. Richard comes to Alice's assistance by marching into the living room and sharply reprimanding the children, thereby starting their cleaning effort. It is clear that his presence and booming voice carry authority, for the children are deadly silent when he speaks. Alice comes to the living-room–kitchen archway to back Richard up, though she says nothing. When the children start their cleaning effort, she returns to the kitchen for her breakfast and her book. She reads for what seems like only a moment, and then we hear Nicholas asking for her help because Carrie is hitting him. Without getting up, and without taking her eyes from her book, Alice calls sharply to Carrie and commands her to stand in a corner in the kitchen for five minutes. Carrie skulks into the kitchen, goes to the corner and faces outward. Although displeased, Carrie does not seem to take the punishment very seriously. However, when Alice insists that she face the corner, she begins to whimper. Richard, who is near the sink, asks her if she wants a spanking. Looking petulant, she turns toward the corner for the moment.

James then comes into the kitchen and asks for help from Alice in their cleaning effort. Alice indicates she will help them when she is finished. At that point Richard says he is going to sleep, and without further ado walks into the bedroom and closes the door. James asks Alice what Dad is going to do, and in a tired voice that sounds used to such questions, Alice tells him that his father's going to sleep. Not satisfied, James asks why, and Alice perfunctorily tells him, "Dad's tired." She continues to read her book, but I wonder how much reading she is getting done. James asks why Carrie is in the corner. By this time Carrie is sitting on the floor in the corner playing with the vacuum cleaner—she has managed to turn a punishment into a playtime. James is playing in the sheets on the kitchen floor. Alice asks James to leave and give her some peace and quiet—she sounds even more tired, even more drained. James resists this idea but finally goes into the living room, only to retrieve his blanket to lie down on the kitchen floor near Alice's feet. (Later Alice tells me how much this behavior bothers her, since it indicates to her that the children aren't "coping.") Meanwhile, Carrie is still sitting in the corner playing with the vacuum cleaner; she is now "mouthing" the tube. Alice doesn't seem to notice this and tells her she can leave the corner now (five minutes have not passed). Carrie dallies there. In yet another attempt to create her space, Alice tells Carrie and James to go and play "something" or they won't go outside with her when she goes to the store. At this point Nicholas comes into the kitchen wearing a rain hat and carrying a purse. Alice and I smile at each other. Nicholas asks to sit in Alice's lap, but she says, "Not now." James asks Alice what Nicholas has on his wrist. Alice answers curtly, "It's a watch." Nicholas's entry seems to activate Carrie, who leaves for the living room. She has changed places with Nicholas. Alice still does not have the space she has been trying to create for herself for the last fifteen minutes.

9:15 A.M.

James is still lying at Alice's feet in the kitchen. Nicholas whispers to Alice that he wants to sit in her lap. Alice says no and sighs. Once again she tries to read her book. James sits down at the table near Alice. Nicholas asks Alice to fasten his wristwatch. She does so while continuing to read. James and Nicholas try to talk to her, but she reminds them curtly that she is reading. Carrie comes into the kitchen, inviting Nicholas to play with her; Alice supports this idea by suggesting that he do so. Carrie has brought some toys into the kitchen, and Nicholas and Carrie begin to play on the floor very close to Alice's feet. Alice reads. Carrie is directing the play. James is momentarily drawn into this activity, but he soon returns to his chair, announcing for Alice's benefit that he will sit on the chair. Alice sighs audibly and does not respond. Carrie and Nicholas seem to have come to the end of their activity, and Carrie approaches me, implicitly inviting some interaction. When I don't respond, Carrie and Nicholas begin to hover restlessly around Alice; Nicholas tries to initiate a conversation with her. She doesn't respond to this attempt.

Carrie and Nicholas chat briefly as they "read" on the floor. James says happily to Alice, "We colored there." Alice's response is a distracted "yeah." "Can we cut them?" asks James. Alice rises and rounds up some scissors. She has now given up trying to read—her "break" is now at an end. The other two children get into the action and become involved in James's book. Alice wipes the kitchen table and warns them that they can cut the magazines, but not the books. Alice asks Carrie to sit down. Nicholas is cheerfully talking to himself about the numbers and animals he sees in his book. James is now telling Carrie what he plans to cut out, and Carrie reciprocates. Alice looks further for scissors, finds another blunt-edged pair, and hands them out. She sets Nicholas up at the table too. James discusses his scissors with Carrie.

Alice now goes into the bedroom, where Richard is asleep, to get her own clothes—she is still in her bathrobe. She goes into the bathroom briefly. Nicholas then asks for help in using the scissors, and Alice comes out to arrange his fingers for him. As she does this, James complains that he can't use his scissors. Alice moves around the table to put his scissors "on" also. She asks James and Carrie to trade scissors, an event that occurs without incident. In the meantime, Nicholas's scissors are off his fingers once again. While Alice is suggesting to James how he might cut out the pictures,

144

Introducing the Bernards: A Day in their Lives

Nicholas is playing with the scissors near his face. Alice doesn't notice. Nicholas tells James not to pick his nose. Alice moves to the sink, her back to the children, to wash dishes.

9:30 A.M.

Alice then decides that pens might be better than scissors, and she gives them to Nicholas and James, warning them sternly to color on the paper only. Alice continues to wash her dishes. Nicholas loudly and cheerfully talks about what he is doing. Alice insists that James not write on his hand, which he is now doing.

James asks Carrie if he can cut out pictures from her book; Carrie refuses. He asks Alice, who also says no. Nicholas drops his scissors and announces the fact loudly to Alice, who tells him to get them. Three times he tells her proudly that he's got the scissors; twice she doesn't respond. The third time she responds tiredly in acknowledgment. Nicholas begins to talk happily, again, to no one in particular.

James addresses Alice, but she doesn't hear him. She is humming quietly to herself as she washes the dishes. Nicholas tells Alice, as if asking for her approval, that he is going to color the eyes. Without paying much attention, Alice says, "OK," distractedly, turns on the radio, and goes downstairs to the laundry. During all this time Carrie has been quietly cutting out her pictures. James and Nicholas have been talking to themselves, sometimes addressing Alice.

James announces to the general audience that he has to go to the bathroom. When Alice comes up from the basement he tells her and asks for help with his overalls, which she undoes. She notices that James has ink on his face. "Are you going to spank me?" he asks. "That's right," she answers in a slightly teasing voice as she puts the toaster away. James goes off into the bathroom, and Nicholas begins to write on his hand, as if the idea had been implanted by the exchange between Alice and James. Alice insists that Nicholas stop this. She wipes his hands and face and takes away his pen, replacing it with crayons. James rushes into the kitchen bare-bottomed and smiling. Slightly amused by this display, Alice pulls up his pants and fastens his overalls. James then asks for his pen. Alice asks if he wants crayons. "OK," he responds. She returns to the dishes and Carrie asks for her crayons, as if to get some of the attention James and Nicholas have received. Alice tells Carrie to get them. James and Carrie rush off into the play area and get their crayons. Once again, Nicholas proudly asks for some approval from Alice, which she distractedly gives him. James shows me his crayons as he comes back into the kitchen. Alice continues washing dishes.

9:45 A.M.

James asks Alice when she is going to shower. She indicates that she will do so after she does the dishes. James tells her he wants to wash the dishes, and then Carrie pipes up that she wants to wash them too. Alice tells them no, but that when Dad has his day off, James can be first. Carrie insists that she wants to be first, but Alice abruptly reminds her that she is first in a lot of activities. This involves James and Carrie in an argument about who is first, and Alice raises her voice to insist that they stop bickering. Carrie has a final word by saying that James "started it." James starts to whimper about the dishes. Alice is quite irritated by now and threatens to have him stay home while she goes out. He continues to whimper and she suggests that he color. James says he's too tired and then wanders over to the stove, becoming distracted by what is behind it. He begins to play with the wires.

Meanwhile Carrie has returned to the table; she is now cutting her crayons. Nicholas is still quietly coloring. James sits on the vacuum cleaner, and Nicholas begins to chat loudly. Alice very sternly asks James not to play with the vacuum cleaner, but he ignores her and continues to "ride" it. Carrie is now cutting her crayon box, while Nicholas is attempting to put his crayons into his box. Carrie becomes restless; she stands up, goes over to the vacuum cleaner hose and walks on it momentarily as if she were a tightrope walker. Soon bored, she returns to the table and begins playing with James's crayons—lining them up in her hands. Meanwhile, Nicholas is none too successful with his crayons, as they are falling out of the bottom of the box. James gets off the vacuum cleaner to put his crayons away. Noticing this, Carrie innocently returns to her own seat at the table.

Alice finishes up the dishes and attempts to wipe the hand James wrote on. He resists, insisting that it hurts. Nicholas announces that he is getting off his seat. Realizing that his crayons are missing, James asks Carrie where the rest of his crayons are; she doles some out to him. He asserts his right to his crayons and goes to Alice for help. Immediately, Carrie gives him his crayons, some of which are rather short and broken in two. James asks Alice for tape to fix his crayons. She gets some adhesive tape and then Carrie asks for tape. Alice indicates sternly that the tape is not for purposes of play but for repair. She puts the tape on the table, and James goes for it. Alice quickly warns James not to play with it; he backs off. Meanwhile, Nicholas has moved from his seat to a position on the floor near the stove, where he has begun putting his crayons into his purse. Now Nicholas begins to whimper, as he is not being very successful in getting his crayons put away. Alice stoops to help him. Nicholas asks for her help in closing his crayon box correctly. Alice answers that she can't, as the box is torn. She rises and goes downstairs to the laundry.

The telephone rings and Alice rushes up from downstairs. It's a female acquaintance. The children have become quiet, perhaps waiting to learn who it is. As Alice begins her conversation, she sits down. Carrie discusses James's piece of tape with him, while Nicholas is now shoving his crayons out of the bottom of his box. Carrie has two pens; James asks for one, but Carrie refuses him. Alice must have been listening with one ear for, while

146

continuing with the phone conversation, she intervenes nonverbally and gives James one of Carrie's pens.

Alice tells her friend that things have been "topsy-turvy" because Richard is on the midnight shift. She complains that he doesn't get enough sleep and laughingly comments that when she feels angry about his shift she imagines suing his employer for negligence, as she's afraid he'll fall asleep behind the wheel.

10:00 A.M.

Meanwhile, Carrie and James have begun playing together—they are writing on a book on the floor. Nicholas gets a book and lies down next to them. All three are quite close to Alice. James takes his own book. James gets excited about something, and Alice tells him abruptly to stop it and to sit down at the table. James does, but seems angry. Meanwhile Carrie has disappeared into the bathroom; Nicholas is whimpering out of frustration and is throwing his books around. When Carrie emerges from the bathroom she asks James if she can write with him; he says no. Carrie is annoyed and taps him lightly with her pen. She asks him two times more and he says no. Carrie hits him lightly and tells him he's bad and mean. Nicholas has quieted down since he's discovered his scissors again. Meanwhile Alice complains to her friend on the telephone about having forgotten an appointment with a mutual friend, complaining that with Richard on the midnight shift, everything is "screwed up."

Carrie has gotten a plastic play hard hat from the bathroom and is standing in it. Restless and probably still angry, she begins to write on James's arm. Alice sees her and, still on the telephone, spanks her lightly and admonishes her to stop. Alice complains to her friend that Richard doesn't get weekends off, and then says that she can't call a friend long distance because of the expense.

James whimpers. Appearing restless, he gets his blanket from the table and lies down with it on the floor near Alice's feet. Nicholas moves his things from the table to the floor near the stove. While continuing her conversation, Alice silently insists that Nicholas take his crayons out of his mouth; he does. James approaches Nicholas who protests. Carrie tells James to leave Nicholas alone. Alice then finishes her telephone conversation and organizes the children to watch television. Carrie and James go into the living room, with Nicholas remaining behind. Alice tells me that usually "all hell breaks loose" when she's on the telephone.

Alice notices that James is at the television plug and warns him off. Nicholas is still in the kitchen. Alice begins to pick up the toys the children had brought into the kitchen. Nicholas starts to walk into the living room with his crayons, but Alice tells him to put them in his box; unhappy now, he resists. Alice threatens him with not going out. Nicholas whimpers, sits down, and goes through the motions of putting his crayons away. Actually he is playing with his crayon box. Meanwhile, Alice has gone down to the laundry. She returns shortly and helps Nicholas put away his crayons. She tells him he should go watch "Sesame Street." She puts away his scissors and he protests through some tired tears. To comfort him, Alice picks him up and asks if he wants to help her take a shower, and he quiets down. She then puts him down, and he begins to whimper again. Once again she picks him up; he whimpers. She tries to distract him with another object. James rushes in and asks for a particular game. Alice asks, "Will you help me take a shower so that we can go out soon?" James wanders into the living room and then returns to the kitchen. He starts an interaction with Nicholas who cries out loudly. Taking on her mother's role once again, Carrie calls out loudly from the living room for James to behave himself. Not pleased, Alice tells Carrie to be quiet.

Alice spanks James lightly; he whimpers and disappears into the living room to get his game. Nicholas goes into the living room, where Carrie is. Carrie is heard to cry out. Alice marches into the living room, spanks Carrie, and tells her, "You're too old for that." Carrie is sent to stand in the kitchen corner for "ten minutes," her second time this morning. Carrie protests, "Nicholas said I could play!" "You couldn't really have understood him," responds Alice, obviously not believing Carrie. Carrie whimpers a quiet protest and goes to the corner Alice has pointed out. Meanwhile, James and Nicholas are watching "Sesame Street." Several minutes later, Alice has decided the punishment is enough and tells Carrie she can come out of the corner now. Carrie goes quickly into the living room to watch television.

10:30 A.M.

Alice now goes into the bathroom to shower and dress. She had brought her things in earlier. Nicholas comes to the bathroom door and plays with the knob. The door is ajar and he disappears into the bathroom. Carrie and James are sitting—each on one sofa—with their blankets, watching television. As Alice emerges from the shower I hear her greeting Nicholas, who responds happily. Twice he asks her where Daddy is. Alice tells him he's sleeping. Then they play a teasing game to determine whether Nicholas's diaper is wet. Carrie comes into the bathroom, followed by James. Alice asks, "Who's watching TV? If no one is watching, it should be turned off." She asks James to turn it off; he rushes into the living room and quickly reports back to Alice that he has accomplished his mission. She thanks him. James then insists that he wants to eat. Alice tells him that it is not time—they just ate; he'll eat again in a little while. Carrie asks when she'll be going to nursery school; Alice tells her in a little while. (Alice's spirits seem to have lifted and she appears much more attentive to the children now that she is not doing chores or trying to dress them.)

The children become active and noisy. Alice tries to keep them quiet because "Daddy is sleeping." They respond momentarily to her request. She asks James to get her a diaper. He goes into the bedroom where Richard is sleeping and gets one. I hear Alice admonishing Carrie to stop picking a fight with Nicholas, to find something else to play with. Then I hear her roughly warning Carrie that she will slap her if Carrie looks at her "like that." All the children are in the bathroom, which is small, with Alice. Alice can be heard admonishing James roughly while she is brushing her teeth. He comes out, goes into the living room for a moment—as if the situation were too explosive—and returns. I hear Alice say, "Just a moment. Do it my way or not at all." Then she admonishes Carrie regarding an interaction with James. James asks Alice if hair combing hurts. She assures him that it doesn't hurt her, it's Carrie who doesn't like to have her hair combed. James and Nicholas sing briefly. Alice asks Nicholas to "stop fighting" and tells Carrie to leave him alone. (Presumably, they were in an altercation.) She scolds Nicholas and Carrie. Carrie leaves the bathroom, goes into the living room, and turns on the television. Nicholas becomes noisy in the bathroom and Alice tells him to "keep it down." Nicholas asserts himself with a no and Alice is shocked. "What?" she insists. Nicholas apologizes.

Alice diapers Nicholas as he protests. Alice asks James to get her something; he searches in the living room while Alice tries to quiet the protesting Nicholas. Meanwhile, James has forgotten his errand and becomes distracted by the television. Alice sends Nicholas in search of the pegs to James's game or else the "game is ruined." Nicholas goes off into the living room. Alice emerges from the bathroom, combed and dressed in a wool sweater and blue jeans.

10:45 A.M.

Nicholas rushes into the kitchen crying. Alice says, "Want to tell me about it?" in a soothing voice. Nicholas tells her that James has written on his back. Alice laughs and kisses his head.

The new task is to dress the children for going out. Going out is something they all seem pleased about; it is a task that is accomplished quickly. Alice brings their coats from the pantry to the kitchen. Nicholas begins to stamp his feet—he's excited. When Alice says, "Get your coats on," he gets joyful and then disappears. James comes into the kitchen for his coat. Alice unplugs the television set. She asks James if his nose is running. Nicholas wants to know if he has to wear his boots. Alice then asks Carrie if her nose is running. She puts on Nicholas's coat. James asks Alice to help him with his coat—I offer my help but he refuses. James asks her for help in being buttoned, while Nicholas asks her to hold him. She helps James but doesn't hold Nicholas. The children are finally coated and booted. Alice is the last one to put on her outdoor clothing.

We leave through the kitchen door and pile into the car, which is in the barn. I sit in the front seat; the children are in the back, playfully interacting. After a fifteen-minute ride, Alice parks her car on a main street in the small town where she likes to do her shopping. We link hands as we cross the street, with Alice carrying Nicholas under one arm. The first store we visit is the bakery. As we enter the store the children become excited and rush into the back area and disappear. Meanwhile, Alice purchases several breads and one large sugar cookie for the children. Alice too, seems glad to be out; she appears to me to be much less concerned now with their excited activity. When the children come to the front of the store, Carrie asks for a specific cookie. They are happy. Alice tells them she's already gotten one for them. Carrie gets excited thinking that I had chosen a surprise for them. I comment that Alice has chosen it.

Outside the bakery the cookie is divided into three pieces and each child gets one. They run along the sidewalk, stopping to admire some enormous chocolate Easter bunnies in a store window. As we walk along, Nicholas lags behind and Alice urges him on twice.

Alice remembers that she has to get some paper and ribbon for a birthday party she and the children are going to tomorrow. We reverse direction and head for a gift shop. Alice tells me that she doesn't like going into the store because the salespeople there are nervous about the children breaking things. Consequently Alice is also nervous about it, and before we enter the store she makes certain that each child has heard the admonishment: "Be careful. Remember, don't touch anything." She says this firmly and matter-of-factly, with less irritation than earlier in the day. We also cannot enter the store with food, so she urges Nicholas to finish his cookie. We wait while he finishes up, then go in.

In the store, Alice chooses her paper and card quickly, although she tells me later that she likes to browse in gift shops. The haste, it would appear, is in consequence of the children's presence. As we enter, the children discover a large basket with fuzzy Easter bunnies in it, and Carrie and James immediately handle them. Next to the basket is a two-foot image of Snoopy, a favorite character, and Nicholas examines it. It almost tips over, but Alice catches it. Carrie is also fingering some delicate-looking plaster animals, and Alice tells her not to touch them. She also tells the boys not to touch, but they only halfheartedly obey. Paying quickly for her purchase, Alice hurries the children out.

We drive to a small store where Alice buys some milk and ice cream. The children express interest in the gum machines. She provides a penny for each of them. I help James and Nicholas get their gum while Alice pays for her purchases. The visit goes smoothly.

We then drive to a supermarket. As we leave the car the boys are placed in a shopping cart near the parking spot. We then go across the lot into the store. Carrie hangs onto the side of the basket, making the cart more difficult to wheel. Alice makes several sarcastic remarks aimed at Carrie, indicating that the basket would be easier to maneuver without her hanging on. The shopping through the supermarket is peaceful and uneventful. Alice is in-

150

volved in conversation with me about what it means to be a woman and about a particular checker at the market, and pays little attention to the children. James zeroes in on the candy as we pass, but Alice tells them she is not buying any and we move on. At the checkout counter, the candy is placed at child height. James asks if he can buy some M&M's but Alice says no. Still, he tries to sneak a pack onto the conveyor belt, but Alice sees it and puts it back. She gets slightly irritated in admonishing him. On the way out the door with the groceries, James becomes interested in the automatic "in" door and does not come out with us. Alice gets irritated at him, as she is worried he could get hurt by someone coming in. He finally comes out and then becomes involved with the bike rack. Again, Alice admonishes him to hurry up.

Alice tells me that this was an unusually peaceful trip. Usually, the children fight in the car. (I wonder how much of this "peace" was because she was talking with me rather than attending to them.)

12:10 P.M.

We return to the house and the children are undressed quickly and peacefully. They all cooperate, and Alice begins to hurry to prepare lunch for them as she wants to leave for Carrie's day-care school by 12:45. Carrie goes to the toilet, accompanied by James and Nicholas. Alice then sends the children to watch television. They run into the living room, turn on the set, and sit down to watch, holding their blankets. Alice runs down into the basement to do laundry and then hurries up. The children can be heard discussing the television characters. From the kitchen Alice calls to Carrie: "You want liver sausage?" Carrie: "Yeah." "James, what do you want?" He doesn't answer and Alice goes into the living room, making her question "felt." James indicates he wants bologna. Alice asks Nicholas. I don't recall his response. Carrie initiates an interaction with Alice, who responds passively and returns to the kitchen to resume her lunch-making activities.

12:15 P.M.

Alice is preparing lunch. The children are watching "Bugs Bunny." Nicholas and Carrie are on the floor with their blankets. James is on the sofa with his. The children are particularly quiet now.

As Alice begins to put their food on the table, James comes in and asks if it is time to eat. Alice says yes and asks him to get napkins. James: "Where?" Alice: "You know where. Get four." (I had indicated to Alice that I wanted to observe during lunch and therefore wouldn't be eating with them.) He pulls some napkins out of the cupboard and asks, "Is this four?" Alice, hurried and irritated, says, "You know how to count four." She then calls the others, at which point James runs into the living room. Alice says, "Turn the TV off," which Carrie does. Carrie and James come into the kitchen and sit down. Alice indicates "Dad's chair" for Carrie. Alice then calls for Nicholas, who wanders slowly in, intrigued by the bells on his shoes. (Their shoes had been left on for the trip out again.) Finally, Alice impatiently picks him up and seats him. Alice says, "Come on, let's eat. We have to get Carrie off to school." Nicholas asks his mother a question several times but Alice doesn't respond. She is at the sink. Nicholas spills some milk and tries to tell Alice. She brings them bananas and wipes up Nicholas's spill, telling him not to worry about it, "just eat."

12:30 P.M.

Finally, Alice brings her own sandwich to the table and gets herself a napkin. James had not brought enough. She asks James if his sandwich is hard to chew. Nicholas tells her about his "apple"; Alice tells him it's a banana. Nicholas continues to chatter. Alice urges them to eat more quickly as they have only fifteen minutes left. James starts to choke on his sandwich and Alice pats his back. Alice tells Carrie she can't go out at the nursery school break until her ear is better. Carrie protests that none of the other children have to stay inside, but Alice insists. Then, "Nicholas, use two hands," as his milk is about to spill. Carrie complains that her crust is hard and, rather tiredly, Alice explains that's the way bread is. James starts to complain about something too; Alice tries to understand him, then gives up and simply asks him to eat. She turns her attention to Nicholas, feeding him and playing "handsy" with him. Finally, she threatens him: "Eat or you can't come." She asks James to use his napkin and then again tries to get Nicholas to eat or "stay home." Carrie makes a comment about school, about which Alice inquires.

Alice finishes her sandwich first (she has eaten very quickly, it seems) and goes to the sink, rinses out a cloth, and wipes up her place at the table. She tells Carrie to finish her sandwich and urges Nicholas onward. She tries to feed him. Carrie asks, "Can I still work at my school?" Alice indicates that she can but "not outside." Carrie then decides that she won't miss the fun. Nicholas says "Oscar Meyer" and Alice acknowledges him absentmindedly, urging him to eat. James announces that his ears don't hurt and Alice says, again distractedly, "Good." Alice asks Carrie if she's done and James says he's done too. Alice tells Carrie to wash herself, but to brush herself off before she leaves the kitchen. Carrie obliges. Alice gets a cloth to wipe up the boys. As she wipes James's face, he asks her, "Why?" "Because you're so cute," she replies. She asks James to wash his hands, but he indicates that he's already done that. "Do you have to go to the bathroom?" James goes into the bathroom and Carrie comes out. Alice says to Carrie, "Did you go to the bathroom?" In response Carrie tells James, "Don't flush, I have to go." Nicholas says he has to go to the bathroom as Alice removes his partially eaten sandwich. James emerges from the bathroom bare-bottomed and announces again that his ears don't hurt. He checks with Alice to make sure he is going too, and Alice reassures him. Carrie comes out of the bathroom singing "Yankee Doodle," which the others pick up. Carrie plays atop the vacuum cleaner while James and Nicholas clap. Alice is wiping the table and urges Nicholas to "finish this milk, OK? Please." She seems harried and rushed. He complains about spilling milk and she says, "OK, finish your banana." His complaint probably indicated to her that he didn't want to finish his milk.

James asks Alice why the vacuum cleaner is "that way," a question which makes little sense in and of itself. "Because," Alice replies. Alice begins to sweep the kitchen; James volunteers to help her and gets her the dustpan. Meanwhile, Carrie shows me her ring, which I admire. Nicholas announces that he's done and Alice wipes his hands. She asks Carrie to go into the bedroom "quietly" to get Nicholas's pants. James starts to "sweep," and Alice gets annoyed. "Please!" and she puts James into the corner. He whimpers. Alice picks up the broom. Nicholas announces that he's ready and Alice tells him to "be patient." James announces that he wants to leave the corner but Alice doesn't respond. Alice removes Nicholas's overalls and asks Carrie to get her a diaper. "Daytime?" "Yes." Carrie and Nicholas run into the living room and small bedroom. Alice wipes the kitchen table again, while James is playing with the vacuum cleaner. Carrie brings in the diaper, and Alice asks her to put it on the bathroom floor. Alice begins to sweep again, and James asks her if he can leave the corner now. Alice says, "OK, but don't touch the stuff." "What stuff?" asks James. "None of your business," responds Alice. The children are in the kitchen as she continues to sweep.

12:45 P.M.
Still sweeping the kitchen floor, Alice acts annoyed as she tells the children to "move." The children go into the living room. She tells them it's time to put their coats on. She picks Nicholas up and takes him to the bathroom to diaper him. He protests loudly. Alice asks, "Carrie, did you shut the bedroom door?" I answer "yes," as Carrie can't hear her; she's in the living room.

Alice dresses Nicholas. James asks for his hat. Alice says, "OK, one moment." Nicholas begins to jump up and down at the prospect of going out. James and Carrie are getting their coats on. Just as Alice gets one shoe on, Carrie asks for her "school socks." The three of them are standing in the pantry. Alice takes off her own shoes before going into the house and rushes off to get them. She then remembers to restart the washer. Finally, we get off, but it is 1:00 P.M. or so. Alice comments to me about always being late.

On our way to Carrie's day-care center, once again Alice and I are involved in conversation. However, this time there is more commotion in the back seat. Nicholas finds some gum on the floor and chews it. Alice insists he take it out of his mouth. Carrie pulls James's hat off; James complains and Alice yells at Carrie. Nicholas complains of a runny nose. At the day-care center Carrie is dropped off and I am introduced as Alice's observer. Nicholas and James become involved with the toys near the door and James is reluctant to leave them. Alice has to urge him on. On the way to the car, James dallies over a penned animal outside, and Alice admonishes him to hurry.

We then drive to the bank. Alice has to cash a check to get James's new clothes out of layaway. She remembers that the cleaner is nearby and that she forgot to bring Richard's uniform along. She tells me she used to iron all his shirts but no longer does. During the wait for the drive-in teller at the bank, she tells me about her upcoming trip to see her sister and about her differences with Richard regarding the spending of money.

After the bank business is completed we drive to a local shopping center where she has put a deposit on some clothes for James at a children's clothing store. She also has to buy a birthday present for the little girl whose party is tomorrow. She alternately contemplates a sunsuit and a terry coverall and searches for the boys, who are enjoying making Mother look for them. The racks are all at adult height, so the little ones are easily lost to view. She tells me that James has begun to pick out his own clothes and seems very proud of this adultlike behavior. Alice is concerned with Nicholas's hiding, as he has been known to walk out of stores. In fact, at one point she has to restrain him from marching blithely out of the store. James and Nicholas have discovered the children's books (at child level) and are looking at them, pulling the books off the display. They are sitting on the floor near the cash register where Alice is picking up the clothing items. She reprimands them once, but then, involved in her conversation with me and the cashier, soon forgets them. They continue their activity. When it is time to leave Alice notices that the books are all pulled out, and she asks them to put them back. James does pretty well; Nicholas tries, but the task requires more coordination than he is capable of. Alice soon helps them. James discovers some more toys but Alice insists that they go. Nicholas starts to fuss, as he doesn't want to leave, and Alice picks him up and carries him out the door. I carry her package.

She then heads for a treat shop near the clothing store. She deposits Nicholas on the counter; James wants to get up too. She obliges him and orders a "Coke to go." James gets interested in a cookie being sold on the counter, but Alice reminds him that he is getting a Coke. When the Coke arrives Alice loosens her hold on Nicholas in order to get at her change. He begins to wiggle around on the counter. She grabs onto him again.

In the car Alice asks for some Coke and James passes her the cup. During the ride back, the boys become cranky and start to complain and whimper. Alice suggests that they wave out the back window, which works for a brief time. Nicholas spills Coke on himself, whimpers, and I give him a napkin. James insists he can't see out of his eyes, and Alice playfully goes along with it. The boys bicker about the middle space behind the front seat, and Alice gets annoyed, admonishing them roughly to both vacate the space as she can't see and could get into an accident. To humor James, Alice asks him to make a face for her—a mad face, a sad face. He teases her by making his monkey face, and she laughs. Nicholas is still cranky. Alice assures him they'll be home soon. Nicholas whimpers and falls asleep on the back seat.

2:25 P.M.

Alice carries Nicholas into the house and puts him to sleep in the bedroom. She then unwraps James's package in the kitchen. They look at his new clothes and admire them. However, James is a little out of sorts and Alice says, "I don't understand you today. Do you have to go to the bathroom?" She says it's time for sleep soon. She shows him the pants he has chosen that have zippers and buckles that make noise. (They remind me of the paraphernalia Richard has on his uniform.) It's quiet and Alice seems peaceful.

2:30 P.M.

James retrieves his blanket and lies down on the kitchen floor at Alice's feet. James says something that Alice doesn't understand. Patiently, she asks him about it. They have some exchanges about it. Alice explains about the birthday present and birthday party. James wonders why they don't go over to his friend's today and Alice explains. Alice spanks James playfully. Slightly concerned, James asks about its meaning, and Alice explains that it's a "love pat." Alice goes into the bathroom followed by James. Alice says she has to go downstairs to put Richard's pants in the dryer. James complains that it'll take too long. Alice sighs audibly and, sounding exasperated, says, "It won't." She goes into the basement, returns with some dry laundry, and goes down to make another trip. James asks when she will be finished, and Alice tells him to be good, that she has just one more trip. When she comes up again, James announces that he was "good," and Alice says, "That's good." James is lying on the floor with his blanket. Alice says to James, "Time to go. Let's go, James." James resists physically. Alice picks him up and he starts to cry. He's obviously tired. Alice says, "Sshh, quiet. Dad's asleep. I'll go with you." They disappear into the bedroom for their naps. All is quiet except for the sound of the dryer.

2:35 P.M.

I sit down on the sofa to write notes and soon fall asleep myself. At 3:00 P.M. the telephone rings and I answer it. A detective is calling for Richard. He needs an accident report Richard wrote up that is misplaced. He needs to be called by 5:00 P.M.

3:50 P.M.

Richard wakes up first and comes out of the bedroom. I tell him about the telephone call. He nonverbally communicates disgust about it and proceeds to return the call, explaining where he thinks the report is. The telephone call is short. Alice gets up and Richard tells her his class starts in half an hour. Alice says, "Oh, I'm sorry," and asks him if he wants a sandwich. He doesn't. (Her apology suggests that they see it as her responsibility to wake him up.)

4:00 P.M.

Alice and Richard chat with me. Richard is concerned about getting his chores done, and he makes a sarcastic comment that "Alice will do the chores." She gives him a dirty look. He responds half kiddingly and with some implicit hostility, "But you like those eggs and bacon." Alice responds, "You're baiting me, but I won't respond," and continues with the ironing she is doing. Richard does not give up and makes some comment about her vacation plans, to which she doesn't respond. Alice then asks if we want ice cream and prepares ice cream for us. This ice cream is expensive, but she explains to me it is her favorite kind. Richard comments with lightly veiled hostility about the cost of the ice cream.

4:30 P.M.

The three of us are chatting at the kitchen table. The children are still asleep during most of this time. We talk about religion—Richard has a friend who is a born-again Christian and Richard is interested in his conversion. He also talks about his anger at the police department—he feels the men on the beat are doing the detectives' work but don't get credit for it. He reports he is beginning to feel quite fed up with the whole thing. Alice is folding laundry while we chat.

James comes into the kitchen with his blanket and seats himself in Alice's lap. He is still sleepy. When she gets up to see Richard out by going to the back door with him, he whimpers. Alice says, "One minute." James becomes quiet and lies with his blanket near the kitchen window. Alice comes back to the table and James sits in her lap again, playing with some plastic toy sunglasses. Alice and I discuss religion and her desire to protect herself from having another child.

5:10 P.M.

Carrie arrives home. She was brought home from the day-care center by one of the workers there whose husband is also on the police force.

Alice warns James not to break the glasses he is playing with. Alice says to James, "We have something to show Carrie," and James opens his box to show Carrie his new clothes. Carrie then tells Alice she wants to look at *her* clothes (bought some time ago). Alice opens her box and both admire them. Carrie asks to try them on and Alice agrees; in fact, Alice acts very pleased with these purchases. James also asks to try on his clothes, and Alice tells him, "OK, as long as you take them off." Alice then asks James to bring her his new shirts so that she can take the pins out. "These?" he asks. "Yes." He brings her the shirts from the box and she takes out the pins.

156

Introducing the Bernards: A Day in their Lives

Meanwhile, Carrie has gone into her bedroom and changes into her new swimming suit. She comes into the kitchen and Alice admires it. Carrie is pleased and smiles. Alice asks Carrie if she likes it; Carrie indicates that she does.

5:15 P.M.

James asks Alice for help in putting on his new clothes and she helps him. He asks her a question about his new clothes and she answers him in a friendly manner. She puts his new shirt on; he wants it to jingle and wants the pins to remain in. Alice says no. Alice then admires his new clothes and suggests he stand up on the toilet in the bathroom and look at himself in the mirror; he leaves for the bathroom. She admires him again when he comes back. Carrie tries on a shirt. James wants to know where his new pants are. Alice says she will get them. James asks for "keys" for his new pants. Alice says, "Daddy will get them." Nicholas can be heard crying—he is up. James informs Alice, and he and Carrie go with Alice into the bedroom to fetch Nicholas. Alice carries Nicholas back into the kitchen and sets him on her lap. James asks further about the keys, and Alice patiently explains that she doesn't have any, but that Father might. When James asks about them again, Alice begins to lose patience and answers him in an irritated way. Carrie puts on clean tights and Alice says that she can't. Carrie resists Alice's instructions. Carrie wants to stay in her shirt and James wants to keep his new pants on. Alice wants them to take off their new clothes, but they resist. Alice explains why she wants them to undress; James argues and resists. Alice sighs loudly; she is losing patience. James tries to get into her lap, unsuccessfully, as Nicholas is already there. Carrie finally changes her clothes.

The telephone rings. Alice answers it, carrying Nicholas. James hovers near her while Carrie goes into the living room and turns on the television set. James gets his blanket and, still in his shorts, begins to watch television.

The telephone call was from the head of the department where Richard works. He wants to talk to Richard. Alice is very worried now, as this is the first time he has ever called. She thinks Richard will be upset; she obviously is.

5:30 P.M.

In the meantime, Nicholas has gone into the living room and hurt his head. Carrie announces it loudly for Alice's benefit, and Alice goes into the living room and picks him up. She tells Carrie to pick up her clothes, which are in a pile on the living room floor, and to hang them up. Carrie follows her to the kitchen, whimpering. Nicholas sits on Alice's lap. He tries to talk to her but Alice indicates gently that she doesn't understand him. She calls out to James in the living-room area. He comes into the kitchen, and she tells him he has to take off his new clothes. He cries and lies down on the floor. Alice tries to persuade him gently. When this doesn't work, she becomes more forceful. She sends Nicholas in to watch television and warns James that *she'll* cry if he doesn't listen to her. She then tries to undress James who forcefully hangs on to the clothes she is trying to remove. Being stronger, Alice is successful in undressing him. James insists he wants his shorts. Alice explains that it is not summer, but that he can wear them in the summer. James is very unhappy and cries. Alice comforts him and tells him he can hold his shorts. This solution does not satisfy James, who insists he wants to wear them. Alice says, "Sorry, you only can hold it." Again, a battle ensues between Alice, who insists that he hold the shorts, and James, who wants to wear them. James is very petulant and whiney; Alice is forceful and annoyed. She dresses him in his overalls and he goes into the living room.

The telephone books James uses to sit at the kitchen table are on the floor and Alice picks them up. The children are in the living room watching television, sitting with their blankets. James and Carrie are on the sofa; Nicholas is on the floor. Alice folds up their new clothes.

5:45 P.M.

It is quiet, as the children are absorbed in the television program. Alice tells me she is worried about the telephone call and begins to pace in the kitchen. Carrie comes in for her medicine. Alice tells her to get the spoon. James comes in and watches Carrie receive her medicine. Alice asks Carrie about a friend at the day-care center, and they chat briefly about this person.

Alice goes into the bedroom with the new clothes and puts them away. Carrie goes into the living room. James follows Alice into the bedroom and then Carrie follows them. Alice is in the doorway between the living room and the bedroom; Carrie and James stand nearby and the television program catches their attention. When Alice starts to move toward the kitchen, James runs ahead of her.

The telephone rings and James runs to it. Alice answers it; it is for Richard. Nicholas whimpers while Carrie runs into the kitchen and James runs into the living room. Again, the call is from Richard's superiors. Alice is very worried now; these telephone calls are very unusual—he's never been called at home by such "high-ups."

Alice begins making dinner, which consists of breaded pork chops. The boys are in the living room. Carrie goes to the bathroom and then to the sink where Alice is working. Carrie tells Alice about her day. James comes into the kitchen to the sink where Alice is, and as he does so Carrie approaches me (I am sitting near the doorway between living room and kitchen). James begins to "ride" the vacuum cleaner. Carrie follows Alice around the kitchen, while she prepares dinner. Alice asks Carrie, "What do you want?" and Carrie asks something that I cannot hear. Alice responds, "Yeah." Carrie goes into the living room and James soon follows. Carrie is about to turn off the set when Alice says, "Nicholas is watching TV; you don't have to turn it off." She sounds worried and preoccupied. Carrie brings a stool in from the play area to sit next to me.

Introducing the Bernards: A Day in their Lives

Alice is getting increasingly worried about the telephone calls and tries to call Richard's classroom but can't reach him—there is no answer. Nicholas is hanging on to her leg as she makes the telephone call. James joins Carrie on the stool next to me, talking to me about why I am writing. I read my notes back to them. Alice picks Nicholas up and asks Carrie to turn off the television set, which she does. To Nicholas she says, "Don't push me, Nicholas!" Alice is worrying out loud about Richard and the telephone calls. She asks James and Carrie to put their stools back in the play area, as "they don't belong [here]." She seems anxious and worried. She warns James not to drag the stool as he starts to maneuver it out of the kitchen. James asks, "Why doesn't it belong here?" and Alice answers, "Because I said so." The stools are replaced, and Carrie and James return to the kitchen.

6:00 P.M.

Alice puts the plastic sunglasses on Nicholas, playfully, and he whimpers and complains that they hurt. Alice kisses his hand and Nicholas still whimpers. He shows Alice his hand and she examines it, more for his benefit then for serious medical purposes. Meanwhile, James and Carrie are playing with the clothing boxes on the kitchen table. Alice says she might want to use the boxes in the future and tells Carrie to put away the adhesive tape. James sits on Alice's lap and asks her about his clothes. Carrie tries to make herself comfortable on my chair next to me. Nicholas drags in the two stools from the play area and Alice admonishes him, telling him they belong in the play area. Nicholas whimpers in protest, and Alice and James go with Nicholas to return them to the play area. Alice and James return to the kitchen, and Nicholas returns with the stools. When Alice insists he put them away he protests, and Alice threatens to get "Dad's strap." Distressed, he cries out, "No!" and proceeds to replace the stools. He returns and approaches Alice, who then thanks him. Alice is restless and tells me she is worried about the telephone calls. She is standing near the back window. She recalls a past incident when some police officers were fired from the department; she feels the department doesn't support them enough. Clearly, she is worried about the possibility of Richard's losing his job. The children also are active and seem restless. James attempts to climb on the vacuum cleaner as Alice tries to put it away. Carrie starts to climb the rungs of my chair and Alice tells her to get off.

Carrie goes to the table and plays with the clothes box, pretending it's a cookie box. The boys are nearby and there is a little struggle. Alice tells Carrie that if she's pretending, she has to share. She also tells her to keep the box on the table. James and Carrie then drag the boxes onto the floor. Alice says she needs those boxes and takes them away. Carrie asks why she needs them. "For work," is the answer. Nicholas drags a box out of the cupboard, and Alice tells him to put it away. James tips back a chair and Alice reprimands him. Alice seems nervous.

Alice tries to reach Richard at school again. Carrie and James stand near the telephone and then begin to play near it. James starts yelling playfully, and Nicholas bangs on the window, near the telephone. Alice asks James to be quiet. He asks, "Why, is someone sleeping?" Again Carrie tries to sit next to me on my chair. She tells Alice that James is spitting. Alice reprimands James, who continues. Carrie "spanks" James, and Alice reprimands Carrie, sending her to her corner, but she doesn't go and says something in protest. "What?" insists Alice, and Carrie quickly says, "I'm sorry." James plays with the telephone cord; Carrie and Nicholas are at the kitchen window, giggling and yelling at the cat outside. Again Alice tries to get through to Richard, but she has no luck. Alice sits down at the table and Carrie hugs her, followed by James who also hugs her. Nicholas is still at the window, playfully and happily interacting with the cat. Carrie approaches me and James climbs on the back of Alice's chair. James teases Alice by calling her "Mary Hartman" and then calling her by her maiden name. Alice is amused. Alice comments to James that his nails need cutting. "No!" he protests and starts to yell as he climbs onto the kitchen table.

Alice sends the children to the play area to play "birthday party or barber shop." They run into the area and become loud and excited. Alice tells me that she wishes Richard worked days because he can control them. We hear yelling. Alice reprimands Carrie: "Leave Nicholas alone. Fix the table." Carrie complains that she has to do everything.

6:15 P.M.

Nicholas comes into the kitchen with a book and sits on Alice's lap. James soon follows, with Carrie immediately behind him. Alice says in an exasperated voice, "Can't you find something to amuse yourself?" Nicholas is on Alice's lap and James tries to climb on too. Carrie approaches Alice and then comes over to me. Alice kisses James. Both James and Nicholas are seated on Alice's lap. Carrie hugs me and snuggles up to me. Then she goes to play with a kitchen chair—tipping it backward.

Alice plays with James while Nicholas "reads" a book. They no longer are seated. She asks if they are ready for the party tomorrow. James and Carrie get excited. They surround Alice. Carrie asks if she can bring her toys. Alice tells her she won't need them there. James burps; Alice says, "What do you say?" James denies the burp and blames Nicholas. Alice asks James to bring the listing of television programs to see if there is anything special on television, which he does. Carrie shows off her jumping jacks to Alice, who admires her and asks for the "Carwash" dance, which Carrie then demonstrates. James runs the length of the kitchen and falls down, while Nicholas asks for a Band-Aid. Alice examines his finger and kisses it. She then suggests some music for them to dance by. She turns the radio on; the music is slow.

Alice tells them it's time to clean up and goes into the play area with the children. They begin to whimper in protest as they all go into the play area. Alice begins to organize their activities—trucks here, books there. James

160

protests and becomes preoccupied with a bag. Alice tells Nicholas to hang up something in the bedroom, which he does; he announces his completed task to Alice, who gives him another task. Carrie is standing in the corner with a toy in her mouth. Alice tells James to get the toys that are under the sofa, which he does. He has to move the corner table slightly to do so. Nicholas sits on his stool and rocks back and forth. Carrie picks up books. James puts some toys in his mouth, and Alice insists, "Let's get going. Nicholas, put the puzzle together!" Alice insists that James pick up the game, but he resists and she sternly says, "Now!" James straightens his chair. Carrie brings in some books and straightens the benches. Nicholas hurts his hand, whimpers, and Alice kisses it. Carrie complains that her back hurts; she stops working and turns on the television. Alice tells her to turn it off—they are not finished.

6:30 P.M.

James and Carrie struggle over a drum. Alice sends Nicholas to throw something away, which he does, and then she breaks up the struggle between James and Carrie by telling them to stop and get to work. She sends James to throw something away. Carrie goes into the television area.

Alice goes into the dining area, followed by James and Nicholas. Carrie turns off the television set and also goes into the kitchen. Carrie asks for some music; Alice turns on the radio. She asks James to put his picture away and compliments the picture. She asks Nicholas to put something away on the television set; he does and returns to the kitchen. She picks Nicholas up and hugs and kisses him. James asks for some hugs too. Alice picks him up and hugs and kisses him as well. Meanwhile, Carrie has her blanket and is trying to sit on my chair with me. Alice asks James if he wants to watch a television program. He says no, but Nicholas wanders into the living and turns the set on. Alice also goes into the living room, followed by Carrie and James. The three of them sit on the sofa, and Carrie and James complain that Nicholas, who is sitting on the floor, is "in the way." Alice tells him to move. She tells Carrie not to suck her fingers. I go into the living room to sit on the sofa. Carrie comes and sits down next to me.

It is now quiet. James is next to Alice on the sofa. All the children hold their blankets as they watch television. Alice asks James to turn off the light in the kitchen. At first he protests, but then he complies. Nicholas climbs on Alice's lap, and Alice thanks James when he returns. Carrie snuggles closer to me on the sofa. She reads her book. Alice plays with Nicholas's hair as James and then Nicholas talk about the television show. Alice does not seem to listen. She tries to get James and Nicholas not to suck their thumbs, telling them it will make their teeth stick out. Carrie pushes her teeth back and says that it hurts to do it. Alice and Carrie discuss whether Carrie will be able to walk to school. Alice tells me she's nervous about her children taking buses to school. Alice asks all the children to stop sucking their thumbs, an activity

161

that clearly disturbs her, but they ignore her. She tells James that his being able to play football is contingent on his stopping. Carrie then says that she wants her bed back—the one that James and Nicholas are using to sleep on.

6:45 P.M.

Everyone is raptly involved with television. James and Carrie indicate concern about a child on television who they think is injured. Alice responds vaguely to their query. Again, Alice discusses thumb sucking with Carrie and James, who protest her urgings that they stop. Carrie climbs on the back of the sofa where we are seated. Alice says, "Stop," but when Carrie doesn't comply, Alice ignores her. Again she notices that Carrie is still climbing on the sofa and occasionally admonishes her. Finally, Carrie straightens the sofa pillows and hugs me. Carrie goes over to Alice and plays with her hair, then jumps around in the play area behind the sofa on which Alice is seated. Alice goes into the small bedroom momentarily, followed by James and Nicholas. She returns to her seat on the sofa, followed by James and then Nicholas, who soon goes into the play area. James is snuggled up next to Alice on the sofa. Behind the sofa, Carrie is dancing and singing, while Nicholas plays with a balloon. Alice notes that they might have to eat without Dad. James repeats what she said. Nicholas brings his balloon into the living room, and then returns with it to the play area.

Alice sings to James and tickles him; he's delighted. Carrie is still singing in the play area while Nicholas dances with his football in front of the television. James pokes at Alice who tells him to stop, as he is hurting her. James then notices the insignia sewn onto his pants and demands that she remove it. Good-naturedly, Alice says that she can't. She suggests to James that he sing the "ABC song," but James refuses. Alice prompts him by teasing him, saying that he doesn't know it. He teases back. Finally, when Alice stops asking about the song, James begins to sing it quietly. Carrie is still singing (but not getting attention for it) while Nicholas comes to sit next to Alice and gives her some imaginary cookies, which she accepts and pretends to eat. She suggests to him that he make some more, and he goes into the play area to "make more." Meanwhile, Alice and James are involved in some affectionate play, and then James goes to get some more cookies, saying that he ate them all. Nicholas brings more imaginary cookies. Carrie is playing by herself, singing. Nicholas and James are all over Alice, with Nicholas feeding her pretend cookies. James also pretends to eat and Alice sends Nicholas off to bake some more. James says that he will and rushes off to the play area. This upsets Nicholas, and Alice suggests to James that he make some ice cream.

James is the first to notice the lights of Richard's car and announces excitedly, "Dad's home!" Alice jumps up and turns the television set off—she also was anxious to have him home. The children become agitated in the play area—playing aggressively and then becoming quiet. Carrie asks me if it's "OK to hide for Dad." I tell her it's up to her. Alice has gone to the door to tell Richard about the telephone calls he received from work. James is running around in a circle in the play area. Carrie goes into the kitchen, followed by James and then Nicholas. James rushes back to tell me, "Daddy's home!" There is excitement in the kitchen as Richard tells them he brought some applesauce. He gets on the telephone immediately to return the calls. He instructs the children loudly, "Quiet!! I'm on the phone."

7:05 P.M.

(I also get caught up in the excitement of the homecoming and forget to note the time.) Alice sends Carrie and James into the play area to play. Richard teases Carrie when she passes through the archway by putting his foot out. He giggles as she encounters the obstacle. They love his teasing and are excited. In the play area James and Carrie are yelling and playing noisily. Alice shushes them, as she is trying to listen to the telephone call. Nicholas is being quiet in the kitchen. From the play area we hear James protesting something with loud whimpering; Alice comes to the door and hushes him. James comes to the archway between kitchen and living room, where the telephone is, with a toy. Carrie comes to me, asks me to read my notes, and then kisses me. The children commence excited activity. Carrie starts banging on blocks, and Richard firmly sends her into the play area.

The telephone call is short, and Alice and Richard briefly discuss it. Richard prepares to go out to feed the animals. James says, "Good-bye, see you later," and Richard kids him in return. Nicholas repeats, "Good-bye." Before he goes, Alice asks Richard about getting a key for James. (Does she want to keep him there a bit longer?) She tells him about the new clothes and brings out James's clothes. Richard admires them. James takes his overalls off and puts on his new shorts. Richard is playing with and teasing Carrie. Nicholas talks about a key, but no one is attending to him. Finally, Nicholas comes up to Richard and asks about a key. James shows him the place where he needs the key on his new pants. Carrie also asks for a key, but Richard says there is just one key for James. Alice has gotten some keys from the other room and all the children hover around Alice and Richard as they discuss which key they can spare. Richard shows James a key and helps him put it on his pants. For some reason James is not satisfied and whimpers. Alice says to James that she doesn't understand what the problem is as he said he wanted a key, and she removes his key. Richard tells her he's not hungry as he had a sandwich at school.

7:15 P.M.

Alice sets the table, while Richard is in the back pantry. She asks James whether he asked his father if he likes the clothes they bought. James rushes off to the pantry to ask him. Richard says that he does. Richard comes in and asks Alice when his supervisor called. I look it up in my notes and tell him.

163

Carrie and Nicholas are sitting at the kitchen table now—they are discussing "Daddy's place." James takes off his new clothes. Alice and Richard are near the sink, discussing the sandwich Richard ate at school. Alice then helps James with his shirt and admires it. She asks Richard if Carrie has shown her new clothes to him. Hearing this, Carrie rushes off to get her new swimsuit and shows it to Richard, who admires it. Alice and Richard briefly discuss the purchase of the suit. Then Carrie rushes back toward the bedroom in excitement. James asks that his clothes be put on—he's in his underwear. Nicholas is whimpering at the kitchen table; Alice asks him if he's hungry, but he indicates that he's not. He's unhappy about something. Alice suggests to Carrie, who is back, that she show me her jewelry, which she does. James then shows me his new key. Richard is heating up water for his animals in the back pantry. Alice turns on the radio. Carrie gives me a present—a cutout picture of an animal. Richard says he's not hungry and tells Alice that he's going outside. Meanwhile, Carrie and James have gone into the play area. Alice calls them into the kitchen to eat. They are seated when Carrie announces, "We're missing someone!" She smiles and looks around knowingly. She did not hear Richard say he was going out. Alice answers, "He's not hungry." The boys then specifically ask about Daddy—if he's eating with them. Alice tells them he ate. Carrie also asks about me; I tell her I've eaten. (I had eaten a sandwich earlier, while observing.) Nicholas gets off his chair and asks for a napkin. Alice is serving food and shushes the children; she seems tired. The children, however, are still full of energy and are talking all at once. Alice says, "Let's say grace," and they repeat grace with her.

As they begin to eat, it becomes quieter. Alice worries to me that her anxiety about Richard's telephone call is being "let out" on the children. Carrie asks for some ketchup. Alice tells her that she's annoyed that Carrie puts ketchup on the food, but she gets up and provides Carrie and James with some ketchup. Somehow, Carrie hurts herself and gets food all over herself. Alice is annoyed at Carrie, who protests that she didn't do anything. Alice tells her sharply to get her pants off and wash her hands. The boys are quiet and Alice is very serious as she asks Carrie how her plate tipped over. Carrie offers some explanation. Alice asks Carrie if she wiped her hands (she did—in the bathroom), and Alice gives her a rag to "wipe up the floor," which she does.

7:30 P.M.

Nicholas shakes his head back and forth playfully; Alice tells him to stop. He asks for more applesauce, but Alice tells him to finish his meat. James and Nicholas talk to Carrie. James whimpers and Alice tells the children to finish eating or "no dessert." Carrie asks if it's a "surprise," and Alice tells her to pull her chair in properly.

Introducing the Bernards: A Day in their Lives

Throughout the meal, Alice is urging the children on. She repeatedly reminds Nicholas and James to eat their peas. Carrie tries to identify singers on the radio and Alice helps, seeming pleased. Nicholas repeats words that he hears Carrie say. Alice gets exasperated with James. He climbs off his chair and the telephone book falls off. To Carrie, Alice says, "Sit straight; eat with your mouth closed." This seems more a response to James's than to Carrie's behavior. Alice insists that Nicholas eat a pea. He does and she praises him. James has gone into the bathroom. He emerges with his bottom bare and Alice pulls up his pants. (He came to her with an implicit expectation.) Alice tells him to sit down and to turn off the bathroom light. She tells Carrie to finish her dinner. Nicholas shows Alice his plate and she tells him to finish some more peas. She urges Carrie and Nicholas to eat. Carrie dallies over her food.

Richard had gone outside. At the back door he asks Alice for his keys. She gets up to look for them, gives them to him, and he goes out the kitchen door. She sits down and urges James on with his dinner or "you can forget about the special dessert." Carrie asks, "How special?" and Nicholas asks if they are cookies. Alices tells them it's ice cream. Nicholas stands up in his chair. Alice angrily snaps her fingers at him: "Get down, or no dessert!"

7:45 P.M.

Alice urges James to clean off his plate, and she carries hers to the sink. She has cleared off her own place. Nicholas stands up in his chair; Alice does not notice, as she is momentarily in the pantry. Nicholas calls to her. Richard comes in and asks if anyone else has called. Alice indicates that no one has. Carrie and James talk to me briefly. Alice tries to feed James, while Nicholas stands up again. Again, she threatens him with no dessert. She then gets out the ice cream purchased that afternoon and brings them all bowls of ice cream. James and Nicholas comment about the ice cream. Carrie asks for a napkin and Alice tells her there's one next to James.

Richard comes into the kitchen, and Alice asks him if he wants any ice cream—he does. Richard teases Alice by saying that Alice will tell Laura, her friend, that Alice talked to the police chief. Alice agrees and tells me that this will impress her friend even though she thinks it is silly. When Richard walks into the kitchen, the children initiate a guessing game with him. Richard asks where James's pants are and James explains. Alice is at the sink with the dishes, while Richard sits down at the kitchen table to eat his ice cream.

Alice and Richard discuss how many eggs Richard is selling and to whom. It is quiet as the parents talk. Then Richard and Alice discuss the telephone calls; Richard indicates that it is nothing to be concerned about. James complains about the peanuts in his Rocky Road ice cream, and Carrie says she will eat them. Alice turns out the light in the sink area and enters the dinette. She asks Richard if he will sleep before work; he says he will. Alice

165

and Richard discuss whether to bathe the children. Richard asks her to leave him some hot water, as he might want to wash before he goes to work.

8:00 P.M.

Richard is still at the table with the children, and he plays "patty cake" with Nicholas. Alice wipes James's face, then Carrie's, and then Nicholas's. James and Carrie get up from their places. Carrie comes over to where I am sitting, followed by James and then Nicholas. Carrie shows me her new outfit. Richard asks Carrie to put on her robe. When she puts on her dress instead, Richard insists that she put her robe on, which she does.

Alice comments out loud that James's nails need cutting. She sits down with him on the floor and cuts a few nails, while he whimpers. She threatens to bite his nails instead. Richard says teasingly, "If we cut off your fingers, we won't have to cut your nails." Nicholas goes into the living room and turns on the television set. Richard wipes the kitchen table. Alice then begins to cut Carrie's nails. There is a slight accident and Carrie cries. Richard asks if Carrie had her fingers in her mouth today. Alice says, "She made a mistake and wants another chance." This comment seems designed for Carrie's benefit. Carrie comes over to me. All the children surround me while Richard and Alice discuss the telephone call further. Richard asks the children if the toy area is clean. All agree that it is. Richard tells James to pick up a small toy and tells Nicholas to pick up his shoes. Richard vacuums in the kitchen. The children ask me what my notes say. Carrie kisses me repeatedly. Richard asks Alice how much money is left and Alice tells him.

Alice has taken out the present she bought for tomorrow's birthday party. She starts to wrap it and all the children surround her, wanting to help. She tells them they can watch. As Richard walks by to go into the living room, Nicholas playfully lunges at his legs, and Richard picks him up and carries him into the bedroom. They are playing tag, for Nicholas runs laughing back into the kitchen, chased by Richard who also is laughing. Alice is getting irritated as the children insist on helping her with the wrapping. Alice persuades them to get some toys to wrap. Richard is in the pantry, getting ready to go out again. James and Carrie rush out to the play area and return with some small toys. Alice gives them small pieces of wrapping paper to wrap their toys in. She does not do this with any great enthusiasm; her goal seems to be to get the children out of her hair. Richard comes back into the kitchen briefly, in preparation for going out again. Alice also gives the children some tape and they work at the wrappings—Nicholas at the table, James and Carrie on the floor. James starts to complain because his paper is too small for the toys. (The paper is becoming smaller as he works with it.) Alice tells him she can't give him a bigger piece and suggests that he wrap one toy instead of two. He accepts this advice and proceeds. James gets up, and Nicholas, who seems to feel that his territory has been invaded, begins to whimper in protest. Alice admonishes Nicholas. She seems to be getting

166

progressively more irritated. Carrie stands up to get some of the Scotch tape Alice has put around the table for her own use. She admonishes Carrie for not asking for the tape. She gives all the children some more tape and announces that she is not willing to give out more. Alice becomes annoyed at Carrie, who is told to "stay cool" when she puts up a minor protest. It appears to me that Alice herself is beginning to get hot under the collar and is fighting her own irritation.

8:20 P.M.

James hears Richard enter the back door and rushes to tell him that it's Pam's (their little friend's) birthday party. In the pantry, James and Richard have some conversation about this coming event. Alice finishes wrapping the present. Nicholas wants a piece of paper, and Alice tells him that she needs to use it. She asks if he's ready to brush his teeth; he says no but goes into the bathroom. James comes into the kitchen from the pantry and announces that he was talking to his dad and his dad's "in." From the bathroom, Alice calls James to brush his teeth. She also admires his wrapping effort, which he shows her as he goes to the bathroom door. He comes out of the bathroom with his toothbrush, and Alice calls him back and tells him to brush hard. Carrie goes into the bathroom also. She has been quietly wrapping during this time. Alice comes out of the bathroom, goes to the refrigerator, and sighs audibly. Richard asks her when she and the children will be leaving tomorrow, and she tells him. At the bathroom door, Nicholas complains loudly about James. Alice comes to the rescue while James goes to his father who checks his teeth ("Let me see your teeth") and tells James to wipe his mouth. Carrie is back on the floor again, wrapping her toys. Alice has gotten a bottle from the refrigerator and asks, "Who wants "Pepsi water'?" (Water is kept in a large Pepsi bottle in the refrigerator.) Nicholas drinks some while James visits with his father in the pantry. Richard tells him to go to the bathroom before bed. Carrie approaches Alice for some water. James takes his father's advice and goes into the bathroom, coming out shortly thereafter—bare-bottomed—to announce, "I can't." Alice tells him to go talk to his dad "real fast" and then to go to bed. To the going to bed, he says, "No!" Yet he gladly rushes to talk to his father, who is in the pantry.

Nicholas runs away from his mother—asserting himself about not wanting to get ready for bed. She turns it into a game. He laughs with pleasure. While they play briefly, Carrie is wrapping and James is still talking with his father. Alice captures Nicholas, who alternately laughs and whimpers as Alice tries to get him ready for bed. He is on the floor. He whimpers as she tries to change his clothing, so she tickles him. When this tactic does not work to distract him, she threatens to cry herself. He laughs at this; she tickles him and plays with him, trying to distract him so she can get him undressed and diapered for bed. But still he protests. She jokes; he laughs, giggles, and protests his pajamas. Alice tries again to tickle and distract him.

Carrie complains to Alice that she is unable to wrap the little toy chest. Alice, still working with Nicholas, suggests she get something smaller.

8:30 P.M.

In the bathroom Alice begins to work on removing Nicholas's diaper; he fusses and then quiets down. Richard and James are still conversing quietly in the pantry where Richard is polishing his shoes and belt. Alice gets up from the bathroom floor to throw away the diaper and Nicholas calls her. Carrie asks for my help in tying her package and then shows her success to Alice, who responds lukewarmly with "very nice." She then shows her accomplishment to Richard, who admires it briefly. James leaves the pantry and approaches Alice, followed by Carrie. Meanwhile Alice has congratulated Nicholas for his success on the potty and tells him to tell his father. He rushes over to the pantry and announces proudly, "Stinky!" "Good boy," responds Richard. Alice works on preparing Carrie for bed, while both boys visit with their father in the pantry, where he is still polishing his shoes and belt for work. Carrie brings her nightgown into the kitchen.

Alice retrieves James from the pantry; he protests. She warns, "You won't go to Pam's party!" He begins talking about the party as Alice undresses him further and sends him for pajamas and clean underpants. Alice puts pajamas on Carrie, and James comes back without clean underwear. Alice admonishes him about this, while he insists his pants are clean. At this, she laughs and goes with him to get his underwear and pajamas. When she returns, she asks Carrie to hang up her "dress-up things" and then gives each of the children a piece of ribbon, with which they seem pleased. James goes to see his father in the pantry, shows him his ribbon, and comes back to say that "Dad wants a ribbon." Alice yawns and begins to pick up the variety of toys and wrappings on the kitchen floor.

Meanwhile, the children are all with their father in the back pantry. Alice announces that she will read a story. They all emerge from the back and go into the play area to select a story for reading. Richard comes into the kitchen now, carrying his polished belt and holster. Alice is on the sofa reading them a story, to which they respond and about which they talk.

8:45 P.M.

Alice tells them to "come in to kiss Daddy good night." They do so and also kiss Alice. Carrie also kisses me good night. They go into the bedroom. Carrie goes to sleep on the large bed.

Alice begins to iron some blouses. Richard is at the sink washing some eggs and putting them in cartons. It suddenly becomes very quiet. I can hear the children in the bedroom whispering and talking to each other.

9:00 P.M.

There is crying in the bedroom. James comes out and Alice yells at him to go back. Richard and Alice and I sit down at the table and talk. The children can be heard talking. Once again, James emerges and Alice asks Richard for a stern word for them. Richard gets up from the kitchen table and sends James sternly back to bed. Next, Nicholas comes into the kitchen and asks for cookies. Richard sends him back. James comes into the kitchen and asks for a particular game. Richard sends him back. Nicholas emerges again. Alice and Richard sternly say, "Good night," and Richard stands up threateningly.

Richard returns to putting away his eggs. James comes in and asks for tape. Alice says, "We'll talk about it tomorrow," in a no-nonsense voice. Nicholas emerges from the bedroom. It appears that Richard has had enough. He marches into the bedroom, and I hear a stern warning and then children's cries and commotion. "Get in bed," we hear Richard warn. Soon, however, James comes out for a Kleenex. During this time Alice has been ironing her blouses.

9:30 P.M.

Richard decides to go to sleep. If Alice goes to sleep, Richard might oversleep, so she plans to stay up. She tells me she feels guilty about having him go off to work while everyone is sleeping, because he doesn't like to go. Richard asks her to wake him before 11:00. James calls for his father, and Richard goes into the bedroom.

Alice and I talk until 11:00, when she wakes Richard up. She tells me that if I were not there she would have worked on her needlework. Richard gets up. He's very groggy and unhappy-looking. He gets dressed. Alice sees him to the door. His partner has come to pick him up for work.

11:30 P.M.

Richard leaves, and Alice, looking tired, begins to prepare for bed. I leave.

Commentary

Figure 7-2 gives an overview of where family members were in relation to each other during the Base Day. It is useful to put this day in the context of other days in the Bernard household. Richard might have stayed up until 10:00 A.M. and eaten breakfast with the children. If he had something to do on the farm and it was a sunny day, he might have stayed up until 2:00 P.M. to work outside. Alternatively, he may have gone to court for much of the day and returned home in the late afternoon in order to sleep before going off to work again. He is especially tired in the days following a court appearance, which may occur several times a month. If he had not gone to class he could have eaten dinner with the family before taking his nap. The weather, the incidence of court days, and how tired he feels seem to determine how much Richard sleeps during the day. According to Alice, for her the day was typical.

Figure 7-2. Time Available for Family Contact during Base Day

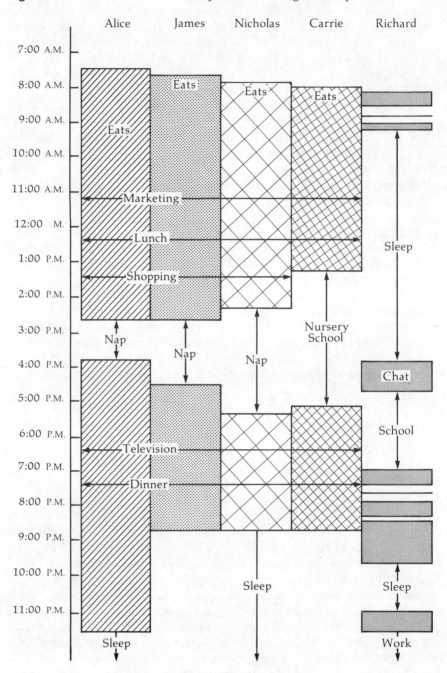

CHAPTER 8

Richard Bernard, "Righteous Warrior"

More than any other research participant, Richard Bernard chose work that was personally meaningful. For him, becoming a soldier and then a police officer can be understood in the context of his personal history and, in particular, his relationship with his father. In Chapter 6, I suggested that the process of acquiring a work identity may be connected with the visibility of parental work roles and how they are talked about. Whereas Richard was vague about what his father did for a living, his father's military experience was discussed with interest, pride, and affection.

> RB: What I always remember is that he used to play a . . . band marching thing, and being kids, we used to get up and march to it. I can stilll remember it. I can't tell you what song it was, and I've heard the thing about three or four times in my lifetime since then, and I can just nearly stand up like a kid and march around. And then he had a book in his library about the division he was in, and it showed different campaigns over Japan and it would really show, it would show dead bodies and stuff like this and I got it in my mind that that's what you've got to do to be a man. . . . I guess my dad just kind of built it up unconsciously. Like we were in the Cub Scouts, we were in the Boy Scouts. . . . Dad works for these things for the military, how can it be that bad?

Richard joined the army during the Vietnam War partly to gain the respect of his father. "I guess I had to be my father's son," he commented about his enlistment. As a soldier he would make up for his father's disappointment in his not being a conscientious student.

Joining the police academy also was a "feather in [his] father's cap." Richard connected an experience he had during late adolescence—when work identity begins to crystallize—with his choice of a career in law enforcement. On a camping trip, he was stopped by state troopers.

RB: Here these guys were straight and narrow as could be; their uniforms were spotless; they were courteous; they stopped by; they took time to talk to us and this is what I wanted to be.

It would not be too far-fetched to suppose that the state troopers represented to Richard both his ideal self and the idealized internal image of his father, whom he wanted to be like and be close to.[1] The police uniform symbolized goodness, strength, masculinity, and power. As an observer on patrol with Richard, I experienced some of the power associated with the uniform and saw both the respect and the fear it inspired. This is reflected in the stimulation Alice reported upon seeing Richard in uniform.

AB: There's something very attractive about a man in a uniform, be it military or what, and I found it very pleasing to see him looking very sharp, very neat, and going off like this—what?—the Roman gladiator or something, going off to fight the war, big and strong and brave, and I think that's what got the women all hyped.... There is something very exciting, I think, about the righteous warrior, something very good.

The job of police officer met Richard's need for order, structure, and the conviction that he was working for the forces of good. Power and strength on the side of goodness were a powerful combination for both Richard and Alice. The priesthood also appealed to Richard, for it represented the other side of the coin: as a priest he would have saved souls; as a policeman he could protect the innocent while punishing wrongdoers. In being a "righteous warrior" he could live according to his ideals.[2]

Changes: Becoming a Police Officer
In Carleton City, the process of socialization into police work was intense. Rookies were put on the afternoon shift to give them experience. As a result, their social networks changed. Soon Richard and Alice found that their friends were primarily policemen and their wives. A number of police families lived on their street. The police world became all-encompassing. Richard took his training seriously. He described himself as a "hard charger" for whom right and wrong became clearly delineated; to him "there's no gray area in between."[3] This intense

1. From his experience as a psychiatrist and consultant to police, Symonds (1970) has noted that policemen have preserved an attitude of awe and respect toward authority, bypassing the stage of adolescent rebellion. In his view, joining the police force represents an unconscious wish for approval by a father they would have liked to have had.

2. In their study of one hundred patrolmen, Kroes, Margolis, and Hurrell (1974) encountered the image of the "white knight" crime fighter. Symonds (1970) also has noted the idealism of young police officers.

3. Reiser has termed this development the "John Wayne syndrome." He wrote: "The symptoms of this malady are cynicism, over-seriousness, emotional withdrawal and cold-

socialization and the immersion in the experience of power began to carry over into the home setting. In his individual interview, Richard described the process:

> RB: At work, because you carry that badge and that gun, you tell somebody to do something and nine times out of ten they're going to do it. . . . So when you come home, you say that you want steak today instead of hamburgers. The steak's in the freezer and the hamburger's already thawed, you know. [*Laughs*]

This interpersonal style was congruent with his view of how his own father had behaved. Alice also described the new isomorphism between Richard's interactions at work and processes within the family.

> R: What did you argue about?
>
> AB: Oh, it was basically his attitude. Basically, the way he was treating me and the children. . . . Rather roughly—he didn't take time to listen. He didn't want to even take time to try to understand. . . . Question-and-answer sessions were like the third degree. . . . Things almost became very businesslike. . . . There wasn't very much affection or whatever. He became very cold.
>
> R: He hadn't been like that?
>
> AB: Oh, no. . . . I've just thought of a word to describe his behavior. It's just really hard. It's just hard towards anything. Things didn't affect him. I mean, bloodied bodies didn't bother him at one point. At first they did, but he reached a point where it was just, "ah."

We can imagine that Alice and the children felt like the citizens Richard interrogated at work—angry and intimidated.

Since police work was so close to Richard's identity, the separation of role and self did not take place in these early phases of his career. However, now he attempts, with "training," not to bring his work life home, for "divorces among law enforcement people are just so high. That's why I have a tendency to do my job at work, and when I come home, it's me—it's not the patrolman that comes home, it's Richard." In other words, like other research participants, Richard now tries consciously to separate work from family life in an attempt to protect the family system from the tension created by the carry-over of interpersonal style.[4]

Richard's world view also underwent changes, for he had contact

---

ness, authoritarian attitudes, and the development of tunnel vision. This is a nonocular condition in which there are only good guys and bad guys and situations and values become dichotomized into all or nothing" (1974, p. 158).

4. In further commenting about the "John Wayne syndrome," Reiser (1974) noted that the police officer may become emotionally cool to his wife, with the consequence that she feels alienated. However, after several years the policeman gradually "loosens up" and rediscovers his family.

with people under the most adverse conditions—when they were in trouble or when they were suspected of a crime.[5] Richard described himself as becoming less "open-minded": "I wasn't supposed to do any thinking, and for a long time, that's the way it happened." Alice described the changes she saw in him:

> AB: He became much more cynical, cynical of everything. He didn't trust. He lost all of his, really lost all of his faith in people in general. He almost expected people to prove themselves to him. Like you better show me that you're a good person, you know. . . . He's pretty much changed back to what he was before. I mean he'll never be the same person, but the traits that I liked about him are surfacing again, just because there isn't the pressure in this particular area . . . because he's in a nice little community and the vicious things don't occur with regularity. . . . It's not like he's meeting the bar owner who's been "B and E'd" [i.e., breaking and entering]. He's just meeting people just because they're there and not because—just because he's run into them on the street, not because he had to take a report from them under an adverse situation.

Seeing people at their worst colored Richard's attitude toward people in general. In our discussion about the way his work affects his outlook, Richard pointed out a crucial difference between us: whereas I will find a rotten apple in a barrel and assume I simply found one rotten apple, he will assume that the entire barrel is bad. As we talked it became clear that as a police officer he is safer believing the worst of people. Trust can be dangerous. As we shall see, this vigilance is still an issue for him.

The Glory That Came and Went.   For the first two or three years of law enforcement work, Richard imagined that he would be quite content remaining with the Carleton City Police Department for the rest of his life. Eventually, he thought, he might even become a captain; certainly, he would put in his twenty-five years of service and retire with a comfortable pension. Alice, too, had "great expectations" about this job. However, changes in the political and public climate caused him to become disillusioned and angered. For Richard, the ultimate validation of his efforts comes from seeing the person he apprehends brought to trial and convicted. The trial is a form of clear feedback about his performance—it ensures that the fight for good against evil is won on at least one front. If he has handled his investigation well, then he will obtain a conviction. Richard perceived the new "liberalism" in the court system as undermining his efforts:

5. As a police officer on patrol, Richard must deal most frequently with offenses classified as "street crimes." As Eisenberg (1975) has observed, such crimes do not involve white-collar criminals. Thus, those with whom Richard came into contact in the course of his work were mostly the poor and uneducated.

RB: Four or five years ago when you caught somebody breaking into a man's car, you knew that this guy was going away. Right now, today, if you catch this guy breaking into a car, you can try your hardest, do the best you can, advise him of all his rights, follow everything up in the most professional way you know how, and the guy is still going to be walking around the streets before you're done with him. . . . You think you did the right thing and the next thing you know you go in front of a judge and he says, "We've reviewed your case from a month ago. We've had a month to study it, and we've decided you did the wrong thing."

Such a change had many meanings for Richard. It meant that he could no longer help the victims of malfeasance, for criminals were set free. This state of affairs violated his sense of the basic order of the world. Richard never questioned himself—he was an impassioned crusader with a sense of mission. To see his mission undermined made him bitter and angry.

R: You used to get angry about it?

RB: Oh, I'd see things that happened right in front of my face and go to the judge, try to get a warrant or something and he'd come up with the goofiest things about why he couldn't grant you a warrant or give you a conviction on the case.

R: How did you express your anger?

RB: Oh, I kept expressing to myself that I wanted to get out of the job. I kept saying, "Well, it's not for me. I tried it and it's not for me." Well, here I am five years later, still with it.

The function of the system, of course, is not only to protect the community from lawbreakers, but also to protect individual citizens from misuse of the power of the state. Richard, as an individual, only saw his work being unrecognized and wrongdoers going unpunished. "Lenient" courts have been noted by a number of workers in the field as stressful to police officers (Eisenberg 1975; Kroes et al. 1974).

Not only did the judges set free those whom Richard apprehended, but he felt that the general public also disdained him. The first inkling he had of the public view was when he entered the police academy.

RB: Even when I worked for the employer where I worked before and I was thinking about getting into law enforcement, I lost a lot of friends that way. . . . They just didn't want to be seen with me. It was the unpopular thing to do—being associated with governmental agencies or people that want to branch off in that field. That was the first hurt that I felt as far as this career.

Another "hurt" Richard experienced was being called "the 'Man' or . . . all the other things that they call him." A warrior needs public validation of his deeds, of his service to mankind. Perhaps Richard's feeling of utter disappointment is best expressed in his comment, "I was so proud about this thing that I thought I was doing this for mankind, but mankind just kind of sat back and said, 'What are you doing?'" Like Henry Johnson, Richard was in a difficult "boundary position." Community relations has been mentioned as a major stressor for police officers (Eisenberg 1975; Kroes et al. 1974; Symonds 1970). Not being understood and appreciated was an experience Richard was familiar with, for when he returned from Vietnam he saw the public turn its back on those who believed they had fought for their country. In part, the deep cynicism that Alice described stemmed from this blow to his passionate commitment to police work.

Breaking Out. Richard began to look for solutions to his discontent. In Chapter 3, interorganizational mobility was mentioned as a possible solution to job stress. For most research participants, changing job assignments by moving to another work organization was not a real alternative. They were locked into their jobs by years of seniority and the lack of other alternatives. The Bernards, on the other hand, experienced benefits and high pay as a potential "trap."

> AB: It's like you're a rat in a trap, and you're just scratching to get out, and they start giving you more benefits, and you feel more compelled to stay, and you get this false sense of security and, really, what is security? It's none of that. I mean really. We thought we were secure. Do you believe that? Look at that. We thought we were really secure. We had a home. We had good schools that we knew we'd be able to send the children to, and good hositalization, insurance, and all this kind of bull. I mean when you don't even feel safe driving down the expressway, that's not secure, but you're beguiled almost. It's like the mermaid luring you in and you're just trapping yourself. It's horrible.

Unlike most other participants, Richard had little seniority in the police department, and he also had a marketable skill. Therefore, he did not feel locked into his position, and he was not yet prepared to resign himself to giving up his sense of purpose and accepting the new liberalism. His solution was to apply for a job in Centerville, where I came to know the Bernards. Centerville, Richard believed, was still immune to the liberal elements that he perceived as eroding his efforts. Still, the decision to move was not made lightly. In his family of origin, stability and "settled living" were highly valued. Someone who moved from job to job was considered a "bum." His uncles and grandfather had worked at one job for their entire lives; as the oldest son, he was supposed to uphold the tradition of respectability and serve as a model for his younger brothers. A job move threatened him with a loss of status in his family. Still, countervailing forces encouraged the Bernards to make a move to the Centerville area. They saw their neighborhood in the city deteriorating, and they worried about their children's safety. When they finally moved to his new job, Richard accepted a 30 percent pay cut. The search for a solution to job discontent created yet other stresses for the Bernards, for they had not foreseen the financial pressure such a salary decrease would entail. They have not yet recovered from this financial setback, and Richard, as we have seen, is obliged to take on extra jobs to support his family.

New Hopes, New Disappointments

In Centerville, Richard suffered new disappointments; not only was he not safe from the liberal element, but his new job had its own sources of stress. Autonomy and a sense of personal responsibility are job characteristics that most participants mentioned as being important, and they are features of police work that Richard particularly values. However, with the institution of new rules designed to protect the work organization from citizen complaints, Richard felt his autonomy eroded. Rather than leave the disposition of an incident up to the discretion of the individual officer, new rules required that he make a report on every incident. Richard experienced this requirement as a challenge to his judgment and as a devaluation of him.

The theme of being insufficiently valued also arose in his comment that he was treated like a rookie again when he made the move to the Centerville Police Department. As Richard put it, "When I came out here, I started at the bottom again, which was kind of a sore point for me and my feelings. Here I came from a larger city which gives you so much more experience and you start out right from the bottom no matter where." Work organizations often use monetary compensation as an implicit statement about a person's value to the system. Caplan et al. (1975) have cited "inequity of pay" as a job stressor. By starting at the "bottom," Richard's several years of experience are unrecognized, undervalued, and even negated, for suggestions he makes for improving the job go unheeded. In hierarchical work organizations, change comes from the top rather than the bottom; Jesse Jones and Chuck Simpson also felt that their ideas were discounted. To Richard, fellow police officers are significant others. When they dismiss his knowledge and experience they are dismissing him. His solution to the hurt and anger this situation generates is to render them less significant—they are simply foolish and rigid.[6] However, this devaluation of the work organization has its price, for it makes it more difficult for Richard to develop pride in his association with it.

6. Commenting on the idealism and loyalty of police officers, Symonds noted, "Even the men who express cynical feelings about the department seem like rejected suitors" (1970, p. 158).

The "Wonder Workers." Inadequate resources to do one's assigned job can also be a source of stress (Kahn et al. 1964). While he thinks of himself as a knowledgeable professional, Richard also feels that he is required to solve problems for which he has no training.

> RB: I think that they expect too much out of me. A policeman nowadays is supposed to be a marriage counselor, a lawyer; we're supposed to be a who-did-it, a jack-of-all-trades. More often, I'm put into situations where I can't handle it. A lot of times, I'm having troubles enough with just me and my wife getting along, then for me to go to some guy yelling at his wife, and they're fighting in front of us, and telling them how to get their marriage problems taken care of. . . . Like we're supposed to be wonder workers. If somebody hits your car during the night and nobody saw it and if there wasn't any damage, enough damage done to his car so that you could identify it, such as maybe hitting a green car, and there was green paint on his red car, something to link these two cars together, or we get an eyewitness there. . . . We'll tell them that we'll put out an all-points bulletin and all this other stuff.

As a front-line worker he represents the police department to the public. Like Henry Johnson, he is supposed to make the customer happy without the resources to do so. His solution is either to pretend to solve problems or to avoid them. "Don't care if they have an accident three miles down the road, just get them past your area." As did other participants, we see Richard learning not to care as a way of managing stress. But in not caring, Richard Bernard is giving up the possibility of realizing his ideal self through his vocation.

Job Insecurity and Powerlessness. When I interviewed him initially, Richard's dissatisfactions with his work were not fully acknowledged. As the research progressed they came closer to articulation. With the gratification Richard derived from his work decreasing, so his dissatisfaction with "hygiene factors" (Herzberg & Hamlin 1964) increased. ("Hygiene factors" include variables such as pay and working conditions that are extrinsic to the work activity itself.) I have described his anger over inadequate pay and lost seniority. Of greater concern to Richard at present is his sense of insecurity about his future. "Job future ambiguity" is a source of job-related stress that refers to "the amount of certainty the person has about his job security and career security in the future" (Caplan et al. 1975, p. 45).

Richard's first taste of powerlessness and the ensuing insecurity came when he was threatened with a layoff after his first few months on the Centerville police force. He then found himself transferred—suddenly and without warning—to another station. If they could transfer him suddenly, then he could be sure of nothing, and his feeling of having a secure place was shaken. As a mere patrolman, he is at the bottom of the organizational hierarchy. Such powerlessness contrasts with the deference with which he was treated by citizens during the night I observed. No one overtly questioned his power and authority; everyone was polite and even fearful. The public power he has highlights his powerlessness in the work organization.

Future job ambiguity also stems from Richard's perception of how the organization rewards officers for their hard work. He feels, as do some of the other officers I heard talk, that movement upward in the system depends on political favoritism. This theme also was repeated in the interviews with those who worked in large corporate organizations. When a new police chief was appointed, Richard saw some officers reduced in rank while others were promoted. He concluded that he might work hard to be promoted, only to be demoted to "dogcatcher" with a new administration. Rewards are capricious. Such ambiguity about his future emerged as a central concern during the research period.

Managing Job Stress

How workers manage job-related stress is central to understanding the nature of the psychological relationship between work and family life. Richard is angry, hurt, and disappointed because he feels undervalued and unsupported by the court system and insufficiently appreciated by the public. Sometimes he is convinced that he is a man out of place and time: an earlier century might have been more appropriate for him. One of the ways in which Richard is trying to manage these strains is through the process of disengagement, described in Chapter 5.

> RB: I understand that beating my head against the wall isn't going to solve anything. . . . I have gotten out of the front-row seat and drifted back a little.
>
> R: What do you mean by that?
>
> RB: Well, before, I was a hard charger. Either it's right or wrong; there's no two ways about it. But that's working in the city. . . . Well, now it's—I don't get worked up about things. If I feel I have a good case, I'll try to pursue it, and if I lose it, I lose it.
>
> R: You accept defeat?
>
> RB: Right. Different things make the world go round. It just doesn't revolve around my personal interests anymore.

I have suggested that the process of disengagement occurs over time. In Richard's case, the progression is particularly evident. When he began police work, he cared about it intensely; to him it was more than a job—it was a vocation that expressed his vision of himself and the world as it should be. Disengaging on a daily basis began as a way of managing

179

the threat to his marriage stemming from the carry-over of his interpersonal style into the family system. At first he attempted to deal with his increasing disappointment with the court system and with the public's attitude by looking for an alternative job situation. But this solution failed him, for he encountered yet other difficulties in his move to Centerville, including job insecurity and inadequate pay. When he experienced his powerlessness, the process of disengagement began in earnest, for he did not want to beat his "head against the wall." Feeling angry and frustrated was simply self-defeating, and like other participants, he did not want to endure the pain.

During the six-months of data collection, I watched Richard struggle with his anger and sadness about the loss of his vocation, for learning not to care meant that Richard had to give up his dream of being a "righteous warrior." He commented that others view this process as accepting reality, but Richard is not sure that this is a reality he wants to live with, for giving up his commitment to personal meaning in his work is a deep loss. But more and more, Richard is considering police work as an instrumental activity—a way of making a living—and, like other participants, he has come to subscribe to the idea that, for him, work and personal life are separate.

Managing Anger

The painful and unhappy process of disengagement is bolstered by other coping mechanisms. Some of the hurt and anger Richard feels is expressed in the workplace itself. For example, after he was abruptly transferred, he expressed his outrage through a work slowdown, making only a minimal effort. Such passive-aggressive tactics are used when we feel we must protect ourselves from the wrath of those at whom we are angry. To declare anger against supervisors openly would have resulted in dismissal, and Richard's dependency on his job would not permit it. Other participants also had silent ways of expressing anger at work that had to be carefully hidden.

I observed a more communal form of ventilating anger and hurt during the forty-five minute period when officers in three patrol cars stopped to talk to one another (see entry for 1:40 A.M., Chapter 7). Through this activity, they asserted their autonomy from "supervision"; however, this independence and power was illusory, for one patrol car occasionally called in a false position in order to appear busy. During this forty-five minute period, almost all interaction consisted of joking and ribbing. Joking is a very complex form of communication. Meissner (1976) has suggested that joking at the workplace allows for the impersonal expression of deep hurts and injuries, while emphasizing solidarity of circumstances in what is experienced as a no-exit situation. Direct expressions of personal pain would be threatening in Richard's police world. There, masculinity in its traditional form is highly valued, as evident in the gratuitous remarks about homosexuals made by the police officers I observed. Richard likened a partner to a mate, for he spends more time with his patrol partners than with Alice. To such close associates, open displays of painful feelings would be especially threatening. Joking offers a communal and acceptable expression of anger and hurt.[7] However, joking itself reveals the officers' powerlessness in that it serves simply to ventilate feelings, while the organizational sources of stress remain unchanged.

Some of the joking I heard was barbed and was aimed at each other. It seemed to prevent the outbreak of open conflict, for one could always feign humor. But mostly it concerned their supervisors and those moving up in the organizational hierarchy. The content of the jokes reflected some of the feelings Richard had spoken of. Those who were moving up in the hierarchy were described as "brown-nosers" and were uniformly disdained. In fact, suspected "ass lickers" were held in contempt by many of those I interviewed. This contempt was mixed with their own despair about not being able to progress within the work organization without abdicating their scruples about such activity. Richard told me that a civil-service procedure for advancement would be welcomed by the officers. Moreover, the aspersions on the competence and knowledge of their supervisors reminded me of Richard's feeling that his own knowledge and competence were ignored and undervalued.

Richard's Farm

In Chapter 3 I suggested that some people may try to manage job-related stress by creating psychological and physical space for themselves. For most participants, such space was carved out of the family's home environment. Richard Bernard's space surrounds the family home, for his "haven" is his farm and, to a lesser extent, the small pantry off the kitchen where he cleans his eggs and prepares his animals' food. It was his farm that he referred to when he talked about relaxing after work and getting "away from it."

> RB: When I leave, I don't want to talk about shop. I want to talk about milking cows or feeding pigs or something. I give enough to my work when I'm at work. When I work, I try to do my best when I'm there. And it's not the fact that they don't pay me to do more; it's just that when I'm away I would just like to relax and get away from it.

The Bernards rented the small farm approximately at the time that Richard was again disappointed by his paid work and realized how

---

7. Lewis (1973) and Reiser (1974) have suggested that the intense *esprit de corps* helps defend against the stress of danger in their work. Reiser added that internal organizational strife may threaten the camaraderie. A change in administration may have intensified the griping I observed and the officers' psychological balance. The theme of danger in police work is discussed in Chapter 9.

insecure he was within the police department. Perhaps farming, even on a small scale, served as an alternate activity that he could throw himself into. Farming also had personal meanings for Richard, for he remembered running free on his grandfather's farm and also recalled the warmth and friendliness shown him as a teenager by a farmer who gave him a drink of water while he was on a hunting trip. The importance of farming to him is underscored by his taking me to see the surrounding farmland on our way to the shopping center during the night I observed his work activity. He also gains satisfaction from providing his family with fresh eggs and meat that is uncontaminated by chemicals. At one time, he dreamed of farming as an alternative to police work, for he had not yet given up his search for meaning in work. We might infer that he replaced one dream with another. This dream can never be realized, for the capital investment required to buy a farm is beyond the Bernards' means.

Richard's farming also allows him to relieve job strains, decreasing their carry-over into the inner life of the family. I have described Richard as a man of action rather than words. Physical exertion is a preferred mode of managing feelings. For example:

RB: Well, my routine now is that I'll come home, and I'll get busy on my chores right away. So I just blow off the whole thing. . . .

R: Blow it off?

RB: Right. Well, I've got a friendly steer out there who thinks he's a puppy. He jumps all over you. Here he is six, eight hundred pounds and I'm constantly knocking him around and he's pushing me. Well, this may sound strange, but we'll wrestle. I do it mostly in the shed because I know Alice would be mad about it. . . . And I carry things. During the winter months, it's laborious because I have to carry the good water from up here and take it down there in buckets, and they drink quite a bit of water a day, so that's constantly carrying buckets and slowly burning myself out.

Not only can he work off frustration, but the farm provides him with a place away from people, who are always a potential threat and toward whom he maintains a constant vigilance. He is not sure why he feels "peaceful" when he looks over the fields, but we can imagine that the "mob" he feels is after him no longer exists there. He "could spend hours" looking out over the land, he remarked. The psychological space that farm work provides him may be as therapeutic as the physical exertion such work entails.

Conclusion

I have described Richard Bernard as a man with a lost vocation. He has been disappointed in his work and over time has begun the slow and painful process of putting distance between himself and his work role. As other research indicates, the stresses he experiences are not dissimilar to those felt by other police officers. But Richard has not entirely given up the search for personal meaning through work. At the end of the research period he was considering what other jobs he might like to have and how he might improve his satisfaction with the Centerville job. Moreover, it is evident that Richard feels his work still has much to recommend it in comparison to other jobs he might obtain. He enjoys the autonomy, the variety, and the opportunity it offers to think and use his judgment. Despite his deep disappointment with his job, he still derives more satisfaction from his work than many other research participants. His anger stems partly from the fact that police work still holds meaning for him.

In Chapter 9 the interfaces between Richard's work and the family's psychosocial life will be discussed. Final consideration of these relationships, however, must await the examination of Alice Bernard as household worker.

Interfaces: Paid Work and Family Life

In Part II, I suggested that the barriers created by time and space can affect the patterns of intimacy family members establish among themselves. I also suggested that the space the wage earner makes for himself can affect his availability to the family system. In the Bernard family, Richard's farm activity, the number of hours he works, and the fact that he works the midnight shift all contribute to family members' difficulties in regulating desired distances among themselves. Figure 7-2 shows the amount of time Richard spent at home on the Base Day. Not including time spent sleeping and outside on the farm, he was physically present for approximately two hours. In his interview, Richard commented that he would like to spend more time with his family, a wish often repeated by other participants.

Like other participant families, Alice and the children do not visit Richard at work. Although Alice says she can reach him easily, like other participants she will call him only for what she considers to be emergencies. During the Base Day (see 5:45 P.M.), she tried to call Richard at his class but was unable to reach him. Unlike the situation of the Turner family, the time Richard spends at work is time lost to the family. Space serves as a barrier to contact. Alice expressed great curiosity about my observations of Richard's work, for I represented a bridge between her world and his.

The Structural Interface: Selling Time

Including his part-time job at the shopping center and the class he attends once a week, Richard works about fifty hours a week outside the home. In working these additional hours he is not unique. As reported in Chapter 2, one study found that during one month in 1975 30 percent

184

of men between the ages of 20 and 54 worked forty-one hours per week or more at their principal job, excluding travel time (Hedges 1976). With rising inflation such increases in working hours may become more common.

Like other participants, Richard feels locked into the occupational structure. While he would love to farm, his responsibilities to his family make that impossible. In Chapter 4, I described how the birth of children can lock a worker into his job. Richard is explicit in stating that the responsibilities of a family, especially three young children, prevent him from attempting to realize his particular dream. Sometimes he imagines what his life would be like if he were single. His fantasy takes him into a northern wilderness, living a life of austerity and simplicity. Not only dreams but concrete alternatives also have become limited for him. Before Carrie was born, Richard sometimes stayed home from his job in a department store, feeling he could afford such holidays. He no longer has that luxury and, instead, works two extra jobs to support the family. Still, the Bernards feel financially pressured. In introducing them, I noted that most of their overt conflicts were related to how money is to be spent. The most explicit conflict I witnessed between them during the home observation occurred around the use of scarce financial resources (see Base Day, 4:00 P.M.). Richard's jokes about Alice's vacation and about her favorite ice cream were chastisements fot the way she spends money.

Richard's underlying resentment about being bound into the occupational structure occasionally is expressed toward Alice. For example, he does not like to use an alarm clock, so that on the Base Day, Alice stayed up late in order to wake him up for work. Since he resents going to work, he wants her to share some of his discomfort. On one occasion he "tested" her to see if she would wake him on time and a lengthy argument ensued. Alice understands that Richard may resent the pressure to provide. She thinks that men have a more difficult time than women because men have "fewer outs." A man cannot simply stop working, she noted, and it is a "hassle going to work day in day out for thirty years." Alice accepts the displacement of his anger. She apologized for forgetting to wake him up in time for class, indicating that she also sees this as her responsibility (see Base Day, 3:50 P.M.). When I asked her why she had apologized, she answered that she feels guilty that he has to go to school, that is, to work. Whereas the wife of a professional might feel envious of her husband's gratifying work, Alice feels guilty knowing that Richard is working to support the family at a dangerous job that he is disenchanted with. Consequently, she thinks she is better off than he because, after all, she does not "work" and the family needs his wages. Similarly, Paula Doyle reported feeling guilty about being able to sleep late on Saturday when Tom had to go to work.

In these undercurrents of resentment and guilt, family members personalize structural constraints placed on them because they must sell time. We are rarely taught to look at social structure and its effect on our lives. Anger and resentment search for outlets, and sometimes a wife is a willing scapegoat. Yet we sense that while she cannot express her anger directly, there is an unspoken hostility for being the object of his resentment. Twice during the research period, Alice smiled as she commented that she had forgotten to take Richard's uniform to the cleaner. Passive aggression, again, is a technique sometimes used when people are fearful of expressing their anger directly. We shall see that, for a variety of reasons, Alice is reluctant to express anger toward her husband directly.

The dependency on Richard's job that the Bernards feel is evident in the panic that struck Alice when she received several telephone calls from Richard's place of work during the observed day (see Base Day, 5:45 P.M.). She was frightened because it was extremely unusual to receive telephone calls from work and even more so to be called by the police chief. "I have a constant fear that he'll get fired," she commented, and she recalled an incident in which citizens' complaints had resulted in the dismissal of several officers in the department.[1]

Personal Time and Space

In Chapter 5, I suggested that a worker's leisure activities can have implications for the whole family. Insofar as the farm is Richard's personal hobby, which provides the personal space he needs to help him manage strain, the time he spends in solitary activity on the farm takes away from time spent with his family. For example, on the Base Day approximately one-third of the time Richard spent awake and in and around the house was spent on his farm. While he was outside, he was essentially physically unavailable to the family. The pantry is on the margin between outside and inside; farm-related activity there makes Richard marginally available. The children tended not to approach him in the pantry when he was doing farm chores, for he moved in and out of the house quickly, making sustained contact impossible. In contrast, we see that when he was polishing his shoes and holster—a sustained activity—the children eagerly approached him (see Base Day, 8:20 P.M.). Unlike a hobby that can be left at will, the farm makes concrete and daily demands on Richard, for the animals are dependent on him for food and water. In this sense, the farm also is work in that it helps to provide the family with fresh food.

---

1. Reiser (1974) has mentioned the police officer's "double jeopardy." Not only is he criminally and civilly liable for his misdeeds, but he also faces departmental punishment. Richard experiences the necessity of making quick decisions as stressful because of the possibility of disciplinary measures against him, a stressor also noted by Eisenberg (1975).

Interfaces: Paid Work and Family Life

The farm has different meanings for the family at different seasons of the year. During the cold months the animals require increased care, and Richard spends even more time tending to their needs. Moreover, during the winter the children cannot easily be outside with him. In contrast to the home observation made on the Base Day, when snow was still on the ground, the following observational data were gathered on a warm day.

"On the Farm" (April 11)

Alice is in the kitchen sorting laundry. The children are outside playing. Alice *hears one of the children asking for their father.*[2] She knocks on the window for their attention. "He'll be out soon." Alice goes into the bedroom. I hear Richard waking up and getting dressed. Alice comes back to the kitchen and goes outside briefly. I hear her scold *Carrie, who asks, "Where's Daddy?"* "He's getting dressed now," Alice tells her.

Richard looks sleepy as he goes into the bathroom. Alice begins putting the clean clothes into the bedroom. James comes to the back door; Alice hears him, and goes out to the porch. He asks for help with his clothing. Richard comes out of the bathroom and goes to the back door of the kitchen, leading to the porch. James, who is still at the back door, comments to his father about his football, while Richard sleepily begins to prepare for his chores. Nicholas, too, comes to the door. Richard is still yawning. Finally, Richard greets Nicholas. James says, "Come with me, Dad." "In a minute," Richard answers.

The boys now come onto the porch where Richard is removing feed from the freezer for his animals. James asks whether the food is for the cows, and Richard tells him it is. James then tells me that pigs bite. Nicholas picks up a bucket and Richard tells him to "put it down." Carrie arrives at the porch and Richard asks her, "Who brought you home [from the day-care center]?" "Mommy," she replies. James plays with the animal feed. The children are standing around the bucket Richard is filling. "James, don't!" Richard warns him against playing with the feed. Meanwhile, Carrie picks up the cat and shows her to me.

Richard goes outside into the yard to lace up his boots, and the children follow. Nicholas begins to play with the buckets next to Richard, while James plays on the lawn chair. Nicholas then interests himself in the cat, picks it up, and pulls its fur. Richard asks Nicholas, "How come your face is dirty?" Carrie explains that they had ice cream for dessert. Richard walks to the side of the house with his bucket and places it on the ground. *Nicholas follows with an enormous bucket that he can hardly walk with and places it next to Richard's.* James plays with the hose while Carrie plays with the cat. With Nicholas beside him, Richard stands at the side of the house for some time, waiting for the bucket to fill with water, and then returns to the porch area. He looks out over the field. Then James and Richard walk hand in hand to the side where the bucket is filling. Nicholas follows them, and Richard suggests to James that he carry Nicholas's bucket, as Nicholas is struggling with it. Richard fills his bucket while James carries the empty bucket around. All the children follow their father into the barn to feed the cows, with James dragging the empty bucket behind

2. For the reader's reference, themes to be discussed are set in italics.

him. Richard walks slowly, either because he is tired or because it makes it easier for the children to keep up with him.

In the barn Richard opens up the back door and tells me to watch as the cows come running. They do, and he begins to feed them their hay. The children are all around him, watching happily. He strokes the nose of his dairy cow and James and Nicholas do too. The hog comes up to try to get some food and Richard kicks him away. James is very interested in the idea that this pig is dangerous and mean and comments to Richard about it. Richard responds that it is mean and that it can eat him, warning him to "be careful." James backs away cautiously. Richard comes back into the barn to prepare the feed for the calves, which he proudly shows me. Nicholas indicates he wants to see too, and Richard lifts him onto a pile of bricks so that he can see them. James and Carrie are playing in the hay. Again, Richard goes out back and all the children follow him. Richard asks Carrie, "What does a red sky mean?" Carrie gives some sort of an answer and he laughs. He tells me it should be "sailor's delight."

Richard is still tired as he does his chores, but we see here that the children have an opportunity to make contact with him, to imitate him, and to engage him. Seasons, therefore, are an important dimension of the structural interface for the Bernard family. In some families, summers may mean less time with fathers who are engaged in solitary leisure activities.

The Marital Duet: Time for Intimacy

Being with Richard is important to Alice, and she professes some "twinges of resentment" over their lack of contact. In considering this aspect of their marital relationship, we need to think both about what does occur between them and about what does not. On the Base Day, approximately forty-five uncoded and coded interactions were observed between Richard and Alice. Moreover, they did not spend any extended period of time simply being with each other. In contrast, Alice nostalgically recalled the time when she was pregnant with Carrie. Richard was excited about being with the Carleton City Police Department, and he and his partner would drop by at lunchtime to joke and cheer her up.

In Chapter 5, I suggested that husbands and wives may find themselves in different "worlds," knowing little of each other's life experiences. It is precisely this development that Alice fears. She is concerned that when the children are grown, she and Richard will have very few common experiences and interests, a phenomenon she has seen in her own parents' relationship and does not want to repeat. Finding time to be together, she thinks, is a particular problem for "lower-middle-class families who have to hustle to make a buck."

The timing of Richard's work shift also makes Alice's attempts to become closer to him difficult. In the evenings he is either at his part-time job or catching extra sleep before he goes off to work. Thus, they lack quiet evening hours together after the children are in bed. Another time period that couples may have together is the time before retiring. I would suspect that the bedtime chat is not uncommon; Alice reported that this time is particularly important to her. She feels comforted and "close" just lying next to Richard. It is not simply quantity of time together that is at issue but quality and meaning. The midnight shift also limits their opportunities for socializing and going out together. Furthermore, their differing daily work experiences also result in different needs regarding how they spend the time they do have together. As we shall see in the discussion of Alice's work experiences, she feels trapped in the house with small children and wants to "go out." Richard, on the other hand, prefers to remain aloof from people toward whom he feels constantly vigilant. Alice experiences her dissatisfaction with the companionship features of their marital relationship in what she calls a "periodic discontent."

Alice is unhappy with Richard's midnight shift in part because it interferes with her ability to be as close to him as she would like. Yet, as we shall see, Richard himself has ambivalent feelings about the night shift because it is more interesting than day work and because he has more autonomy then. We see here a conflict between the ways in which Richard tries to enhance his job satisfaction—thereby minimizing his disgruntlement—and the needs of other family members. This theme emerges again in regard to Richard's farm activities. The scarcity of time Richard has at home places Alice in direct competition with the farm for his time and energy. Since his paid work is essential to their survival, it is from his farm that Alice tries to steal time. During the Base Day, I wondered whether Alice was trying to keep Richard from going outside to do his chores when she suggested that the children show him their new clothes (see 7:05 P.M.). She responded to this suggestion by telling me, "I do this all the time. . . . I use special means like, 'Oh, guess what I cooked for you?' or I tell him his favorite show is on." But the issue of time is not openly discussed. Instead, they participate in veiled negotiations around the allocation of his time and energy, as is evident in the following observational segment.

"Negotiating Time" (April 11)

The family sit down to eat at the kitchen table. Alice and Richard are annoyed at Carrie who is playing with her food. Richard cuts the meat and discusses its texture with Alice. Alice has placed the vegetables on the plates. Richard puts meat on each plate. Grace is said. Alice asks me if I've eaten. I tell her that I have. Richard discusses the car's performance with Alice.

Alice asks Richard if he's planning to sleep tomorrow. Richard asks, "Why?" Alice wants to pick up the baseball bat that Nicholas won at a local drawing. James goes to the bathroom. Richard says, "OK" (in reference to James's going to the bathroom). James wants to close the door but Alice says no. Richard says,

"Just hurry up." Alice urges the children on: "Come on Nicholas, eat. Let's go, James." *Alice asks again about picking up the baseball bat and a wall poster she is interested in. Richard asks about the weather.* Alice answers, "It'll clear up but not until the afternoon." Richard turns on the radio. James returns to the kitchen. Alice says, "I didn't hear the toilet flush." Richard says to James, "Go on, go on," and James goes into the bathroom. I hear the toilet flushing. Richard says, "Wash your hands real fast." Richard says something sternly to Carrie concerning her table manners, as Carrie is playing with her food. Alice quietly tells Carrie to eat, but Carrie complains. Alice threatens her with no dessert. James returns from the bathroom. Richard fixes Nicholas in his chair and then fixes James in his chair. James begins to eat with his hands and Alice tells him, "Pick up your fork! Use your fork!" There is a struggle between Alice and James. James begins to use his fork. "That's right," Alice says. "Don't use your fingers, stick it in your mouth." She tells him twice to eat with his fork.

Richard asks Alice what time the store opens. Alice answers. Alice tells James to "come on." Richard points an admonishing finger at James's plate indicating that he should eat. Alice admonishes Carrie and tells her, "Carrie, put that in your mouth!" *Richard gets up and goes into the pantry for eggs, which he brings to the counter and lays out.* Carrie asks Alice something and Alice responds, "Carrie—just eat." Alice sounds tired. *Richard is going back and forth between the kitchen table and the counter with the eggs.* Alice says to Nicholas, "Eat your carrots!" She warns him, "Do you want to go to bed?" Carrie asks Alice a question. Alice answers her quietly. James talks to Alice. Alice says, "Nicholas, eat." When he does not she says, "OK, no dessert, just Carrie and James." Nicholas whines. Alice responds again, "Ok, eat." When he does not, she warns, "Nicholas won't get any dessert."

Richard returns to the table. Carrie is talking about a child at her day-care center. James tries to interrupt. Richard asks which child Carrie is talking about. Alice answers him. *Richard gets up briefly and then sits down again.* When he does, he says in a friendly tone, "Hi, Nicholas." Alice gets up and tries to feed Nicholas. "Open your mouth," she says. Again she threatens him with no dessert. She tries another tactic: encouraging him. "It's good; Carrie ate hers." When Nicholas again resists, Alice says, "No dessert." Finally, Alice sits down and Nicholas starts to eat. But when she comes over to him again he resists. Richard takes some food from Nicholas's plate and eats it himself. Alice approaches James to feed him. Carrie chats with Richard. Alice tells James, "Come on, hurry up and I'll make ice cream." Nicholas gets excited at that but Alice reminds him, "Not for you!" Richard adds, "Come on, eat" to Nicholas.

Alice gets up for the ice cream. James asks her what flavor and Alice tells him. Carrie asks for a cone, but Alice doesn't have any. Carrie tells Richard, "I got a lot of stars today." Alice notices that James is not eating and says to Richard, "Dad, James will eat if he gets a little help." Richard starts to feed him. Again Richard urges Nicholas, "Come on Nicholas, eat this." Nicholas resists. "OK, no ice cream." [A crying scene ensues because Nicholas is not allowed his dessert.]

In the dinner scene above, we see a series of maneuvers between Richard and Alice that involved them in silent negotiations about how time will be allocated between Richard's sleep time, farm time, and time with Alice and the children. We can see that Richard was carefully considering the allocation of his scarce time and energy. He asked about the weather because if it was going to be sunny and warm, he would have preferred to be up and about rather than asleep. However, nice weather might mean that he would want to work on the farm. Timing considerations also become important because he might be able to accompany Alice and the children to the store immediately after he came home from work.[3] Since time with Richard cannot be stolen from sold time, it must come from either farm time or sleep time. Alice verified this when she returned from her two-week trip to visit her sister and excitedly told me that she and Richard were spending more time together. As we talked about where they found this time, she indicated that it came from sleep time and farm time. It is doubtful that Richard could further decrease the number of hours he sleeps, for even now he complains of insufficient rest. Insofar as the farm helps him cope with work-related strain, time away from there would also take its toll.

What is significant about the above observational segment is the veiled way in which the negotiations were managed. Richard did not give Alice a direct answer, and Alice did not pursue her interest. Yet, if the conflict between Richard and Alice was muted, it was intensified with the children ,and the conflict between Alice and Nicholas escalated. We might suspect that their involvement with the children's mealtime behaviors was a way in which they avoided a direct confrontation between them about the general issue of time together. (We can also understand the conflict around Nicholas's eating as connected to their recent discovery that he is underweight, but this interpretation does not invalidate my original suggestion that this issue was used to divert the conflict from Alice and Richard.) A preoccupation with the children's eating habits diverted their attention and filled the silence left by the unspoken tension in regard to time.

Since Alice has some resentment over Richard's not spending more time with her, the excerpt above suggests that Alice does not express her needs or her anger about this issue directly. Another example further supports this interpretation. On the Base Day, she was waiting anxiously for Richard to return from class. That she was waiting dinner for him is evident in her comment that they might have to eat without him (see 6:45 P.M.). When he finally arrived, he told her that he had eaten a sandwich and was not hungry (see 7:05 P.M.). We can imagine Alice's disappointment, for Richard had not eaten breakfast with her either. Nevertheless, she did not overtly acknowledge her feelings. If we

---

3. Jesse Jones complained that Sandra wanted him to "rip and run" with her in the mornings. The Healys and the Ellisons also described time-synchronization problems.

look at Table 9-1, we also see that Alice does not express anger directly to Richard. Of Alice's initiations toward him, none is Negative. The analysis of "Negotiating Time" also suggests that some of this anger is expressed instead in her relationship with her children. In Table 11-1 we shall see that 43 percent of Alice's initiations toward the children are Negative. The discussion of Alice's work in the home will attempt to clarify these negative interactions further.

Alice stated that Richard's irritability, which she attributes to loss of sleep because of the midnight shift, makes it difficult for her to approach him directly. Most likely, she also fears that open anger will drive him yet further toward the edge of the family system and onto the farm, an interpretation with which she concurred. In "Negotiating Time" we also saw Richard move between kitchen table and counter. Perhaps he used this activity as a way of escaping the escalating tension.

Fathers and Children

In Chapter 6, I suggested that ordinary father absence and daily separations pose special tasks for children. From the Base Day, we can

Table 9-1. Quality of Initiations between Richard and Others as Percentages of Coded Initiations

INITIATION	RICHARD TO ALICE $N = 32$[a]	ALICE TO RICHARD $N = 35$	RICHARD TO CHILDREN $N = 86$	CHILDREN TO RICHARD $N = 71$
Positive				
Base Day	12%	21%	59%	75%
All Days[b]	16	17	45	66
Neutral				
Base Day	71	79	9	7
All Days	72	71	9	8
Negative[c]				
Base Day	6	0	15	7
All Days	6	0	26	8
Influence Mild				
Base Day	12	6	18	14
All Days	6	14	24	20
Influence Strong				
Base Day	0	0	9	0
All Days	0	0	8	0

Note: Percentages total more than 100 because each initiation could be coded in more than one category.
[a]The total initiations coded for All Days.
[b]*All Days* refers to percentages of total initiations coded, including those on the Base Day.
[c]*Negative* includes the category of *Influence Strong*.

192

see that the Bernard children are sensitive to their father's absence. After Richard went to bed without saying good-bye to them, both James and Nicholas inquired about his whereabouts (see Base Day, 9:00 A.M. and 10:30 A.M.). Later the same day, Carrie noticed her father's absence at the dinner table, and the boys also became concerned that he was not eating with them (see Base Day, 7:15 P.M.). Both of these absences were sudden and unexpected, and Richard did not engage in rituals of separation with them.

Richard's departures also can make the children anxious. For example, soon after James asked for his father he began to hover anxiously around his mother, retrieving his blanket from the living room and lying on the kitchen floor at her feet (see Base Day, 9:00 A.M.). In the following informal, uncoded observational segment we again see the children become anxious after Richard leaves.

> "A Separation" (February 3)
> Richard is preparing to leave for his part-time job at the shopping center. He kisses the children good-bye, and, as he is leaving, James gets his blanket and becomes whiney, insisting he wants more buttons, with which he had been playing. As soon as his father leaves, James—seeming quite unhappy now—crawls into his mother's lap, with his blanket still in hand. Meanwhile, Nicholas has momentarily gone into the living room, becomes quickly frustrated, begins to complain, and as he walks into the kitchen with his blanket, bumps his head and starts to cry. When Alice begins to comfort him, she displaces James, who complains. Both boys have their blankets now and become very demanding and whiney. Both try to sit on Alice's lap, and she tries to accommodate them. Meanwhile, Carrie also has retrieved her blanket and is hovering nearby. Finally, she sidles up to me and I place her on my lap. Alice tells me that she is pleased I am staying, as she gets anxious when Richard is out in the evening.

Alice verbalized her anxiety at Richard's absence to me; the children appeared to act it out.[4] We might infer that the children were made anxious by Richard's leaving because they are unsure about where he had gone. Blankets may serve as "transitional objects" for children to help them manage separations (Winnicott 1958), for the blanket represents the absent parent. Clinging to Alice and their blankets can be interpreted as a sign of the children's insecurity about their father's whereabouts. Although they may know that he has gone to "work," such work remains vague and abstract. Their difficulty in concretely imagining him there—that is, seeing him in their "mind's eye"—would make it more difficult for them to ward off the dread that he has simply disappeared.

4. The notion that parental anxiety is communicated to children is implicit in much of the family therapy literature. This empathic induction of anxiety is central to Sullivan's (1953) interpersonal theory. However, he himself could not illuminate this subtle process.

193

Not only are the children sensitive to their father's absence, but their desire for contact with him is evident in their approach behaviors toward him during the Base Day. For example, when Richard came home, the boys followed him into the bedroom while he undressed and then followed him out again (see 8:00 A.M.). Alice told me that this is their usual way of greeting him in the morning—which is to say that this is ritualized behavior (see also Lennard & Lennard 1977). When Richard closed the door to the bathroom, their sudden loss of visual contact with him made them anxious (see 8:15 A.M.). The children also behave as if contact with their father is a special event. When he came home from class (see 7:05 P.M.), his arrival was greeted by excited activity that could hardly be contained. They began to rush about, yell, and run in circles. It was as if they had no other way to express their joy, and Alice's, at his presence. We might also hypothesize that they were expressing some anger at his not coming home sooner in this flurry of excited and aimless activity.

Of the three children, James appeared most concerned with his father's absence. During the time I observed, he consistently was the first child and usually the first family member to notice his father's arrivals (see Base Day, 8:00 A.M., 7:00 P.M., and 8:20 P.M.). He often became joyful and radiant when he saw Richard, even wanting to share his excitement with me (see Base Day, 6:45 P.M.). Of the three children, he most often sought out his father and tried to close the distance between them (see Base Day, 8:00 A.M., 8:15 A.M., 8:20 P.M., and 8:30 P.M.). James's concern with his father's whereabouts is graphically illustrated by the following edited observational segment, which spanned a forty-five-minute period.

"The 'Daddy Duck'" (April 21)

[Richard has just left for his job at the shopping center. He has kissed the children good-bye. Alice and the children are in the living room. She is preparing to read them a story.] Alice settles down on the sofa to read.... James and Carrie sit next to her while she begins to read the Ugly Duckling story. Carrie is totally engrossed; while James is distracted and begins to look at another book. Nicholas is quietly sitting on Alice's lap. He is yawning. Alice reads quickly; the children are quiet. James turns his attention to the story and the pictures in the book. *Suddenly, he looks up at Alice and asks, "Where's the daddy duck?" Alice answers that "he's somewhere swimming around"* and continues to read....

[Alice has prepared the children for bed. They now sit down in the living room to watch "I Love Lucy" on television.] James is playing with his father's belt on the sofa, next to Alice. *As they watch the program, he asks Alice in a worried tone, "Where's the daddy?"* He is responding to a scene where Lucy is engaged in a rivalrous interchange with another woman. Lucy's little boy is with her, as is the other woman's small son. They are using their children in the interchanges between them. No man has yet been seen on the screen, and there has been no mention of a daddy. Alice's somewhat amused reply to James is, *"He's off at work playing the bongos."* This answer seems to satisfy James. . . .

[They are still watching the show. Alice is warning Carrie about the danger of thumb sucking, telling her she might cut the inside of her mouth. Although the conversation is primarily between Alice and Carrie, James expresses concern about these threatened effects of thumb sucking.] James worries out loud to Alice about the dangers of thumb sucking and Alice agrees that, indeed, these things might happen. This discussion occurs while they are still watching the television show. Then, *in reaction to nothing I can see on the screen, James asks, "At work?"* Alice absentmindedly indicates yes. *Then, when Desi finally appears on the screen with Lucy, in a satisfied tone James remarks out loud, "That's her daddy."* [Soon afterward, James plays being his father by telling Carrie that if she does not go to sleep, he will spank her with a belt. The belt he was using to threaten her with was what Alice has referred to as "Daddy's belt."]

Neither Alice nor I could see any obvious reference to a father in either the story or the television show, but James was attuned to precisely this absence. The story and the situation comedy served as projective devices upon which James could express his concern about the person who was missing—the daddy. "Work" became a legitimate place for the television father to be, but James's anxiety about the missing father was not allayed until he actually saw him. His own father's absence was never explicitly discussed during the evening.

Both the television show and the story that triggered James's concern about absent fathers portrayed mothers alone with their children. He, too, was home with his mother. We can better understand James's special sensitivity to this familial constellation by reference to the psychoanalytic theory of psychosocial development and male identification (Freud 1949). According to this theory, because of his close relationship with his mother, a little boy comes to feel threatened by injury and punishment from his powerful father.[5] Consequently, he gives up his mother as an object of his special love and identifies with his father. Because of his stage of psychosocial development, James is becoming attached to and identified with Richard.[6]

In this context we can also understand why James lay on the floor when his father left and why he wanted to be held by his mother. By

5. James's concern with cuts and injuries may reflect this psychosocial stage, for when he saw me with a Band-Aid on my finger, he become so apprehensive that I had to remove it in order to assure him that my finger was intact.

6. Kohlberg, in contrast, has argued that "the boy's preferential attachment to his father as against the mother proceeds from, rather than causes, basic sex-role identity and basic tendencies to imitate the father preferentially" (1969, p. 432). In other words, the attachment stems from the boy's understanding that both he and his father are members of a fixed category of males.

195

becoming a younger child again, he moves back to a time when the oedipal triangle was not yet important. Although this theory of identification is problematic in many ways, it does help us to understand why James would be made particularly anxious by mother–child constellations when the father is absent.[7]

At present, the relationship between Alice and James is densest in that most interactions occur between them (see Table 11-2). We could predict that in the next several years he will move from this relationship toward greater involvement with Richard, whose presence or absence will become even more central to him. Assuming that the Bernards stay at their present location, being able to work with Richard on the farm may become especially important to James, as was Charles Turner's time at work with his father. We would predict that Nicholas will show further tendencies to overtly imitate Richard, tendencies already evident (see "On the Farm"), and that Richard's presence or absence will become increasingly significant to him as well. We also might expect that Richard's absence will contribute to the children's idealization of their father (Bach 1954), as reflected in Carrie's proud comment to me, "We get paid for cleaning up when Daddy's here."

From the hospitalism studies of the 1940s through the maternal-employment literature of the 1960s, there has always been a great deal of attention paid to mother deprivation and absence. But because they are viewed as normal and usual, we have overlooked the normal and daily father absences due to selling time to external work organizations. This issue is an area for further research.

Numbers

Richard's presence or absence also changes the ratio of children to adults in the family system, a numerical relationship to which both Alice and Richard feel sensitive. Richard experiences being alone with the three children as being with a "pack"; he told me he becomes irritable, and it is "easier for [him] to go out of control." During a brief breakfast observation, when James spilled milk on himself Alice commented that if the other children had been awake and present, she would not have reacted so calmly to the incident.

Their subjective experiences of the child-to-adult ratio were confirmed by my own observations. During an evening interview, for

7. Kohlberg (1969) has noted that a psychoanalytic theory of identification cannot account for everyday imitative behaviors in children. He has explained imitation, in part, in terms of effectance motivation. Social learning theorists would explain imitation of the same-sex parent in terms of reinforcement theory. Still, in this case, James's sensitivity to the television show followed by his assuming his father's role vis-à-vis his sister (he will spank her with the belt) seem best accounted for by the psychoanalytic theory of psychosocial development and identification.

example, I noticed that Alice became increasingly agitated when first one child and then two children approached her from the bedroom. It seemed to me that the agitation was connected not only to their being up when they should have been asleep but also to their numbers. I also noted a particularly peaceful interchange when Alice and James were alone on the Base Day (see 2:25 P.M.). Almost 20 percent of Alice's Positive initiations toward James on that day occurred during this ten-minute period of time. The importance of the child-to-adult ratio is also suggested when we compare the following scene, which occurred when Richard was at work, with the preparation for bed that took place on the Base Day with Richard present (see 8:20 P.M.).

"Preparing for Sleep" (April 21)

Alice tells Nicholas, "Take your socks off, Nick," and again she admonishes James to put away the vacuum-cleaner attachment. She tells him to take off his socks, but he protests that he's not tired. "I don't care, take them off!" she insists. He protests, "It's not dark yet." Alice yawns and says that the birdies are going to sleep. This comment intrigues James, who talks about it with obvious interest. Alice says, "Take your shirt off," and he answers that he can't. Alice remains seated and shows him how. She turns it into a game and they laugh. Carrie also laughs loudly from the bedroom. Alice says to James, "You've got to learn to do it. I'm tired of doing it." He then finishes the job of undressing. Carrie emerges from the small bedroom in her nightgown and hands Alice the television program guide. Alice looks through it and says there's nothing special on television. She tells James to put his clothes in the hamper, but he ignores her. She scolds him and then begins to undress Nicholas, playing a game with his "piggies." He laughs with pleasure. She asks Carrie to get a nighttime diaper for Nicholas, which she does. She tells James to get his nightshirt, but he ignores her. After her second request, he goes into the bedroom and brings back two shirts. Alice asks him to put one back. Alice asks Nicholas to put his clothes in the bathroom hamper. When he does not move she says, "Do something around here." He becomes stubborn, refuses, and begins to whine. Alice becomes angry and spanks him. *She then threatens to get "Daddy's belt"* and goes into the bedroom to get it. Alice sternly warns Carrie to get onto the couch and then insists—*with the belt in hand*—that Nicholas pick his clothes up off the floor. He does and Carrie begins to laugh. Alice insists that she stop. She then angrily insists that James "get over here!" She puts his pajamas on while Nicholas puts his clothes into the hamper in the bathroom.

James has found a toy ladybug, and he plays with it and sings while Alice dresses him. Alice goes into the bedroom to get Nicholas's pajamas and tells Carrie twice to "settle down." Then she insists that Nicholas "get over here!" When he doesn't respond, she warns, "*OK. I have Daddy's belt.*" At this, Nicholas runs away in fear. Alice then sternly tells Carrie to "come here and put these books away." Alice sounds very annoyed now. Carrie puts them away and tells me, "We get paid for cleaning up when Daddy's here." Alice tells James to put away Carrie's tights, which he does. She picks Nicholas up and takes him to the bathroom to diaper him and tells James, who has followed them, to "make potty, just in case," but he is unsuccessful. Meanwhile, Carrie has disappeared into the play area. Alice calls her to wash up, and she wanders slowly into the bathroom. Alice has to admonish her; she wants to wash her. Nicholas tries to escape, and Alice sternly states, "I'm the boss here." They say their prayers in the bathroom. They now want to leave, but Alice has to keep them there in order to wash their hands. She then makes loving noises to Nicholas and washes their hands at the tub. She tells them to dry their hands but has to urge them on to do so.

With Richard present, Alice could prepare Nicholas and James for bed individually, while the others interacted with their father as he polished his shoes and belt for work, another special ritual. His presence served as a child-care resource. In contrast, in the observational segment above, she had to work with them simultaneously and, in her attempt to manage this work overload, became authoritarian and punitive. Richard's presence was introduced by means of his belt, and thus he became the agent of control when her own authority failed her.

The difference in emotional tone between the bed preparation above and that of the Base Day also is evident in the quantitative analysis. During the preparation for bed when Richard was present on the Base Day, 59 percent of all initiations and responses within the total family system were Positive and 21 percent were Negative. During the above "Preparing for Sleep" segment, 45 percent of initiations and responses were Negative, whereas only 17 percent were Positive. Although these two episodes may represent random occurrences, they do correspond to Alice's and Richard's experience. Golden (1975) also found that the quality of family interactions varied with the number of family members present. Thus, Richard's presence or absence may affect the functioning of the whole family system. Systematic research with families could investigate this proposition by comparing similar situations for which the child-to-adult ratio varies (see also Knox & Wilson 1978).

The Psychological Interface

I have suggested that Richard's physical presence affects individual family members and transactions within the family system in a variety of ways. Intertwined with such structural variables are psychological ones. I have already described the carry-over of interpersonal style into the family when Richard first joined the police force. The psychological interface relationship also was implicit in the discussion of time spent on the farm insofar as it serves Richard as a "haven" for coping with strains related to work. Alice also commented that when Richard does not get enough sleep he is crabby and irritable with her and the children. This irritability was accentuated when he began to work the midnight shift. It is difficult for him to sleep during the day because the children are noisy. He feels fortunate, he told me, if he gets a "good" four hours of sleep each day. As a result of his being tired and irritable, Alice began to feel as if she were "walking on eggs." His edginess made her reluctant to talk about the problems of time and timing, and she worried that he lacked patience with the children and would "lose control" with them. (As we shall see in the discussion of Alice and her work, she has this worry about herself as well.) When she once asked him why he hated her, he reportedly answered, "I hate everyone on midnights." Moreover, when he has court duty—which requires his presence during the day as well—his lost sleep begins a cycle of further physical exhaustion, and it takes some time for him to recuperate. This physical exhaustion becomes a link between structural and psychological dimensions of the interface relationships. The midnight shift confronted the Bernards with a new set of dilemmas to cope with.

When I collected the observational data on the Bernard family, the usefulness of homecomings as an indicator of the psychological interface pattern was not yet apparent to me. Consequently, only two observational segments of Richard's coming home from police work were collected. Two observations are insufficient to allow us to make definitive statements, but the data are suggestive and do allow us to draw some tentative conclusions.

During the observations, I did not witness the type of irritability Alice spoke of. In fact, if we consider the time period between Richard's arrival at 8:10 A.M. on the Base Day and his going to sleep at 9:10 A.M., we are immediately struck by what appears to be a paucity of evidence about Richard's state of mind and the quality of his interactions with family members. He did not talk about his feelings and, unlike Ezra Turner or Henry Johnson, was not obviously joyful or upset. Yet, later in the day, Richard talked to me about his anger at the fact that he was doing the work of the detectives without getting credit for it. In fact, this issue had arisen during the previous night. And true to his word about not bringing his problems home, he neither talked about it when he came home nor behaved angrily. But the absence of overt anger did not instead bring joy. It is precisely this apparent lack of affect—what is not there—that suggests depletion and an energy deficit pattern on the Base Day.

Availability

In Chapter 3, the concepts of emotional and interpersonal availability were introduced as helpful in understanding how work experience can be expressed in the family system. Interpersonal availability had both a response and an approach component, as well as an affective dimension. In the Turner family, Ezra's interpersonal availability was indicated by examining the number of initiations Ezra made when he came home and their emotional quality. We can make a similar analysis of Richard's homecoming on the Base Day.

Richard's first two initiations were Positive, which leads us to hypothesize that he was interpersonally available when he first came home. However, soon afterward he went outside to work on his farm. An additional component of interpersonal availability is how sustained it is. One difficulty in measuring Richard's interpersonal availability, in comparison with other family members', is that during the morning time period he moved in and out of the house several times. His initiation rate therefore reflects his physical absence. With this limitation in mind, we find that, until he went to sleep Richard initiated 7 percent of all family initiations, both verbal and nonverbal. These initiations were distributed evenly among Positive, Neutral, and Negative ones. In contrast, he was the object of 26 percent of initiations by others. In other words, Richard was sought after by other family members—especially James—an analysis in keeping with the previous interpretations. Although Richard was available to respond to family members who approached him, he did not move actively toward them. Even his responsiveness was limited in that it consisted of short statements that were direct responses to questions. Thus, the pattern that suggests itself for the Base Day is one of personal depletion and energy deficit. We might speculate further that Richard withdrew into himself in order to cope with the anger and frustration he was experiencing, feelings that emerged later in the day when talking to me.

If we consider the homecoming on the Base Day further, several other hypotheses suggest themselves. We notice, for example, that Richard did not initiate an interaction with Alice until 9:00 A.M., when he asked her a brief question that was Neutral in emotional quality. In fact, we see in Table 9-1 that the majority of their interactions on the Base Day were Neutral. Similarly, in Table 10-1 we see that the majority of their interactions were related to household matters. There are several ways we might understand the limited number of interactions between Alice and Richard, and their quality and content. Perhaps they avoided more intimate interactions because of my presence. However, Golden (1975), who observed marital pairs she knew very well, also found that their interchanges were frequently "objective." I have already suggested that Alice and Richard are avoiding discussing the issue of time together; presumably household topics are less emotionally tinged. We might suppose, too, that given the limited time they do spend together, it would upset their relationship to deal with more difficult, affect-laden subject matter. In addition, when time and energy are limited, pressing issues of the household may be given priority over difficult emotional

200

problems of the marital subsystem.[8] Alice herself suggested such an interpretation when she worried that intimacy has been lost in the daily routine they are caught up in.

This interpretation about limited time and personal resources and their careful allocation might also help us understand why Richard greeted James and Carrie when he came home but did not make an overture toward Alice until much later. It may be that Richard, like other participants, is especially sensitive to his children's need for contact with him. When other adult participants worried about insufficient time with their families, children were often singled out as a special concern. Perhaps, when his emotional availability is limited, Richard deploys his attention where he feels it is most necessary. Since Alice is an adult, Richard may assume that she can sustain herself. Moreover, Richard himself becomes "charged up" by his children's excitement at seeing him. Most likely, Alice would not give him such a rousing welcome. In fact, he reported that his children's delight at his arrivals momentarily counters some of the depletion he feels.

The difference in Richard's behavior toward Alice and the children suggests that psychological interface patterns are not uniform for all subsystems within a family. This distinction was implicit in the discussion of the Healy family in Chapter 3; Mike was angry with his wife but not with his children. In the Bernard family two patterns suggest themselves. In relation to Alice, the interface pattern is one of personal depletion, withdrawal, and unavailability—that is, a pattern of energy deficit—thereby further depriving Alice of contact with Richard. When he becomes irritable and angry, distance between them is increased. With the children the pattern differs. Their joy in seeing him charges Richard. When he becomes tired the depletion pattern is activated and he begins to withdraw. If he stays up too late he becomes irritable and easily angered. In fact, on the Base Day, his first two Negative initiations toward the children occurred just before he went to sleep. We may have been seeing the onset of the negative carry-over pattern.

For the most part, Alice reports that Richard is in a good mood when he comes home and that he spends at least a few happy minutes with the children. This suggests that when Richard is not feeling depleted or upset, joyful interactions with the children are possible. We can contrast his homecoming on the Base Day with the following interchange with James on the morning after the night on which I observed him at work. That night, a Sunday, was relatively stress-free, and he had had the opportunity to sleep before he came home.

8. Lopata (1971) found that women she studied ranked the role of husband as less important than that of father and of breadwinner.

CASE STUDY: THE BERNARD FAMILY

"Training in Toughness" (April 25)

Richard greets James cheerfully: "Hello, Jamey!" He calls him by a pet name. Carrie and Nicholas are asleep. Richard, James, Alice, and I sit down at the kitchen table. Alice has placed their breakfast on the table. Richard has some cereal, as does James. Alice is having waffles. James spills milk down the front of his pajamas and looks questioningly at Alice. Alice wipes him up, and she and Richard smile at each other. Alice, Richard, and I are chatting about the night's events. Richard wants to make a telephone call. Since James is sitting at his usual seat—on a large pile of telephone books—Richard lifts him up and puts him on his lap and begins to leaf through the book. James is delighted to be on his father's lap and is smiling happily. He starts to slide off and Richard holds him more firmly, and they discuss whether he is really going to fall. James is worried, but Richard assures him that he is safe. Richard becomes playful. He pretends to bite James's elbow, and James squeals in delighted protest. Richard then playfully pretends to grab James around the neck in a stranglehold and, again, James is thrilled and excited. When Richard stands up to make his telephone call, James asks to sit atop his shoulders. Richard lifts him up, and James is happy because his head is touching the ceiling. Richard asks, "Do you want to touch the ceiling?" Alice tells him, "He's already doing it." Richard then asks James if he wants to play the "bounce game." Usually, they play this game over the bed (Richard lets him drop and bounce). James agrees, and Richard holds him over the floor as if to drop him there. At the last minute James loses trust in his father and grabs the neck of his T-shirt, hanging on for dear life. Richard is amused by this and tells him to let go, that he won't drop him. But James will have none of it and continues to hold on, all the while squealing in excitement. Richard puts James down and Alice and Richard walk me to the back door. As we chat briefly there, James climbs up the front of Richard's legs—with his father's help—and becomes increasingly excited, crying "More! More!" [Richard went to sleep soon after I left.]

In this excerpt we obtain a glimpse of the playful interactions that are possible when Richard is not overtired or angry. They contrast with the lifeless reunion I observed on the Base Day. I have suggested that these different homecomings reflected his different experiences at work the night before. In Chapter 3, I noted that psychological interface patterns can be mixed. Insofar as any individual has variations in work experiences from day to day we would expect the interface patterns to change with them. Thus, for any family we would predict a range and mixture of patterns. Further observations of Richard's homecomings might establish a particular, predominant pattern for him. From what Alice and Richard both say, and from what I observed, the pattern that has evolved from the midnight shift has been one of short bursts of energy upon arriving home followed by withdrawal and depletion. If he stays up late, he becomes irritable.

The quality of the interactions between Richard and James during the above observational segment also are significant in their implications for the interface relationship. The teasing manner in which Richard

202

showed James his affection reflects both Richard's "dread of tenderness" (Henry 1965) and his desire to toughen James. Difficulty in expressing affection to a male has its roots in his family of origin, but it appears to be reinforced by his occupational culture. I suggested that joking was a way the police officers expressed their disappointment and hostility. Such joking also was used to express affection, which must be veiled because of their close contact at work. Toughening James through play also seems related to his occupational world view. When I asked Richard why size and toughness were so important to him, he was astonished that I did not immediately recognize the asset they were in his work, for they make him less vulnerable to attack. Through his play with James, Richard is teaching his son the importance of being unafraid in a world created, in part, by his occupational experience.

Denial of Danger and the Subtle Communication of Dread

Denial and repression are two ways in which people attempt to manage disturbing feelings. We also know that these defenses require psychic energy and that such attempts to manage conflict and strain are not always successful. Both Richard and Alice acknowledged that, in some ways, the research process disturbed the accommodation they had made between their work and their personal and family lives. Initially, when I interviewed him, Richard appeared unruffled and in control. In a subsequent interview he described himself as a "spinning egg"; even though the outside stops spinning, the contents are still in motion. To communicate his feelings to me he used images such as being "bottled up" and "in high gear." The research process itself made the repression of feelings less tenable, for the questions I asked would sometimes lead to their uncovering. The data collected with the Bernards covered a six-month period, during which the feelings described here were slowly articulated.

The tenuousness of attempts to deny strain is most evident with regard to the issue of the dangers inherent in police work. Danger is not simply a problem for those whose line of work puts them directly under fire. The possibility of injury and bodily damage through one's work was mentioned as a concern in five of the other twelve research families. In every case wives and children worried privately, while husband-fathers denied their concerns. Richard initially disclaimed any distress about this feature of his work. When I inquired directly about it, he denied and dismissed worries or fears. At first Richard answered me by saying, "The experience I had overseas really cushioned me for all this over here. This is mild compared to what was over there." As Bermann (1973) has noted, ours is a death-denying culture in which fear of death can surface in insidious ways. To admit one's fears openly—to face death without defenses—can be incapacitating to those who must manage the threat of injury in their everyday life. Kroes et al. (1974) also have suggested that in police work physical dangers must be kept from consciousness both for psychological well-being and in order to do one's job. I would add that such a dynamic would be operative in any job where personal injury is an experienced possibility. (See, for example, the discussion of Jesse Jones in Chapter 5.)

Despite their defenses against it, some concerns about danger slowly began to surface. For example, in our first interview, Richard briefly mentioned that one of the reasons he tries not to talk about his work while at home is that "I don't want my wife aware of all the strange situations that I see somewhere." When I asked about his meaning, he passed quickly over his comment. "Well, there's a risk factor. I don't know." In telling me that he does not like to talk about work problems "because I don't like to drag my dirty wash home," he went on to describe an incident in which he entered the scene of a murder and realized that he had known the dead man. He became so ill that he "thought of calling in sick a couple of days." Thus, I had a sense of the constant defensive stance he must maintain to protect himself from concerns about death and destruction. In the incident he described, death touched him too closely, and his coping mechanisms failed him.

The topic of constant vigilance against fear again was hinted at when describing how relieved he was not to be allowed to take his gun across the border on a visit to Canada. He felt "relaxed" and unguarded. In contrast, as a police officer he must be available for duty twenty-four hours a day. Even off-duty, he must carry his gun. In her first interview, Alice also talked of her feelings about Richard being a police officer around the clock.

AB: There was this one instance when we were just on the road, just a highway, and this was when, this was just about the time when Richard decided it was time to get out because we were almost run off the road by a bunch of goofs, and the same bunch had almost run an old man off the road and a bus, and they just really were acting crazy. So, Richard was angry, and this is how it really carried over. He got angry, pulled up next to the car, and motioned for them to pull over. I'm in the car with my 2-year-old child and expecting another one. . . . And he always has to carry his gun. . . . This is what they teach them. You're a policeman twenty-four hours a day. This is something that you can't put away in your locker at quitting time. . . . So he motions for them to get over, pulls the gun out of his pants and sticks it in his jacket pocket. I was dying. I thought, "Oh my God, I'm going to be a widow!" You know, because there were three guys in this other car and I was just freaking.

R: Did he have his uniform on?

AB: No. And I was pleading with him, "Please don't!" in tears, "Just drive away." He went, "Did you see what they did? They could have killed us," and all this other kind of stuff. He got out of the car, and I guess they saw the handle of his gun sticking out of his pocket because one guy got out of the car, and I thought that they were going to start actually fighting, and the guy saw it and jumped back into the car and they sped off. Well, we had, we really had quite a discussion about this. In fact, we were at odds. . . . We were at odds for about a week after that. You know, don't ever do that to me again.

R: What was his position?

AB: He felt that he had to uphold the law. The thing is that he was completely caught up in the whole thing, and he really thought that he was a policeman all day, everyday, and he's not.

R: How long had he been working?

AB: I guess it was about three years.

During this time Richard was still a "hard charger." Here the potential dangerousness of his work was communicated to Alice in a striking and horrifying way.

The midnight shift has increased Alice's concerns about Richard's safety. During the Base Day, we saw her tell her friend that she is afraid he will fall asleep behind the wheel and that he is not alert enough to deal with the situations that may arise (see Base Day, 9:45 A.M.). Although she laughed when telling her friend, in her subsequent reading of the observational notes she recalled the inner turmoil and "multitude of emotions" she has about this issue, emotions that she found difficult to articulate.

Richard's constant vigilance, his feeling that the world is a potentially dangerous place, that he is always a target became clear during the observational period. Noticing a young man in a store, he remarked to me that he has to be careful because there are people released from prison who would like to "get" him. Shortly afterward he mentioned that he knew of a man living in the vicinity of the shopping center who carried a grudge against police officers. Whereas other participants saw their home space as a haven, Richard's vigilance extends even there. He does not publicly disclose his occupation for fear that someone will think he keeps guns in the house and break into it. During the evening I observed, he drove by his house to see for himself that all was well. When he is particularly anxious he may drive by several times a night. He then becomes concerned that someone might notice this interest and decide there is a reason to break in. The more he worries about this occurring, the more he drives by; he becomes caught in a vicious circle of anxiety. During Alice's out-of-town trip, Richard slept with his pistol next to his pillow. Whereas Ezra Turner feels that the world is basically benign and safe, for Richard people are a potential threat from whom he must protect himself. Thus he feels as if there were a "mob out to chase" him, perhaps representing those he thinks would like to wreak revenge on him. As Richard becomes more disillusioned with his work and its lack of rewards, the necessity for such constant vigilance becomes less tolerable.

In Chapter 5 I suggested that even when people think that they are leaving work-related concerns at the job by not talking about them at home, such worries may nevertheless be communicated unconsciously. During one of the final joint interviews with the Bernards, Alice described her night fear and her dislike of sleeping alone. As we saw in Chapter 4, night fear was common among women whose husbands worked late-afternoon or midnight shifts. Alice's fear takes the form of vivid fantasies whose basic plot remains constant. In her fantasy two or three men are trying to break in the front door while she and the children are sleeping. Richard is at work. She does not know how to operate a gun and her major concern is to hide her children. Most of the fantasy involves her obsessively considering various places to hide them. After hiding them she crawls to the telephone to try to call Richard at work, but just as she gets there, the men break in and her fantasy ends. In her detailed concerns about where to hide the children, we can see Alice trying to be the protector of the family, just as Mary Ellison felt she had to be the protector in her husband's absence. We also can see Richard's own concerns about someone breaking into their house. As Alice talked about these fears, Richard recalled an incident several years earlier when a police officer's wife was shot in revenge for an arrest the officer had made. "See," Richard commented, "You arrest people and they take it personally." Alice was shocked that she had repressed the story.

We can make some guesses about the dynamic that underlies this process of subterranean communication. Although Richard wants to protect Alice from the "strange situations" he sees and his own fears about revenge seekers, his fear has nevertheless been communicated to her in his stories about what happens to other police officers and their families. Similarly, Jesse Jones, who suppressed his worries about being injured on the job, told Sandra about accidents that happened to others, and Sandra then worried about Jesse. Talking about what happens to others can be a way of trying to master one's own fear without acknowledging it. Personal dread still is a taboo subject; consequently, Alice and Richard cannot discuss their worries openly. We know that when feelings are troublesome they can make themselves known through our dreams and fantasy life. Thus, Alice has fantasies triggered by Richard's absence and by her own feelings of vulnerability that condense both the more common night fear and the special fear to which she and Richard are subject—that someone may seek revenge on him. The process of subtle communication is reflected in Alice's comment that she had begun worrying about Richard's safety two years earlier. "As long as he felt confident, I felt confident," she remarked. It was two years earlier that Richard realized that the Centerville job would not meet his needs. Perhaps his disappointment also made it more difficult to sustain his defenses against fear. Alice later commented that if Richard were injured in the course of his work, it would be more difficult for her to tolerate now because he no longer "believes in" his work.

Alice's and Richard's anxieties about danger and death also are reflected in their concerns about preventing their children from viewing violence on television and from playing any games involving guns, topics about which they talked uneasily with me. The children are not allowed to watch most police programs on television. Alice worries that even in nonpolice shows "a policeman is presented in some sort of 'situation' and sometimes they have questions about it." Alice and Richard must find it difficult to answer their children's questions about the "situation" without a name, for they, too, are troubled by it. Alice went on to complain of the violence in cartoon programs, displacing her anxieties about the "situation" to a more tolerable topic.

Richard and Alice have not allowed toy guns into the house and, as yet, the children have not asked for them. They worry that such play will somehow harm the children because of Richard's work. Many parents probably have similar feelings about violence on television and about violent toys, but for Richard and Alice such play has special meaning. The following excerpt is from an interview that occurred late in the research process.

RB: They broke a toy the other day. . . . There's a series of little hinges on the back. Well, they ripped off the back panel, and there's all these L-shaped little hinges. So now James and Nicholas run around the house with these L-shaped hinges and play "guns." [*He makes shooting noises to imitate them.*]

R: I see. And that bothers you?

RB: Well, it bothers me when they run up to your face and go "Pow-pow, I kill you!" and stuff like this. I mean, they're probably saying this because they see it on TV or something. . . .

R: You have mentioned . . . that you don't like when they use the word "kill."

RB: The service time was bad, you know? Trouble is, when I came back over here, it just didn't stop. It continued because of the career I'm in.

R: You talk about the good things you got out of the service, but on the other hand, there seems to be stress.

RB: I think it is stress. With just the word—you know, whenever I think of the word, I think of it—it should be capitalized, you know. Big block letters, right? People just don't realize how [*pause*] how threatening it is! Just to snuff out somebody's life is just, you know. . . .

R: Uhum. So when the children are playing, they're innocently using a word that is very upsetting to you.

RB: Yeah. I don't like it. It catches me off guard. I react to it, you know. . . . I usually take the things that they're shooting away, and I tell them not to use the word. [*Pause*] I don't know; I don't know if the day will come when we're going to have to buy James a holster set with a gun in it, or, you know. . . . But then, it's just [*pause*] being a boy. . . .

R: So it could be that [their play] has something to do with your uniform and your gun, but it also could be innocent child's play and you don't know . . .and it upsets you anyway.

RB: There's the phase there.

R: And you're not sure what is going on, so you get upset.

RB: Well, it upsets me because they see the gun, you know what I mean? [*Pause*] And, maybe, because of—they'll come up and say, "Just like you, Dad. . . . Just like you in your uniform. Just like the gun you use at work. . . ." And probably that's what, you know, gets me. . . . James is always saying, "You're carrying a gun to work so you won't get killed." This is one of the things [*chuckle*] that he has picked up. I say, "No, I don't carry it to work so I won't get killed. I carry it to work because sometimes you need it. . . ." I can sit down and think about it and then, you know, I'll say, "Well, I'll do this when it happens." Well, two weeks will pass and I'll say, "Boom!" It'll come up, and it'll catch me completely off guard again. And I go, "Well, what is it I was gonna say?" You know, I forgot what I was gonna say, you know.

R: When has it struck you?

RB: Well, like, I'll be getting dressed, or I'll be in a hurry to get dressed or get out to work and all of a sudden they'll go up, and they'll start grabbing for the gun. And then they'll run out and get their toys and pretend they're shooting, you know. . . . I was laying on the couch the other day, and they came up and [*chuckle*] started sticking these things in my face and shooting. I mean. [*Pause*] I haven't thought very highly of having things pointed at me for a while.

Richard also worries about the danger of having his police revolver in the house.

We can make some inferences about the underlying dynamics here. The children's play can be understood in a variety of ways. Of the three children, James is most interested in gun play, although Nicholas has begun to show greater interest in it more recently. James and Nicholas are at ages when active imitation of and identification with their father are beginning to accelerate.[9] In Chapter 6 I suggested that the visibility

---

9. The conceptual distinctions between imitation and identification are not clear. Although we need not assume that imitative behaviors are always indicators of a deeper process of identification involving structural change, here we are assuming that—for the older children at least—their imitation of Richard indicates the beginnings of an identification process.

of the work role may facilitate the process of identification. In Richard's case, the symbols of his work—his gun, holster, belt, and uniform—are very concrete and visible to the children, even if their meaning is not entirely understood. The uniform very much symbolizes Father, and during the home observation I noted that Nicholas would sometimes hover near Richard's uniform or play with it. The pair of shorts that James chose for himself and tried on (see Base Day, 5:15 P.M.), with its hooks and brass attachments, reminded me of Richard's belt with its brassware. The gun also symbolizes Father's power, and James reportedly was very excited on the occasion when he watched Richard shoot a small animal. He also told me quite proudly, "Daddy has a gun." When little boys try on their father's role, they are also trying on his power and testing to see that their own assertive activity is permitted. The process of paternal identification is indicated in James's reported statement, "Just like you, Dad." Since the play is sometimes activated by Richard's putting on his uniform, we might infer both the process of identification through imitation and the boys' managing the separation by playing out in fantasy their images of Daddy's work and where he is going. Unlike me, they have never been on patrol with Richard. We should recall, too, that Richard identified himself with his father through his emulation of his father's military connections. We can also interpret some of their play as a form of aggression against Richard, as in James's pretending to shoot him. During the observations, direct aggression against Richard was almost nonexistent. Of the children's coded initiations toward him, only 8 percent were Negative (see Table 9-1) and, of those, all were distress or unhappiness initiations rather than assertions of anger or aggression.

According to Alice's reports, Richard initially encouraged the children's imitation of him by putting his police hat on them and letting them run around the house with handcuffs on. Not only could Richard thereby control the content of the imitation, but he played out with them his inner image of what is desirable about police work: he brings criminals to justice. By wearing both his cap and his handcuffs, they were at once both the good policeman and the bad criminal. Alice also thought that Richard was trying to make light of his work by playing at it with them, so that they would not come to think of him as the "big heavy out to get everybody." Now, however, the content of the imitation and the play associated with it have moved out of Richard's control.

The insufficiency of Richard's defenses against danger are reflected in the extent to which these developmentally appropriate imitative and play behaviors on the part of the children are personally distressing to him. While he initially told me that his military experience accustomed him to death, clearly this defense is tenuous. Not only is he upset by his children's use of the word "kill," but he himself referred to it as "the word." We know that words can sometimes be experienced as so powerful that the distinction between saying and doing are blurred. To Richard, his children's play may be too similar to reality, evoking intense feelings that he finds difficult to manage or even to acknowledge. His solution is to try to discourage the play, but he worries that he is discouraging age-appropriate activity, and Alice is concerned that he is inducing anxiety about their play. Paradoxically, because of the public attitudes toward police, Richard and Alice worry that their children may reject their father by not seeing him as a desirable identification figure.

Finally, we should consider the hypothesis that the children themselves are acting out and attempting to master in their play the family's unarticulated concerns about Richard's safety, as in James's reported comment to Richard, "You're carrying a gun to work so you won't get killed." The children's play reminds Alice and Richard of a reality that they must themselves deny. Research on the play of children whose fathers are in occupations perceived as dangerous would be helpful in clarifying these phenomena. But we do know that despite Richard's best efforts to keep himself and his family immune from worries about his safety, the concern nevertheless is expressed within the family system. Though the subject of danger and police work is a dramatic illustration of the process, we see portrayed here the way in which work-related stress can intrude on a family's inner life, despite assiduous efforts to keep work and family life distinct.

Unfortunately, the situations that are particularly dangerous are also more interesting to Richard. The most exciting shifts are the afternoon and night shifts, as that is when most criminal activity—which would involve a patrolman like Richard—occurs. In discussing his work in the city, Richard contrasts night work with day work:

RB: It was a different kind of work at that time of night.

R: How was it different?

RB: Oh, it was more or less a high crime area and it kept us busy, and when you're busy, the time flies. If you're doing what you want and what you enjoy doing, time seems to pass for me.

R: You enjoyed the night work?

RB: Oh, I preferred working nights myself, if it was just for myself. . . . Like working days, things were very dry. You're more of a public relations person during the day. You represent the department. Whatever the problems, you have to handle them very diplomatically. You have to show them the best side. It's the brassy side of the job working days.

Richard prefers the excitement of night work to the dry diplomacy of days. The shift I observed was unusually "slow"; it was a rainy Sunday night. I was surprised to see how boring police work can be, as my image of police work was based on what the media portrayed. Having a purpose, whether it was stopping a car for a traffic check or investigating vandalism, came as a relief to me. Moreover, Richard has greater autonomy on the midnight shift, as there is less supervision then. To increase his own satisfaction with his work, Richard is in the dilemma of making a choice that may have detrimental effects on the family system.

Summary

I have suggested the ways in which Richard's presence and absence in the family affect the patterns of intimacy family members can develop. Alice wishes she had more time with Richard but is reluctant to make her anger over its lack explicit for fear of moving him further to the periphery of the family. Three-year-old James is particularly sensitive to his father's absence and tries to make contact with him whenever he is at home. Richard is responsive to their approaches, but personal depletion makes it difficult for him to move out to others for extended periods of time. I also suggested that what personal resources he does have are made more available to the children than to Alice. Thus, it appears that there is not enough of Richard's time and energy to meet the needs of other family members. During the warm weather the children can spend time on the farm with Richard, but Alice is still in competition with it for Richard's attention. Richard, too, wishes he could spend more time with his family, but the Bernards' financial status requires that he work extra jobs to make ends meet. The farm is psychologically important to Richard as his personal area and the haven in which he works out, through physical effort, some of the frustration from work that he is reluctant to bring into the home space. I have also argued that despite Richard's best efforts to keep work concerns out of the family system, through the subtle communication of dread they are expressed there.

In suggesting these interface dynamics in the Bernard family my intention is not to highlight the extraordinary or the unusual. Rather, I would argue that the Bernards' experience is quite ordinary. Among the research families, husband-fathers wanted more time with their children, and children were sensitive to the comings and goings of their fathers. Moreover, while the theme of danger certainly is more dramatic for the Bernards, it nevertheless emerged as significant for other families as well. In the following discussion of Alice's work experience, we will consider further the effect Richard's availability has on the interface between the household subsystem and the emotional life of the family and how Alice's work experience determines, in part, what she needs from Richard.

CHAPTER 10

Household Work
and Its Discontents

The discussion of the interface between Richard's work life and relationships in the Bernard family remains incomplete without a fuller examination of transactions within the Bernard home. Just as we asked how Richard's relationship to his job affects the nature of interactions within the family, we can ask how Alice's work experiences affect family processes. And just as the structural region between work and family systems was mapped, structural relationships at the interface of household and family subsystems can be considered. The sensitizing concepts and method of analysis introduced in Part II will be helpful in our examination of this new interface relationship. In so doing, the traditional framework, which considers only the position of the paid worker and the connections between paid work and family life, will be expanded. We shall then be in a better position to understand how work, both paid and unpaid, influences the emotional dynamics of family life.

Two Work Worlds: Expanding the Framework

Kahn et al. (1964) have defined a work organization as a purposeful, open, dynamic system "characterized by a continuing process of input, transformation, and output" (p. 12). If we consider the industrial plants in which many of the research participants work, these features of a work organization become clear. The purpose of these work systems is to generate profit through the output of tangible products such as carburetors, shock absorbers, car bodies, etc. The input includes human time and energy—labor—and machinery to transform the raw materials into these commodities. The purposes of the law enforcement agency that Richard Bernard works for include providing protection for the citizens of the community. In so doing it uses labor, cars, weapons, and

212

an elaborate communication system, all of which become transformed—via training, discipline, and rules—into a service for the community.

The Household: Home as a Work Setting

Ordinarily, when Americans think about forming a family, they consider love, affection, and companionship as crucial features. Such is the modern romantic ideal. This view of families characterizes not only popular culture but also the writings of clinicians, historians, and social scientists who consider the family as a haven; as a last refuge in a cold, impersonal world; as a place where people can express their feelings openly. Thus far, I too have been concerned primarily with the emotional dynamics of family life as it occurs within in the home. However, such a portrayal obscures another important aspect of home life that interests us, namely, household activity. The emotional dynamics of kin relations—of families—can be distinguished conceptually from the dynamics of household relations.

In Chapter 1, the homes of American families were described as containing a household, where material resources and labor are used to generate the goods and services that maintain and reproduce human life.[1] It was also noted that, in our society, it is women who generally perform this work, even when they are simultaneously employed outside the home. If we look at the observations of a day at home with the Bernards, we can see some of the work that was performed there. Alice fed and clothed her children, looked out for their physical well-being, cleaned the house, and went shopping. In terms of the definition proposed by Kahn et al., we would say that Alice used her labor, in conjunction with tools such as the stove, washer, car, vacuum cleaner, and various raw materials, to provide products and services for her family. Her "output" includes the meals she cooks, as well as services such as housecleaning, laundering, and marketing. Alice provides services that are less material than an engine block; however, if her services were withdrawn, the Bernard family would be quick to notice their absence.

Because Richard is paid, we think of what he does as work. However, Alice is also a worker. Using "time budget" data, the yearly market value for the total household labor performed by a family with three young children was estimated at $10,362 in 1973 (Burns 1975). Based on a modest annual inflation rate of 6 percent, the market value of this work in 1977 was approximately $12,900. Since Richard and the children contribute little to the work done, most of it falls on Alice's shoulders.

Using the household work record devised by Walker and Woods (1976), a rough estimate was made of the total amount of household

1. The Marxist analysis stresses the production of labor power, that is, workers, for capitalism.

work Alice performed on the Base Day reported. We found that she spent approximately 8.8 hours in household work; this figure does not include break time or watching the children while she was resting. In the Walker and Woods sample, nonemployed women with three young children averaged 8 hours of household work per day. Thus, Alice's workday can be considered typical. Husbands averaged 1.4 hours of household work per day. This figure contrasts with the .08 hours we estimated for Richard on the Base Day. However, Richard was not physically awake much of the day; when he is home and alert, he performs tasks in the house without being asked.

In many ways, this general period in the Bernard household is particularly busy because of the presence of three young children. Walker and Woods found that household work increases with the addition of children to the family; the first child adds three hours of work per day to the household work performed (see also Knox & Wilson 1978). Moreover, the younger the children are, the more time is spent in the very time-consuming household work activity of physically taking care of family members. At this time of increased work load, Richard works outside the home for more than fifty hours each week.

The Content of Home Interactions. In the case of the Bernards, the characterization of the home as containing a household is supported by an analysis of the content of interpersonal interactions among family members. Looking at Table 10-1, we find that on the Base Day 44 percent of all coded family interactions were related directly to Domestic matters. (This figure is not a measure of household work *activity.* See the Methodological Appendix for an explanation of the Content codes.) If we examine only Alice's interactions with family members, we find that 50 percent of her interactions with the children and 63 percent of her interactions with Richard were Domestic. We have already seen the primacy of Domestic interactions between Alice and Richard. Domestic interactions retain their important position on other observed days as well.

Even though Alice considers such activities as reading to the children and providing them with crayons as part of her household work, such interactions were not included in the Domestic count, as a balance to the uncoded periods of observation. Domestic interactions did not occur uniformly throughout the day but took place primarily around mealtimes, waking times, and bedtimes. Social and Play interactions occurred primarily after breakfast and between the afternoon nap and dinner time. Thus, life in the Bernard household has a rhythm structured by eating and sleeping. These findings cannot be generalized beyond the Bernard family. However, data from the studies by Golden (1975) and Bermann (1973) indicate that in the families they observed, a

214

Table 10-1. Content of Family Interactions as Percentages of Total Coded Interactions

INTERACTION BETWEEN	CONTENT OF INTERACTION			
	Domestic	Social Interaction	Play	All Other
All Family Members				
Base Day	44%	34%	15%	10%
Other Days[a]	49	33	17	13
Richard & Alice				
Base Day	63	9	0	40
Other Days	52	32	0	16
Alice & Children				
Base Day	50	32	13	12
Other Days	58	26	12	12
Richard & Children				
Base Day	23	60	9	11
Other Days	30	48	10	20
All Children				
Base Day	9	42	47	3
Other Days	0	41	66	2

Note: Percentages total more than 100 because each interaction could be coded in more than one content category.
[a]*Other Days* refers to percentage of total interactions coded on days *other* than the Base Day.

substantial proportion of the interactions were "objective." We might infer that such "objective" interactions also relate to the business of everyday living.

Even without further data, the finding is sufficiently strong and the sense of the day as measured by time budget studies sufficiently typical to support those who question the structural-functionalist notion of the home as primarily the "expressive realm" (Parsons 1955). In this latter view, the mother-wife is the expressive leader, who is responsible for nurturing, soothing emotions, and reducing conflict, while the husband-father is the "instrumental" leader. Such a view neglects the household work performed in the home by the wife-mother. Moreover, in the Bernard family, household work activities affect the content of transactions that occur there. Alice's involvement is highly instrumental. It is her work that keeps the household running, and her Domestic interactions with family members reflect this fact. The high frequency of Domestic interactions may displace other, more expressive interactions. In contrast, only 23 percent of Richard's interactions with the children on the Base Day were Domestic, whereas 69 percent were Play and

Social (see Table 10-1).[2] This finding is supported by the naturalistic research of Dyck, who also found that "fathers' social contacts exceeded mothers' in their per cent of occurrence" (1963, p. 95). In ignoring the home as a work setting, structural-functionalist theory seems to be little more than an idealized vision of what some social scientists think family life—and woman's place in it—should be, rather than what it actually is. The nature of the family transactions reflects the fact that a great deal of work gets done in the Bernard household. The nature of the connections between such instrumentality and expressive interactions is ultimately the question to be considered here.

Traditionally, the position of the wage earner who interpenetrates both work and family systems has been highlighted in the study of their interconnection. This perspective was used in the analysis of the interview data presented in Part II. However, as soon as we begin to view the home setting as a workplace, a new interface position suggests itself. Even though they overlap in time and space, for heuristic purposes we can think of the household organization and the emotional life in families as different subsystems, with the household worker at their boundary. The conceptual confusion surrounding the roles of housewife, wife, and mother results from her interface position. When a woman is being a mother, she may be attending to her children's emotional needs, or washing and feeding them, or doing both simultaneously. The dual codings of family interactions were designed to reflect these multiple meanings of family interactions (see Methodological Appendix).[3]

In the discussion to follow, the term "household worker" will be used to denote Alice as a worker in her home. When the terms "wife" and "mother" are used, it will be with the understanding that these roles include both work and emotional dimensions.

Interlocking Household and Paid Work Organizations

In Chapter 4, I described how family systems and paid work organizations are interlocked because, in capitalist societies, individual family households are dependent on the wages brought in from the external work setting; the breadwinners are thus bound into the occupational

2. The proportion of Domestic interactions rises slightly to 30 percent for an observational period during which he was home for a greater length of time, suggesting that the more time Richard spends at home the more household business he engages in.

3. In some homes these activities might be performed by different people. For example, a family might have a paid housekeeper and cook. The adult female in the family might still be called a "housewife," insofar as she manages her paid employees, but her activities as wife and mother would be primarily companionate, emotional, and socializing. Even socialization activities might be given over to a nursemaid. Still, in most families emotional tasks and work tasks, including socialization, are performed by the same person.

structure. This structural reality establishes the context in which interface negotiations occur in the Bernard family and in other research families. This schema can be expanded to include the household work subsystem.

Unless families have independent wealth or can purchase household services with their income, nuclear family units must distribute the required household and wage and salary work among their members in order to maintain themselves adequately. Since the occupational structure discriminates against women, participants generally felt that men's wages are more important to the maintenance of the family system. Richard Bernard stated that because he can earn more money than Alice, he is the one who works outside the home. Alice does not think she would be able to secure a paying job, for she considers herself as having no marketable skills. Through her household labor, Richard's wages are turned into commodities and services that can be used by family members. It has been argued that through her labor the household worker serves as an adjunct to the external work setting because she performs the work more cheaply than it could be purchased in the marketplace. For example, children and the elderly are maintained more cheaply in the home than in other institutions (Women's Work Study Group 1976). If workers had to purchase such services, wages and salaries would have to be higher, or the families would suffer a reduction in their standard of living. Thus when Richard's time, effort, and skill are purchased, Alice's labor is indirectly included as a form of subsidy to the law enforcement work organization for which he works.

No Exit: Locking-In the Household Worker. This interlocking of household and external work systems means that nonemployed women and their children are dependent on the wages earned by husband-fathers (see also Chapter 4). This dependent relationship is one way in which household workers are also locked into their jobs. Despite Alice's feeling that she has more "outs" than Richard, as a household worker she also is tied to her work, both by her obligations to her young children and by her own dependence on the wage system. Alice's feeling of total dependence on Richard's earning power is reflected in a fantasy that used to occur when he became angry at her. She would imagine herself working the afternoon shift as a waitress in an expensive restaurant, but earning very little. In her fantasy, Carrie, James, and Nicholas are staying at her parents' home; they have no place of their own in which to live. Alice understands this fantasy as the expression of her fear of being abandoned by Richard. The fantasy plays out the consequences of such an abandonment. We are reminded of her reluctance to express anger toward him, for without Richard she would be unable to provide financially for herself and the children. Alice's anger at Richard creates problems for her, as her worst fear is that he will leave. Her conclusion is that she would be unable to manage without him. "What am I good at?" she asked herself. Her answer came quickly: "Giving birth."

In Alice's fantasies of making her way without Richard, the children loom as very important. In Chapter 4 I noted that it was the birth of children that locked men into their jobs. Insofar as women view children as their responsibility, they also bind women to the household. Perhaps Alice could support herself, but she could not support three children. The women's movement has educated us to understand better how women come to feel responsible for the care of their children. Alice cannot articulate the details, but she is aware of the process of socialization.

> AB: It's like a baby trap. You've had it programmed into you since day one, maybe not by your parents, but by outsiders, that this is the thing to do: you get married and you have children. Now, I genuinely wanted children, but there are days when I go, "Why, oh, why?"

I finally broached the subject more directly.

> R: Do women feel trapped by their children?

> AB: Yes, definitely. In fact, I worry about it that much that there was a magazine in the back of the church, a family-type magazine with big headlines that said, "Why Do Mothers Feel Guilty?" [*Her eyes get large and expressive. She laughs.*] It was interesting because, of course, the situations they pointed out weren't identical, but there were some similarities. Yeah, I think that can happen, that a female can feel trapped by her children.

Even though Alice laughed as she remembered her feelings, they are nonetheless real, for sometimes she resents the fact that Richard can leave the house alone, but the children are always with her. Children are ties that bind household workers and paid workers to their jobs. The ties are not simply economic and structural. They are formed by years of learning and the internalization of a sense of responsibility, as well as by the love that develops among family members. This point of view was expressed even more explicitly by Pamela Gates.

> PG: One time I think it got to me so bad this summer that actually I felt like walking out! I just felt like packing the bags and going away for awhile—no kids, no husband. Good-bye. See ya! In fact, I almost got to the step where I put the luggage in the car. Then I started thinking, "Well, wait a minute. Who's going to take care of the baby?"

As both a household worker and an employed worker, Pamela felt doubly trapped.

218

Like Richard and many other young participants, Alice sometimes imagines what it would be like without children. Her fantasies are modest. She imagines waking up one day without the children being there and spending the day as she pleases. To borrow a phrase from Henry (1965), she imagines "unbound time." She would wake up whenever she pleased, meet a friend for lunch, and go window shopping.

Alice also recalled a more desperate time when she wanted to escape from pressures she still could not openly articulate. After Carrie was born, she faced, as do many young mothers, the new fears and stresses that accompany such a significant change in who she was and how she lived her life. Her relationship with Richard underwent changes as well, for he paid less attention to her now that Carrie had become his little princess. As we shall see, she found that she hated midnight feedings and many of the tasks associated with infant care. One evening she ran aimlessly into the night, carrying Carrie. Richard was confused and came after her in his car, begging her to return home. Alice still does not understand why her outburst occurred and explained it to me by saying she was "childish." She still cannot forgive herself for being overwhelmed by her feelings of distress and entrapment, and she cried as she related this incident. For a woman to abandon her home is unthinkable; such women are looked upon with horror. Chesler (1972) has suggested that some women escape into madness to flee the "female role."

Like Richard, Alice occupies a boundary position between work and family subsystems. In her case, the work organization is the household. And like Richard, Alice is locked into her job as household worker—at least for the present time. The interlocking of household and external work organizations is the context in which the negotiations among all interfaces occur.

The Discontents of Household Work

In analyzing the psychological interface between paid work and family systems, I examined sources of job stress and job gratification, as well as ways in which stresses were managed. In Chapter 1, I noted that researchers' efforts have recently been directed to the job satisfaction and the mental well-being of household workers. While I had not originally begun the research project with household work in mind, in Alice Bernard's interview the themes that were emerging more slowly in the interviews with other women could no longer be ignored. In filling out the personal data sheet with which the interview began, Alice balked at the question asking her to list her "occupation." With this, the importance of household work and its relationship to family life emerged as a central issue of this study, for among the participants Alice was most outspoken about her troubled feelings concerning her job.

Like many of the women interviewed by Oakley (1974a, 1974b), Alice finds housework boring and monotonous.

> AB: I got into the whole thing really fast, whereas a lot of my friends worked for five years, then started having children. . . . So I'm at the point where I'm just tired of it, and they're still kind of digging the whole thing. . . . I absolutely hate it. I want to have enough side interests that it can be part of life that has to be done and that I don't dread it, and I can do it quickly and just get it out of the way.

These feelings were readily and easily admitted. However, it was only after some time that she confided to me her similar dislike of taking care of children. Though she easily told me that she hates washing dishes, her mention of her negative feelings about midnight feedings and the boredom of child-care activity was accompanied by shame and guilt. It appeared that the more distance there was between household work activities and family members, the less troubled Alice was by her negative feelings about her tasks. Most of the research on the job satisfaction of household work has bypassed child care in favor of housework. Yet the care of children, too, can be a source of distress.

The difficulty Alice had in verbalizing her discontent with child-care work must be understood in the context of a culture that obscures this work role. LeMasters (1957) and E. D. Dyer (1963) have documented the shock of reality for young parents when first babies are born. Although they did not focus on household work per se, the majority of factors cited as stressful for young mothers involved the work components of parenthood. There was little "anticipatory socialization" to prepare them for this new work role.

Not only is the work of motherhood obscured, when it is talked about, the work done for family members is described as a "labor of love." This fusion of work and family spheres makes the household worker susceptible to the feeling that her attitudes about her work reflect upon her feelings toward her children, for it is through her work that she is supposed to express her love for them. Whereas a wage earner might feel pride in making sacrifices for his family by working at a job he dislikes (Sennett & Cobb 1972), the household worker is not allowed to dislike the work or acknowledge her dislike. Alice learned not only that she was supposed to be a wife and mother but also that she was supposed to love the role.[4] When, during her last pregnancy, Alice turned to Coomes's *Mother's Manual*, a religious publication, in search of

4. As Bernard has noted, "We expect every woman not only to want babies but also to love motherhood. If she does not, we make her feel deviant" (1975, p. 31).

spiritual comfort, she read, "Motherhood is a sacred thing. When a mother has borne a child, she has fulfilled a sublime and holy role" (1969, p. 45). Rather than provide support, such assertions upset and depressed her, for they reinforced her feelings of guilt at not loving the work that comes with being a mother.

It is her interface position and the lack of clear barriers between household and emotional subsystems, that make it easy for a woman like Alice to accept the notion that to dislike one's work implies inadequate loving of one's children. Since every activity as a household worker can have meaning within the family's emotional subsystem, this multiplicity of meaning turns against her. Rather than acknowledging her boredom with many of the activities associated with child care, she equates this distaste with unholy feelings about being a mother; she feels inadequate and guilty (see also Bernard 1975). Of the issues stirred by the interviews, these feelings most troubled and depressed Alice. Coming to accept them was one of the most important personal outcomes of the research process for Alice.

Household Work and the Threat of Self

In Chapter 3 I suggested that boring work can be experienced as a personal threat because it does not allow a person to develop his or her abilities or to realize his or her internal image of an ideal self. I also suggested that Richard Bernard's anger and disappointment about police work stemmed partly from his difficulty in living out his personal dream of being a "righteous warrior." The theme of how boring work can be experienced as an assault on one's ideal self became more explicit in the interviews with Alice.

Chesler (1972) has commented that most women "forget" their dreams of individuality when they marry. Alice has not: "I want people to see me for my works, not see my children as projections of me. I think a lot of women can lose themselves in their children." Alice is afraid of "losing her self," a theme that was reflected in two images that recurred throughout her discussion of household work. On the one hand is the person she is and further aspires to be: vital, bright, and interested in life. Although she does not read the feminist press, she repeated the sentiments of the liberal women's movement when she talked about housework as not providing the opportunity for self-expression or the stimulation necessary for personal growth:

> AB: You do not grow with housework. And housewifery is such that you've got no outlets. . . . One time I got in a discussion with a friend about the whole business of, ah, I hate to call it liberation because it's become so clichéd, but just individuality, not losing yourself to your wax floor. . . . I'm not saying that these things [i.e. playing with the children] aren't worthwhile, especially the contact with the children and spending

time [with them]. That's definitely worthwhile: But you need stimulation to grow. . . . It doesn't take any personality to clean a house. It doesn't take any personality to bake. It's all very mechanical. Anybody can do it.

Counterposed to her image of life and vitality is that of the "housewife," a poor old woman who has become mindless and dormant, her personal version of the "cabbage" described by Oakley's (1974a) respondents.

AB: You tell people you've got three children and it's kind of, "Wow!" [*She imitates surprise.*] They expect this poor woman to come in with a wheelchair and crutches, just gray at the temples and barely able to get around. I do not fit into people's notion of what a woman, a mother of three, would look like or was supposed to act like. . . . I would much rather have people be surprised that I have three children than have them be able to take one look at me or listen to me speak and just—"Wow, she must have a brood!"

R: You see mothers as beaten down?

AB: Right. Right. Just kind of mindless.

The image of the old woman is an image of death, of a loss of an ideal self. We saw that Tony Johnson also talked of being "dead" if he lost his dream. Those household activities through which Alice is supposed to express her love for her husband and children threaten her self ideal; only women "made of some super stuff" can withstand the danger. Thus, Alice is torn between two internalized ideals: the "child-centered" mother and the vibrant, intelligent, attractive young woman. These ideals are, to her, contradictory. In many ways, Alice thus personifies the dilemma of modern young women who learn conflicting role expectations. On the one hand they are to be the "complete" mother, and, on the other hand, they have learned the goal of self-actualization.[5] Alice tries halfheartedly to reconcile the two for, after all, "If you become dormant, you can't offer your children too much."

The housewife that Alice fears becoming is not simply an image derived from the popular media. She experiences the threat more directly. The women becoming old before their time—women lacking interests outside the home—are embodied in her friends. Alice talked of them with compassion, knowing she is like them and can share their fate.

AB: I've been to friends' homes where the husbands make remarks in very condescending tones, like her brain has turned to mush over the years. Whereas when they married them, I'm sure they selected them because they were bright and vital and interesting. But if you spend too many

5. I am not arguing that such goals are necessarily contradictory. The college-educated women Lopata (1971) interviewed tried to make housework and child care a "creative activity," thereby reconciling these goals for themselves.

years at home without any other interests, I don't know. . . . I see it more and more in my friends and it's upsetting. I don't like to see that because these are girls I went to high school and college with and they're bright girls. When their husbands give them a little pat on the head for remembering to put stamps on an envelope and mail a letter for them. . . .

Her compassion and concern for them also is mixed with anger and contempt:

AB: One day we were out, I was with a friend, and she had two of her friends that I didn't know or hadn't met until that day, and we had our children. So, they started talking, and I generally just kind of sit back for awhile, case the situation and then sort of join in. So, I was just kind of sitting back, watching the flow of the conversation and then I just got so angry. It was like, "Oh, so-and-so got basket furniture for her little girl. Oh, it looks like yours but there's a little different hue." The whole conversation was about furniture, food, and children's clothing. I didn't say anything. I was fairly quiet through the whole thing and my friend kept saying, "What's the matter? What's the matter?" and I just said, "Oh, I'm feeling a little out of sorts today." I went home and I was so mad.

R: Who were you mad at?

AB: Women in general. And I was telling Richard that I was in a rage by the time I got home. Of course he went, "What's your problem?" I said that it was no wonder that people have this conception of housewives as addle-brained zeros. They can sit for three hours and talk about this stupid, trivial stuff and be really getting into it. I'm ready to quit the human race.

Alice's anger at "women in general" serves to distinguish herself from them, thereby reassuring herself that she is different. Her anger thus serves as a defense: the danger of becoming an "addle-brained zero" is too real, for she, too, is a household worker. This same implicit identification with these women makes her angry at what she sees as their succumbing to being "just housewives." Their resistance would give her allies in her personal struggle; their victory would be hers. In many ways, the ambivalent feelings she has toward these women are a reflection of the feelings she has toward herself. She vacillates between acceptance of herself and compassion for her situation and self-contempt for being "just a housewife."

This ambivalence is also experienced toward her mother and grandmother, who bring the threat of losing her self still closer. Whereas Alice saw her grandfather and the other men in her family as strong and "vital," in her eyes the women were worn out and shapeless. She felt that her mother knew little about the world because she spent all her time at home. She reported that as a teenager she used to think, "What does she know? All she does is stick around here. She doesn't know what's happening out there." We must wonder to what extent her youthful contempt for her mother stemmed from a deeper disappoint-ment that, through her example, her mother did not adequately prepare her for another life.[6] To reject her mother and grandmother, however, is to reject herself, for she too is a household worker. Alice feels some shame, now, at this flippant dismissal of them and is beginning to understand the difficulties they faced as household workers in large families. But Alice's fearfulness about becoming like them is expressed in her own concern about her appearance and in her apprehension about looking "old and fat."

The Public Image

In her image of the old housewife, Alice shares the public's lack of esteem for the job of the household worker; this, too, is a source of stress for her. We saw that Richard feels angry and disillusioned because "mankind" does not appreciate his efforts. Similarly, Alice feels her work goes unvalued and unappreciated.

> AB: There's no pay structure, there are no benefits. I'm fortunate because I married a decent man, but friends of mine that married less-than-desirable sorts are really taken advantage of. Their work is treated with almost no regard. A woman can spend an hour and a half washing her floor and her husband will come in with his muddy boots and say, "So. It's no big deal." This is the case with a lot of my friends. . . . Another thing that I'm up in arms about is that so little credit is given to women who raise children. It's a job and I don't think that a lot of men or even women who have decided not to have children really realize what it involves.

Household work is "invisible" (Oakley 1974a) in that it neither has pub-lic status nor is publicly rewarded. Husbands who could be in a position to appreciate the work done in the home share the public view. Invisible work comes to public attention when it is left undone. Richard agreed that he expects a clean house, but he comments to Alice about her housework only when it is not done—when he lacks a clean handker-chief or notices dust on the furniture. This phenomenon was dramatized for me during one of the observations when Richard asked Nicholas, "How come your face is dirty?" In contrast, Richard did not admire or notice Carrie's and James's clean faces, which Alice had recently wiped. Not only does household work go unnoticed until it is undone; in the form of dirty laundry or unkempt children it always is undone. As Betty Johnson remarked, "Everything gets dirty again and nobody gives a damn."

6. Chesler has described the profound ambivalence daughters feel for their mothers who "have put brooms in their hands and romantic escapist illusions into their heads. Daughters can have no pride in their sex, which seems to survive and fatten on its domesticity" (1972, p. 265).

While up in arms about the devaluation of her work role, Alice nevertheless had internalized the public view. Her ambivalence is reflected in her feeling that she does not want to become "mindless." She is angry that her brother thinks that once a woman has "started having kids, you just don't exercise your brain all that much." Again, we see an internal conflict between valuing her role and wanting to dissociate herself from it. I would guess that it was possible for her to defend her work and express anger at its devaluation because I implicitly indicated interest and respect for what she did. However, much of the time she devalues herself as she devalues the role.

Being Housebound

Being spot-bound and place-bound was considered by a number of paid workers in the study to be a job stressor. Such boundedness implies a loss of autonomy over self, and the ability to move at will was valued. During the observational period with Richard, he also mentioned liking to walk around rather than simply sit for an eight-hour shift. Similarly, being housebound is a source of stress for Alice (see also Gavron 1966). During the Base Day, Alice spent over three-fourths of her waking time in the home. Few of her interactions with other family members concerned matters outside the home. Approximately 4 percent of her interactions with others while at home pertained to such subjects as jobs, school, or church. Moreover, except for shopping trips, her brief interchanges with Richard, and her few telephone calls, with my presence excepted she had no other conversation with adults. Conversation with the children was limited to one or two interchanges. Since she works and lives in the same setting, for Alice her everyday world is largely encompassed by the four walls of her home. This fact creates some conflict between herself and Richard concerning the type of social activity they engage in when they do have some time together. Feeling "trapped" and "caged" were among the metaphors Alice used to describe her feelings of being housebound. She felt that the house becomes "stale," whereas the out-of-doors represents freedom and vitality. The staleness of the house implies a lack of movement and a stagnation—death, if you will—that parallel the images she used to describe her fear of becoming an old woman. Being housebound comes to symbolize the lack of opportunity for personal growth and the feeling of being locked into her job.

The Stresses of Work Overload and Role Ambiguity

I have been describing Alice's experience of her work as boring, unrewarding, and lacking potential for her personal growth. As such, her work seems to have no real challenge for her. Yet, such a portrayal remains one-sided, for in the social production of children—their so-

225

cialization and personal development—Alice feels overloaded and overwhelmed by the task. In the description of Henry Johnson's relationship to his work, we saw that work overload can be an important source of stress. The overload Alice experiences can be understood through the concept of "objective role ambiguity." Kahn et al. (1964) have noted that there is some "normal" need for clarity about job performance that involves knowing what is expected of one, having the information to know how to perform, and having a way to evaluate one's performance. Lack of such clarity, or what they termed "objective ambiguity," can lead to tension and anxiety.

Alice does not lack a standard. "Everybody wants to be a perfect mother," she told me, and "I get depressed when I feel I'm not being effective as a mother." This standard of perfection is a hard taskmaster, for it remains ambiguous.

> AB: The whole motherhood thing is such an open kind of thing that you are grasping for something to kind of attach yourself to, try to look up to.

Alice feels that she is required to be perfect in this aspect of her job as household worker, but she is unclear about what being perfect entails, nor has she been given the skills and knowledge to do the job perfectly.

> AB: People expect you to be the perfect mother, but nobody teaches you how to be a perfect mother. They'll give you lessons in child care, but not in child rearing. When you seek professional help through books, there's so many, it's such a "hand throwing" argument. There's so many conflicting opinions. That's distressing to me.
>
> R: The many articles reinforce the idea that you must be better.
>
> AB: Right. That's true. [Laughs] That's true. That's true. But you know, it's exhausting trying to be the perfect mother because you're human. I get depressed when I feel like I've had a bad day. I've got a friend who lives just ten minutes away from here, and I'll talk to her and she says, "Well, Dr. Spock says—" And the thing is that I don't even want to hear what these people have to say because they're just as human as I am and generally they just upset me more. I prefer to follow my own instincts.

The conflicting opinions about appropriate performance cause Alice to feel anxious. In the language of "role ambiguity" we would say that she is made anxious by the lack of clear information that would enable her to perform her job in a manner she deems adequate. Her anger has turned toward those experts who seem to demand that she be perfect but who do not provide her with adequate knowledge to meet that goal. So she dismisses them, but the deprecation is also turned toward herself. More significantly for Alice, she feels that she is somehow personally lacking for not knowing what to do or how to do it. She recalled that, as a young girl, she was told that she was "good with children" and that she would "make such a good mother." The implication of these communications is that the job is not learned but is rooted in destiny and in identity. Failures, therefore, are more readily experienced as final statements about the inadequacy of the self.

The extreme privatization of child care in the nuclear family contributes to the lack of information about how one goes about rearing children and obscures the fact that these work activities are learned. Laslett (1973) has described how the separation of work and home life has made family members less accountable for the behavior that occurs within the privacy of the home. However, such privatization also has the effect of removing people such as Alice from the social support and learning opportunities that come from seeing other parents solve day-to-day problems. Sandra Jones, for example, sought her mother's help after Billy was born because "I don't know what I would have done, because she actually had to show me everything. I learned how to fix bottles down [there]." Alice does not turn to her mother for help because she worries that her mother will dismiss her concerns or make her feel inadequate.

When Alice does have the opportunity to hear other women talk about their child-care work, these afternoon visits are often sources of anxiety rather than support. Alice's friends' attempts to publicly validate their work by talking about their children's accomplishments result in Alice's feeling even more inadequate. The anxiety surrounding the performance of her job makes it difficult for her to share her doubts and concerns because she is convinced that only she has such feelings. The privatization of child care extends to the privatization of feelings about it, and Alice is unwilling to share her secret shames and worries. She returns home from such visits feeling depressed and vowing not to return.[7]

Evaluations. Inadequate feedback about one's performance is also a feature of role ambiguity that can be stressful. Alice has no supervisor from whom she will obtain a written evaluation, nor will she receive a bonus at the end of the year for a job well done. The inability to evaluate how she is doing is an additional source of stress. Kahn et al. have noted that ambiguity increases as objects and events recede in time, because it becomes more difficult then to predict the consequences of one's actions. In Alice's own words, "I think the satisfactions of motherhood are long-term, you know. It's like, it's what the finished product.... But I guess the ultimate satisfaction is seeing this fairly well-adjusted

7. One of the most significant outcomes of the research process was that Alice was finally able to share some of these feelings with her friends, including the fact that she did not enjoy child care.

adult. . . . I think that's when I feel really overwhelmed because I think . . . my terms are too distant." In other words, Alice must wait until her children are adults to determine how she has performed.

Even in the short run, Alice finds it difficult to evaluate her performance because the consequences of her actions remain unclear. Although the experts have convinced her that the way she rears her children is important for their well-being, she does not know which actions lead to which consequences. For example, recently Carrie began to lie, a behavior common in her age group. The question of how to deal with this new behavior involved Alice in a minor crisis. Should Carrie be spanked? Ignored? After several weeks of worry she finally found what she considered a viable solution. Thus, her children's every developmental step can be a source of new anxiety and stress.

The invisibility of child-care work contributes to Alice's difficulties in evaluating her performance. As Golden (1975) has noted about other mothers, Alice does not take the normal developmental gains of children—learning to walk, talk, control their bowels—as marks of successful job performance on her part. Oblivious to her successes, she translates her anxiety about doing a poor job into a heightened sensitivity to her possible failures. Signs of such failures are carefully monitored. Alice worried when James stuttered and wondered whether her children's habits of thumb sucking and holding their blankets indicate that they are not "coping." Other women in the study worried about their children's bed-wetting, school problems, or toilet training.

Job performance, and its evaluation, is especially critical in the area of child care because the outcome is so important. Bearing responsibility for persons is a potential source of job stress (Caplan et al. 1975). Lopata (1971) has aptly commented on how modern ideological developments have made women responsible for their children's physical and emotional well-being. Alice articulated this additional source of worry.

AB: I think, too, that many people my age or women my age get more and more caught up in this mother-guilt sort of thing because there are so many things working against you now. It would have been so much nicer to live in simpler times. I don't want to fall into this thing where things were so much better way back when because they had their problems then too, but I don't think as many.

R: Bigger expectations now?

AB: Right. [Laughs] Sometimes I really think that ignorance is bliss because the more you evolve, the more you've got to worry about. [Laughs] I mean, now we know that those first five years are so important to the final outcome, right? And you go, "Oh my God! Three years to go. What have I done?" [Laughs] Whereas, I think that before they knew it, and they just took it a day at a time, but we're seeing the whole picture now. We're seeing how too much affection can be smothering, not enough depriving.

R: A burden?

AB: It is. That's it exactly. It is a burden. That's it. You can see the whole picture now, whereas before I think that people just took it one day at a time.

Because Alice has internalized the ideology that defines child rearing as women's work, she feels this dilemma more acutely than does Richard. As far as he is concerned, she is "doing a fine job," but Alice heard this statement as a dismissal of her concerns. His well-intentioned support was heard as lack of understanding for the anxiety and strain that she was experiencing.

Thus, the socialization of children represents for Alice a source of job stress without seeming to provide tangible satisfaction. The results are long-term, she noted, and her feelings of being overwhelmed obviate, at present, gratification. We will see that Alice is not alone in these feelings. However, the privatization of the socialization process, at least of young children, means that these worries are not shared but are seen as secret badges of failure that must be hidden from view.

Managing Discontent

I have suggested that the psychological link between work experience and emotional life in families is mediated by the way the worker attempts to manage stress and strain. For example, we saw that for Richard Bernard the physical effort required by his farm chores helps him vent his frustration. Similarly, in order to understand the impact of Alice's experience of her work on the psychological life of the Bernard family, we need to consider how she attempts to manage her discontent, anger, and frustration.

No Exit

The discriminatory wage structure, sex-role ideology, and the necessity for the family unit to support the household combine to bind Alice to her work. Unlike Richard, Alice lacks the alternative of changing her job assignment in an attempt to create a better fit between her personal needs and her work. She cannot "bid" on another job within the household, and her extraorganizational alternatives are limited by her lack of marketable skills and the fact that her children are young. By definition, being a household worker in her family specifies the household into which she is locked. Moreover, the hours Richard works make it difficult for the Bernards to distribute household work more equitably. Alice would like more help with the children. She worries, however, that Richard's exhaustion from working the midnight shift makes him so irritable that he might lose control with the children if he spent extended periods of time alone with them. The solutions she must devise to deal with her work discontent lie within the home and within herself.

Managing Boredom
Because they are constrained by technology and hierarchical social relations of production, workers in the study who complained of monotony and boredom in their paid work could do little to reduce this source of strain. When circumstances allowed it, a common solution was to perform one's work quickly in order to steal rest time. Oakley (1974a) has pointed out that one way that household workers feel they are more fortunate than their wage-earning counterparts is that their freedom from supervision and their ability to determine their own work rhythms give them more autonomy. Alice can lessen the monotony of household work by varying her routine or by trying to avoid routine altogether. By not committing herself entirely to doing her chores in a regular way, she tries to prevent being captured by the rut she dreads.

> AB: Sometimes I think . . . that I'm not organized as my way of rebelling. I refuse to write shopping lists. I go shopping and I will forget at least a half a dozen things. I think that unconsciously I just don't want to.

Recalling her morning's activities on the Base Day, we can sense the rebellion Alice described as she flits from washing dishes to vacuuming and back again. Even though she may have more control over how and when she performs her chores than do many of the paid workers interviewed, external constraints on her ability to vary her routine still exist. Alice must feed the children in the morning as biological needs dictate, do her vacuuming before Richard goes to sleep, shop when the stores are open, and fix dinner when Richard comes home. The fact that we can talk about varying a routine indicates its existence. She herself recognized these constraints when she observed, "It's like I have to adjust my schedule to meet everybody's needs here."

Self-Rewards and Invisible Work
For work that is invisible goals are not clear and, therefore, a sense of achievement is difficult to attain. Some of the participants who did very routine work with few visible goals reported that they created their own goals in order to reward themselves. For example, the elder Mr. Turner prided himself on producing the smallest pile of metal shavings of any machine operator in the industrial plant where he worked. Jesse Jones sets personal production standards for himself so that he has a goal to work toward. Sometimes workers compete against each other as a way of creating visible goals. Oakley also has found that women who work in the home will substitute their own reward system by establishing performance standards, often based on those of their mother. By

230

meeting these standards, women gain a feeling of accomplishment and achievement.

Alice Bernard also has housekeeping standards; she calls herself a "perfectionist." However, the presence of young children makes it difficult for her to meet the goals she establishes. She feels fortunate to be able to clean two rooms a day. Her situation limits the self-rewards she is able to obtain through meeting her own expectations. Alice has found a partial solution to this dilemma by locating her need for cleanliness in one room—the bathroom; she gains some satisfaction from seeing a spotless bathroom.

Managing the Threat to Self

I have suggested that the boredom and monotony of household work threaten Alice because she experiences household work as endangering her ideal image of herself. One way she attempted to manage this threat was by enrolling in an accounting class the previous summer. School not only helped her to escape from being housebound, but it also offered expression to an identity that was an alternative to that of a housewife.

> AB: I started back last summer, and it was terrific! The work was piling up on me, but I loved it because I felt motivated. . . . I have to feel that the wheels are working or it bothers me. For some it could be like joining a club or getting into quilting or something like that. But there's got to be more!

Tony Johnson also described a feeling of being "charged" by being challenged and motivated, and Eric Cooper talked of how important school had become to him to counter the depletion he encountered at work. School similarly allowed Alice the opportunity to achieve and to express herself.

The research interviews were conducted during the winter and spring months. Alice had attended school during the previous summer, and she talked excitedly about returning again the following summer. Ironically, Richard was the family member who attended school during the time the research data were collected. As a veteran, he received money for going to school, and the household needed the extra income he earned in this way. But he would have preferred not to attend, and the time he spent there took him away from his family. The fact that Alice wanted to attend school but could not, whereas Richard attended although he did not want to, indicates how the personal needs of family members are given lower priority than the needs of the household as an economic unit. The Bernards made a decision on how and where to allocate their time and energy based on the household's economic needs. Richard was moonlighting in order to meet their financial obligations. These commitments made his time and energy less available for freeing Alice from some household work while she was at school. "The pace was a bit much," and she stopped attending.

Psychological Disengagement

A defense participants use against the threat to self is to learn not to care about their work activities and their work situations—to disengage from them. To the extent that they achieved this disengagement, male participants could distinguish conceptually between their roles as workers and their roles as husband-fathers, even though in reality there was carry-over from the former to the latter. They could make family roles more important to themselves, even though such a commitment could not readily be realized. Such disengagement was more difficult for men like Richard Bernard, whose work activity is connected to his ideal image of himself.

For the household worker, such disengagement is extremely difficult. Family socioemotional roles and household work roles overlap in time and space and are not easily distinguished. Moreover, being a wife and mother—a "good enough" one, at that—is very much at the heart of personal identity for many women. Alice struggles against this connection, but in the pain she feels, the connection nevertheless makes itself known. Learning not to care about her work would be experienced as not loving her children and husband, and such a blow to her self-esteem would be difficult to tolerate.

Managing Anger

A number of participants reported that anger in a situation of powerlessness is threatening to the self—a form of self-torture and self-destruction. In my view, it is her feeling of anger—what she has called her "resentment"—that Alice has most difficulty managing. This resentment stems from being locked into a job that is boring and threatening to her self-image while being at the same time ambiguous and overly difficult. These feelings were articulated in the process of the study. Previously, the barely acknowledged feelings of being overwhelmed by her job seemed to be expressed by recurring feelings of inadequacy or bouts of what she termed becoming a "cleaning fanatic." By cleaning her house vigorously, Alice tried to regain control—to put her house in order, both internally and externally. However, these solutions were short-lived and doomed to failure, for within hours the external disorder returned. When the children created demands and the house began to get messy, Alice's internal unrest returned as well. The context in which Alice attempts to manage her anger is important for our understanding of interface relationships.

"Defiant Neglect"

In addition to learning not to care, participants also coped with angry feelings by giving vent to them. Richard, for example, alleviated tension by wrestling with his steer. I also mentioned the silent protest he made in the form of a work slowdown when he was transferred to another department without warning. Though reluctant to describe the details, Samuel Coleman mentioned his use of "technical means" to express his disgruntlement at his supervisor. Jesse Jones, as well as Samuel, mentioned lodging complaints through the union hierarchy against supervisors he felt had wronged him. Such expressions of anger may not change the sources of the problem, but they do serve to release inner tension. When feelings of rage and frustration would mount, Alice also reported that she had acted out her discontent with a form of work slowdown.

> AB: I'd go for a week without cleaning the bathroom. I'd figure all this stuff was unimportant, so it could just wait. . . . So I just kind of collected my chores. I'd do it defiantly. It was almost childlike, like, "Oooh, I'm not gonna do that." And then the whole thing would pile up on me, and I'd get really angry that I had done this. . . . It was like a vicious circle—defiant neglect and anger at myself.

Richard could use the slowdown as a silent work protest because its effects were invisible. Similarly, Samuel Coleman's sabotage is invisible because of the impersonality of his work organization. The social nature of the productive process protects him. But household work becomes visible precisely when it is undone. And since it is a solitary activity, the responsibility for doing the work remains clearly with the household worker. The presence of incompleted work served as a constant reminder to Alice. Moreover, those who suffered from its continued neglect were not strangers or disliked supervisors—they were the same people Alice loves and lives with. Because her work is performed in the same setting in which she lives with her family, she cannot leave at the end of a shift. The fusion of her work and family life makes it difficult for Alice to express her discontent through her work.

Griping

Giving vent to anger by talking about it also can give release to personal tension. I described the "griping" that occurred during the night I observed Richard at work. The interview situation also served as an opportunity to gripe, and whether directed at work organization, fellow workers, or management, anger emerged in fifteen of the eighteen interviews with participants who were or are employed.

Griping requires that anger be openly admitted and that it have an external object. For example, Alice can become angry at supermarkets

233

that place candy at child height. She has fantasies of "going berserk," upsetting the stand and throwing things around. When her anger is directed at impersonal objects, it can be vented. For the most part, the venting of anger through griping is not simple for her, as the objects of her frustration are her husband and her children. The employed worker leaves his or her supervisor and fellow workers at the end of the day; Alice must live with those toward whom she feels angry. Not only does she lack a group with which to share her gripes, but we also know that openly ambivalent feelings toward loved ones can result in guilt and a loss of self-esteem. Insofar as she feels that her anger is unjustified, it is even more difficult to express. Though her husband and children lock her into her job, dirty anew what she has just cleaned, and present her with difficult problems, she also knows that personally they are not to blame. Without a legitimate object, Alice is allowed neither to experience her anger nor to vent it through griping. The fusion of working and loving, therefore, makes it difficult for her to release angry tension through the means that paid workers have available to them.

How "Typical" Is Alice?

For a variety of reasons, household work is a source of strain for Alice Bernard. Certain activities such as vacuuming, washing dishes, and the physical care of her children are boring and uninteresting to her. The invisibility of this work limits the social rewards she might obtain from its performance. More importantly, Alice fears losing her self, and the person she wants to be, in her household work. She not only dislikes aspects of her work and feels strain from them, but she also is guilty about not liking them. Child care especially is a source of conflict for her. She has internalized the ideal of fulfilling a "holy role" and being child-centered, yet she fears that such work will result in her losing herself. We can understand why Alice was willing to articulate her feelings to a relative stranger: bringing them into public view was a confession and a relief.

In contrast to the boring features of her work, the tasks of socialization and the social production of children are complex, difficult, and ambiguous for Alice. Lacking clear guidelines on how to proceed, this form of work overload and role ambiguity is another source of stress. She feels responsible for the outcome of her efforts in raising her children, but she cannot evaluate her performance. The invisibility of her work makes her vigilant for failure; she feels alone in her anxiety because these feelings remain private.

As a result of such job stresses Alice feel's angry, frustrated, depressed, and often inadequate. These feelings moved ever closer to ar-

234

ticulation during the course of the six months of data collection and collaboration.

Although Alice is being understood for herself, it also is helpful for us to place her experiences in the context of what we know about how other household workers feel about their work experiences. The recent research on housework has come up with equivocal results about the way women feel about such work. Ferree has noted that the "preference of less educated women for housework over paid work... has been unjustifiably inferred from Komarovsky's finding that better educated housewives are more unhappy at home than less educated women" (1976, p. 435). In her own study of working-class women, Ferree found a high degree of dissatisfaction with their lives and with housework among women who were nonemployed. The low self-esteem and feelings of powerlessness she found are similar to the findings of a study performed more than a decade before (Rainwater et al. 1959). Oakley (1974a) also found a high degree of dissatisfaction with housework among the small sample of women she studied. On the other hand, with a larger sample, Lopata (1971) found that the women she studied were relatively satisfied with the role of housewife.

There are several ways in which we can understand the differences between Lopata's findings—which utilized the largest sample—and those of Ferree and Oakley. Oakley has suggested that she was considering women's feelings about performing household tasks, whereas Lopata was considering their feelings about the social role of housewife—that is, the difference between doing and being. Using an analogy to paid work, we might consider differences in how men might respond to questions about their actual work activities and their satisfaction with the role of breadwinner. We know from studies of paid job satisfaction that the way one asks about work satisfaction can have an important effect on the results (Quinn 1974). When women express satisfaction with being a housewife, they may be expressing satisfaction with their fulfillment of social role obligations, with their notions that women should fulfill these obligations, or with the actual work activities themselves. Expressions of satisfaction also could indicate a lack of dissatisfaction rather than ego gratification. Finally, from Lopata's research we also know that women understand the concept of "housewife" in a variety of ways. She found that "housewife" is seen as a vocational role, as a generic term identifying the whole person, or it is ignored—with its duties and rights divided among other roles such as that of wife and mother. Any assessment of satisfactions must take into account the differences between the phenotypic response and the underlying constellation of roles and activities to which it refers. Further careful research is needed in this area.

Despite these equivocal results, we could say that at least some women are dissatisfied with housework. Most of the housewives Oakley interviewed complained of monotony and boredom. As Bernard (1972) has noted, not all women have the aptitude or inclination to be housewives. The feeling of being "housebound" and tied down by young children is a consistent theme in the literature on housewives (Ferree 1976; Gavron 1966; Komarovsky 1953, 1962; Lopata 1971; Rainwater et al. 1959). Whereas the job satisfaction research does not examine child-care activity directly, it does indicate that some women find child care tedious and unrewarding. Lopata reported that many of the duties associated with child care are "irksome" to some mothers; Oakley found that deep ambivalences about child-care activities emerged in the interviews she conducted. The interview with Alice Bernard lends support to Oakley's conclusion that such ambivalence is so difficult to admit that it cannot be tapped by simple survey questions but emerges in the course of long hours of interviewing. Lopata also found what I have termed the "threat to self"—namely, that many of the women she interviewed felt conflicts between obligations to themselves and the duties of child care. Finally, Lopata reported on the anxieties experienced by young women about their children's behavior—a stressor I described as "role ambiguity." Because I have reported on one person, Alice's discontent may appear dramatic. But there is reason to believe that other women— young mothers in particular—share with Alice a similar constellation of feelings about their work.

The Research Participants

The data on participants' feelings about their household work are scanty, in part because the importance of the household–family interface was uncovered after much of the data were already collected. Moreover, questions about their work did not elicit lengthy responses, perhaps because they did not deem their own work important enough to talk about. Still, enough data were collected to indicate that, while intensity of expressed feelings varied, seven of the ten women interviewed indicated some dissatisfaction with household work or stated a preference for working outside the home.

Reasons for dissatisfaction included monotonous work and a sense of not accomplishing much with their lives. Paula Doyle gains more of a sense of esteem and competence from her paid job than from her household work, although she also worries about her inability to maintain her standards of household work performance while working outside the home. Celia Healy seemed reluctant to express her views openly with Mike present, but she did complain about lacking a feeling of accomplishment in her work and indicated that she sometimes wants to escape from it:

Household Work and Its Discontents

R: How do you feel about your job?

CH: I don't have a job. [*Laughs*] You mean my house job?? [*Grimaces*] Some days I just think, "Get out. Just [leave] it all behind." But I wouldn't, 'cause I love them all too much. . . .

MH: I don't want her to work.

CH: He'd rather me clean the house or do something he wants me to do rather than what I want to do!

MH: I don't want her to work; it's as simple as that. I want all her undivided attention to my kids—

CH: And I can't do that!

R: Why can't you do that?

CH: Because I don't feel like I'm accomplishing anything! I want to do something with my life, like he's going to school and doing something with his. But he don't understand that.

This interchange between Mike and Celia was quite heated and perhaps my presence encouraged her to express these feelings. Among the participants, Betty Johnson was particularly outspoken about her feelings about housework:

R: Some women think of housework as a job. Others see it as something special.

BJ: I hate it! I hate it! And my one dream would be that I would have a cleaning woman. I hate every minute of it because I've been doing it for twenty-five years, and I'm tired of it.

Sandra Jones, who left her office job to care for their new infant, approached the question slowly.

R: You first thought you would like staying home?

SJ: [*Indicates yes and laughs*]

R: What . . . were your thoughts about staying home? . . .

SJ: Well, I thought that I'd probably enjoy getting up early in the morning and cleaning my house and not having to wait until the weekend to do my cleaning. I thought that I'd just . . . enjoy the thought of getting up, watering my plants, and in the wintertime I'd wake up and look at everybody else go to work and not have to get out in the cold. But it turned out different.

R: What were your fantasies about having a little baby?

SJ: No. Well, getting up, enjoying getting up with him and cleaning him, bathing him, and feeding him. But I guess after a time, a year's time, it gets boring.

Sandra hesitated to say that taking care of Billy is "boring." Her feeling of being imprisoned in her home is more explicit.

237

SJ: Sometimes I feel like if I stay in here for long periods of time, then I feel like the walls are closing in on me. Sometimes I go through the house, even like when I'm cleaning, just like it's not clean unless I change it around. I have to change my furniture around, just to get a different appearance in the house. . . . My girlfriend, she changes, she's fickle and she changes I know every week because the living room is arranged differently. She feels the same way I do. She can clean and clean, and it's just not clean unless it's changed around, or she might feel like the walls are coming in on her. She just rearranges.

Sandra and her friend try to deal with their feeling of constriction by creating minor changes of scene. These changes, however, are not real; they are merely rearrangements that never satisfy. Sandra is now considering returning to paid work.

Even without my pursuing the topic in great detail, most of the women I interviewed expressed some dissatisfaction with aspects of their household work. Added to their husbands' discontent with work is their own. In considering the Bernard family, we must ultimately ask about the consequences for families when both employed and household workers are dissatisfied with their jobs.

CHAPTER 11

Interfaces: Household Work and Family Life

Although work activities and emotional activities overlap for the household worker, it is instructive to use the interface concepts elaborated in Part II to analyze the relationships between emotional and household subsystems within the Bernard family home. Such an analysis can help us see, with fresh eyes, what transpires daily between mothers and their children and between wives and their husbands.

The Pattern of Negative Carry-over

I have suggested that anger is among the emotions generated in Alice's relationship to her household work. Anger that cannot be expressed verbally or acted out under nonthreatening conditions still can make itself known. Repression and denial of such feelings are not always successful, and anger can be expressed in duplicitous ways. For example, Alice described becoming nauseous when she attempted to contain anger. Realizing that her "resentment" does emerge in her life, Alice worries that these feelings are expressed in her relationships with family members. They are her most immediate audience, and when she feels unappreciated she expresses irritation at them. For example, she described a time when she was particularly bitter about feeling unvalued.

AB: The way that it will surface may not be directly involved with the problem. It can surface in different ways. . . . It was just this feeling of—[*Long pause*]

R: Displacement?

AB: Right! Right. Yeah.

R: Tell me more about that.

AB: Well, I think it is basically that everybody needs to feel their worth, all right? Now, all I had to show for myself was this, and if my immediate worth was not appreciated by others, taken lightly, then I would get angry about—you know—the toothpaste squeezed in the middle of the tube or something like that. Which is so far out in left field. But then, when you trace it back, that's what it all boils down to.

More specifically, she worries that she expresses these feelings toward her children. For example, she recalled a time when she flew into a rage at Nicholas and found herself on the verge of physically hurting him. Shocked and frightened, she "shut down" for the day, and put herself and the children to bed. That memory is important to Alice, for it reminds her of the undercurrents of her rage. Richard, to whom she had spoken about the incident, had forgotten it. More recently, she described an incident in which resentment over the duties and obligations of her work role expressed itself toward Carrie.

AB: I was having a miserable night trying to sleep and Carrie woke me up about 3:30 crying and I asked her what was the matter and she, "Waah . . ." [*mimics Carrie's wail*]; so she goes to the kitchen and she's standing there sobbing. I said, "What is the matter with you?" And she goes, "I want water!" So I grabbed her hand like this and gave her a dig with my nails, and in a second she's going, "Look! Look!" And I got her the water, and when I got done I said to myself, "Why did you dig your nails into her skin?" You know, I'm angry at her—so what?

Whereas Richard can work out his frustrations on his farm by wrestling with his steer, Alice has no such outlet for her anger. Instead, some of it becomes directed at the children, whom she sees, in part, as connected to her difficulty.[1]

In Chapter 3, displacing angry feelings about work into the family system was described as a variant of the negative carry-over pattern. In Table 11-1, we see that 43 percent of Alice's initiations toward Carrie, James, and Nicholas are Negative. These Negative initiations are primarily Influencing and Disapproving, rather than Blaming–Accusing and Antagonistic. From the definitions of these categories, as presented in the Methodological Appendix, we can say that insofar as Alice acts out her resentment about her work in her interactions with her children, such a carry-over takes the form of, in her words, "ragging." Rather than being punitive with the children or expressing disdain toward who they

---

1. Bernard has suggested that the idealization of motherhood is used to protect children from the rage that mothers feel and that "the anger and irritability [motherhood] fosters in women reverberates on the children" (1975, pp. 14–15). Simone de Beauvoir wrote: "A mother who whips her child is not beating the child alone; in a sense she is not beating it at all: she is taking out her vengeance on a man, on the world, or on herself. Such a mother is often remorseful and the child may not feel resentment, but it feels the blows" (1961, p. 484).

Table 11-1. Quality of Alice's Initiations to the Children as Percentages of Coded Initiations

INITIATION	ALICE TO CARRIE $N = 190^{a}$	ALICE TO JAMES $N = 285$	ALICE TO NICHOLAS $N = 237$	ALICE TO CHILDREN $N = 571^{b}$
Positive				
Base Day	8%	18%	20%	16%
All Days[c]	9	14	17	15
Neutral				
Base Day	9	5	3	5
All Days	9	5	3	5
Negative[d]				
Base Day	39	34	32	38
All Days	39	39	43	43
Influence Mild				
Base Day	47	47	45	43
All Days	45	46	37	40
Influence Strong				
Base Day	10	13	15	14
All Days	12	14	18	16

Note: Percentages total more than 100 because each initiation could be coded in more than one category.
[a]The total initiations for All Days.
[b]This figure does not represent a row total, since one initiation to more than one child was counted but once in this column.
[c]*All Days* refers to percentage of total initiations coded, including those on the Base Day.
[d]*Negative* includes the category of *Influence Strong*.

are as people, she is irritated by what they do and do not do. This irritability about their behavior is reflected in the Base Day observations as well. In Chapter 3, I also suggested that such carry-over can prevent positive interactions from occurring. Table 11-1 indicates that 15 percent of Alice's initiations toward the children are Positive, suggesting that when Alice is feeling edgy and angry, it is difficult for her to simultaneously express warmth and affection.

In the discussion of the psychological interface patterns involving Richard, I indicated that such patterns may vary for different components of the family system. I have already suggested that for several reasons Alice is reluctant to express anger or irritation toward Richard. Expressing such feelings toward him might propel him outside, thereby further reducing their contact. In contrast, as indicated in Figure 7-2, she has constant contact with the children, except for the evening hours. Furthermore, if we look at the patterns of interactions during the Base Day we see, in Table 11-2, that Alice was at the hub of an interactional

Table 11-2. Interaction Patterns on Base Day as Percentages
of Total Coded Verbal Interactions in the Family

INTERACTION BETWEEN	PERCENT OF TOTAL
Alice and Richard	4[a]
Alice and Carrie	21
Alice and James	34
Alice and Nicholas	24
Richard and Carrie	2[a]
Richard and James	5[a]
Richard and Nicholas	2[a]
Carrie and James	5
Carrie and Nicholas	2
James and Nicholas	2

[a]These figures may be a slight underestimate. Parallel play was difficult to code (see Methodological Appendix). Also, some of the uncoded observational segments included time periods when Richard was at home and awake. This latter bias is counterbalanced by two factors. First, some interaction occurred among other family members as well, so that the percentage figures would not necessarily change. Second, Alice mentioned that Richard stayed to chat before going to class and before going to bed *because* I was present. These time periods constituted the bulk of the uncoded observational periods. Thus, my presence induced greater interaction with Richard than would normally have occurred. This interpretation is further supported by the fact that Richard directed most of his comments to me.

network that involved her and the children. Over three-fourths of all coded verbal interactions occurring within the family system on the Base Day involved this quartet. While this figure is not corrected for the brief uncoded periods, it still is striking and corresponds to other research that indicates that mothers and their young children have a high degree of contact, even with fathers present (Dyck 1963). Resentment, therefore, would most easily be expressed in these interactions.

This carry-over pattern is compounded for Alice because she lacks a private place—such as Richard has—to which she can withdraw to ease tension. The need for a quiet space when one is tired from work was a repeated theme in the interviews with paid workers. During these times the needs of children can be irritating; regardless of how Alice feels on a particular day, the children are always there. On the morning of the Base Day we saw her efforts to create space for herself when she sat down with her book and her breakfast (see 9:00 A.M.). Alice had been working hard for over an hour and was taking what would normally be considered a "break," time that is carefully guarded by many of the employed participants I interviewed. Richard had just gone to sleep, and James began hovering nearby. Alice made several attempts to clear some time and space for herself by reading, by asking the children to leave and give her some "peace and quiet" and go "play something," and by ignoring them. Unsuccessful in these efforts, Alice finally resolved that they could remain in the kitchen but that the table was to be hers. This description of Alice's effort to create a physical—and emotional—space for herself hints at the importance of architectural design as it may affect family dynamics (see Lennard & Lennard 1977; Chilman 1978).

Sometimes the children manage the tension themselves by physically withdrawing. For example, on the Base Day both Carrie and James momentarily removed themselves from their mother's presence after she had scolded them (see 10:30 A.M.). However, the children's momentary attempts to ease the tension are limited because they are dependent on their mother for affection and for meeting their needs. Without Richard's presence, there normally are no other adults to turn to. Toward the end of the Base Day, Carrie did turn to me on two occasions (see 6:45 P.M. and 8:00 P.M.).

Children and Household Work

To understand the pattern of Alice's initiations toward her children only as a displacement of her resentment toward her work seemed to me, during the study, an oversimplification of what I had observed. In order to further understand this pattern, interactions between Alice and the children were analyzed thematically. What emerged from this analysis was the hypothesis that, without sufficient resources to prevent it, conflict is built into the structure of current everyday household life with children. This antagonism stems from the fact that alongside the household work subsystem is a children's "world", for the home is also the setting where children may play and obtain satisfaction of their emotional needs. A young child's orientation to the realities of time, space, and things, and his or her difficulty in deferring gratification of needs, place the child's world at variance with the production and service orientation of a work organization. Children are excluded from many employment settings, but the household worker with young children must accomplish her tasks alongside this children's world.[2]

2. Oakley (1974a) similarly noted that it is an unusual aspect of housework as a job that it is carried on simultaneously with child rearing. In her study she found that children were often cited as a general source of frustration for women trying to accomplish housework because of interruptions required by child-care tasks. Children amplified the fragmentation of housework. She has suggested that children not only make messes and interrupt the houseworker, but that the roles of houseworker and child rearer are, in principle, contradictory. Note that Oakley did not include child care as a housework activity (see Methodological Appendix).

In the section that follows, quantitative and observational data will be used to illustrate this structural conflict and to draw out its implications for the relationship between Alice and her children. I will suggest that the tension created by the subsystem antagonisms depletes Alice and makes it even more difficult for her to manage the conflict. By analyzing such ordinary transactions we can learn more about the experiences of what Komarovsky (1953) has called the "overworked young mother" and what such overwork means for family life. Focusing on the relationship between the children's subsystem and that of the household means that other themes present in the data, such as the socialization to obedience, will not be discussed.

Children as Household Aides

Alice does not go about her household work independently of the children. The importance of children to the management of the household is reflected in the fact that on the Base Day, 50 percent of all coded interactions between Alice and the children were related to Domestic matters (see Table 10-1). Of the initiations Alice made to the children, 61 percent were related to household work. The implications of the interface between children's activities and the household for mother-child interactions can be seen if we look at Table 11-3.

Of the Domestic initiations, 64 percent involved Alice in attempts to get the children to do something. In other words, over one-third of all the initiations Alice made to the children on the Base Day were influencing attempts relevant to her work in the home. These figures suggest that Alice depends on her children in carrying out her daily work activities. Sometimes she asks them for help directly, as in getting a diaper or turning out a light. More commonly, she needs them to cooperate with her efforts to get household work completed. For example, she requires that Nicholas lie still while being diapered, that they eat their food, that they not interfere with her goals, such as sweeping or washing dishes, and that they abide by some household rules such as not spilling food and remembering to flush the toilet (see, for example, Base Day, 10:30 A.M., 12:30 P.M., 5:30 P.M., 6:15 P.M., and 7:30 P.M.).

In asking for help in these ways, Alice serves as a household manager. Whereas an adult or a trained older child might understand what needs to be done without explicit direction, Alice must tell the children exactly what she needs. They are still young, relatively untrained household aides. In contrast, I watched 14-year-old Charles Turner take his turn at washing dishes because he knew that was his chore for the day. Not only is Alice teaching her children the rules of the household, but she also serves as an overseer of their activities. This role was most evident when she specifically directed the children during the cleanup of the play area (see Base Day, 6:15 P.M.). When I noted this overseer role

Table 11-3. Alice's Initiations to Children by Content and Quality as Percentages of Coded Initiations

	CONTENT OF INITIATION						
QUALITY OF INITIATION	Domestic	Social Interaction		Play		All Other	
	N = 369[a]	N = 114	(N = 110)[b]	N = 59	(N = 54)	N = 61	(N = 45)
Positive							
Base Day[c]	11%	30%		24%		13%	
All Days	8	39	(41)	19	(20)	15	(16)
Neutral							
Base Day	7	5		0		3	
All Days	6	4	(5)	5	(6)	3	(0)
Negative[d]							
Base Day	35	53		35		21	
All Days	44	46	(48)	51	(50)	28	(13)
Influence Mild							
Base Day	49	19		43		68	
All Days	45	17	(15)	36	(35)	57	(67)
Influence Strong							
Base Day	15	10		11		8	
All Days	20	9	(8)	8	(9)	7	(9)

Note: Percentages total more than 100 because each initiation could be coded in more than one category.
[a]The total number of coded initiations for All Days.
[b]Total number of coded initiations for All Days, with initiations also coded as Domestic, removed.
[c]All Days refers to percentage of total initiations coded, including those on the Base Day.
[d]Negative includes the category of Influence Strong.

during our discussion of the observational notes, Alice responded that she sometimes experiences herself as a "creature with a bullwhip, driving the children on."

For the most part, Carrie, James, and Nicholas comply with Alice's requests for help and cooperation. Table 11-4 indicates that two-thirds of Alice's Domestic initiations toward them were met with either clear positive or quiet compliance. This compliance varies with the age of the child, with Carrie being most compliant and Nicholas slightly less agreeable than James, suggesting that they have become trained in household cooperation and assistance over time. However, in obtaining this compliance, Alice sometimes uses coercive measures. Thus, 20 percent of her Domestic influencing initiations involved some display of coercion or force (see Table 11-3).[3] Noncompliance can upset the smooth running of the household; therefore, the potential for stress and conflict exists. Alice is thus dependent on the cooperation of her children to meet household work goals, and her awareness of this fact is reflected in the value she places on obedience. She lamented the loss of "blind control" over Carrie, who is becoming independent, for household life would be simpler if the children did as they were told.

Colliding Subsystems

Although they can be enlisted in the running of the household, children easily can subvert the work process by not cooperating; since children are not automatons but have their own goals and needs, household life does not necessarily run smoothly. In the observational segment "Preparing for Sleep" we saw tension increase and conflict escalate rapidly when the children chose not to cooperate with Alice. Turning again to Table 11-4, we see that approximately one-third of Alice's Domestic initiations to the children are met with some sort of negativism, either direct or covert; covert Negative responses include avoiding or ignoring her. Removing from other content areas those initiations that are also Domestic, we find in Table 11-3 that over one-third of Alice's Domestic initiations to the children also are Negative, that is, disapproving, scolding, or coercive. The children's Domestic approaches to Alice also are almost one-third Negative (see Table 11-5). In fact, more than half of all Domestic interactions between them involve some negativism, either on the part of Alice or the children. Domestic interactions have little to recommend them as warm and affectionate interactions. In both their initiation and response components they are

---

3. Simmons and Schoggen (1963) also found that mothers are significant sources of environmental pressure on children, and that children comply with about two-thirds of these pressures.

Table 11-4. Children's Responses to Alice's Initiations by Content and Quality as Percentages of Coded Responses

	CONTENT OF RESPONSES			
QUALITY OF RESPONSES	Domestic $N = 334$[a]	Social Interaction $N = 100$	Play $N = 61$	All Other $N = 84$
Positive				
Base Day	18%	30%	36%	37%
Total[b]	16	28	34	29
Neutral				
Base Day	52	34	49	40
Total	49	34	46	49
Negative				
Base Day	35	33	11	29
Total	34	36	15	26
Overt Negative				
Base Day	15	18	4	5
Total	14	22	3	5
Covert Negative				
Base Day	20	15	8	24
Total	20	14	11	21

Notes: Percentages total more than 100 because each response could be coded in more than one category.
[a]The total number of coded responses. See Footnote b.
[b]Total excludes one observation period for which figures are unavailable.

the least positive of all the interactions between Alice and the children. These figures are important because so much of daily interaction between Alice and the children centers around household work.

The differing goals, needs, and realities of Alice and the children became evident when the observational data were analyzed by two judges for the source of household-related conflict and tension. Though the list is not exhaustive, conflict occurred over the younger children's developing sense of autonomy and independence and Alice's goal of maintaining their physical well-being, over their different orientations to time and space, and over their desire for contact when Alice wanted to work (see, for example, Base Day, 8:30, 9:00, 9:45, 10:00, and 10:30 A.M.; 12:30, 6:00, and 6:45 P.M.). Some of these conflicts will be illustrated briefly.

Time. We have seen that time is an important dimension in the structural interface between work and family systems. Time also

Table 11-5. Children's Initiations to Alice by Content and Quality as Percentages of Coded Initiations

| | CONTENT OF INITIATIONS | | | |
QUALITY OF INITIATIONS	Domestic N = 113[a]	Social Interaction N = 151	Play N = 52	All Other N = 58
Positive				
Base Day	7%	39%	35%	49%
All Days[b]	9	38	38	43
Neutral				
Base Day	16	19	5	31
All Days	17	24	4	29
Negative[c]				
Base Day	26	24	19	5
All Days	29	23	15	17
Influence Mild				
Base Day	51	28	54	28
All Days	45	25	62	22
Influence Strong				
Base Day	4	3	0	0
All Days	6	3	0	0

Note: Percentages total more than 100 because each initiation could be coded in more than one category.
[a]The total number of coded initiations for All Days.
[b]*All Days* refers to percentage of total initiations coded, including those on the Base Day.
[c]*Negative* includes the category of *Influence Strong*.

emerges as an important structural variable relating the subsystem of the children and household work within the Bernard home. Alice's work in the household is often accompanied by a sense of urgency and the need to get jobs underway and chores completed. This sense of urgency was apparent on the morning of the Base Day. She rushed to get her vacuuming done before Richard went to bed; she rushed to get the children fed; then she rushed to get Carrie off to nursery school. Work time is measured by the clock. Children follow other dictates and very young children lack any conception of time. Thus, the first Domestic conflict of the Base Day began with a clash about time (see 8:30 A.M.). Carrie was languishing over her breakfast and Alice wanted to get breakfast completed. Alice became an overseer, urging her recalcitrant young daughter to finish eating. A second such conflict occurred during lunchtime, with Alice determined to be out of the house by 1:00 P.M., while the children continued to eat at their own leisurely pace.

Not only are the children differently oriented to time than Alice is in her role as household worker, they also have different ideas about the way time is to be used. Often conflict occurred because the children wanted to play while Alice wanted to dress or undress them, feed them, or involve them in cleaning up. For example, the following excerpt illustrates how conflict can escalate when Nicholas and Alice confront each other over the use of time.

"Nicholas Upset" (April 11)

[The children are outside playing; Richard is working at farm chores.] Nicholas is in the barn, climbing around the back area. It seems dangerous, and I close the gate to prevent him from falling off the back loft. Alice comes out of the house and calls to Richard, "Where's Nicholas?" Richard indicates that he is in the barn. She comes out to the barn to fetch him, and as she enters, she gives Carrie a box and instructs her to pick up the toys. She picks Nicholas up and he begins to scream. Nevertheless, she carries him onto the back porch of the house to take off his muddy shoes. Now he is in full-fledged protest and is screaming loudly. I see that Alice is becoming tense. He strikes out at her as she tries to take off his shoes and jacket, and she becomes visibly angry. She carries him into the bathroom; her anger is clear, for she is using his middle name. "Nicholas Thomas!! Straighten up! Do you want a spanking?"

He is still crying violently as she cleans him up. Carrie and James come in from the yard and examine the Easter lily on the kitchen table. James walks into the bathroom where Alice is washing Nicholas, who is still screaming. Sounding stern, Alice says abruptly to James, "I want the dirty clothes off in the pantry!" James quickly goes off to the pantry. She emerges from the bathroom and says to Carrie, "Carrie Margaret! I want the dirty clothes *off*!" Again she spanks Nicholas, who is still crying. She is extremely irritated. She insists to Nicholas, "Now you will stop!" He is still crying uncontrollably, and she carries him into the living room to deposit him there. "That's enough," she tells him.

She now turns to James, who is in the pantry, and says, "James Michael! Get your jeans off!" "I can't," he complains. "Well, come here," she responds, but instead she goes into the pantry to pull off his jeans. Nicholas, still crying and blinded by tears, comes from the living room and goes into the bathroom, searching for Alice. Finally he finds her in the pantry and, still crying, follows her into the bathroom as she washes Carrie's and James's hands. Alice says sternly, "Nicholas, do you want to go to bed?" "No," he answers through his tears. Alice scolds Carrie briefly. Nicholas is standing next to Alice, still crying loudly. Curtly and sternly, Alice asks Carrie, "Did you put all the toys in the box?" "Yes," Carrie answers quietly. Still not satisfied, Alice asks "Where did you leave the box?" Carrie's reply is meek and satisfies Alice who answers, "OK." She finishes washing Carrie and James in the bathroom and they emerge into the kitchen.

Alice is at the sink; Nicholas, still crying but more quietly now, approaches Alice. "What do you want now?" He quiets down and she says, "Will you behave?" "No," is his answer. He follows her around the kitchen, still crying. Alice sends Carrie and James into the living room. "Come here, Nicholas," she says. "No," he says once more. "Fine," Alice responds. Nicholas stops crying. "What do you want?" she asks. "Water." "OK. Come here. I'll give you a hug."

249

He goes to Alice who hugs him. James comes into the kitchen at that point and asks for water too.

This fifteen-minute incident illustrates conflicts between Nicholas's autonomy and desire to play and Alice's desire to clean him up for dinner and get the family fed. As a result of the escalation of conflict between herself and Nicholas, Alice's irritation carried over into her interactions with Carrie and James: her use of their middle names indicated that she meant business. My impression watching this scene was that Alice was looking for the opportunity to vent her anger at Nicholas's resistance. Carrie might have provided her with the opportunity had she not performed her job properly. Alice seems to be less constrained in expressing anger at Carrie, the oldest and least vulnerable child. Perhaps this scene would have gone differently had Richard been in the house to help Alice with Nicholas.

Spaces and Things. As a household worker, one of Alice's tasks is to maintain the physical plant—the house—in a reasonably orderly way. This aspect of her work requires her to monitor spaces and the things that occupy them, including the tools she uses to keep things and spaces clean. While household goals include cleanliness and neatness, children's orientation to space and things may be quite different. Children use space and objects in play and sometimes rearrange them in the process. These different orientations also result in conflict between Alice and her children. For example, on the Base Day we noticed her chastizing the children when they "rode" the vacuum cleaner (see 9:00 A.M.). To them it must have seemed like a convenient vehicle. Furniture, as well as tools, must be defended from children, as when James climbed over an end table and Alice yelled, "Get off the table." By being stern, Alice hopes to teach him a household rule which, if followed, would ease her household work in the future.

Alice's job in keeping the home livable means to her that things are to be kept in prescribed locations, while certain spaces are maintained free of encumbrances. That is the meaning of "neatness," one of Alice's goals as a household worker. But again, young children lack an orientation to such tidiness and propriety.

"The Toy" (April 21)
[Alice and James are sitting on the sofa, watching television.] James drags a toy from the play area beyond the sofa. Alice admonishes him with a "No!" and throws it back over her head. He rushes off into the toy area and brings it back. Alice again throws it angrily into the play area, over her head.

James's original goal seemed to be to maintain proximity to Alice while playing. However, one of Alice's goals is to maintain the neatness of "at least" the living-room area. What began as a desire to play and maintain contact resulted in a confrontation over control and autonomy. Emotionally meaningful issues thus are expressed through household matters.

A more dramatic example of the conflicting goals of play and contact versus keeping spaces clean occurred on the morning of the Base Day (see 8:45 A.M.). Nicholas had taken his blocks from the play area into the living room, most likely in order to maintain visual contact with Alice, who was in the kitchen where she could not be seen from the play area. James was helping him until Alice noticed this forbidden activity and insisted that they take the blocks back. To protect his autonomy and maintain visual contact with Alice, Nicholas's creative solution was to play on the small table at the boundary between the play and the living-room area. He incorporated the lamp into his play and placed the blocks on and around it. Such play required considerable coordination and effort on his part; yet the rules of the household—designed to minimize Alice's work—did not allow such creative play, and soon he had to put his blocks away.

Another one of Alice's household tasks is to guard her children's physical well-being. Space that seems interesting for play can be dangerous. The following incident illustrates how the children's desire to use space in play conflicts with Alice's goal of keeping them safe, as well as her need to accomplish other household tasks.

"The Door" (April 11)

[Alice is in the kitchen folding laundry. The boys are in the living room at the front door, which is partly ajar. Alice can hear them but not see them.] James and Nicholas are at the front door in their underpants. As I go in to observe them, Alice tells me that they're "probably in some mischief." She follows me and warns them about not opening the front door, which is slightly ajar. [The front door faces onto a highway with much traffic.] James asks her why the door is open. She answers that it's open for the fresh air. She suggests that they play "Emergency" and tells them she'll just be a few minutes. She returns to the kitchen and wipes the table. From the kitchen she asks Nicholas, "Did you get me a diaper yet?" There is no response from him. Despite Alice's warning, the boys have not given up on the door. . . . They have opened it further and Alice has heard them. She stalks into the living room. "James, did you open the door?" He answers yes. "Don't do that ever," she warns sternly and wipes his face. She returns to the kitchen. Nicholas is at the door and has opened it. Playfully, and proudly, he repeats "open" several times. From the kitchen Alice calls, "Who's near the door?" She sounds annoyed. James rushes into the kitchen, "Not me!" Obviously proud of himself, Nicholas announces, "Me!" From the kitchen Alice says, "Nicholas get me a diaper. Come on, so we can go outside." Nicholas ignores her. She comes into the play area and sees the door open and becomes angry. "Oh!" She spanks Nicholas and then James. "Don't you ever do that again," she warns. "Do I have to lock the door? We won't get any fresh air." She puts the chain on the door and Nicholas whimpers. Alice returns to her work in the kitchen and immediately the boys try to open the door. Nicholas gets a chair to stand on and tries to undo the chain. James gets on Nicholas's chair; he can reach the chain, but he can't undo it.

The boys continued to play at and with the door for some time, with Alice moving between the kitchen and play area to watch them. Since it was hot, she was reluctant to close the door. In their play, the boys are learning mastery over objects in their environment. But again, their use of space in play is in conflict with Alice's household goals.

Reducing Distances. The children's desire for contact with Alice also can clash with Alice's performance of household work. For example, James was being friendly to his mother and was imitating her behavior when he tried to help sweep (see Base Day, 12:30 P.M.). But in her rush to accomplish her work, Alice discouraged him. A more emotionally trying episode occurred earlier in the morning of the Base Day (see 9:45 A.M.), when James asked Alice if he could help her with the dishes. We can infer that in making this request, James wanted both to have contact with his mother and to imitate her role. Alice, on the other hand, wanted to finish up the dishes, a particularly disliked task. Involving James would certainly have prolonged it and created additional work. Thus, she did not allow him to help her. Moreover, James's request activated the sibling subsystem and the process of competition for Alice's attention: Carrie piped up that she wanted to wash the dishes as well, thereby initiating a conflict between herself and James. Doing dishes became a prized route of access to Alice. Alice's annoyance at Carrie's involvement and further interference with her task is suggested by her promising James that he "can be first" when Father has his day off, stimulating the competition between brother and sister. Carrie may also have heard her mother's statement about his being first as a preference for James. This incident illustrates how a conflict between Alice's accomplishing a disliked chore and James's wanting to be close to Mother initiates a conflict within the sibling subsystem.

"Two Different Worlds"
These examples of conflict between Alice and the children are not exhaustive, but they illustrate the notion that the home environment contains within it at least two subsystems that are in daily conflict. Insofar as Alice requires both the help and the cooperation of her children, the potential for interpersonal strain exists. The children have their own goals, which can clash with those of Alice as a household worker. Space, time, and things have different meanings to them. Whereas Alice's goal is to protect space and things and keep them clean, the children transform them in play; the door becomes a roadway, the lamp a tower, the vacuum cleaner a horse. Children may behave as if

252

clock time does not exist; in contrast, household work activity is bound by time so that meals are served regularly and errands are completed before the bank closes. This notion of differing goals is reinforced when we look at positive and conflict-free Domestic interactions. They occur when the children and Alice have similar goals, such as going outside or eating dessert. Alice is aware of the conflict.

AB: They have no notion of time or work or anything like that. They don't understand. We're like in two different worlds. . . .

R: They are sometimes in conflict?

AB: Most of the time!

Isomorphism

Alice wondered why she finds it difficult to "lighten up" with the children, even when she is not in direct conflict with them.

AB: I was just thinking. . . . Even when we're in a less oppressive situation, the kids and I, like out doing something that we enjoy, it's like I really don't know how to lighten up. I can just go so far and then part of me is, like holding back.

R: Holding back lightening up?

AB: Yeah. Just really fooling around with them.

R: What is the holding back about?

AB: I can't [pause]. I don't know. It could be one of a dozen things. It could be resentment, who knows? I don't really know. I haven't really examined it. I just thought of it just now. I've noticed that it's—I don't know. Maybe it's [gropes for words] hard to break out of the mold. You know, you're in this, you're like monster woman for three hours and all of a sudden [snaps fingers] you change scenery. It's really hard to just turn it off. . . . Even when I was gone [on my trip] I found that to be true. When I'd really, really lighten up was when they were in bed and somebody else was babysitting, and I was all by myself.

Initially, she wondered if the displacement of her "resentment"—what I have been calling the negative carry-over pattern—was at the root of her difficulty in relaxing around her children. But then it occurred to her that perhaps it was difficult to alter forms of interaction and ways of being from situation to situation.

During one observational period I noticed Alice's attempt to switch rapidly from one type of behavior to another.

"Tumbling" (April 21)

Nicholas is crying in the play area, but initially Alice ignores him. Finally, from her position at the kitchen sink, she calls out, "Nicholas!" harshly. She asks Carrie, "What's going on?" Carrie begins, "The boys are . . ." and she fades off into, "Look at this." Alice goes into the play area and yells at the boys, "If you two can't get along, then you're going to bed!" Meanwhile, Carrie is showing off her tumbling, "Look at this, Mom," she calls. Alice responds tiredly, "That's good, honey."

As I observed this last interchange between Alice and Carrie, I sensed the lack of heart in Alice's praise. I commented to her that it must be difficult for her to switch modes. She agreed and said that "it usually doesn't come off" and that she experiences these responses as "phony."

The concept of isomorphism may be useful in helping us to understand Alice's experiences. Isomorphisms between work and family settings indicate similarities in behavioral patterning. The carry-over of Richard's interpersonal work style into the family was described as an isomorphism between work and home. This concept has been applied only to the relationships between paid work settings and family systems. But we should similarly be able to apply it to the experience of the household worker. In fact, this concept may be particularly applicable to the relationship between household work and emotional life in families because the fusion of working and loving would make it difficult for Alice to compartmentalize work-related interactions.

In addition to Alice's reports of her experience, the quantitative data also suggest isomorphic relationships. We saw that Domestic initiations constituted the majority of the approaches Alice makes to the children. Thus, we might expect them to set the tone for other initiations. We can compare, within each content area, the rank order of the proportion of Positive, Neutral, and Negative initiations to the children (Table 11-3). Examining the percentages for which Domestic initiations have been removed from other content areas, we find that except for the category of All Other, their rank order is the same: Negative is first and Neutral is last. While such quantitative data are only suggestive,[4] they tend to support Alice's sense that the tone of household interactions carries over into other areas of the relationship between herself and the children.

Personal Depletion and Energy Deficit

As a result of the conflict between herself and the children, Alice feels that they have few pleasurable times together. She contrasted her experience with Richard's:

AB: Like I've noticed that he has at least once a day he has a screwing around session where they enjoy themselves. And I was thinking about that and I can't . . . I don't even know when I've had one of those with the kids. It may vary from day to day, but he does have one point where he just fools around with them.

R: You don't have those times?

4. These results also must be interpreted in the light of the limited interjudge accuracy achieved for the Play category (see Methodological Appendix).

AB: No! And I've noticed a lot of days it happens when he comes in. They're up and eating breakfast and stuff. . . . They fool around like that if they're up. . . . Tired or no, when he comes in he will fool around with them for about five minutes. It can go longer if he isn't quite as tired.

R: He says at least a few words?

AB: Yeah!! Like "Hahaha." And I *never* have that—giggles—and I'm going [*Alice makes a tired, grouchy face*]. I notice that even when I come in from somewhere, either shopping or something, and I got all these groceries, and they all greet me and go, "Hi, Mommy," and I go, "Hi" [*simulates low, tired voice*]. And I'm lugging this junk in and I never have that!

Actually, Alice initiated more Positive approaches to the children on the Base Day than Richard did. But for Alice, these warm moments are lost in her experience of being overwhelmed by conflict, while Richard's happy interchanges with the children occur in clearly delineated episodes.

In Alice's image of carrying home groceries and being able to greet her children with only a feeble "hi," she indicates—through a metaphor—her feeling of being burdened by her work, depleted by it, and, therefore, unable to be as emotionally open to the children as she would like to be. In Chapter 3 this pattern was termed personal depletion and energy deficit. I have suggested that depletion can occur when people give time and personal energy to their work while receiving little in return. Moreover, work that is experienced as an assault on the self is particularly enervating. In a variety of ways Alice feels depleted by her work. If we look at her initiations to the children in Table 11-1 we see that over three-fourths are depleting in some way, in that they involve her scolding, disapproving, or trying to influence the children to do something. Domestic initiations are particularly trying. Such interactions are depleting to Alice because constant "ragging" is exhausting, and the children are not always compliant. Alice experiences her depletion by saying that she "gets tired" of "always giving" and she "wants something back." By the end of a difficult day she is particularly exhausted and feels she has little to give, biding her time until the children are in bed.[5]

One consequence of personal depletion, as described in Chapter 3, is that interpersonal availability to family members is diminished. We saw that Alice is a very active member of the family communication network. But in her difficulty in approaching the children positively, in responding with more than a tired "hi," Alice's depletion makes itself known. Thus, only 16 percent of her coded initiations to the children are Positive (see Table 11-1). Her responses, in contrast, are primarily

5. See Bernard's (1975) discussion of the "guilt–stress–fatigue" syndrome.

Positive (43 percent; see Table 11-6), but they are generally short and unelaborated. Thus, Alice sarcastically said, "Some swell mom" when she read one such curt response in the observational protocol.

We also saw that depletion and deficit can readily develop into a "negative" energy pattern when a depleted person is pressed by environmental demands. This dynamic was suggested for Richard, who becomes irritable when he is overtired. When I asked Carrie if she can tell when her mother is tired, she responded, "When I talk to her nice and she yells at me." Alice alluded to such a pattern in her comment about "the vicious circles that develop here. . . . Like children bickering, food burning, work not getting done." Alice is depleted by such "vicious circles" and has difficulty dealing with them because she feels exhausted. As her work and the children press on her, she can easily become irritable and upset.

Alice's depletion also is evident in her interactions with Carrie. I

Table 11-6. Quality of Alice's Responses to the Children's Initiations as Percentages of Coded Responses

RESPONSE	ALICE TO CARRIE $N = 48$[a]	ALICE TO JAMES $N = 159$	ALICE TO NICHOLAS $N = 93$	ALICE TO CHILDREN $N = 209$[b]
Positive				
Base Day	57%	39%	37%	43%
Total[c]	56	42	33	43
Neutral				
Base Day	17	17	16	18
Total	17	16	15	16
Covert Negative				
Base Day	13	23	39	27
Total	15	24	43	29
Overt Negative				
Base Day	9	15	6	12
Total	8	13	8	11
Not Coded[d]				
Base Day	9	3	6	5
Total	8	3	5	5

Note: Percentages total more than 100 because each response could be coded in more than one category.
[a]The total number of coded responses. See footnote c.
[b]This figure does not represent a row total, since one response to more than one child was counted but once.
[c]*Total* excludes one observation period for which the figures were unavailable.
[d]Those responses for which there was insufficient information or which were prevented from occurring were not coded.

have suggested that Richard allocates his time and attention to those parts of the family system that he feels need him most. Similarly, Alice approaches Carrie positively less often than she does the boys because, as the eldest, Carrie is seen as needing less attention than the others. Carrie's desire for adult attention was reflected in the numerous times—more than the other children—she engaged me while I was observing. In over half of such cases, her approaches to me occurred when Alice was occupied with her work and was unresponsive, or when she was paying attention to the boys. Carrie has an independent source of gratification in the day-care school she attends several afternoons a week, an activity that is important to her and that she looks forward to.

Alice's depletion means that the children are sometimes in competition for her attention. This sibling subsystem was mentioned previously. The observational protocol is replete with examples of one child following another to Alice. As we saw in her effort to create personal space for herself, the children see her work breaks as an opportunity to make contact with her. The more intense the conflict between Alice and her children, the more depleted Alice feels; at the same time, the children increase their demands for her attention. These demands lead to further depletion, and thus they are caught in a deficit cycle in which neither Alice's nor the children's needs are fully met.

Reducing Conflict

Kahn et al. (1964) have suggested that when workers find themselves in a situation of role conflict, they try to minimize it by reducing communication and contact with those who are perceived as the source of stress. However, such a solution is not possible when there is a high need for communication with those who are the source of stress and when there is a dependent relationship between them. Neither Alice nor the children can escape from their everyday conflict because the children are dependent on her and because communication between them is necessary. They are forced into almost continuous contact. Alice was envious and resentful about a media presentation of a wealthy woman who simply sent her children off with their nannies when she had had "enough."

Additional resources would help to reduce conflict. Such resources would come either from help with the housekeeping or help in keeping the children constructively busy when Alice is doing other household work. The financial status of the Bernards makes it difficult to buy household help. Moreover, the privatization of the household and the establishment of young couples in their own homes also means that help from community and kin are limited. Richard, therefore, can be an important resource. When he is home, and not tired, he helps Alice by vacuuming in the kitchen and cleaning the table.[6] As we saw in the observational segment "Preparing for Sleep," Richard's presence may have prevented conflict because he met the children's needs for parental contact while Alice accomplished her work. Richard also can help reduce interpersonal tension when it does occur, as the following incident illustrates.

"The Poster" (April 21)

Alice asks Nicholas, "Going to eat?" "No!" is his answer. Alice asks again and when Nicholas indicates his resistance she says, "OK. You are going to leave the table." Alice wipes him up and clears off his place. Now Nicholas, who had been whimpering, produces full-fledged tears. *Richard picks him up and takes him into the bedroom and returns to the kitchen.* Carrie and James are eating their ice cream. Still crying, Nicholas comes into the kitchen, and *Richard tries to placate him, saying "Oh, Nicky."* Alice has started to clear off dishes and is at the sink. Crying, Nicholas goes over to her and she tells him, "Stop it!" Richard is now in the pantry and tells Nicholas, "Don't eat, don't get dessert." Nicholas cries louder. Alice sits down at the table with her dessert, while Nicholas hangs onto her in tears. James makes sure he understands why Nicholas is not getting any ice cream, and he seems somewhat distressed by it. Alice tells him he's right when he says that Nicholas hasn't eaten his dinner. Richard is still in the pantry. Nicholas approaches James's ice cream, whining. Alice tells him, "Settle down! I'll hold you, but no ice cream!" Nicholas stops crying as she places him on her lap. He eyes her ice cream, but she warns him that he's "not getting any." Carrie and James are worried that Alice has taken away Nicholas's ice cream, and Alice worries to me that she appears "harsh and ungiving." She tells James, "Nicholas's ice cream is in the freezer. He can have it if he eats tomorrow. . . ."

Alice gets up, and, as she puts Nicholas down, he begins to get unhappy again. In the meantime, Richard has come back into the kitchen. *He picks Nicholas up and they look out the window. Nicholas becomes quiet.* Alice wipes Carrie, who comes to me and hugs me. She then goes into the play area. Richard, still holding Nicholas, asks if he wants a nap. He takes him into the living room and puts him down on the sofa, "for a little rest." When Nicholas protests, he tells him to "count to ten."

Alice is cleaning in the kitchen and quickly wipes James. Nicholas is still crying now and he comes into the kitchen. Alice tells him, "Nicholas, you'll go to bed if you don't behave." Richard tells her, "Don't tease him like that," and then he himself gets irritated at Nicholas. This time Alice defends him and says, "He didn't sleep long enough."

Carrie shows up in her ballet outfit. Richard goes into the living room briefly and *brings out a poster which he gives to Nicholas. Nicholas quiets down and seems pleased. Richard asks him, "Where do you want me to hang it up?"* Alice suggests that he "hang it up where everyone can see it." *Richard and the*

---

6. Oakley (1974a) has concluded that a housewife-mother whose husband participates in household work is more relaxed in her performance of child care activities.

children go into the bedroom. He positions it on Nicholas's crib and everyone seems pleased. Alice tells me she is "raggy" today.

By picking Nicholas up and distracting him with the poster while Alice completed her chores, Richard served as a tension-reducing resource for the embattled pair. Again we see the implications of the child-to-adult ratio for managing and reducing conflict. Since Richard is gone much of the day, however, his help is not an easily accessible resource for the family and household subsystems.

Television also serves as a household resource, for Alice uses it to occupy the children when she is busy. She explained that it "keeps them out of my hair" and that she does not know what she would do without it. Alice first introduced television on the Base Day when the boys' level of activity began to increase and she wanted to finish her vacuuming (see 8:30 A.M.). She finds their noise, in addition to that of the vacuum cleaner, difficult to tolerate. When she was in a rush to prepare lunch, she also introduced television (see Base Day, 12:10 P.M.), and she again introduced it when a confrontation between herself and James was pending (see Base Day, 5:30 P.M.). Television before dinner also creates a quiet time that Alice looks forward to. Television thus serves as a resource for helping reduce the level of household tension. As such, it can be preferable to involving the children in play. When I asked Alice if she considered it work to set up the children for coloring activity (see Base Day, 9:45 A.M.), she remarked:

> AB: Yes. I classify it under a "Big Pain." [*Laughs*] And it's just because they stay interested in it for such a short time. I mean it would be a different story if they sat there for an hour. But I'm lucky if I get fifteen minutes out of them. So, yeah, it's a big pain.

In other words, the effort that Alice must use does not pay off for her in terms of the quiet and noninterference she thereby obtains. Involving the children with television requires less effort.

Being outside the house is another way in which stress can be avoided, for it is an activity that both Alice and the children enjoy. As a result, their preparations for going outside are smooth and rapid. The children's play and activity can be less constricted outside, and there is stimulation for them that can occupy and interest them, as the following excerpt indicates. During this episode, I was a "participant-as-observer."

"Ice Cream" (April 11)

Alice, the children, and I leave the children's clothing store, and she suggests that it would be nice to have some ice cream because it is hot out. We drive to an ice-cream stand. Alice comments to me that Richard doesn't think the children's appetites should be spoiled for dinner, but she reminds him of how good it felt to have special occasions when he was a child. I treat everyone to an

259

ice-cream cone. Alice is in good spirits. We all sit on the curb, eating our cones. Carrie snuggles close to me and sits between Alice and me as we chat. Since it's warm outside, James's and Nicholas's ice creams are melting too fast for their licking to keep up. Alice licks their ice cream for them, and she laughs as she says people wonder why mothers get fat. Alice gets us all some napkins. James uses his and throws it on the ground. Alice is amused and gets up and throws it in the bin. Nicholas drops his ice cream on the ground, manages to pick it up and continues to lick on. I laugh as I point this out to Alice who goes, "Oh, Nicholas," and then she laughs too. Alice and the children seem in good spirits. Some men walk by carrying motorcycle helmets and James asks about them. Alice explains to him what they are doing. When it's time to leave, the boys run away from Alice in fun, and she good-naturedly chases them and brings them to the car.

The opportunities for being outside as a way of avoiding conflict are, however, limited. There are no sidewalks to walk and play on in their neighborhood, and because they live on a busy highway, the children—Nicholas in particular—must be supervised when they are outside. Alice has "visions of my kids plastered all over the road. Some days they're worse than others because some days they just need to get outside and run. I can't let them out. I got stuff to do." Her household work interferes with her ability to be outside with them. When she is busy and the children become restless, conflict and tension build. Because they are even more constricted in winter, the cold months are particularly stressful. Being housebound has a very concrete meaning in their lives.

Going outside can be viewed as a way of "charging" the mother-child quartet, counteracting depletion and helping to avoid later tension by reducing irritability. Alice is keenly aware of this process and carefully allocates her personal "fueling" efforts. For example, she used to take her shower very early in the morning, but she decided that she was "wasting" this source of refreshment. She now postpones her shower until the late morning, when she is in need of it. On the Base Day, she emerged from the shower and greeted Nicholas cheerfully (see 10:30 A.M.). In reviewing the observational notes, she commented on this interaction:

AB: This shower makes a "new woman" of me. It's really funny. I have little things during the day that kind of revitalize me. That's one of them.

R: Others?

AB: If I take a nap, and I'm the first one up, and I can have a half hour to wake up, I can really be nice [giggles], believe it or not. . . . And I don't even do anything, I just look.

A shower, a nap, time for herself are the events that refresh Alice during the day. When she feels "revitalized," she thinks she handles the incidents with her children with more forbearance. Commenting on the same time period, she said:

> AB: I notice, though, that since I am revitalized, I am dealing with things a lot better. . . . I'm a much nicer person to be with. . . . Like the hassle of getting the diaper and all this other kind of stuff, if it hadn't been right after my shower I would probably have been screaming my guts out.

Both the shower and the quiet time after her nap are times alone. For Alice, personal space to deal with her depletion is at a premium.

Richard, too, is an important source of support for Alice. In remarking about her "twinges of resentment" about his not spending enough time with her, she said, "It feels good just to have him be there. Just his presence is revitalizing." In one of our interviews, when Alice became anxious about appearing never to enjoy herself with the children, she began to talk about an enjoyable episode. What struck me about the incident was that Richard's presence was vital.

> AB: Yeah. Now we had a real positive experience, though. . . . It was warm and we went to the lake. I didn't have to drag Richard, see. He was very cooperative. He wanted to go. Sometimes I have to drag him to go to the lake. [*She imitates a drooping sigh.*] "Huuh."
>
> R: So then, that's just a big burden also?
>
> AB: Yeah. But he really wanted to go. So we finally parked ourselves on the grass; it was really nice. [*Her voice imitates relaxation, relief, letting go.*] It was really, really nice. [*Her voice is very soft now.*] But, like, as we were driving home and the kids were ragging on us, it's like you can feel this motor starting up and [*she imitates a revving motor*] you're going, "ahhah." [*Giggles*]

Being out of the house and with Richard are both sources of revitalization for Alice. However, as she neared their home and the daily routine it represents, she became tense again.

Although I have described the sources of revitalization and ways of lessening the conflict, implicit in the discussion was the notion that these resources are limited. Richard's work takes him out of the home, going outside is not always possible, and Alice's time alone is limited. Thus, the home becomes a stressful work environment for her. The household constrains and impinges upon the children's activities, and when they assert themselves, they collide with the household subsystem. Still, Alice must still do her work. Insofar as Alice and the children are bound together in one space, conflict cannot easily be avoided.

How Typical Is the Bernard Household?

It could be argued that the incidence of conflicting household interactions in the Bernard family are not typical family patterns. We lack sufficient observational data on daily household life to know what is usual. Yet the available evidence suggests that this situation is not atypical. For example, in his home observations of the A. family, Bermann found that Mrs. A. had a considerable percentage of Negative approaches to other family members. He concluded that Mrs. A.'s "low percentage of 'cooperative-affectional' approaches, as well as her relatively high inclination to disapprove, may be attributable to... her intense task orientation, and the attendant premium on timing" (1973, p. 54). Simmons and Schoggen (1963) found that mothers were involved in many oppositional contacts with children and that this fact could be understood by considering that mothers, more than fathers, are involved in daily care and socialization. They found, too, that the conflicts centered around differing goals, but they did not specify the content of these differences. Finally, from her interview studies with household workers, Lopata concluded that the "constant need for 'trying to have patience with children' is difficult for many mothers. . . . The word 'patience' is frequently repeated" (1971, p. 208). And Komarovsky estimated that "one out of every four Glenton mothers has considerable anxiety over her irritability, 'hollering,' and impatience with children" (1962, p. 80). From the analysis of the Bernard household, I would suggest that the conflicts alluded to in these studies stem from the structure of everyday household life with young children.

Personal Blame and the Ideology of Patience

Alice is unaware that many other young household workers "holler" at their children, for the privatization of the household means that she can only imagine what occurs behind the doors of other homes. Her images of household life are derived from what might be termed the "ideology of patience." In Alice's eyes being a competent household worker means that

AB: You run really a tight ship. And by a tight ship I mean things are in order, kids have been read to, the kids have been played with. . . . You're serving well-balanced meals [chuckles] and the house is neat, and you're on top of everything, you know. Nothing gets by here.

In this vision of perfection—the standard against which Alice measures herself—there is no room for anger and irritation, nor for the conflict and tension that are so much a part of daily household routine. Consequently, her own experiences cause her grief.

AB: Every night before you go to sleep, you recount the events of the day and you're constantly—not constantly—but feeling guilty quite a bit for like losing your temper. . . . There are so many thin lines that you don't want to cross. They can be exasperating and you don't want to lose your control too much, although sometimes it's necessary and beneficial. I don't mean the losing of control, but having a real show of anger for behavior that you don't particularly care for at the time.

R: You mentioned that you sometimes feel guilty ... about losing your temper.

AB: Oh, yes!

R: Why is that?

AB: Yeah. I feel guilty because if I'm dealing with adults, by no means do I lose my temper as much as I do with them. And it's really hard to relate to a child. You expect them to comprehend as an adult would comprehend, and they just don't seem to and that's exasperating. You just say, "Why can't you? What is the problem here? I've explained it to you. You can see the mess it makes, so why do you continue to do this?" It's one of these things. So you get angry and—

R: Why feel guilty?

AB: I feel guilty because I don't think that intelligent, civilized human beings have to go that far. They don't have to get angry that much. They should be able to talk things out and work things out that way. I feel guilty when I feel like I've lost my control. . . .

R: Do you think mothers feel guiltier about losing their tempers ... than fathers do?

AB: Yeah. Yes, I do, because fathers don't lose their tempers quite as often because they're not dealing with them on a twenty-four-hour basis like a mother is. See, Daddy's been away all day with adults, talking to adults, and he comes home and the children are a welcome relief. The whole tone changes; the whole mood changes. It's one of "Yippee! Daddy's home!" and everything lightens up. . . . So if there comes a time when he has to reprimand them, it doesn't happen very often and they really, really deserved it. They just have driven him to the point of no return. Where I might bark at them because they've been screwing up all day, and they come to me with something that's really trivial, that's just the straw that broke the camel's back. Whereas, I think a father's anger most of the time is justified, whereas a mother's at time is displaced. It could be that the whole day has been really crummy and this kid comes up with something that is really minor and that's just "it." You can't take it. Whereas, Dad can kind of—it's easier for him to be a little more fair.

Her search for some understanding of the relationship between herself and her children—one in which she experiences tension and not enough good times—leads her to question her own adequacy. Since she has internalized an ideology of patience, loss of self-control and anger are seen as personal failures. Guilt and depression ensue. In recalling her anger at Nicholas some time before, she remarked, "Then I'd get down on myself for the next few days. I guess it was my way of punishing myself for saying that." Depression is symptomatic both of her self-punishment and the loss of self-esteem that comes from not being the patient mother she feels she should be.

While discussing the roots of this "ideology of patience," Alice rushed into the bedroom and returned with two books for me to examine. In Coomes's *Mother's Manual* we found the instruction,

> Neither commands nor corrections should ever be given with a show of anger or with shouting that shows irritation. It is always a mistake to correct a child in a hasty manner or with a show of temper or anger. It is even more a mistake to strike a child in a fit of anger [1969, pp. 147–48].

We then turned to the *How and Why* book series from which her mother had read to her and from which Alice was reading to her children. Inside, we found a picture of a smiling woman baking a pie. The caption that accompanied it read:

> Our home is just
> The Nicest place
> With Mother's
> Gentle, smiling face;
> I'm glad for beds
> That Mother makes
> And pies and puddings
> That she bakes.

Embodied here is the wife-mother of the ideology of patience. De Beauvoir wrote that "the religion of maternity proclaims that all mothers are saintly" (1961, p. 484). In this portrayal, a woman feels no anger or irritation, nor does she dislike her work. Such patience and good will are remote from real interactions between mothers and children and only serve to camouflage the conflicts inherent in household life with young children. This ideology does not allow Alice to dislike her job as a household worker. Whereas other household workers might blame their children for the interpersonal strain resulting from work in the home, Alice blames herself.

CHAPTER 12

A Systems Perspective

In describing the interfaces between work and family life for the Bernards, I have analyzed their experience into its component parts, looking first at Richard's work and suggesting the ways in which it might be affecting family relationships, then at Alice's experience as a household worker and the manner in which household work impinged on her life and that of her children. In this way, two work interfaces have been explored and the traditional orientation, which focuses on the paid worker, has been expanded. We now are in a position to integrate these analyses to reconstruct the family in such a way as to consider the systemic links among work activities, personal life, and the emotional life of the Bernard family as I found them. Such an overview involves us in an ecological mapping of their family life.

Like other families, the Bernards try to achieve safety and security in the world, to build a meaningful life together, and to regulate close-ness and distance among themselves. For the material support without which family life cannot be sustained, Richard Bernard sells his time and energy to external work settings for more than fifty hours each week. Alice and the children are dependent on this work he performs, and, in turn, Alice provides household services, which help to maintain herself, Richard, and the children. Insofar as Richard is strained by his work, depletion and frustration threaten to carry over into the family system. He tries to cope with such carry-over and personal strain in several ways, including trying to disengage from his work, taking personal time and space on his farm, and increasing person-job fit by continuing to work a late shift. Although the department first assigned him to the midnight shift without consulting him about his preferences, he is considering remaining on a late shift to increase any personal gratification he obtains from his work. Insofar as his farm helps him to manage strain, it enables him to continue working for pay. Richard is thus attempting to maintain a satisfactory equilibrium between the psychic and physical effort he expends in his work and the personal returns he obtains.

The way Richard manages work-related strain and the time he spends at his job influences the relationship between household and emotional subsystems in the home. As a household worker, Alice receives little gratification from her work. Unlike Richard, she has fewer ways of coping with personal strain, for she cannot take space for herself nor vent her resentment away from the family. Moreover, Richard's absence from the home increases her work overload and isolation, the family is not financially in a position to purchase household help, and community resources that might benefit women like Alice do not yet exist. Her resentment about her work and her no-exit situation carries over into her relationships with her children, adding to the existing structural conflict between the household and children's subsystems. Such conflict is depleting and makes Alice less emotionally available to the children, who then increase their demands on her and compete with each other for her attention; this further depletes her and makes it more difficult for her to cope with conflict. The lack of resources and paucity of Alice's sources of personal revitalization limit her ability to manage conflict. The children's dependency on Alice means that distance is difficult to achieve. They are caught in an energy deficit cycle wherein Alice is drained of emotional resources. As conflict intensifies and demands increase, irritation builds and turns to anger and tears.

Richard's presence and participation in household and life are important in easing interpersonal tensions. However, his availability is limited by the structural separation of work and home and by the way he tries to cope with personal strain. Insofar as time and emotional resources are limited, Richard allocates them carefully among himself and his farm, the children, and Alice. The majority of his time and effort is bought by the Centerville Police Department. Since the children are young and vulnerable, he tends to allocate attention to them and neglects the marital relationship. Alice's resentment about insufficient contact with Richard and her anger at him are expressed where it is safe—in her relationship with her children. Moreover, the children's reactions to their father's absence result in increased demands on Alice to be interpersonally available to them. The pattern of personal depletion and energy deficit also is exacerbated by Richard's working the midnight shift. Alice sees even less of Richard, and his irritability and tiredness make contact especially problematic. Keeping the children quiet while he sleeps requires her further effort. Thus, the interpersonal conflict between Alice and the children can be understood as the result of multiple forces. Alice also turns anger on herself and becomes depressed.

In these ways, the Bernards were caught in a dilemma between their emotional and economic needs when I first studied them. The structural interlocking of household and work systems and the necessity for Richard to sell his time means that they are constrained in their negotiations at the structural and psychological interfaces. Time at work is time away from the family, and since the distance cannot easily be bridged, desired contact is difficult to achieve.

More than Richard, Alice has difficulty in negotiating a better personal solution. Perhaps if Richard did not have his farm she might create some personal space. However, this solution would have its own price. We see, then, a competition between systems and subsystems for the scarce resources of time, space, and personal energy. The family system and the police department compete for Richard, although—for the family—the battle is partly lost. Alice and the children are implicitly, if not actively, in competition for Richard's attention. More openly, Alice competes with the farm. The children compete for Alice's attention, and Alice has difficulty revitalizing. In the interface between the household subsystem and the children's subsystem there is further conflict over time, space, and energy. The children are too close to Alice and not close enough to Richard.

As a result of such scarcity, the systemic conflicts express themselves in personal and interpersonal strain. Richard is tired, and Alice is often angry and depressed. The children and Alice do daily battle, and the children bicker among themselves. Meanwhile, Alice and Richard are avoiding talking to each other about their lack of time together, and Alice feels some discontent with their relationship. We might say that the systemic conflict between work and family life is absorbed by the family subsystem and reflected there. As a result of these systemic conflicts, the Bernards are prevented from achieving sufficient intimacy and meaning in their life together. Although we have no direct evidence, I would hypothesize further that the external work organization—the Centerville Police Department—remains relatively immune from the consequences of the conflict. Given the relative powerlessness of the Bernards vis-à-vis the police department and their dependency on Richard's job, we would predict that greater strain would be experienced in the family system. Although Richard is no longer wholeheartedly committed to his work, it is clear that in matters such as the allocation of time, the police organization—and the needs of the household—are given priority over the emotional needs of the whole family and of individual family members.

Still, the Bernards care for each other and search for a better accommodation of work and family relations. A lack of awareness of interface patterns makes it even more difficult for families to manage interface dilemmas. The research process contributed to the Bernards' reassessment of their needs. Richard considered a job move, but he and

Alice decided that they could not sustain the severe financial setback of such a move. Richard stopped going to school for the summer and quit his part-time job at the shopping center. The family was able to manage the loss of income these changes entailed by postponing the goal of owning their own home, although they both had learned in their families of origin that renting is not respectable.

As money was traded for time, Richard became more physically and emotionally available to Alice and the children. As a special time together, the family began to go out to dinner after church on Sundays. Alice's younger sister came to live with them for almost two months and took over some of Alice's child-care duties so that Alice and Richard could spend some time alone together. Moreover, the summer meant that the children could spend increased time with Richard on his farm. On Richard's vacation, Alice's mother stayed with the children while Richard and Alice went on a trip. Importing outside resources and trading money for time revitalized the marital relationship and Alice became happier. With these changes and with Richard's increased presence, Alice reported that the tension between her and the children decreased. Alice also tried to return to school part-time in order to further revitalize herself, but this attempted solution created a new problem. Even with household help from Richard and her sister, her homework load initiated another depletion pattern and, after several weeks, she discontinued her class. However, she did take tennis lessons so that she and Richard could play together.

Thus, the interface relations changed when the Bernards postponed their goal of owning a house and they traded cash for Richard's time and energy—options other families may lack. This solution, however, was not meant to be permanent. Richard now plans to go to school during the day and work the afternoon shift, which is more interesting than day work. This change will again entail adjustments in family relationships, as Carrie will be starting school and James will be in day care. Carrie and, perhaps, James will see Richard less often. Alice will not necessarily have less domestic work, because she will be chauffeuring the children to school. Consequently, the interface relationships will have to be renegotiated. These further changes may ease some strains while posing other dilemmas that the Bernards will have to manage. The interface patterns do not remain static. Rather, they must be renegotiated with changes in work situations, in families, and in individuals.

PART IV

Reflections

A major goal of this study was to illuminate the connections between "working and loving" in a small number of working-class and lower-middle-class families. In so doing, I hoped to provide further understanding of the emotional dynamics of life in families and the effect work has on all family members. This goal was shaped by a theoretical orientation by which families are viewed as "open systems" in active interchange with their social environment, and significant social institutions are perceived as related to each other. I began with the assumption that some connections exist between work life and the emotional lives of families. The research design was, of necessity, exploratory because the nature of these connections as they are expressed in the transactions that constitute daily life in families was unclear. My interest lay not in the ways families influence work systems but in the kinds of tasks work life poses for them. Whereas others have examined work–family connections at times of stress and transition (see, for example, Rapoport & Rapoport 1965; Renshaw 1976), I looked for points of strain in the everyday life of "inconspicuous" families who were assumed to be managing these tasks.

Given the limitations imposed by sample size and the exploratory nature of the design, generalizations about the connections between work and family life must be treated with caution. However, even a limited study can suggest what the interconnections might be for other families and the ways in which they might be studied. It also suggests hypotheses that can be subjected to empirical test with more carefully constructed samples. Finally, the findings have implications for clinical practice and for social policy and change.

CHAPTER **13**

Summary and Conclusions

As social systems, families have goals that they attempt to maximize. Although their specific goals differ, participating families can be characterized as trying to achieve some security and safety in the world, to build a meaningful life together, and to negotiate emotional distances among their members. The modern ideology of the family also leads people to expect that emotional needs will be met within the context of family relations. In trying to achieve these goals, family members utilize time and space and rely on their emotional availability to each other. But time, space, and the personal efforts of family members also are used by work organizations for economic ends. Families cannot remain aloof and separate from such requirements, for under capitalism, most families must maintain themselves materially by selling their labor for wages that the household worker transforms into useful goods and services for her family. Many research participants thus experience themselves as locked into jobs—inside and outside the home—that they do not prefer. This structural interlocking of household and employment systems delineates the regions that this study explored.

Two major interface regions were described for participating families. One lay at the juncture of the emotional subsystem of the family and the external work organization, the other between the emotional subsystem of the family and the household work system. It is difficult to distinguish household life and the emotional life of a family, for they overlap spatially and temporally. However, this distinction serves a heuristic purpose for it allowed us to investigate emotional dynamics as they are influenced by household work.

These interface regions were found to have psychological and structural dimensions. Three psychological patterns were described: positive carry-over; negative carry-over; and personal depletion and energy de-

271

ficit. The positive carry-over pattern characterizes the Turners, a middle-class family. The other two patterns were uncovered in the study of the other research families. These patterns were not meant to be exhaustive, and families often exhibited several simultaneously. Personality variables alone seemed insufficient to account for these patterns. Rather, it was suggested that we require a formulation that includes transactions among individuals, families, households, and external work enterprises. Although these psychological patterns were uncovered in the exploration of the interface regions between paid work and family spheres, they also were found to be applicable to the relationship between household and family subsystems.

The psychological patterns are shaped, in part, by the psychological state created in a worker by his or her job experience and ways of managing job-related stresses. For example, personal coping mechanisms can exacerbate negative effects on the family system by reducing a worker's interpersonal availability to other family members. In the case of Alice Bernard, household worker, attempts to manage stress are constrained by limited household resources and by the fusion of working and loving in the home. It also was suggested that families, varying in their psychosocial style and their emotional and material resources, manage work-related stresses differently.

The constructs of emotional and interpersonal availability were useful in helping us conceptualize the processes of psychological carry-over from work to the family system. Emotional availability denotes a psychological state that influences a worker's behavior—his or her interpersonal availability—toward other family members. This latter construct was operationalized by considering a worker's rate of initiation to others and the socioemotional quality of her or his interactions. The consequences of unavailability depend, in part, on the needs of family members for intimacy and contact.

Regardless of the type of psychological patterns that emerged for them, the structural variables of time and space proved important for most participating families. Because the employed family member works outside the home, space and time create barriers for families as they attempt to achieve desired closeness. In the interface regions between the household and the family emotional subsystem, conflicts between Alice Bernard as a household worker and her children appeared to center around differing orientations to time, space, and objects. Without adequate resources to reduce conflict, the household and children's subsystems were viewed as antagonistic. It was hypothesized that their conflict influences the emotional tone of interpersonal interactions between Alice and her children.

Although psychological and structural dimensions were distinguished for purposes of analysis and discussion, they are not independent. For example, in order for a family member to be interpersonally available, he or she must find ways to bridge space and make time. Although time together may be plentiful, the nature of the psychological pattern might not allow the family to utilize profitably the time they do have together; in contrast, a positive carry-over pattern may allow a family to use their limited time well. Time and space also have psychosocial dimensions that become evident during life-cycle transitions. For example, the amount of time husbands and wives could spend together was especially important during pregnancy; the amount of time fathers spend with their children has different meanings for children depending on their psychosocial stage. Thus, particular interface patterns can change their meaning as families and their members change.

The research families have accommodated more or less successfully to dilemmas posed for them by work and family relationships. However, as the foregoing discussion indicates, these accommodations are not static, for the consequences of relationships between work and family life change as the family does. Moreover, there are forces outside the family, as well as within it, that operate to alter existing relationships between work and family life. For example, a change in job assignment meant that Mike Healy began to express work strain in his relationship with his wife, thereby altering the existing interface pattern. As Henry Johnson aged, his job became more stressful and his tendency to worry increased, thereby exacerbating the existing negative carry-over pattern. We can hypothesize that the connections between work and family are dynamic, that they pose ongoing tasks and problems for families, and that the solutions devised are not fixed. The processes of accommodation may be particularly evident during periods of transition, but they appear to be integral to everyday life.

As we saw in the case of the Bernards, families sometimes try to find more satisfying balances between their economic needs and their needs for intimacy. However, their power to negotiate a better balance is limited because they are locked into the occupational structure through their dependency on income from external work organizations and because they have no formal power within the employment setting. Consequently, they have few opportunities to modify their relationships with these work organizations to better suit their changing needs. For example, the Joneses tolerated spending little time together during the first year of their marriage; with Sandra's pregnancy, the lack of contact caused strain. However, Jesse was unable to change or reduce the number of hours he worked, for now the household required all his earning power. For the majority of research participants, it appeared that alterations in the work–family relationships are made to meet, not their needs, but those of the external work organization.

Unable to influence work systems to alter structural arrangements and psychological patterns, some of the research participants developed individual solutions to their dilemmas. One way in which some participants attempt to minimize the daily strains experienced at the workplace and the carry-over of these feelings into the family is through the active process of disengagement from their work. Although a number of research participants themselves subscribe to the "myth of separate worlds," I suggested that such a myth can be understood in the context of this disengagement process. Although the fusion of working and loving makes disengagement difficult for Alice Bernard, some of the paid workers appear to use this defense in order to manage anger, frustration, and what is experienced as a threat to the self.

Still, attempting to disengage is only a partial solution to personal strain and the threat of negative carry-over, for other connections between working and emotional life are unnoticed by participants and remain beyond their personal control. For example, although disengagement can minimize negative carry-over, it remains unclear whether the pattern of personal depletion and energy deficit can be managed in this way. This pattern, and the barriers created by time and space, were generally unnoticed by participants. Although most research participants try to make their family role primary, their actual commitment to this role is limited by lack of time and by personal depletion.

It also was suggested that personal attempts to manage work-related stresses may themselves have unintended effects on family members. Attempts to keep work and home separate by not talking about work might make it difficult for children to learn about work roles and could create gaps in communication between husbands and wives. And despite efforts to suppress work concerns, they nevertheless can be communicated in subtle ways. Creating physical and psychological space, or worrying, or displacing anger each comes with its price for other family members and for the family as a whole.

By considering the relationship between family life and another social system, this description of some connections between everyday work and family life extends an "ecological" conception of families. The structural-functionalist view of the family as specializing in "socio-emotional" functions also exemplifies an ecological perspective, one that assumes a harmonious fit and complementary relationship between families and instrumental work organizations. Similarly, the conception of the family as a necessary haven from the industrial world assumes such a complementarity. Not only are families *required* to provide emotional sustenance, but it is also assumed that they *can* do so.

The ecological perspective does not necessarily entail harmony and fit; tension and conflict also are possible. Although we may expect and require families to satisfy emotional needs, the data presented here point to essential conflicts between satisfying these emotional needs

274

within families and providing for the economic support of households. To the extent that family members depend on time and personal effort to achieve emotional well-being while, under capitalism, they simultaneously must sell their labor to external work enterprises and utilize it in providing household goods and services, we could say that these systems compete for scarce resources. The more time a family must sell, the more stressful is the work family members perform, and the fewer resources families have for decreasing work stress inside and outside the home, the more intense is this competition. Furthermore, work organizations and families are not equal opponents, for households without wealth are economically dependent, and workers and their families have but limited power in determining the way their productive life is organized. Negative carry-over from work may strain family cohesion, but for most research families a stressful job is preferable to no job at all. Family members not only give up time and effort to work systems, but sometimes they have to forgo the satisfaction of emotional needs in their attempts to sustain the family wage earner. It may be that the very conditions of occupational life that require paid workers to find havens in their families makes it difficult for families to serve this function. And to the extent that families attempt to create these havens, the emotional needs of wage earners may be pitted against those of other family members. Since the home is the workplace for the household worker, it may provide no haven for her.

Tensions and conflicts are "absorbed" by families and are expressed in intrapersonal and interpersonal strain.[1] Such strain was evident in the brief stories of the Bernard, Johnson, Healy, Jones, Cooper, and Doyle families, in particular. But because I chose "inconspicuous" families for my sample, at the time of the study they were managing these strains. Occasionally, a participant mentioned that during especially difficult times the thought of divorce or separation occurred to him or her; fantasies of being single were not uncommon. It may be easier for people to change partners and families in a search for ways to meet their emotional needs than to alter work organizations and the work–family relationship. I also suggested that the "myth of separate worlds," by obscuring these connections, encourages people to blame themselves and each other when their needs go unmet rather than recognizing the role that their work lives may play in hindering fulfillment of personal and familial goals. The myth is supported by families themselves, who may want to believe in their own autonomy.

1. It should be noted that some aspects of these conflicts can be described using the language of role conflict and strain. But insofar as the concept of role encapsulates and focuses on individuals (Jackson 1966), it is limited in its use for the analysis of systemic conflicts and dilemmas. Role theory should be but one of the conceptual tools used in understanding the connections between work and family life.

The uncovering of interconnections between work and emotional life in the families participating in this study indicates that we have been too quick to assume that work and family constitute "separate worlds" for working-class and lower-middle-class families. Investigating this assumption was a secondary goal of the study. Although the sample was not truly representative of this population, the findings indicate that the assumption must be questioned.

At the outset of the study a further assumption was made that class is as important as race in understanding the interrelation of work and family life. Race emerged as important when participants discussed their experiences of job discrimination and the difficulties they perceived in finding alternative employment. However, irrespective of race, research participants share much the same goals and concerns and face similar problems. The black families in the study are the Colemans, the Ellisons, the Gateses, the Joneses, and the Turners. The white families are the Bernards, the Coopers, the Doyles, the Healys, the Johnsons, and the Simpsons.

Directions for Theory and Research

The assumption that the connections between work and family life are minimally important for working-class and lower-middle-class occupational groups in part derives from a limited conception of these connections and from worker's self-reports that work does not interfere with their lives. For example, in their study of work and family life in England, Young and Willmott found that between 69 and 75 percent of their sample of married, full-time manual workers reported "no interference" to a question of whether their work interfered with their home life (1973, p. 165). Although we can accept this report at face value, Young and Willmott also found that at least 66 percent of this sample of workers said that their work was physically tiring, and between 40 and 59 percent reported that their work was mentally tiring (p. 164). Assuming some overlap in respondents who reported fatigue and "no interference," we could conclude that their tiredness did not interfere with family life. The data presented here suggest an alternative explanation. We would predict that mental and physical fatigue would result in personal depletion and reduced availability to family members but that this pattern of energy deficit would go unrecognized by workers themselves. Moreover, since they would value their ability to separate their work and home lives, interference would be underreported. In addition to asking workers themselves about their tiredness and the extent to which work interferes with their family life, the findings presented here suggest that we also should ask other family members about the availability of the wage earner or household worker. With the recognition of the patterns described in Part II, we can develop more sophisticated research questions to determine the extent of these patterns within individual families and occupational groups.

Another research finding of theoretical importance is the discovery of important relationships between household work life and the emotional life of families, particularly the relationship between mothers and their children. The traditional framework has examined only the employed husband-father, while the experiences of the household worker have been either ignored or considered primarily as dependent on the husband's work role. For example, using exchange theory, Scanzoni (1970) hypothesized a connection between the way in which a wife fulfills her household obligations and the degree to which a husband fulfills his obligations to provide her with both material wealth and symbolic rewards such as status and prestige gained in the occupational system. The more status and prestige a husband brings to his wife, the more she feels her "rights" are honored and the more positively she performs her instrumental and expressive duties. In this view, the relationship of the household worker to her work has no independent status. Yet in the case study of the Bernard family we saw a more complex dynamic. Alice Bernard's experience of her work in the household has a status separate from Richard's success in the occupational sphere, and her dissatisfaction with her work carries over into her relationship with her children. Rather than make Alice more content in her role as household worker, Richard's success as a provider exacerbates her frustration because the hours he works make him less available to help reduce her work overload and to provide her with needed emotional support. Thus, she experiences further strain and distress, contrary to what Scanzoni's exchange theory might predict.

Scarce finances can cause family strain. The data presented here suggest that extra work to supplement family income *also* can be a source of stress. In their recent work, Aldous et al. (1979) have suggested a similar dynamic. When discussing the tendency of men who are unsuccessful occupationally to withdraw from family life, they noted that for the blue-collar man, withdrawal from family participation can stem from attempts to be *successful* as a provider by taking on extra work. I would argue, further, that the withdrawal of the provider is not merely physical. Insofar as the working-class man works increased hours at jobs that are not personally satisfying, decreased family participation may stem also from his need to recoup his personal resources by creating space for himself. A similar dynamic, of course, could be postulated for employed working-class women. Since household work can be an additional, independent source of familial strain, we need to consider the effects on families when both household and employed workers feel depleted and frustrated by their work.

In their revision of Scanzoni's theory, Aldous et al. have suggested another formulation of the work–family connection that is of interest here. They have proposed a "Success Constraint Theory," which links occupational achievement and marital satisfaction in a curvilinear fashion. Reviewing Scanzoni's data, they have hypothesized that there is less marital satisfaction when the husband is *either* extremely successful or unsuccessful. Lowered marital satisfaction comes from decreased family participation, that is, fulfillment of the family responsibilities or caretaker tasks necessary for the functioning of the family unit. In linking occupational status and family participation, Aldous et al. have proposed a major intervening variable: power and its spillover. Successful men use their occupationally derived power to avoid family responsibilities because time on their job is intrinsically more rewarding to them. Occupationally unsuccessful men lose power, therefore reducing their legitimacy to perform other family responsibilities.

The findings presented here suggest amendments to this formulation. Family participation can be conceived of more broadly to include psychosocial participation in the life of a family. Decreased participation could therefore arise both for the very successful person, who is highly involved with his or her work, and for the person in a job that is not at all fulfilling. In addition to the spillover of power, other variables such as psychological state and time and space can influence participation in the family. It would seem that the connections are sufficiently complex to require a variety of variables in explaining observed phenomena in different families. Most likely, further research will unveil increasingly complex interconnections that will include cultural, psychological, and structural factors. Moreover, we need to study these connections for a wide range of families, including those in which both men and women work inside and outside the home (three-job families), and single-parent families, in which the adult works inside and/or outside the home. Longitudinal studies of families, even over periods as brief as a year, would help us uncover interface transactions.

The findings also indicate that the research on paid work and well-being must include an assessment of workers' families, including individual family members and the family as a whole. We saw that work-related stress, for both paid and household workers, may be reflected in distress exhibited by other family members and by conflicts among them. Generally, well-being is measured through assessments of either job satisfaction or the presence or absence of psychiatric symptoms. When stress is expressed through interpersonal conflicts, psychiatric symptoms—which are based on individual distress—are an insufficient measure. Casting a wider net to include all family members and assessing the quality of their interpersonal relationships would provide increased accuracy in determining the variety of ways in which people can be affected by work stresses. With a broader conceptualization of the relationship of work to mental health, we also could ask about the effect on other family members of the ways in which a worker manages strain. Coping mechanisms that are successful for the individual may be detrimental to other family members and to family relationships.

The theme of danger and injury, which recurred during the interviews, points to the need for studying children and other relatives of people in physically hazardous occupations. We know that such workers are prone to exhibit symptoms of psychological distress (Special Task Force 1973). The findings here suggest that even when dread of danger is not explicitly discussed, it may nevertheless be communicated to family members. We need to know how work situations perceived as dangerous affect *all* family members and how family members cope with such stress. We saw that, even for occupations that we do not normally think of as being dangerous, wives and children reported worrying about the husband-father's safety.

Although most previous research on work and mental health has concentrated almost exclusively on employed men, as noted in Chapter 1, some recent research has addressed the effects of housework on the job satisfaction and mental health of women. As we saw with Alice Bernard, stressors of housework include boredom, monotony, and houseboundness. I further suggested that the fusion of working and loving may make it difficult for household workers to minimize these stresses. The case study of Alice Bernard indicates that child care—in both its physical and nonphysical aspects—may be a source of job stress. Not only does it involve tasks distasteful to some women, but it also is an important, demanding job with few guidelines and little opportunity for evaluating one's performance. We also saw in Alice's case that the ratio of children to adults is important as a stress factor.[2] Although the addition of children increases work, it does not bring a significant increase in household help (Walker & Woods 1976). In fact, husband-fathers may be pressed to work longer hours as children are added to the family.

Bernard (1975) has observed that it is not necessarily motherhood per se that is stressful for women but the way we institutionalize it. She noted Minturn and Lambert's findings that mothers who have primary responsibility for child care and spend a high proportion of their time with their children are especially "unstable" in their emotional reactions

2. Nye, Carlson, and Garrett (1970) found that women's reports of decreased life satisfaction were associated with increasing family size, up to four children.

to their children and tend to exhibit hostility unrelated to a child's performance. Minturn and Lambert concluded:

> The pressures impinging upon the growing child are much more the nature of by-products of the horde of apparently irrelevant considerations that impinge upon the parents. These considerations of household composition, size of family, work load, etc. determine the time and energy that mothers have available to care for children. They determine the range and content of mother-child relationships and the context in which these relations must take place.... Obvious as it may be, these forces have been ignored in many studies [1964, p. 291].

In the study of Alice Bernard we saw how work overload, conflicts over time, space, and things, and lack of material and emotional resources affect Alice's interpersonal availability to her children and contribute to the formation of negative carry-over and energy deficit patterns. This analysis, along with the conclusions reached by Minturn and Lambert, suggests the importance of studying child care in context, as part of household work, with comparisons made for family size and household structure, as well as for access to community, financial, and extended-family resources. Unfortunately, the American ideology of motherhood has made child care particularly invisible as work. It also makes it difficult to research this topic directly, for women do not easily admit their ambivalences to others. This difficulty points to the utility of in-depth interviewing and observational studies.

Citing research about the relative discontent of married women, Bernard (1972; 1975; 1976) has suggested that the privatization of the household, which removes women from contact with and support from other women and gives them exclusive care of children, is detrimental to women. The "little machines" that Young and Willmott (1973) have lauded serve to bind many women to the home. Regardless of the size of the family, in our society solitary women have responsibility for maintaining their households. Just as Minturn and Lambert have suggested that child care must be understood in the context of everyday household life, so must its privatization be understood in the context of its relationship to the larger economic structure.

The privatization of the household also means that its maintenance is dependent on wages earned by its members. As I have suggested, for families with limited resources, conflicts may exist between emotional and economic needs, with the latter often taking priority. The study of the Bernard family further suggests that household workers, in particular, are given short shrift; although Richard's emotional needs are taken care of, Alice's often are not. Oren's (1973) study of the household budget of nineteenth century English laboring families provides an interesting analogy. She found evidence that, in these families, women (and, to a lesser extent, children) ate food of lower nutritional value than did husband-fathers. Since the household depended on their wages and therefore their strength, they were given the best of what was available to the family. The addition of children did not appreciably change this relationship. Although most women no longer starve, it may be that the dependence of the nuclear household on wages, and the conflicts this relationship engenders, results in the emotional undernourishment of women as dependent household workers. The home as haven has special costs for women.

The findings also suggest directions for psychological research. With Golden (1975), I would urge research on the effects of ordinary, work-related father absences on the development of children who live in two-parent families. We also need research on the impact of parents' rotating shifts on children's abilities to manage separations. The significance of the child-to-adult ratio also is a fruitful area for clinical research. To what extent do interface stresses cause problems or exacerbate existing ones in clinically troubled families? We need to determine the links between work and family life in a wide range of family types.

Coupled with intensive interviewing, observations of even two days in the lives of families can help us develop baseline information about them. This study also indicates the viability of gaining entry into families for purposes of observation. Gaining entry was dependent, in part, on the rapport developed in the initial interviews and on the collaborative technique whereby the input of the family was seriously solicited and considered. When the research questions have meaning for them, the procedure is clear, and their assistance is valued, even families without a previous commitment to the goals of research can be enlisted in the research process. Such an approach to research would require open disclosure of its purposes and written end products that can be read and understood by research families. This collaborative procedure would involve research families in the active process of learning about themselves. The potential for change as a result of this process should be made clear to them and be consciously built into the methodology.

Clinical Assessment and Intervention

When mental health professionals assess an individual or a family as a whole, they often ask series of questions in order to assess such variables as communication patterns and ego strengths and weaknesses. With the exception of very poor and "multi-problem" families, clinicians rarely direct their assessments to the nature of a family's (or individual's) relation to other social institutions, even though these relationships may be a source of distress.[3] This myopia stems, in part, from the narrow view of the family—and the individual—as a closed system, but it is compounded by the absence of an elaborated way of thinking about such interfaces. Whereas we have a complex vocabulary for and set of conceptualizations about individual and family pathology, we lack sensitizing concepts with which to assess the work–family relationship for any given family system. One of the implicit goals of this study was to provide such concepts. Such relationships may or may not be important for the clinical understanding of any given family; their significance is determined by making an assessment. In this way we can uncover otherwise obscured work-related stresses and everyday strains.

Using the sensitizing concepts developed here, several assessment questions suggest themselves: How do the adults in the family feel about their work? How stressed are they by it and how are such stresses managed? How emotionally available to family members is the husband-father or wife-mother after a day of work? Does he or she work overtime? How is his or her nonwork time spent, and are other family members involved? Does the family as a whole have time together? How isolated is the household worker? Does she have sufficient resources to do her job? If she also is employed, is this second job a source of gratification or a source of additional strain? What types of work–family relations characterize the family? Are family members in agreement about how work-related stresses should be managed? What kind of patterns were learned in their families of origin? Are the children reacting to father absence and mother overwork? In times of crisis, as when a family member is ill, interface accommodations may be upset so that implicit systemic conflicts between work and family life exacerbate existing difficulties.

The recognition of interface dilemmas and difficulties also can lead to a wider range of strategies for clinical intervention. For example, when a clinician is confronted with what appears to be a "rejecting mother," an assessment of the work–family relation might lead to treatment recommendations that focus on ways to reduce her household work load and the structural conflict between the woman as household worker and her children. Although there are limits to the clinical treatment of interface stresses, identification of these dilemmas might provide individual families with a greater number of options for managing them.

Clinicians also might play a role in the prevention of future difficulties by better educating young people about the realities of everyday work and family life. The romantic ideology of family life and par-

3. In the clinical literature, difficulties at work or in school generally are viewed as symptomatic of an underlying personal or family problem.

enthood does not adequately prepare young people for the realities they will encounter. Since household work is largely "invisible," many young women are unaware of the stresses associated with it. Child care, in particular, is romanticized so that its work components become obscured. Similarly, young men may be unaware of the effects economic presses and work life will have on them and their families. Even though young people may marry for love, intimacy, and companionship, everyday work life may erode their best efforts to achieve their goals. Young working-class families are particularly vulnerable in interface conflict because of the limits of their financial resources. Education about work life and its organization and possible effects on family life may help young people make more knowledgeable choices. However, one must be cautious not to overestimate the efficacy of educative efforts.

Social Policy and Social Change

The picture I have drawn is one of conflict and strain for families and their members. In contrast, Young and Willmott (1973) have presented a more positive vision of the future. In their "Stage III" family—toward which their analysis suggests we are moving—the family primarily will be a unit of consumption and will provide the incentive to work. Workers who are not valued by their employers will be valued at home. "Technology" will pay back its debt to the family by providing each home with "miniature machines" that will make "homes more satisfying to be in" (pp. 263–64). People will become increasingly "home centred" and life more private. Sex-role segregation will decrease and families will spend more time together in leisure pursuits, as nonwork time also will increase. This view represents Young and Willmott's projection of current trends in English professional and white-collar families. In their view, the family and technology will have made a "crucial alliance" (p. 269). A major threat to the heralded Stage III family would occur if technology increased the intrinsic interest of jobs so that work would compete with families for workers' time and energy. Thus, for the family system, it would seem that uninteresting jobs for its members are most preferable.

This portrayal of the future integration of work and family life is questionable for a number of reasons. Increased nonwork time depends on a continued growth economy that can reduce working hours while simultaneously increasing wages and, therefore, the material support for families. If the experience of families participating in this study is any indicator, the future holds a very different promise. Inflation and slowed economic growth would mean that family members increasingly will have to sell their labor to maintain their standard of living. In expending even more of their time and effort for economic maintenance, families will have less time for intimacy. Moreover, the family is not simply a unit of consumption; it also is organized as a household. "Little machines" have not reduced appreciably the work load of the American housewife (Vanek 1974). While home-centeredness may be valued, it may not be realized. Uninteresting jobs that do not compete with the family for the husband-father's or wife-mother's attention are not an easy solution, for they also have unwanted effects. Rather than a reduced conflict between modern capitalism and families, the conflict will increase for the majority of working people, who depend on selling their labor to support themselves. Although the ideal of the home-centered family may be approached by those in quasiprofessional and white-collar occupations when income is satisfactory, people in such occupations too may be pressed to work more hours (see Hedges 1976). Insofar as they are dissatisfied with their work, increased working hours would take a psychological toll.

This less optimistic vision of the future integration of work and family life raises the question of how to assess and reduce familial strains resulting from the conflicts among the needs of families, households, and external work systems. Mental health professionals can attempt to help some individual troubled families to manage these strains better. However, individual adaptations are limited, for they do not address the fundamental sources of conflict as they may affect the majority of working-class and lower-middle-class families. Considering the roots of conflict necessarily leads us to assessments of social policy and to questions about the necessity for basic social change.

The recent interest in the development of family "impact statements" (see, for example, Kamerman & Kahn 1976) on the effects on families of public policy and the government as an employer reflects the growing concern with creating social policy that enhances, rather than detracts from, the quality of family life. A better understanding of how work experiences and the structure of work organizations impinge on families is relevant not only for assessing public policy and public employers, but also for determining the impact of all types of work organizations on families. The implementation of programmatic recommendations such as job enrichment and humanization, mobile pensions, a shorter work week, flextime, paternity leave, increased employment opportunities for women, and community-based day care may reduce strain for many families. Such proposals must be examined in light of a complete understanding of work–family relationships for varieties of family types. For example, insofar as flexible working hours are a partial solution to the problems created for families by time and timing, they may not be available to those workers in highly rationalized occupations and work situations. Part-time employment may improve the mental health of individual women while simultaneously adding to the base of material support for individual households; but, if part-time jobs depress wages and make unionization difficult, they may prove detrimental for working-class families as a group. A full assessment of specific programmatic solutions to family strains that may result from the nexus of work and family life is beyond the scope of this study and my individual skills as a psychologist. However, I would like to raise some broader considerations.

Addressing the fundamental sources of conflict involves us in questioning the basic organization of productive life and household structure, as well as the distribution and allocation of resources and the use of human time and energy. These are political questions. It is my feeling that the problems facing American families like those described in this study cannot be solved as long as productive life is organized for private profit. Still, regardless of the nature of economic arrangements that structure work life, questions about the psychological life of workers and their families, about the organization of time and space, and about the structure of households will remain. Remaining also will be questions about the power workers and their families have in influencing those institutions that affect their well-being.

We have seen that powerlessness is a factor in limiting the research families' abilities to arrange their personal lives in more satisfying ways. An increase in the power of families vis-à-vis work organizations appears critical in altering work–family relationships.[4] Those concerned with public policy and its impact on families are implicitly responding to the issue of family powerlessness. With no spokespersons, no well-paid lobbyists, most families have had to adapt their lives to changes initiated by other institutions (Vincent 1966). As social scientists and practitioners we are concerned for families who cannot act on their own behalf. "Impact statements" reflect this concern. The roles generally suggested for us are those of researchers and analysts of public policy. Yet, by treating families simply as objects of study so that "better" policy can be formulated *for them,* we are essentially reinforcing the initial fact of their powerlessness. Instead of being the unintended victims of policymakers, families become the "objects" of researchers who wish to advise these policymakers. We need to ask ourselves: To whom are we responsible? Can we facilitate family power rather than further undermining it?

As researchers we could help to mitigate the powerlessness of families by considering, whenever possible, a collaborative approach to the research process. Just as community agencies have advisory boards, we might consider developing similar procedures in conducting large-

4. To speak of power indicates the political nature of family research and appears alien to our tradition of scientific objectivity and freedom. However, we know from past experience that family research is political, not only because it is not value-free, but also because it points to concrete social policies (see, for example, Staples 1971).

scale family research. Such an approach would avoid the duplication of family powerlessness in the research endeavor, while simultaneously helping us to avoid the imposition of our values—often male, white, and middle-class—on other families.

Research, however, is but one minor arena in which the powerlessness of people as workers and as members of families is crucial. Ultimately, working-class and lower-middle-class people must engage in collective struggles to gain power over those institutions that shape their lives and to alter those structural arrangements that are detrimental to their well-being. Social scientists can participate in this process by critically examining those myths, such as that of "separate worlds," that hide the social relations connecting families and personal life to other institutions. Research such as that reported here, which describes some connections between work and emotional life in a small number of families, is only one step toward raising these issues for public discussion and increasing our understanding of the forces that shape everyday life at the workplace and in the home.

Research as Process

Among those factors that distinguish scientists from others who also pursue knowledge about everyday life are an explicitness about the way in which they proceed to know and the public communication of the data-gathering and inference processes they have used. Describing our procedure is important not only for purposes of replication but also as one way of enabling others to judge the soundness of the study's findings. For the social scientist, these findings are embedded in a complex network of social transactions that represent the conditions of our knowledge. The knower is part of the process. Yet the social ecology of the research enterprise often is lost in the final public reports of the procedure (see, for example, Hammond 1964). What emerges is not research as process, but reconstructed research in which the knower is eliminated—thereby giving the findings an air of total objectivity—with imperfections and difficulties smoothed over. Exploratory research is especially messy because the path is not clearly marked; when this exploration occurs in natural settings the difficulties are compounded, for the researcher as guest in a setting not of his or her own making has little control over what occurs there. Thus, the temptation to present a clean public face is especially strong in the case of naturalistic, qualitative research, which is already criticized for its apparent lack of methodological rigor. Not only does this idealization of the research process obscure the real conditions in the context of which the findings must be understood, but it also mystifies the procedure for those who wish to try their hand at such research in the future. In accordance with the belief that the most useful discussion of methodology requires a description of the social conditions of the study, the real process will be presented here along with the ideal.

Choosing a Method

Social science research involves the self-conscious and publicly articulated investigation of human life in its social form. How we proceed is determined by the questions at hand and the type of knowledge we desire, and what we learn is shaped, in turn, by our procedure—our methodology. The research problem here was to consider how work life may affect the emotional lives of families. Because what we know of whole families is still rudimentary (Handel 1965), the knowledge to be generated included sensitizing concepts and analytic descriptions of work–family relationships in the daily lives of a small number of families.

The method that predominates in the sociological research on work and the family is deductive; connections between these institutions are hypothesized and then tested empirically. Operationalizing the hypothesized connections involves the selection of several discrete variables, which are then measured. For example, Kohn (1963, 1969) hypothesized that because of their differing occupational experiences, social classes develop different world views. More specifically, he hypothesized that objectively different occupational situations result in values placed on self-direction or on conformity and that these values are expressed in parents' socialization attitudes. He then compared working-class and middle-class parents on these attitudes.

At the inception of this study, such a method was still of limited use to the clinician interested in the complex lives of whole families. The act of framing hypotheses requires that we are guided by theory; yet, it was precisely such an elaborated theory that was lacking. Further, the premature isolation of specific variables and exclusion of others may have precluded gaining an understanding of the family as a complex system. At any one time we may be witnessing a confluence of multiple, contemporaneous, and reciprocally influential events such as life-stage concerns, conflicts that originate in families of origin, and reactions to a depressed economy, as well as stresses occasioned by work. Some family theorists have eschewed notions of causality, while others prefer models of "circular causality" and "feedback loops" (Jackson 1966; Kantor & Lehr 1975). Premature selection of independent and dependent variables may have prevented our learning about the full complexity of the interrelationships that were of interest here.

It was hypothetically possible to study the relation of work and family life by utilizing an inductive method that does not begin with specified hypotheses. Survey studies generally rely on delimited responses to structured questions. However, the framing of survey questions involved the similar predicament of knowing what to ask about. The problem of the survey procedure is compounded by the "myth of separate worlds" described in Chapter 1, for posing a simple question such as "Does your work affect your family life?" does not take into account the prevailing ideology. Thus, straightforward questions that may appear valid on their face would have obscured complex processes that needed to be explored in greater depth. While it is important to know what people think about the issue, it is equally important to know what lies behind a simple yes or no answer. Formulating more sophisticated questions would have required adequate knowledge of the processes at the work–family interface and of their indicators.

The Naturalistic Approach and Qualitative Method

Since our knowledge about the dynamic processes that connect "loving and working" for families was sparse, an inductive, exploratory design was chosen that would allow for us to assume as little as possible, include as much information as could be managed, and maintain the integrity of people's real life experiences. The goal was to know people "face to face" (Lofland 1971). Qualitative and naturalistic research methods are generally used for generating such close knowledge.

In a naturalistic approach, what is to be studied is not created by the researcher for the purpose of scientific investigation. She or he does little to interfere with the phenomena to be examined, neither manipulating "antecedent conditions" nor imposing units on the outcome variables (Willems 1969). The data-gathering procedures often used in naturalistic research are those that generate "qualitative" understanding: unstructured interviewing and observations of people as they live. These procedures were used in the study in the context of an inductive methodological framework based on Glaser and Strauss's (1967) grounded theory model. One of the major features of this model is the "discovery" of theory from the data themselves rather than its logical deduction from a priori assumptions. Implicit in the model is the naturalist's assumption that there are structures in everyday life that can be uncovered. Gutmann stated this position eloquently:

> For me, the crux of the naturalist's method is that it does not treat nature as passive. The naturalist's assumption, in any field, is that intrinsic orders exist "out there" and that these regularities will organize and drive events even though our theories take no notice of them.... His a priori theories tend, like his methods, to be conditional; they are ways of getting into the phenomena, ways of jogging nature into a response, so that it will declare itself and make explicit the terms in which it can best be understood. Thus, the techniques and instruments of the naturalist are aimed at bringing out, at highlighting, some implicit order in the domain of his interest, and toward turning the implicit order into explicit data. Where the task of the theorist is to explain data, the special task of the naturalist is to generate data. What was hitherto unattended, cognitively neutral, is suddenly seen

as the signature of some important principle—it becomes data [1969, p. 162].

The naturalist's "discovery" stance was especially appropriate for a research area that we knew so little about and that aimed at identifying patterns and developing sensitizing concepts that could form the basis for further research.

This approach conceives of research as an ongoing process; hypotheses and concepts come from the data and are worked out in relationship to them. While Glaser and Strauss have advocated that one come to the data with no assumptions, such a blank-screen approach is not possible and is not necessarily desirable. Instead, ideas serve as "working hypotheses" to be discarded, modified, or validated and elaborated. In this case, the conceptualizations from the existing literature—including concepts of time and energy, segmentation, carryover, and compensation—served as such working hypotheses. However, we can expect constant modifications in the investigator's notions of what is significant. Elaborations come from the "constant comparison" (Glaser & Strauss 1967) of differences and similarities. As Bakan has noted, "Truly good research means that one allows the investigation to be guided by the experiences of the investigation. And this cannot be predicted" (1969, p. xiv). While the grounded model does not require qualitative research techniques, they especially lend themselves to research as an ongoing analytic process.

Because people are known directly, qualitative research is costly. Consequently, such studies usually involve very small numbers of people or even a single case. Because of the small number of cases involved, qualitative research is criticized for not being "generalizable." This criticism misjudges the goals of small-numbers and qualitative research, which aims at description and the formulation of theoretically relevant generalizations, using criteria of large-scale, quantitative, or hypothesis-testing research, which aims at generating knowledge about magnitudes and frequencies of phenomena in specified populations or at testing existing theory. While small-numbers research cannot claim to provide statistical generalizations or "proof" of theory, it can, by assuming that people are not entirely unique, generate *theoretical* generalizations and significant descriptions about complex processes and relationships (see also Hess & Handel 1959).

Description is often dismissed as the province of journalists and as inferior to "explanation," which is the task of science. However, description is indispensable to the scientific enterprise, for theories and explanations must start from careful observation and description of what is there. Description of family life is especially important given the present state of our knowledge. Moreover, a clear distinction between description and explanation is difficult to make. Scientific description is not simply a running account of what occurs before the eyes of the researcher; it is analytic. That is, scientific description uncovers structure and orders the data in such a way as to make sense of human experience and activity. As Kaplan has noted, "The true beginning of scientific activity consists in describing phenomena and grouping, classifying and correlating them" (1964, p. 78). When descriptions help us to see relationships that had previously escaped notice, they are pointing to an explanation. A description of patterns and relationships is therefore a type of explanation, although it is not a proof. It is precisely in its description of patterns of relationships and processes that the qualitative research endeavor can contribute to advancing understanding.

Much significant psychological theory that has generated interesting research has come from the study of small samples. Freud's and Piaget's work serve as outstanding examples of such an approach. Generalization can come from knowledge that accumulates over time. Even without generating revolutionary new theory, small-scale qualitative research can prove valuable. It can establish a phenomenon as worthy of study by focusing attention on it. Even a single observation can be significant, for a "surprising observation" can compel us to search for new explanations and new theories or can indicate some more general phenomenon to be explored (Barton & Lazarsfeld 1969). Furthermore, by applying existing concepts to concrete data, small-sample research can clarify and revise theory or develop typologies. Thus, small-sample research and qualitative techniques are especially appropriate to research problems that require exploration and the discovery of patterns, hypotheses, and theory rather than their validation. (See also Hess & Hardel 1959.)

At the heart of the debate on generalization is the issue of "significance." Given that small-numbers research aims at descriptive or theoretical knowledge, how can we know that what is described in a single case is "significant"? In psychological research, the question of significance is approached statistically, using tests to indicate the likelihood that associations between variables or found differences between samples would have occurred by chance. Tests of significance are best applied to problems with discrete variables and empirically testable hypotheses. Therefore, careful conceptual work must be done before such tests are useful. Moreover, statistical significance does not insure theoretical, social, or clinical significance.[1] We must still ask whether our findings help our understanding or have social meaning or enable us to "see" with new eyes phenomena previously obscured. In addition, a

1. We all have had experience with statistical significance that has little relevance, and if the sample is large enough, statistical significance is highly likely (Bakan 1969).

finding sometimes is considered significant when the phenomenon is extensive enough to be worthy of our attention. The extensiveness of a phenomenon is an important question whose answer must rely on other kinds of research strategies. However, even unusual and deviant cases can be theoretically and clinically informative.

Once the problem of statistical significance and generalization is clarified, the ubiquitous question of sampling begins to be resolved. Critiques about insufficient sampling similarly rest on a confusion about aims. For research that requires generalizing about frequences and magnitudes of a phenomenon in a population, how the sample was formed is crucial. In fact, the entire enterprise rests on a carefully chosen sample. However, in research that aims at describing only a small number of cases and at generating analytic dimensions, the sampling issues are different. In generating descriptive theory and hypotheses for further study, we do not have to sample the whole field randomly, for a single case can tell us that an important phenomenon *can* occur. The sample is chosen for its relevance in revealing what is under consideration. Inevitable sampling bias is treated as a condition of the discovered relationships—it does not invalidate them (Glaser & Strauss 1967). In this study, it was assumed that we could learn something about the interconnections between work and emotional life in families through the study of *any* family.

Collecting Data: Interviews and Observations

Locating Research Participants

The research problem, as described in Chapter 12, delimited an ideal "theoretical sample" (Glaser & Strauss 1967). To investigate the assumptions of compensatory home-centeredness and segmentation of work and family life, the sample was to be composed of families in which the breadwinner was employed in a working-class or lower-middle-class occupation. In order to allow us to focus on everyday connections between work and home life, families were to be "inconspicuous" to social service, educational, and government organizations, with the assumption that such families would be functioning adequately. For purposes of comparison, families were to vary in their stage of the family life cycle and in their attitudes toward the way in which work life affected them. Because much research has centered on "hard living" families, breadwinners were to be stably employed. Given the precariousness of much working-class life, stability was difficult to define. It was roughly operationalized to include men without obvious breaks in their work history who had been employed for the past year. The tenuousness of employment stability is reflected in the fact that one research participant lost his job several weeks after the interviews.

While this idealized sample was defined by theoretical considerations, the actual group of research participants was shaped by reality. Limited by a lack of resources, I found that locating such families to volunteer their time presented a major difficulty. They were not represented in the university subject pool of undergraduates,[2] and their very inconspicuousness meant that they could not be found through mental health settings. As Handel (1965) has noted, locating nontroubled families is especially difficult for the clinical researcher. Moreover, I had no immediate access to work settings. As a result of these limitations, I used a form of "convenience" sampling, relying on my personal resources and contacts for sources of research participants. Several participants were referred to me. I also interviewed the parents of some participants to explore the issue of intergenerational influences. However, the majority of participating families were solicited through students at an adult education program in which I had taught. All the students I approached agreed to participate. Of the thirty research participants, eight were former students of mine and an additional thirteen were their family members. In all, thirteen husband-fathers, ten wife-mothers, and seven children living at home were interviewed. In three cases, wives were not interviewed. In one case, the husband felt his wife was under stress from a new baby and he did not want me to approach her. In a second case, I chose not to interview the wife because she worked outside the home. In a third case, the wife did not agree to be interviewed; her husband was someone who had been referred to me. That the majority of spouses agreed to be interviewed suggests that, for those participants with whom I was acquainted, I was viewed as someone trustworthy.

I used several criteria in soliciting volunteers. For pragmatic reasons, I approached those who were accessible to me. Also, participants had to fit the general theoretical criteria. Initially, these criteria were relaxed because I was concerned about having enough cases for comparative analysis. Consequently, I interviewed members of several dual-employee families and one family in which the husband-father was employed in a skilled white-collar position. Finally, I approached those students with whom I had some minimal rapport because I had known them for some time.[3] Moreover, one middle-class family, the Turners, were included specifically for purposes of comparison and contrast.

2. See Rosenthal (1965) for a discussion of the implications of using sophomore volunteers as the basis for a psychology.

3. One more recent student and his family were included when he expressed some interest in the research project.

This procedure for generating the actual research sample deserves further comment. A random sampling technique would have eliminated the biases inherent in utilizing a convenience sample. However, such a procedure would have been prohibitively expensive, and it is doubtful whether the cost would have justified the information to be gained in order to generate descriptive knowledge and conceptual understanding. Although randomization would have eliminated the biases that may have resulted in my being acquainted with some of the research participants, we must assume it would have made it difficult to achieve the depth of understanding desired (see also Lewis 1959). In other words, the bias introduced by including some participants with whom I was acquainted is not necessarily an entirely undesirable condition of the study, for such prior rapport can be viewed as an aid to achieving its goals. The depth of knowledge achieved by Golden (1975) in her study of two families was a direct consequence of the fact that she knew them intimately before she began her research. Similarly, my prior relationship with some participants seemed to facilitate establishing the rapport and understanding that were necessary to gather in-depth knowledge. The potential problem of "over-rapport" (Miller 1952) was minimized because we did not have a friendship relationship that might inhibit the discussion of topics threatening to it.[4]

In describing my research project to potential participants I stated simply that I was studying work and family life and that I was interested in talking both to people who felt that their work did not affect their families and to those who felt that it did. Unfortunately, I did not directly question motivation to participate, but in some cases it can be inferred. Some participants seemed to see their participation as a personal favor to me. For example, when I asked Samuel Coleman if he would be interested in being interviewed he answered, "Sure, I'll help you out." Some commented that they hoped the research would be helpful to other families as well as to me personally. These motivations changed as the research progressed.

The Where, How, and What of Interviewing

I conducted all but one interview, which was conducted by a research assistant. In addition, this assistant, a black woman, was present during interview data collected with one black family in the sample whom she knew personally. We felt her presence was necessary to sanction the research and to help the family discuss their feelings openly.

4. Since Golden's study of her close friends appeared to facilitate the discussion of sensitive issues, perhaps the important distinction to be made lies in the *quality* of the relationship that exists between participant and researcher.

I offered to conduct the initial interview in participants' homes or in more neutral settings. The latter were chosen by three participants: one participant did not tell his wife he was being interviewed, another's wife did not want to participate and he felt he could be more open elsewhere, and a third chose a location convenient to his work. Allowing the participant to choose the locale was important in helping him or her feel some control over the interview procedure. My impression was that the home interview allowed participants to use familiar ways of coping with stress and anxiety that arose during the sessions. Sometimes, when distressing material was being discussed, a participant would offer me a cup of coffee, or scold a child, or rush to put in some laundry. Without these naturally available coping mechanisms and distractions, they might have withdrawn or simply terminated the interview. In one case, a participant left abruptly to shave and shortly returned. In a research setting he might have terminated the interview to manage distress that the interview created.

I tape-recorded all initial interviews. I felt that I would be unable to reproduce faithfully several hours of interview and that I would be able to attend more completely to what was being said if I were freed from extensive note-taking. People's familiarity with tape recorders, which have become cheap and common, may have made inhibiting reactions less of an issue than in past research.[5] Permission was always solicited in using the recorder, and the indifference with which such permission was generally granted indicated that recording was not important for the majority of participants. With two exceptions, I could detect no qualitative differences between recorded and unrecorded material.[6] One participant who initially experienced the recorder as a "third person" later mentioned that she preferred that I tape-record, as she felt my note-taking was distracting, and she worried that she talked too fast. I think the decision about whether or not to record interview data must rest on an understanding of its effects on the participants, as well as a weighing of its costs and benefits for the study.

Not having decided a priori what was important, I let the participants lead the way. I began simply, with an open-ended question such as "Tell me about your day" or "Tell me about your job" and followed the participants' meanderings into the corners of their lives. Thus, each interview followed its own course. Since we were talking about daily

5. McCall and Simmons (1969) have argued against mechanical means of recording interview data, because of the expense and its possible reactive effects. They have advocated making mental notes instead of note-taking, which also can be distracting to both the researcher and respondent.

6. In one case, marital tensions were discussed after I had turned off the recorder at the close of the interview. In a second case, the participant asked that the recorder be turned off when sexual issues arose.

life, the interviews had the tone of everyday conversation and often continued when the recording stopped. After several such interviews I began to develop more detailed ideas about what was important and constructed a list of topics and questions to guide the interviews. However, with this latter approach, I exercised too much control over the process and the participants' own identities were obscured. My final solution was to combine these approaches by beginning with open-ended questions, which imposed as little structure as possible on the course of the interview, and then using the topics on the list for further "pinpointing" (Strauss, Schatzman, Bucher, Ehrlich & Sabshin, 1964), either toward the end of the initial interview or at a second interview. Thus, while my interview technique was primarily nondirective, I also probed and suggested ideas. Sometimes these more directive questions gave participants permission to talk about their feelings.

Such an unstructured approach raises the problem of the lack of standardization of the interview and therefore possible difficulties in replicating findings. However it is useful to distinguish the interpersonal condition of the interview and the form of interview questions and responses. If we wish to make frequency statements based on interview data, it is important that each interview present similar stimuli for the interviewees and that the data generated be easily compared. But careful standardization of questions does not address the nature of the variability of interpersonal transactions, which cannot be standardized and in whose contexts the interview data are generated. When the goal is depth of understanding, the focus shifts to this relationship between the researcher and the participant. Rapport is the sine qua non of research that aims at knowing people "face to face." Gutmann (1969) has called such rapport the "true" standard condition.

Once we are aware that the crucial procedural feature of qualitative research is to establish rapport and understanding between participants and researcher, the personal characteristics of the interviewer become, not another source of unreliability, but a possible asset to establishing the relationship. For example, one participant commented that although she is usually wary of professionals, I was easy to talk to because I reminded her of her sister. Moreover, she recalled that I seemed shy and therefore unintimidating the first time she met me. My age made me less threatening, I think, to a mature black couple who might have been wary of an older white woman. Instead we developed a warm relationship that had features of daughter-parent interaction, as reflected in their greetings and the small kindnesses offered me. The comfort achieved with some research participants was shown by the invitations to their homes beyond the requirements of the research. Interviewer "effects" are important insofar as they affect the relationship established between researcher and participant and the consequent depth of understanding achieved. I would assume that another researcher would have developed a different relationship with the people participating in the research, without necessarily affecting the conclusions reached.

Although the majority of participants, including the seven children living at home, were interviewed once, twelve were interviewed on at least two separate occasions. Under ideal conditions—when time and expense are not at issue—the scheduling of at least two interviews can prove invaluable. It enables the investigator to review the first interview for important areas missed or insufficiently discussed and permits misunderstandings to be corrected. For example, because I knew some of the participants in another context I would sometimes assume prematurely that I understood what was being said. Reviewing the initial interview allowed me to be more sensitive to such lapses and to correct them. With some participants important themes emerged quickly in the first interview; others presented nontroubled surface, but perturbations became evident in the second interview.

Since resources were limited, the decision to schedule a second interview was based on an assessment of the quality and type of information such an interview would provide. Glaser and Strauss (1967) have pointed out that once a theoretical category has been "saturated," collecting further information is unnecessary. During the later phases of the data-collection process, decisions could be made on that basis. Moreover, the type of working alliance established and the degree to which participants were willing and able to discuss their feelings and their lives also entered into the decision. Still, the possibility of further interviews was left open with every participant.

Most initial interviews were conducted with family members separately, as I felt it would be easier for me to attend to one person at a time. Often the spouse not being interviewed would hover near us for a few moments in order to see what we were about. Quickly satisfied, she or he usually left or occupied the children while we talked, although finding privacy was sometimes difficult. I also was concerned that once a couple put its "best face" forward, to me and to each other, an individual would be reluctant to admit divergence from this public presentation. This process became dramatic in the case of the Bernards.[7] Throughout the first joint interview I was very much aware of the feelings left unexpressed. After this interview, Alice telephoned me to tell me that she and Richard felt that they were not completely honest with me and with each other. It was because we had a working alliance that they were able to articulate the issue of their own public face.

Still, the "simultaneous collusion" that would be required to put up a monolithic public performance is rarely possible (Vidich 1956). Joint

7. I had interviewed each of them separately and at length.

interviews therefore should not be dismissed, as they are very revealing of familial processes, a fact that became evident in the several cases where I conducted interviews with two or more members of the family present. In two cases, time limitations made it improbable that interviews could be conducted separately. In one case the family norm of "togetherness" was communicated to me when I arrived and all family members, except the teenage daughter, were present.[8] The physical formation assumed by the family during the course of the interview also reflected the family valuation of "closeness"; they rested against each other as they talked. In another case I had completed all interviews with the wife and arrived to interview her husband. After I gently suggested that it might be better for me to interview them individually, her husband reminded her that she had had her own interview. However, she neither moved nor said a word. As indicated in her interview, she was very dependent on her husband, felt lonely and housebound, and was not about to give up her time with him to another woman.

What people were able and willing to talk about was, in part, a function of the interview context and the motivations it stirred, how they perceived me and the research, as well as who they were. Since our contract was not a therapeutic one, I was implicitly not sanctioned to ask about very intimate matters such as sexuality. However, in our interviews alone women sometimes spontaneously brought up sexual concerns in their marriage. In general, women were able to talk more freely than were men about their feelings concerning their marriages. In contrast, men tended to gloss over features of marital life, while being able to talk at length and in great detail about their workday life.[9] I do not think the fact that I was a woman accounted for this difference; in fact, my gender appeared to facilitate the discussions that did occur. It may be, as research indicates, that men are more satisfied with married life than are women. Furthermore, as a woman, I could be very naïve about the men's job situations, and they patiently answered my many questions. Surprisingly, several of the men were able to talk freely about wanting to be "the boss" and their desire to have their wives remain in the home. I inferred that my status as a professional woman was not particularly threatening to these participants because I did not have young children and therefore was not yet violating cultural norms. In fact, I was asked several times when I planned to have children—the assumption was always that I would indeed do so. A sensitive issue that emerged with two men concerned their relationships with a parent. When I unwittingly probed into these sensitive areas I was told straightforwardly that they preferred to let sleeping dogs lie.

8. Teenagers were especially difficult to involve in the research project.

9. Komarovsky (1962) encountered a similar phenomenon. L. B. Rubin (1976), however, found that men welcomed the opportunity to talk with her about their feelings.

Participants' Use of the Interview. As Vidich (1956) has noted, people do not only participate in a research project on the terms specified by the researcher. They also use it for their private purposes. The unstructured nature of the interviewing procedure used here encouraged this process. Two women said they hoped that their husbands would "open up" to me since they rarely discussed their worries and problems with their wives. The women felt that it would be beneficial for their husbands to talk to someone, and they implicitly wanted me to act as their surrogate. Alice Bernard found that the interviews helped her to sort out and articulate feelings and make sense of her experience. Once she realized this benefit from the interviews, her willingness to commit her time increased. As the interviews progressed, others saw them as an opportunity to talk about and reflect upon their lives and their relationships with family members. For example, after our interview, a participant decided to call an aunt he had not talked to in years. As Cannel and Kahn (1953) have noted, people can be motivated to participate in research when they can realize some direct gratification in speaking to a person who is sympathetic and accepting. In general, I found that interviews were more fruitful when participants indicated some personal benefits from the research process.

Sometimes participants wanted support for their point of view regarding an altercation with a neighbor or spouse. Insofar as I was seen as an "expert," they occasionally looked to me for validation of a decision they had made concerning a problem with a child or for suggestions for how to deal with such problems. Sometimes I became a "model" for what was possible. One participant who missed her mother a great deal was very interested in how I had solved the problem of living away from *my* mother. Attempts to triangle me (see Bowen 1976) were most evident in joint interviews in which one spouse would sometimes try to draw me into supporting his or her stance against the other.

Generally, the personal uses to which the interview situation could be put were most obvious in these joint interviews. In some of these interviews, spouses used the occasion to talk to each other through me about things they had not talked about privately. There are unspoken feelings in every relationship. Since the interviews were unstructured they often touched these areas of people's lives, and participants would give vent to previously unexpressed feelings. For example, one participant cried as she recalled an incident that occurred twenty-three years ago, which she had never openly discussed with her husband. A striking example of this use of the interview situation occurred in one of the families mentioned above. After his wife silently refused to leave the room, a participant announced that the interview situation forced him to be honest. The subject of his wife's calls to him at work quickly surfaced and the couple began to talk about her worry that he was with another woman. At times my presence encouraged participants to express

299

feelings that they had not previously articulated. For example, during a home visit to the Bernards, Alice cried as she told Richard about her sadness at not being with a sister and her joy at being able to tell her sister that she loved her. Later, she told me that my presence made her "braver." The presence of a "witness" seemed to assure participants that feelings would not overwhelm them, that the situation would remain controlled; thus difficult family issues were defused.

When sensitive emotional issues did arise, as they often did in the course of the interviews, my goal was to help the participants deal with their feelings immediately rather than encouraging further uncovering. Instead of the more removed stance I would have taken as their therapist, I gave support and sometimes shared personal experiences. Since my relationship with them was not long-term, I had to be responsible for the effects the interview process had on those involved.

Selection of Family and Paid Work Settings for Observation

Although they had expressed some interest in being observed, one research family was immediately excluded from possible observation because I felt they would be unable to tolerate close scrutiny (see also Bott 1971). My clinical impression was that they might be using the observations to solve problems of loneliness and dependency. Other families were eliminated because they had two wage earners, or only one spouse had been interviewed, or the wage earner was retired. Four families were finally noted for possible observation. As indicated in their interviews, these families differed in their feelings toward the work–family interface; they also varied in their stage in the family life cycle and in the type of occupational setting in which the wage earner worked. Included among them was the "contrast case" of a middle-class family—the Turners—who reported a particularly positive integration of paid work and family life.

Entry. I had already been allowed into the families' physical interiors; however, I wanted access to their "backstage" (Goffman 1959). From accounts in the literature of how families are "bastions of privacy" (Laslett 1973; Rapoport & Rapoport 1971; Skolnick 1973), I assumed that gaining entry to home settings would be more difficult than acquiring access to paid workplaces. After all, the latter are more "public" and impersonal. This initial assumption proved to be unfounded; as Goffman has wisely pointed out, workplaces have their own backstage areas.[10] And just as do families, they have their own gatekeepers and rules concerning entry.

10. Richard Bernard's police partner described the police car as the only place they could be away from the public eye.

In two of the four families being considered, the wage earners worked in large industrial plants, and I confronted several difficulties in my attempts to gain entry. As would be expected in my sample, research participants were at the bottom of the organizational hierarchy and had little power over entry. Moreover, the work organizations had many gatekeepers; locating the most likely access points was difficult. Given my research orientation, I decided that I would not fare well with corporate gatekeepers. After all, my study was not aimed at increasing productivity, I would be underfoot, and someone's time had to be taken up showing me around while protecting backstage areas. Consequently, I attempted to locate key gatekeepers in the union herarchy. Because unions are highly bureaucratic, the gatekeepers themselves were guarded by others. Moreover, they are not in the business of helping university researchers; messages left with secretaries may not be answered. If I was accepted by one gatekeeper, I was blocked by another. Being a young female seemed a double-edged sword for workplace entry. On the one hand I was perceived as harmless; on the other hand I had no power and, therefore, no foreseeable benefits could accrue to those who helped me. In contrast, for the family system there are only two primary gatekeepers—the adults—who were readily accessible by telephone. Moreover, the implicit criteria guiding entry are more personal here: I had merely to be seen as someone trustworthy and nonjudmental.

Given these endless and unsuccessful attempts to negotiate entry to participants' industrial workplaces,[11] I chose to approach the two families for whom my access to the paid work setting was least problematic. In the case of the Turners—the middle-class "contrast" family—Ezra Turner himself was the gatekeeper. As a supervisor in control of his own area in a research hospital, he could give me permission to observe there. The law enforcement agency for which Richard Bernard worked as a policeman had an established role for observers and a simple bureaucratic procedure was required for gaining entry. As it happened, the gatekeepers in this latter organization changed, and with that the rules for entry were made more stringent. However, because of a history of having had observers, access was still possible. Interestingly, both these workplaces are nonprofit, governmental organizations. Using such a pragmatic criterion to select families for intensive study introduced another bias into the study. However, if we assume that the work–family interface is of interest in all families, it is valuable to study any family. Moreover, these efforts at gaining entry also served as data about the workplaces themselves. We know, for example, that Ezra

11. I finally found a way into an industrial plant, but the timing made it impossible to collect observational data for inclusion in the study.

Turner has power in his work setting that other participants lack and that he works in an organization that can integrate observers easily.

Ezra Turner and Richard Bernard readily agreed to be observed at work. Ezra Turner also spontaneously suggested the possibility of home observations. However, I viewed the household workers as the primary gatekeepers of the home setting. Consequently, I approached Alice Bernard and Isabel Turner about gathering observational data there. Just as I had asked their husbands for permission to observe them working, I asked them for permission to observe their household work. Alice and Isabel expressed some initial concern that I would be bored by their day, and I had to make clear that I respected the work they performed within the home.[12] Alice took several days to "think it over." She was concerned that she might have to "entertain" me; her only role models for home visitors were guests. She finally agreed to participate (as did Isabel) on the ground that she herself might find the experience valuable. Alice became interested in the prospect of helping others to understand that household work, too, is a job.

Formal Observational Periods

As noted in Chapter 2, Ezra Turner was observed at work for a full day and the home setting also was observed. Richard Bernard also was observed at work and the Bernard family was observed at home (see Chapters 2 and 7). Although each setting was observed for a limited time, the assumption underlying the observations was that even such short forays into the field would be informative because home and workplace are nonrandom systems. There are structures inherent in everyday life in these settings: these structures occur within time. In other words, with Lewis (1959), it was assumed that even one day reveals systemic structures that can be elaborated by the interview data and by the participants' own perceptions of their daily lives. Generally, the longer the observational periods, the more certain we can be that we are not mistaking parts of structure for the whole.

The rationale for observing a whole day was to obtain a "baseline" for what occurred in the settings over time and therefore to minimize time-sampling biases. The settings had their daily rhythms. For example, in both the Bernard and the Turner homes, mornings were busy with the activities of cleaning and dressing, marketing was done after-

---

12. Berk and Berhaide (1977) have discussed their difficulty in gaining entry to homes for the purpose of observing household work, and they interpreted this resistance as a reflection of a woman's low evaluation of her own work. I think the importance of the initial interview phase cannot be overestimated. In Blood's (1958) observational study, the first home visit provided the family the opportunity to become accustomed to the researcher. Here, family members could assess me during the course of the interviews. I assume that their assessment resulted in their agreement to be observed.

wards, and late afternoons were "quiet times." Because one of my interests was in the work process, observing these work rhythms was important. In the case of the Bernard family, which was studied more intensively, further observations of the home setting were made to observe family constellations and activities not seen during the Base Day.

Seasons were not equally sampled; observations took place at the end of the winter and in the spring. Moreover, the days chosen for observation were not randomly chosen in that I did not suddenly arrive at the family's door without warning. Perhaps if I knew the families very well such a plan might have been feasible. The families tended to control access to which day I observed; however, their decisions were based on a consideration of my research needs. For example, in the Turner family I asked to see a day in which Ezra was home in the evening; Isabel picked the first such available day. Ezra Turner chose a day at his workplace when he would not be escorting visitors around or attending meetings. In the case of Richard Bernard's work setting, the decision was made for us. I observed on a day his supervisors, for bureaucratic reasons, had chosen. In discussing possible times with Alice, I asked to see a fairly "typical" day. She chose a Monday, when things were not unrealistically quiet or hectic. She cancelled a subsequent observation period during a time in which she felt too much strain. Within such limits I could specify the type of activity I was interested in. We can assume that the times observed, though not randomly chosen, were not unusual for the families.

During the observational periods, whom to follow also involved further selection. Observations at the paid work settings posed no difficulties, as only one family member was present. In Richard's case I was required to remain in the police car during traffic checks. At home when family members went into different rooms I followed several guidelines. I tried to move myself into position to see and hear as many family members as possible. Otherwise I would follow the household worker, since I was interested in her work. However, if I had oversampled her activity, I would observe a family constellation whose interactions I had not yet observed.

Observer Roles. R. L. Gold (1958) and Schwartz and Schwartz (1955) have described the various stances an observer can take. At one extreme is the complete participant who takes an active role in the setting and whose identity is hidden to those she or he is studying. At the other end of the continuum is the passive observer, who remains entirely removed from social interaction and hidden from those in the setting. Between these two extremes stand the roles adopted in the present research. The observer-as-participant role involves the researcher in formal observation; she or he is not actively involved in the

303

setting but is known to those being observed. This is the role I assumed most commonly during the course of the field observations. I would arrive at the setting with a notebook and seat myself in a chair from which I could observe what was occurring. During such periods of formal observation, children sometimes would try to engage me in conversation. My stance was to be responsive but not inviting,[13] so that their approach behaviors were not reinforced. When I inadvertently responded to a child's antics by laughing, I found the performance repeated for me several times.

Ultimately, perception is selective. In gathering the observational data the effects of bias were reduced because I did not know what was important. My goal was simply to note as much activity and interaction as possible. Although other observers have recommended making mental notes for as long as one hour of observation (Bermann 1973; Golden 1975),[14] my rationale for taking notes during the observing periods was to increase the reliability of the observational record. While on patrol with Richard Bernard, note-taking was prohibited so that I would be prevented from serving as a witness against Richard and his partner. Consequently, I had to reconstruct an eight-hour stretch of time that occurred between midnight and 8:00 A.M. This observational record is therefore the least complete and least reliable. In Ezra Turner's work setting, note-taking was not entirely unusual, as it was a research environment with students present. An additional rationale for note-taking was that I did not want to make any pretense about my research role and the fact that I was, indeed, noting what occurred. Blood (1958) has suggested that note-taking while observing can even facilitate the observer role by providing him or her with something active to do and thus decreasing the extent to which family members feel they must entertain the observer.

Family members' presumed curiosity about what I was writing was satisfied in two ways. Sometimes I casually left my notebook unattended and in full view to indicate that what I was writing was not "secret." Considering that I was entering their "backstage," it is interesting that adults were too polite to ask about what I was writing. Children, however, were more direct. Parents were often in earshot as they asked why I was writing and what my notes said. I responded as straightforwardly as possible by telling them that I did not trust my memory sufficiently and read aloud the words to which they pointed.

One difficulty in attempting to be open to all stimuli for an entire day is the mental fatigue that results. For example, although I do not

13. Blood (1958) also found it best to be brief and factual, rather than being a "bump on a log."

14. The observer then jots down notes on what was observed.

usually sleep in the afternoon, when the Bernard family napped I fell asleep on their sofa. One solution to the problem of exhaustion was to slip into a second role of participant-as-observer, participating more actively in the setting. These periods were subsequently reconstructed.[15] I also assumed a more participatory stance when I went visiting or marketing with the women.

An important benefit of such increased participation was the informal interviewing that took place then. The activities of everyday life can elicit the expression of important family themes. For example, while I was helping a female participant hang up her laundry, bed-wetting was introduced; when helping her to fill out school reports, I was told about difficulties with the children's school performance. When folding laundry with another I learned about standards for clothing care. On a trip to the bank, the subject of conflicts about finances was first broached. These topics were brought up in a natural context over which the participants had control. I was not asking them questions; they could choose what they wanted to tell me. Information emerged slowly and comfortably in this way.

Observer Effects.   An issue that inevitably arises in the course of naturalistic observation is that of "reactivity": does the observer disturb the field under study? My assumption is that whether we are observing, interviewing, or studying people in laboratories, the act of research affects, to some extent, the phenomenon being studied. The nature of naturalistic observations precludes a rigorous determination of the extent to which a system is functioning entirely in habitual ways. Even with observer effects, however, we can assume forces that pull systems into their private, habitual manner of operating. One such force in both home and workplace settings arises from the fact that work must be accomplished. To change a household routine in order to attend to me meant that beds would not be made, children would remain unfed, etc. Similarly, the purposes of the employment settings pulled participants into their regular modes of operation. When the setting allowed freedom from work requirements, as during the lunch break at the laboratory where Ezra Turner works, more attention was focused on my presence. Henry (1965) also has noted that children exert pressures toward habitual behaviors because their inner needs are not controlled. Even when company is present and their parents would like a good public performance, children tend to behave as they usually do. The forces of children and daily work duties seemed to exert the most pressure to ignore my presence as an observer in the home. Adults were most likely to engage me in conversation when neither was present.

15. They were not coded. See Chapter 7.

Henry also mentioned habituation to the observer as minimizing reactive effects, and Golden (1975) has argued strongly for using as observers people already familiar to the family. However, I think that the association between temporal habituation and reactivity is not linear. I would suggest a three-step sequence that was most evident in the way children responded to my presence. In the stage of orientation, they seemed to be taking a silent "reading" of the situation. While a decision was being made as to how to proceed, habitual behavior predominated and, in the case of one teenager, even appeared to be exaggerated. When they became accustomed to me as a benign presence they tried to engage me. Would I participate? Could I be counted on for help? After this testing stage came boredom, when I seemed to lose stimulus value and was of less interest. We might hypothesize a similar sequence for adult members in both home and external work settings.

The strongest argument Henry made for habitual behavior rests on the idea that families are stable environments with their own cultures. Similarly, workplaces also have such cultures (Meissner 1976). The culture is resistant to change; altering it requires effort and imposes strain. Moreover, it is not clear that system members would know which behaviors to conceal from the observer. From my experience I would also suggest that the more people are present, the less capacity the system has for deliberately changing the behavior of its members quickly. Since family members have interlocking modes of interacting, a major change in any one member would reverberate through the social system. Thus, the force is toward normalcy. Though some surface manifestations might be altered, it is assumed that the underlying forms are similar (Reams 1975). In other words, systems will reveal themselves even in the ways in which they try to change or conceal themselves. This proposition rests at the very heart of naturalistic observation as a research tool.

To minimize observer effects, I tried to be as inconspicuous as possible. As described above, in the home settings I attempted to be discrete, moving around only to follow family members into different rooms. In Ezra Turner's work setting I was given a white lab coat and therefore could look much like other female research assistants. Integrating myself into Richard Bernard's work setting was far more difficult; everyone else was uniformed, and most police officers were male. I remained quiet and sat in the back of Richard's patrol car throughout most of the observation time. When possible, I followed him outside to do an investigation. In all settings, I was introduced to others simply by my first name or, when necessary, as someone studying the family. For other members of work settings who understood that I was doing research, it was important to indicate that I was not studying them. Still, I was not a covert observer, and we can safely assume that there were reactive effects of my observations.

One can assess some of these observer effects. In Richard Bernard's work setting, for example, no one overtly acknowledged my presence at the police station. I felt "invisible," but Richard indicated that others were well aware of me. At one point Richard's partner commented that I did not seem like an "ordinary" observer because Richard was behaving in an unusually relaxed manner in my presence. What he meant was that Richard was allowing me to see and hear about the backstage area normally hidden from the public. The partner then followed suit; I was sanctioned as someone trustworthy. This attitude seemed to generalize. When Richard and his partner stopped to talk with other police officers, they asked about me, and his partner indicated that I was "all right." Soon backstage gossip emerged. Later, Richard surmised that my not reacting visibly to their stories and my quiet manner made the observation remarkably unreactive. Having seen other observers,[16] Richard and his partner could assess the comparative effects of my observation.

My presence in the Bernard home also eased some strain between Alice and her three children. After making a telephone call, Alice spontaneously commented that my presence was helpful in preventing "all hell from breaking loose." In another instance, Alice mentioned that she liked to have my company in the evening when Richard was at work. Moreover, she liked to have an adult around during the day. Comments about the effects of the observer served as data on the family. Further information about the family system came from noting how and when the Bernard children interacted with me when I was observing. The children approached me at various times during the observational periods; an analysis of these approaches was useful in understanding the workings of the family system.

I also asked Alice Bernard directly about the effects of my observations. She had worried that she would be required to entertain me and was relieved when she learned this concern was unfounded. She also indicated that the observations neither annoyed nor irritated her, because we had "hit it off," and that she did not feel judged, indicating to me that she had anticipated having these sorts of feelings. The interviews before the observations, therefore, proved crucial. Regarding one specific interchange between Alice and Richard, I asked how the conversation might have gone differently had I not been there. Alice's answer indicated that while the specific words she used to respond to him might have been different, her intent and meaning would have been the same.

"Data Slices"

The data-collection techniques utilized were designed to provide multiple perspectives on possible patterns of relationship between work

16. Observers occasionally rode with patrol cars.

and family life. Data were derived from interviews with participants and naturalistic observations of the home and paid workplaces of two families, from the researchers subjective experience of these settings, and finally from the participants'—especially the Bernards'—reactions to the research data and the emerging analysis. Collecting such "data slices" (Glaser & Strauss 1967) gives us more information than would any single approach. Multiple methods of knowing about a phenomenon help mitigate the biases inherent in any one approach.

Data Analysis and Interpretation

The integration of the "data slices" is the task of the researcher. Just as the data were collected in different ways, more than one mode of analysis was used to provide differing viewpoints.

Coding the Observational Data

Again, reality intruded. Because of time limitations only the observations of verbal interactions in the Bernard family home were systematically coded[17] using two a priori coding schemes. Because coding and quantification can provide a condensed way of imparting information, they can be particularly useful in obtaining overviews of what occurs in a system. It is tempting to put all one's faith in such prior schemes; however, they also have their own biases, for what one uncovers depends on the initial categories. Since the data were also analyzed thematically (see below), the limitations of this approach were minimized. The resulting quantification was not aimed at testing rigorous hypotheses but at illustrating themes and suggesting new directions for understanding. In other words, the results of the coding were integrated with the thematic analysis.

Quality-of-Interactions Code. The coding scheme used was based on Bermann's (1973) adaptation of a system developed by Charlotte Bühler (1939) specifically for use with observational data gathered in home visits. This scheme is of manageable size yet is dense enough to account for much family interaction. As used here, family interactions were coded into sequences with two parts: an initiation aspect and a response aspect. Because of resource limitations, the researcher alone coded the entire observational protocol into these interactional sequences. Bias was minimized because there were, as yet, no explicit hypotheses about the family. In order to obtain a measure of reliability, a second judge—a graduate psychology student—coded a random sample

17. As noted in Chapter 7, some observational periods were not coded.

of eight fifteen-minute segments of the observational protocol. An interjudge "estimate of accuracy" (see Barker & Wright 1955, p. 271) was used to determine agreement on the creation of interaction sequences. Achieved interjudge accuracy for the segments was 91 percent. Within agreed-upon interactional sequences, 97 percent agreement was obtained on initiators and 94 percent agreement on respondents.

This way of "punctuating" interactions implicitly reflects a stimulus–response paradigm, and the analysis of interactions remains an important problem in family research that aims at going beyond linear, causal models (Greenberg 1977). To some extent, the stimulus–response model violates the natural structure of human interactions. Barker (1963) termed fragments of behavior selected or created by the researcher "behavior tesserae" to distinguish them from "behavior units," which are inherent in the stream of naturally occurring behavior. Because the observations were also analyzed thematically, natural structure was preserved there.

The coding categories, slightly modified, are described below. The reader is referred to Bermann (1973) for full coding instructions. In order to preserve the natural complexity of experience, each interaction could be coded more than once, as interactions can have several meanings. Following Bermann, interactions in which the observer participated were not coded.

A. *Initiations toward Another*
1. *Cooperative–Affectional:* Friendly, warm, cooperative, smiling, hugging, expressions of nurturance, helpfulness; cooperation in mutual endeavor
2. *Pleasure–Joy:* Overt pleasure, joy, excitement, glee, strong approval
3. *Conversational:* Expressions of opinions, gossip, entertainment, telling stories
4. *Objective:* Questions, explanations, informing communications, exchanges of informations that are neutral and devoid of personal valence or attitude
5. *Mild Influencing:* Trying to get another to do something by convincing, suggesting, urging, directing, asking permission
6. *Strong Influencing:* Insisting, demanding, threatening, showing force, coercing others to do something
7. *Disapproving:* Critical negative communications about behavior that are short of blame and contempt
8. *Blaming–Accusing:* Disapproving and holding another responsible; includes scolding and punishing

9. *Antagonistic:* Hate, disgust, contempt directed at the other person
10. *Unhappiness–Distress:* [18] Unhappiness, distress, crying, pouting, worry

B. *Responses to the Initiation*
1. *Positive–Direct*: Direct, straightforward responses to the social initiation of another; without negativism
2. *Positive–Cooperative:* [19] Friendliness, warmth, giving; mutual or joint activities that involve a smooth flow of interaction
3. *Overt Pleasure:* [20] See Pleasure–Joy above.
4. *Objective–Passive:* Compliance, going along, obeying
5. *Avoidant:* Negativism in an indirect sense; oblique, diverting
6. *Ignoring:* Extreme avoidance; not responding in any visible way
7. *Negative:* Direct refusal, negation, obstinacy, opposition
8. *Disapproving:* See above
9. *Blaming–Accusing:* [21] See above
10. *Antagonistic:* See above
11. *Unhappiness–Distress:* [22] See above

The greater number of negatively toned categories simply allows for greater differentiation of such initiations and responses and does not introduce a coding bias. All interactions were coded by the researcher and a second set of judges—undergraduate and graduate students in the social sciences. The coding was done with minimal training. Since each interaction could be coded more than once, Barker and Wright's "estimate of accuracy" was used to determine interjudge reliability. Overall accuracy was 76 percent; reliability for each category is presented in Table A-1. Disagreements were resolved either through a third judge or through discussion.

To simplify presentation of the results of this analysis, these codes were collapsed into general categories, with the more differentiated codes retrievable when needed. Initiations were collapsed into *Positive* (Cooperative–Affectional, Pleasure–Joy, and Conversational); *Neutral* (Objective); *Mild Influencing* and *Negative* (Strong Influencing, Disapproving, Blaming–Accusing, Antagonistic, and Unhappiness–Distress). Responses were collapsed into *Positive* (Positive–Direct, Positive–Cooperative, and Overt Pleasure); *Neutral* (Objective–Passive); *Covert*

18. Added to allow for coding behaviors of small children; c.f. Golden (1975), p. 82.
19. Bermann called this category Cooperative–Affectional.
20. Added to allow for coding behaviors of small children; c.f. Golden (1975), p. 82.
21. Disapproving and Blaming–Accusing have been added.
22. Bermann called this category "Embarrassed–Withdrawal."

Table A-1. Interjudge Estimate of Accuracy by Category

Quality of Interaction Codes			
INITIATIONS	PERCENT ACCURACY	RESPONSES	PERCENT ACCURACY
Cooperative–Affectional	81	Positive–Direct	82
Pleasure–Joy	66	Positive–Cooperative	46
Conversation	77	Overt Pleasure	62
Objective	74	Objective–Passive	83
Mild Influencing	82	Avoidant	53
Strong Influencing	70	Ignoring	78
Disapproving	70	Negative	75
Blaming–Accusing	62	Disapproving	43
Antagonistic	63	Blaming–Accusing	0
Unhappiness–Distress	77	Antagonistic	0[a]
		Unhappiness–Distress	69
Positive	85	Positive	87
Neutral	74	Neutral	83
Influence–Mild	82	Negative–Covert[b]	76
Negative	89	Negative–Overt[b]	82

Content Codes	
INTERACTIONS	PERCENT ACCURACY
Domestic	91
Play	66
Social Interaction	83
All Other	77

[a]The low reliability of these categories may be a consequence of the low frequency of responses coded as Blaming–Accusing and Antagonistic ($N = 7$).
[b]A general Negative category would show greater agreement, since the majority of disagreements concerned whether a response was overtly or covertly negative.

Negative (Avoidant and Ignoring); and *Overt Negative* (Negative, Disapproving, Blaming–Accusing, Antagonistic, and Unhappiness–Distress). Overall interjudge estimate of accuracy of these larger categories was 83 percent. Specific category reliabilities also are presented in Table A-1.

Golden (1975) has noted some of the limitations of this scheme for coding family interactions. One such problem is that the codings are not adjusted for time. For example, picking up a child and cooing at him would be coded as one interaction sequence even though the child might be held briefly or at length. Second, parallel play—where children or family members do not interact overtly—also is not codable. I also found that some of the Bernard children's nonverbal behavior, such as sidling up to their mother or following her around without saying anything, was not directly codable. These codes, therefore, are most useful for coding verbal interactions. Since all the children in the Bernard family use language, the coding proved useful.

Content Codes. The manifest content of observed verbal interactions also were coded. Four general categories were developed. As with the quality-of-interaction codes, interactions with the observer were not coded, and each interaction could receive more than one content code. Generally, no more than two primary content codes were used for an interaction. The overall estimate of interjudge coding accuracy was 82 percent. Figures for each category are presented in Table A-1. In developing content categories for family interactions about household work (Domestic), the codes developed by Walker and Woods (1976) as a measure of household work activity were utilized. The content categories are listed below.

1. *Domestic:* Food preparation such as meal preparation and after-meal cleanup. House cleaning, including straightening and yard and car care. Clothing care, including laundry, ironing, sorting, gathering. Marketing, including putting away purchases and travel time. Management, including making shopping lists, planning meals, supervising the work of others, banking, figuring out the budget. The physical care of a child or adult, including bathing, dressing, feeding, taking family members to the dentist, care of the sick and elderly. The nonphysical care of an adult or child, including chauffeuring to school, helping with lessons. Self-referent statements about a biological need.[23] Miscellaneous domestic.
2. *Play:* Interactions pertaining to play activity.
3. *Social Interaction:* Statements about relationships, about identity, about behavior; greetings and other ritualistic behaviors. Can be positively toned or negative.
4. *All Other:* Includes reference to an absent family member, references to school, church, employment, and other outside events. References to television programs. Miscellaneous other.

Since one area of interest was the home as a household, care was taken to include a category (Domestic) that would allow us to obtain a measure of the interactions related to household work matters. The difficulty lay in deciding what content was to be considered Domestic. There would be general agreement among sociologists of housework that vacuuming, cooking, and ironing should be considered household

23. This category was added to the Walker and Woods household activity codes.

work (Lopata 1971; Oakley 1974a), even though these activities involve work other than the direct maintenance of the house. Therefore, references to these activities would clearly come under the definition of household tasks. Where confusion arose was in the treatment of child care.

Because of the psychosocial aspects of child care, sociologists have remained unclear as to whether child care should be considered as household work. To deal with this problem, child care has been regarded as "conceptually distinct" from household work (see Ferree 1976) and as an activity belonging to another role—that of mother (see Lopata 1971; Oakley 1974a).[24] Yet such distinctions between child care and household work activities and roles remain problematic. In relegating child care exclusively to the mother role and in excluding it from household work activities, it can too easily be accepted as nonwork. Moreover, actual attempts to make clear distinctions between child-care activities and household work remain unsatisfactory. Thus, Oakley had to include a chapter on "Children" in her book on housework because the women she interviewed constantly brought up child care when they discussed housework, and Lopata recognized that the housewife and mother roles overlap in the physical care of children.

If we examine the conceptual base upon which the distinction rests, the issue becomes more clouded. One implicit distinction appears to be made between activities done *for* children and those done *with* them. Thus, ironing a child's clothes would be considered housework but dressing that child would not. However, doing laundry for the physical maintenance of children is only one step removed from dressing them. If household work is taken to include the production of goods and provision of services for maintaining and reproducing human life (see Chapter 10), then the physical care of children would be coded as household work, that is, in the Domestic category. This does not deny the emotional transactions that occur when parents take physical care of their children; the simultaneous quality-of-interaction coding allowed us to include this emotional component.

A more complex difficulty arises when we consider other activities associated with the care of children, such as their socialization and education. Although such activities are necessary to maintain and reproduce life that is human, it is more difficult for us to categorize them as Domestic because they rest upon and blend with the purely emotional relationships between parents and their children.[25] Walker and Woods (1976)

24. Glazer-Malbin (1976) has wondered about the utility of these distinctions but does not discuss the issue further.

25. It should be noted that the problem arises because of our need to measure interaction by using discrete categories for dynamic, complex processes.

recognized that activities such as reading to a child presented coding difficulties, since some people would consider it work, while others would not. The rule they developed to deal with such cases was to allow the mother to classify the activity. The solution utilized here was more conservative. Although Alice Bernard considered reading to her children to be work, in order not to inflate the Domestic category and to be conservative about its interpretation, references to activities of this kind were *not* coded as Domestic. This represents a measurement, but not conceptual, solution to our problem in adequately understanding socialization processes. In the discussion of Alice's experiences of her work, socialization and educational activities were included.

Thematic Analysis

In contrast to the coding of the observational data according to structured categories, the object of thematic analysis is to allow the data to "speak for themselves" without the prior imposition of a researcher's schema. But the researcher is not merely an empty vessel through which the structure inherent in the data is carried into public discourse. Such an analysis involves a dialectical tension between the process of accomodation, whereby the conceptual schemas are created and modified by the data, and assimilation, whereby the data are fit into the emerging conceptual framework.

Initially, material was labeled with descriptive captions, which then became themes. In the early phase, no shred of evidence was dismissed as too insignificant to become a theme and a "working hypothesis." The original assumption that families are both different from and similar to each other was evident in these emerging themes. Some themes reappeared in the various protocols in slightly different form; others were unique to the particular families studied. These themes or "working hypotheses" began to group themselves into clusters of increasingly economical descriptive and analytic categories. In generating the major categories, the method of "constant comparison" of cases and themes was used (Glaser & Strauss 1967). Those categories for which the evidence was sparse and which were unimportant to the emerging patterns eventually were set aside. Occasionally, a theoretically important category would emerge late in the data collection period. When this situation arises the ideal solution is to return to the field to gather more data. Since new data collection was not possible, the data already collected were reexamined for those newly noticed themes (McCall & Simmons 1969). The observational protocols were analyzed, keeping in mind the categories generated by the interviews. The themes that emerged from the observational data offered new insights and complemented the data gathered in interviews with the Bernard and Turner families. Observations and interviews informed each other.

314

Inference and Interpretation. The language of qualitative data is incomplete, complex, and multifaceted, and the researcher must bring all his or her understanding to bear in order to comprehend it, remaining open-minded and disciplined all the while. Thematic analysis and the process whereby analytic categories are generated from qualitative data require inferences about and interpretation of data. In psychology, inference involves us in surmising meanings, feelings, and structures from observable behaviors. Kaplan (1964) has noted that some inference is involved in all observation; in "direct" observation, inferences are so common and so sure that they are made without awareness and remain unproblematic. Interpretation relies on inference; it is a type of explanation that occurs when the datum is viewed both as "fact" and as symbol (Kaplan 1964). Developing a pattern description that has theoretical relevance necessitates such a process. In fact, all research activity requires that the researcher make inferences (Bakan 1969). In qualitative research the inferences cannot be hidden behind the cloak of quantitative analysis.

In thematic analysis a lone researcher is handicapped by his or her limited perspective on the data. A solution sometimes used to limit judge bias is to have more than one person make independent judgments about the data; the judgments are treated as valid when there is agreement about the interpretation of the data. Resource limitations did not allow for the extensive involvement of external judges in the process of thematic analysis. However, as described in Chapter 2, the collaborative procedure was based on the assumption that the researcher has allies in the research participants themselves. This procedure of comparing the researcher's interpretations of the data with the participants' and discussing the interpretations with them is similar to what occurs in psychotherapy. Therapy that relies on interpretation of underlying processes assumes that the patient has an "ego" with which the therapist can ally, no matter how involved the patient is in the treatment. While the ends differ, we also can make a "working alliance" in the course of the research process (Raush 1969).

At times, my interpretation of the interview and observational data was strikingly similar to those independently offered by the participants themselves. However, it is important to recall that interjudge agreement must itself be subject to interpretation. It may mean, for example, that both judges are subject to the same idiosyncratic bias. Agreement in qualitative research also might mean that the participants are trying to please the researcher (Dean & Whyte 1958). When participants responded with a flat "yeah" to one of my working hypotheses, I was suspicious of their assent, surmising that they were not listening, were trying to please me, or were being defensive. Their agreement was given more weight when they elaborated my hypothesis by providing further supporting data.

Differences in interpretation of data among family members and between participants and myself sometimes occurred. In a search for interjudge reliability, such differences pose problems for data analysis. However, here the data was approached with the assumption that there are many ways to interpret the data at hand, depending on one's vantage point. The "Rashomon effect," with which family therapists are familiar, has been observed in research with families (Bernard 1971, 1972; Lewis 1959; R. G. Ryder 1970; Safilios-Rothschild 1970). Different family members will describe apparently different, but equally real, families. If we add the researcher's perspective to that of the participants, the Rashomon effect is compounded. For example, Richard and Alice Bernard described Carrie as the instigator in fights among the children. However, from my observations Carrie appeared no more or less an initiator of squabbles than the other children. Thus, not only do we have the researcher's interpretations of what happens in the lives of families studied, but we also have interpretations made by participants about their own lives.

It was assumed that these differences in interpretation would become sensible if we take into account the position of the person offering it. Rather than viewing them as sources of error, these differences were viewed as aids to the process of data analysis. When disagreements arose between myself and participants, for example, I asked myself several questions. Did I misunderstand the situation? Am I or is the family invested in seeing the event in a particular way? Furthermore, by focusing on conflicting accounts and interpretations of events, the researcher is forced to arrive at an understanding wherein these differences are subsumed, reconciled, or made intelligible. The altered understandings gained through such a dialectical process can then be checked against new data.

More commonly than clear agreement or disagreement, I found—as did Strauss et al. (1964)—that when I suggested interpretations, participants modified them or offered alternative understandings. The resulting synthesis often was more complete than the original hypothesis. For example, in reading my observations of the Bernard home setting, Richard commented that he regretted that he was still engaging in roughhouse joking behavior with his children. He was trying to eliminate this behavior because he felt it was misunderstood. I had noticed this behavior both at home and when he was with his fellow workers, and I had developed two alternative working hypotheses. One was that the joking behavior was a form of communication functional in the workplace and carried over into the home; the other was that joking was a behavior learned earlier in life. When I suggested the first hypothesis to him, Richard said that he had related to his male relatives in this way, offering evidence for the second hypothesis. At this point, Alice entered the conversation, and what ensued was a more complex discussion of the forms of communication at work, Richard's adolescence, and his relationship with family members. Neither working hypothesis alone was correct; the hypotheses needed to be synthesized.

Research as an Intervention

In describing research as an active process that involves both researcher and participants in a collaboration, the issue of research as an intervention emerges. Rubin and Mitchell (1976) have described the "unintended effects" of their study of couples. They surmised that their study had a significant impact on more than 50 percent of the relationships they studied and concluded that researchers intentionally should view couples research as couples counseling and should make this effect clear to people before they participate in our studies. Even carefully controlled experimental studies are forms of intervention, and Raush has commented on the "fiction of objectizing," that "peculiar form of repression that allows us to think that people can be put on shelves, can remain unaffected by the surroundings, and, if handled with usual laboratory precautions, can be taken down later, unchanged" (1969, p. 135). The ways in which the research process intervened in people's lives was alluded to in the discussion of participants' use of the interview situation. The process of intervention was pronounced with the Bernards, who were studied most intensively.

Rubin and Mitchell have suggested two processes that they think intervened in the relationships of those they studied: processes of definition and processes of disclosure. In the process of definition, asking people to put labels on their relationship sometimes leads them to view or define it differently. This act of labeling feelings and attitudes is familiar to therapists, for it is assumed that the recognition of feelings and their articulation can lead to change. Alice Bernard described the impact the questions I asked had on her:

> AB: It's like a mirror. It's like demanding of you to deal with it *now*. I mean, like, "sort this out; you're not going any further until you get this taken care of." It's like I can't put these things off anymore.

Thus, Alice saw the research process as a way of confronting herself and who she is. The process also was useful to her in that "it feels so cluttered sometimes. You need someone to help you to sort things out." The articulation of difficult feelings, especially about herself as a mother, brought relief, insight, and control.

> AB: It was all like just below the surface [*pause*] and instead of me being irrationally angry, I can now determine generally what is making me angry and . . . I have found myself stopping a little bit more instead of

317

jumping immediately. [*Pause*] I find myself reflecting a little bit more; not all the time . . . but enough that it makes me feel a little better, you know, like a better person.

As in therapy, however, the feelings uncovered during the course of the research also further depressed her. "Like I get really depressed now, I think more depressed than I ever really allowed myself to get. I particularly don't like it, but I got to do it." These depressed feelings emerged as she began to discuss openly her feelings about herself as a mother. As she worked them through during the research study, she began to accept herself and like herself better. Discussing the research findings and reading the observational protocol also had their effect. She consciously began to change her behavior toward one of the children, and my written interpretation helped her to feel more accepting of herself.

Richard also described the processes of definition and self-reflection as the research progressed.

> RB: Sometimes when you tell somebody something, and you really try and be honest, you get to look at yourself in a different aspect. I'm the one who can really baffle myself or confuse myself, and tell myself something which is wrong is right. But if I look at it or try and tell somebody else—well, I usually try and tell people the truth. And I realize, too, when you're telling somebody the truth, this must really be right. So I get to look at myself in a different view. . . . Sometimes it's not so [*pause*] glorious, and sometimes it makes you feel good.

Richard learned something about himself in trying to express his feelings to me. Initially he had been intrigued by the prospect of examining himself. At times, however, what he learned overwhelmed him: whereas he could generally look over the "things" in his inner "closet" one at a time, the research process made him "look over the whole closet." This process occasionally depressed him, as well.

> RB: Last time we talked I knew about two or three days afterward a very severe feeling of depression. And the reason for that was all very—all our lifetime woes—we can handle them as they come, but when we talked, we brought them all out. They were all on the showcase. It was depressing for me.

Because Alice and Richard tried to be honest with me, they talked about issues that were important in their lives. Sometimes, they became depressed as a result, and the working through of these feelings caused them to reconsider their goals as individuals and as a family.

The "process of disclosure," whereby couples exchange feelings about each other, also affects relationships. During one of the research interviews, for example, Richard and Alice became aware of how indirect were their expressions of affection. During the course of the interview, they told each other of their affection directly, an exchange that seemed to strengthen their relationship. The research findings also helped initiate new discussions about Alice's needs. Sometimes they viewed me as a "troublemaker," at other times they saw me as a "facilitator" and as an informal "therapist." This process indicates how important it is for the researcher to be able to provide support over time. Rubin and Mitchell also have commented on long-term responsibilities and on providing referrals or informal counseling.

It is presumptuous to think that while those we study change, we ourselves—as researchers—remain untouched by the process. Research that is "mensch to mensch"[26] implies that the researcher, too, is touched, and I found that my interviews with participants affected me as well. Professionally, I became increasingly interested in the psychology of women and in the study of children and families. These interests reflected deeper personal changes. As I struggled to understand the participants, I came to understand my own family of origin better. I recalled my own father's experiences with his work and its impact on our lives. As I thought about Alice Bernard as a household worker, I came to perceive my mother in new ways that drew us closer together. And as the research progressed and came to encroach on our home, my family was able to utilize what I was learning about other families to better manage the interface between work and family as it affected our own lives.

Summary

At the outset of the discussion of research as process, I distinguished between the ideals of qualitative and naturalistic research and its realities. The methodological limitations of this study are clear: the sample of families might have been solicited on a more representative basis. Still, such a selection procedure may have interfered with the establishment of essential rapport. Observational data on a larger number of families would have enhanced the analysis. Although frequency of occurrences does not necessarily establish a phenomenon as psychologically significant, it would have been helpful to have more observations on the Turners and the Bernards in order to determine how significant the observed patterns were and how reliable the observations were.[27] Finally, the thematic analysis of all the data should have been subject to extensive interjudge reliability analysis. Despite these limita-

26. This was the way my father understood qualitative, "face to face" research.

27. Stability over time is one indicator of the reliability of our measurement operations, but since families are assumed to change over time, such reliability must be treated with caution. In fact, too little change in interaction patterns over time might indicate family pathology.

tions, the analysis presented here helps us to conceptualize new phenomena for further study, aids mental health professionals to think about the problems some families face in their everyday lives, and furthers discussion about the interrelationships between work and emotional life in families. In future research some of the relationships described can be systematically tested.

References

ABERLE, D. E., & NAEGELE, K. D. Middle class father's occupational roles and attitudes toward children. *American Journal of Orthopsychiatry*, 1952, *22*, 366–378.

ALDOUS, J. Occupational characteristics and males' role performance in the family. *Journal of Marriage and the Family*, 1969, *31*, 707–712.

ALDOUS, J.; OSMOND, M.; & HICKS, M. Men's work and men's families. In W. Burr, R. Hill, F. I. Nye, & I. Reiss (Eds.), *Contemporary theories about the family*. New York: Free Press, 1979.

AUERSWALD, E. Families, change and the ecological perspective. *Family Process*, 1971, *10*, 263–280.

ARONOWITZ, S. *False promises*. New York: McGraw-Hill, 1973.

ATTNEAVE, C. L. Social networks as the unit of intervention. In P. Guerin, Jr. (Ed.), *Family therapy: Theory and practice*. New York: Gardner Press, 1976.

BACH, G. R. Father-fantasies and father-typing in father-separated children. In W. E. Martin & C. B. Stendler (Eds.), *Readings in child development*. New York: Harcourt, Brace, 1954.

BAKAN, D. *On method*. San Francisco: Jossey-Bass, 1969.

BARKER, R. G. (Ed.). *The stream of behavior*. New York: Meredith, 1963.

BARKER, R. G., & WRIGHT, H. F. *Midwest and its children*. Evanston, Ill.: Row, Peterson, 1955.

BARTON, A. H., & LAZARSFELD, P. F. Some functions of qualitative analysis in social research. In G. J. McCall & J. L. Simmons (Eds.), *Issues in participant observation: A text and reader*. Reading, Mass.: Addison-Wesley, 1969.

BATESON, G. Minimal requirements for a theory of schizophrenia. *Archives of General Psychiatry*, 1960, *2*, 477–491.

BELL, J. E. The future of family therapy. *Family Process*, 1970, *9*, 127–141.

BELL, J. E. *Family therapy*. New York: Jason Aronson, 1975.

BELL, N. W., & VOGEL, E. F. Toward a framework for functional analysis of family behavior. In N. W. Bell & E. F. Vogel (Eds.), *A modern introduction to the family*. New York: Free Press, 1960.

BERK, S. F., & BERHEIDE, C. W. Going backstage: Gaining access to observe household work. *Sociology of Work and Occupations*, 1977, *4* (1), 27–48.

BERMANN, E. *Scapegoat*. Ann Arbor: University of Michigan Press, 1973.

BERNARD, J. Marital stability and patterns of status variables. *Journal of Marriage and the Family*, 1966, *28*, 421–439.

BERNARD, J. The paradox of the happy marriage. In V. Gornick & B. K. Moran (Eds.), *Woman in sexist society*. New York: Basic Books, 1971.

BERNARD, J. *The future of marriage*. New York: World, 1972.

BERNARD, J. *The future of motherhood*. New York: Penguin, 1975.

BERNARD, J. Homosociality and female depression. *Journal of Social Issues*, 1976, *32* (4), 213–238.

BLAUNER, R. *Alienation and freedom*. Chicago: University of Chicago Press, 1964.

BLOOD, R. O., JR. The use of observational methods in family research. *Marriage and Family Living*, 1958, *20*, 47–52.

BLOOD, R. O., JR., & WOLFE, D. M. *Husbands and wives*. New York: Free Press, 1960.

BORDIN, E. S. A theory of vocational interests as dynamic phenomena. *Educational and Psychological Measurements*, 1943, *3*, 49–65.

BOTT, E. *Family and social network*. 2nd ed. New York: Free Press, 1971.

BOWEN, M. Theory in the practice of psychotherapy. In P. J. Guerin, Jr. (Ed.), *Family therapy: Theory and practice*. New York: Gardner, 1976.

BOWERS, K. Situationism in psychology: An analysis and a critique. *Psychological Review*, 1973, *80*, 307–336.

BOWLES, S., & GINTIS, H. Class power and alienated labor. *Monthly Review*, 1975, *26* (11), 9–25.

BOWLES, S., & GINTIS, H. *Schooling in capitalist America*. New York: Basic Books, 1976.

BRADBURN, N., & CAPLOVITZ, D. *Reports on happiness*. Chicago: Aldine, 1965.

BRAVERMAN, H. *Labor and monopoly capital*. New York: Monthly Review Press, 1975.

BRYANT, C. D. (Ed.). *The social dimensions of work*. Englewood Cliffs, N.J.: Prentice-Hall, 1972

BÜHLER, C. *The child and his family*. New York: Harper, 1939.

BULLARD, F. N., & NEADERHOUSER, F. M. (Eds.). *The how and why program: Steppingstones for little feet*. Cleveland: L. J. Bullard, 1951.

BURNS, S. *Home, Inc.* Garden City, N.Y.: Doubleday, 1975.

CANNELL, C. F., & KAHN, R. L. The collection of data by interviewing. In L. Festinger & D. Katz (Eds.), *Research methods in the behavioral sciences*. New York: Staples Press, 1953.

CAPLAN, R. D.; COBB, S.; FRENCH, J. R. P., JR.; HARRISON, R. V.; & PINNEAU, S. R., JR. *Job demands and worker health: Main effects and occupational differences*

References

(USGPO Catalog No. He20.7111:J57, USGPO stock No. 1733-00083). Washington, D.C.: U.S. Government Printing Office, 1975.

CAPLOW, T. Occupation and the family. In T. Caplow (Ed.), *The sociology of work.* Minneapolis: University of Minnesota Press, 1954.

CHESLER, P. *Women & madness.* New York: Avon, 1972.

CHILMAN, C. S. Habitat and American families: A social-psychological overview. *The Family Coordinator,* 1978, *27,* 105–111.

CHINOY, E. *Automobile workers and the American dream.* Boston: Beacon, 1955.

COOMES, A. F. *Mother's manual.* 3rd ed. N.p.: W. J. H. Litho Co., 1969.

CRAWFORD, M. Retirement and disengagement. *Human Relations,* 1971, *24* (3), 255–278.

CULBERT, S., & RENSHAW, J. R. Coping with the stresses of travel as an opportunity for improving the quality of work and family life. *Family Process,* 1972, *11,* 321–337.

CUMMING, E., & HENRY, W. E. *Growing old: The process of disengagement.* New York: Basic Books, 1961.

DEAN, J. P., & WHYTE, F. How do you know if the informant is telling the truth? *Human organization,* 1958, *17* (2), 34–38. Reprinted in G. J. McCall & J. L. Simmons (Eds.), *Issues in participant observation: A text and reader* (Reading, Mass.: Addison-Wesley, 1969).

DE BEAUVOIR, S. *The second sex.* New York: Bantam, 1961.

DUBIN, R. Industrial workers' worlds. *Social Problems,* 1956, *3,* 131–142.

DUBIN, R. Work in modern society. In R. Dubin (Ed.), *Handbook of work, organization, and society.* Chicago: Rand McNally, 1976.

DYCK, A. J. The social contacts of some midwestern children with their parents and teachers. In R. G. Barker (Ed.), *The stream of behavior.* New York: Meredith, 1963.

DYER, E. D. Parenthood as crisis: A re-study. *Marriage and Family Living,* 1963, *25,* 196–201.

DYER, W. G. The interlocking of work and family social systems among lower occupational families. *Social Forces,* 1956, *34* (3), 230–233.

EHRENREICH, B., & ENGLISH, D. The manufacture of housework. *Socialist Revolution,* 1975, *5* (4), 5–40.

EISENBERG, T. Job stress and the police officer: Identifying stress reduction techniques. In W. H. Kroes & J. J. Hurrell (Eds.), *Job stress and the police officer: Identifying stress reduction techniques.* U.S. Dept. of Health, Education & Welfare, Public Health Service, December 1975. HEW Publ. No. (NIOSH) 76–187.

ERIKSON, E. *Childhood and society.* 2nd ed. New York: Norton, 1963.

FAIRBAIRN, W. D. *Object relations theory of the personality.* London: Tavistock, 1954.

FELDBERG, R., & KOHEN, J. Family life in an anti-family setting: Critiques of marriage and divorce. *The Family Coordinator,* 1976, *25* (2), 151–154.

FENICHEL, O. *The psychoanalytic theory of neurosis.* New York: Norton, 1945.

FERREE, M. M. Working class jobs: Paid work and housework as sources of satisfaction. *Social Problems,* 1976, *23,* 431–441.

FREDERIKSEN, N. Toward a taxonomy of situations. *American Psychologist,* 1972, *27,* 114–123.

FREUD, S. *An outline of psychoanalysis.* New York: Norton, 1949.

FRIED, M. *The world of the urban working class.* Cambridge, Mass.: Harvard University Press, 1973.

FURSTENBURG, F., JR. Work experience and family life. In J. O'Toole (Ed.), *Work and the quality of life: Resource papers for work in America.* Cambridge, Mass.: MIT Press, 1974.

FURTH, H. G.; BAUR, M.; & SMITH, J. E. Children's conception of social institutions: A Piagetian framework. *Human Development,* 1976, *19,* 351–374.

GAVRON, H. *The captive wife.* London: Routledge & Kegan Paul, 1966.

GECAS, V. The influence of social class on socialization. In W. Burr, R. Hill, F. I. Nye, & I. Reiss (Eds.), *Contemporary theories about the family.* New York: Free Press, 1979.

GECAS, V., & NYE, F. I. Sex and class differences in parent-child interaction: A test of Kohn's hypothesis. *Journal of Marriage and the Family,* 1974, *36,* 742–749.

GLASER, B., & STRAUSS, A. *The discovery of grounded theory.* Chicago: Aldine, 1967.

GLAZER-MALBIN, N. Housework. *Signs,* 1976, *1,* 905–922.

GOFFMAN, E. *The presentation of self in everyday life.* New York: Doubleday Anchor, 1959.

GOLD, M., & SLATER, C. Office, factory, store and family: A study of integration setting. *American Sociological Review,* 1958, *23,* 64–74.

GOLD, R. L. Roles in sociological field observations. *Social Forces,* 1958, *36* (3), 217–223. Reprinted in G. J. McCall & J. L. Simmons (Eds.), *Issues in participant observation: A text and reader* (Reading, Mass.: Addison-Wesley, 1969).

GOLDEN, S. Pre-school families and work. (Doctoral dissertation, University of Michigan, 1975.) *Dissertation Abstracts International,* 1975, 13969. (University Microfilms No. 15347)

GOLDTHORPE, J. H., & LOCKWOOD, D. Affluence and the British class structure. *Sociological Review,* 1963, *11* (2), 133–163.

GREENBERG, G. S. The family interactional perspective: A study and examination of the work of Don D. Jackson. *Family Process,* 1977, *16,* 385–412.

GRØNSETH, E. The familial institution. In L. T. Reynolds & J. M. Henslin (Eds.), *American society: A critical analysis.* New York: McKay, 1973.

GUERIN, P. J., JR. Family therapy: The first twenty-five years. In P. J. Guerin, Jr. (Ed.), *Family therapy: Theory and practice.* New York: Gardner, 1976.

GUNTRIP, H. *Schizoid phenomena, object relations and the self.* New York: International Universities Press, 1969.

GURIN, G.; VEROFF, J.; & FELD, S. *Americans view their mental health.* New York: Basic Books, 1960.

References

GUTMANN, D. Psychological naturalism in cross-cultural studies. In H. L. Raush & E. P. Willems (Eds.), *Naturalistic viewpoints in psychological research*. New York: Holt, Rinehart & Winston, 1969.

HALEY, J. An interactional description of schizophrenia. *Psychiatry*, 1959, *22*, 321–322. (a)

HALEY, J. The family of the schizophrenic: A model system. *Journal of Nervous and Mental Diseases*, 1959, *129*, 357–374. (b)

HAMMOND, P. (Ed.). *Sociologists at work: Essays on the craft of social research*. New York: Basic Books, 1964.

HANDEL, G. Psychological study of whole families. *Psychological Bulletin*, 1965, *63* (1), 19–41. Reprinted in G. Handel (Ed.), *The psychosocial interior of the family* (Chicago: Aldine, 1967).

HANDEL, G., & RAINWATER, L. Persistance and change in working class lifestyle. In A. B. Shostak & W. Gomberg (Eds.), *Blue-collar world*. Englewood Cliffs, N.J.: Prentice-Hall, 1964.

HARRÉ, H., & SECORD, P. F. *The explanation of social behavior*. New Jersey: Wittlefield, Adams, 1973.

HAYGHE, H. Families and the rise of working wives: An overview. *Monthly Labor Review*, 1976, *99* (5), 12–19.

HEDGES, J. N. Long workweeks and premium pay. *Monthly Labor Review*, 1976, *99* (4), 7–12.

HENRY, J. *Pathways to madness*. New York: Random House, 1965.

HERZBERG, F., & HAMLIN, R. M. The motivation-hygiene concept and psychotherapy. *Mental Hygiene*, 1964, *47* (3), 384–397.

HESS, R. D., & Handel, G. *Family worlds*. Chicago: University of Chicago Press, 1959.

HILL, R. Modern systems theory and the family: A confrontation. In M. B. Sussman (Ed.), *Sourcebook in marriage and the family*. Boston: Houghton-Mifflin, 1974.

HOFFMAN, L., & LONG, L. A systems dilemma. *Family Process*, 1969, *8*, 211–234.

HOFFMAN, L. W., & NYE, F. I. *Working mothers*. San Francisco: Jossey-Bass, 1974.

HOWELL, J. T. *Hard living on Clay Street*. New York: Anchor, 1972.

JACKSON, D. The study of the family. *Family Process*, 1966, *4*, 1–20.

KAHN, R. L.; WOLFE, D. M.; QUINN, R. P.; & SNOEK, D. J. *Organizational stress*. New York: Wiley, 1964.

KAMERMAN, S. B., & KAHN, A. J. Explorations in family policy. *Social Work*, 1976, *21*, 181–186.

KANTER, R. M. *Work and family in the United States: A critical review and agenda for research and policy*. New York: Russell Sage, 1977.

KANTOR, D., & LEHR, W. *Inside the family*. San Francisco: Jossey-Bass, 1975.

KAPLAN, A. *The conduct of inquiry*. San Francisco: Chandler, 1964.

KASL, S. V. Work and mental health. In J. O'Toole (Ed.), *Work and the quality of life: Resource papers for work in America*. Cambridge, Mass.: MIT Press, 1974.

KNOX, D., & WILSON, K. The differences between having one and two children. *The Family Coordinator*, 1978, *27*, 23–25.

KOHLBERG, L. Stage and sequence: The cognitive-developmental approach to socialization theory and research. In D. A. Goslin (Ed.), *Handbook of socialization theory and research*. Chicago: Rand McNally, 1969.

KOHN, M. L. Social class and parent-child relationships: An interpretation. *American Journal of Sociology*, 1963, *68*, 471–480.

KOHN, M. L. *Class and conformity*. Homewood, Ill.: Dorsey, 1969.

KOHN, M. L., & SCHOOLER, C. Occupational experience and psychological functioning: An assessment of reciprocal effects. *American Sociological Review*, 1973, *38*, 97–118.

KOMAROVSKY, M. *The unemployed man and his family*. New York: Dryden, 1940.

KOMAROVSKY, M. *Women in the modern world*. Boston: Little, Brown, 1953.

KOMAROVSKY, M. *Blue collar marriage*. New York: Random House, 1962.

KORNHAUSER, A. *Mental health of the industrial worker*. New York: Wiley, 1965.

KRANZBERG, M., & GIES, J. *By the sweat of thy brow*. New York: Putnam, 1975.

KROES, W. H.; MARGOLIS, B. L.; & HURRELL, J. J. Job Stress in policemen. *Journal of Police Science and Administration*, 1974, *2*, 145–155.

LANDES, J. Women, labor and family life: A theoretical perspective. *Science and Society*, 1977–78, *41*, 386–409.

LASCH, C. *Haven in a heartless world: The family besieged*. New York: Basic Books, 1977.

LASLETT, B. The family as a public and private institution: An historical perspective. *Journal of Marriage and the Family*, 1973, *24*, 480–494.

LASSEN, K. *The workers*. New York: Bantam, 1972.

LEMASTERS, E. E. Parenthood as crisis. *Marriage and Family Living*, 1957, *19*, 352–355.

LENNARD, S. H., & LENNARD, H. L. Architecture: Effect of territory, boundary and orientation on family functioning. *Family Process*, 1977, *16*, 49–66.

LEVINSON, H. Emotional toxicity of the work environment. *Archives of Environmental Health*, 1969, *19*, 239–243.

LEVISON, A. *The working-class majority*. New York: Penguin, 1974.

LEWIN, K. *A dynamic theory of personality*. New York: McGraw-Hill, 1935.

LEWIS, O. *Five families*. New York: Basic Books, 1959.

LEWIS, R. Toward an understanding of police anomie. *Journal of Police Science and Administration*, 1973, *1*, 484–490.

LIEBOW, E. *Tally's corner: A study of Negro streetcorner men*. Boston: Little, Brown, 1967.

LOFLAND, J. *Analyzing social settings*. Belmont, Calif.: Wadsworth, 1971.

LOFLAND, J. Styles of reporting qualitative field research. *American Sociologist*, 1974, *9* (3), 101–111.

LOPATA, H. Z. *Occupation: Housewife*. New York: Oxford University Press, 1971.

References

MADDISON, D. Stress on the doctor and his family. *Medical Journal of Australia*, August 31, 1974, pp. 315–317.

MAGNUSSON, D., & ENDLER, N. S. (Eds.). *Personality at the crossroads: Current issues in interactional psychology.* New York: Halstead, 1977.

MANNINO, F. V., & SHORE, M. Ecologically oriented family intervention. *Family Process*, 1972, *11*, 499–505.

MARCIANO, T. D. Middle class incomes, working class hearts. *Family Process*, 1974, *13*, 489–502.

McCALL, G. J., & SIMMONS, J. L. (Eds.). *Issues in participant observation: A text and reader.* Reading, Mass.: Addison-Wesley, 1969.

McKINLEY, D. G. *Social class and family life.* New York: Free Press, 1964.

MEISSNER, M. The long arm of the job. *Industrial Relations*, 1971, *10*, 239–260.

MEISSNER, M. The language of work. In R. Dubin (Ed.), *Handbook of work, organization and society.* Chicago: Rand McNally, 1976.

MILLER, D. R., & SWANSON, G. *The changing American parent.* New York: Wiley, 1958.

MILLER, S. M. The participant observer and "over-rapport." *American Sociological Review*, 1952, *17* (1), 97–101. Reprinted in G. J. McCall & J. L. Simmons (Eds.), *Issues in participant observation: A text and reader* (Reading, Mass.: Addison-Wesley, 1969).

MINTURN, L., & LAMBERT, W. W. *Mothers of six cultures: Antecedants of child rearing.* New York: Wiley, 1964.

MINUCHIN, S. *Families and family therapy.* Cambridge, Mass.: Harvard University Press, 1974.

MISCHEL, W. Continuity and change in personality. *American Psychologist*, 1969, *24*, 1012–1018.

MISCHEL, W. The interaction of person and setting. In D. Magnusson & N. S. Endler (Eds.), *Personality at the crossroads: Current issues in interactional psychology.* New York: Halstead, 1977.

MOORE, W. E. Occupational socializaiton. In D. E. Goslin (Ed.), *Handbook of socialization theory and research.* Chicago: Rand McNally, 1969.

MOOS, R. H. Conceptualizations of human environments. *Human Psychologist*, 1973, *28*, 652–665.

MOTT, P. E.; MANN, F. C.; McLOUGHLIN, Q.; & WARWICK, D. P. *Shift work: The social, psychological and physical consequences.* Ann Arbor: University of Michigan Press, 1965.

MYERS, J. K., & ROBERTS, B. H. *Family and class dynamics in mental illness.* New York: Wiley, 1959.

NEFF, W. S. *Work and human behavior.* New York: Atherton, 1968.

NIMKOFF, M. K. Technology and the family. In F. R. Allen, H. Hart, D. C. Hiller, W. F. Ogburn, & M. K. Nimkoff, *Technology and social change.* New York: Appleton-Century-Crofts, 1957.

NYE, F. I.; CARLSON, J.; & GARRET, G. Family size, interaction, affect and stress. *Journal of Marriage and the Family,* 1970, *32* (2), 216–226.

OAKLEY, A. *The sociology of housework.* New York: Pantheon, 1974. (a)

OAKLEY, A. *Woman's work.* New York: Pantheon, 1974. (b)

OREN, L. The welfare of women in laboring families: England, 1860–1950. *Feminist Studies,* 1973, *1* (2), 107–125.

OVERTON, W. F. On the assumptive base of the nature-nurture controversy: Additive versus interactive conceptions. *Human Development,* 1973, *16,* 74–89.

PARKER, S. R. Industry and the family. In S. R. Parker, R. K. Brown, J. Child, & M. A. Smith (Eds.), *The sociology of industry.* London: Allen & Unwin, 1967.

PARSONS, T. The American family: Its relation to personality and the social structure. In T. Parsons & R. F. Bales, *Family, socialization and interaction process.* New York: Free Press, 1955.

PERVIN, L. A. Performance and satisfaction as a function of individual-environment fit. *Psychological Bulletin,* 1968, *69* (1), 56–68.

PLECK, E. Two worlds in one: Work and family. *Journal of Social History,* 1976, *10* (2), 178–195.

PLECK, J. The work-family role system. *Social Problems,* 1977, *24,* 417–427.

QUINN, R. P. Locking-in as a moderator of the relationship between job satisfaction and mental health. Unpublished manuscript, 1972, Institute for Social Research, University of Michigan.

QUINN, R. P. Job satisfaction: Is there a trend? *Manpower Research Monograph,* 1974, *30,* U.S. Department of Labor.

QUINN, R. P. & SHEPARD, L. J. *The 1972–73 quality of employment survey.* Ann Arbor: Survey Research Center of the Institute for Social Research, University of Michigan, 1974.

RAINWATER, L. Work, well-being and family life. In J. O'Toole (Ed.), *Work and the quality of life: Resource papers for work in America.* Cambridge, Mass.: MIT Press, 1974.

RAINWATER, L.; COLEMAN, R. P.; & HANDEL, G. *Working man's wife.* New York: Oceana, 1959.

RAPOPORT, R., & RAPOPORT, R. Work and family in contemporary society. *American Sociological Review,* 1965, *30,* 381–394.

RAPOPORT, R., & RAPOPORT, R. *Dual-career families.* Baltimore: Penguin, 1971.

RAPP, R. Family and class in contemporary America: Notes toward an understanding of ideology. *Science and Society,* 1978, *42,* (3), 278–300.

RAUSH, H. L. Interaction sequences. *Journal of Personality and Social Psychology,* 1965, *2,* 487–499.

RAUSH, H. L. Naturalistic method and clinical approach. In H. L. Raush & E. P. Willems (Eds.), *Naturalistic viewpoints in psychological research.* New York: Holt, Rinehart & Winston, 1969.

REAMS, H. R. The functioning of the psychiatric care worker in interaction with adolescents in residential treatment. (Doctoral dissertation, University of

References

Michigan, 1975). *Dissertation Abstracts International*, 1975, 13608. (University Microfilms No. 14869)

REISER, M. Some organizational stresses on policemen. *Journal of Police Science and Administration*, 1974, 2 (2), 156–159.

RENSHAW, J. R. An exploration of the dynamics of the overlapping worlds of work and family life. *Family Process*, 1976, 15, 143–165.

RISKIN, J. M., & FAUNCE, E. E. An evaluative review of family interaction research. *Family Process*, 1972, 11, 365–455.

RODMAN, H. Middle-class misconceptions about lower-class families. In A. B. Shostak & W. Gomberg (Eds.), *Blue-collar world*. Englewood Cliffs, N.J.: Prentice-Hall, 1964.

ROE, A. Personality structure and occupational behavior. In H. Borow (Ed.), *Man in a world at work*. Boston: Houghton Mifflin, 1964.

ROSENTHAL, R. The volunteer subject. *Human Relations*, 1965, 18, 389–406.

RUBIN, L. B. *Worlds of pain*. New York: Basic Books, 1976.

RUBIN, Z., & MITCHELL, C. Couples research as couples counseling. *American Psychologist*, 1976, 31, 17–25.

RYDER, N. B. The family in developed countries. *Scientific American*, 1974, 231 (3), 123–132.

RYDER, R. G. A topography of early marriage. *Family Process*, 1970, 9, 385–402.

SAFILIOS-ROTHSCHILD, C. The study of family power structure: A review, 1960–1969. *Journal of Marriage and the Family*, 1970, 32 (4), 539–552.

SATIR, V. M. The family as a treatment unit. *Confina Psychiatrica*, 1965, 8, 37–42.

SCANZONI, J. *Opportunity and the family*. New York: Free Press, 1970.

SCHWARTZ, M. S., & SCHWARTZ, C. G. Problems in participant observation. *American Journal of Sociology*, 1955, 60 (4), 343–353. Reprinted in G. J. McCall & J. L. Simmons (Eds.), *Issues in participant observation: A text and reader* (Reading, Mass.: Addison-Wesley, 1969).

SENNETT, R., & COBB, J. *The hidden injuries of class*. New York: Knopf, 1972.

SHERMAN, H. Dialectics as a method. *The Insurgent Sociologist*, 1976, 6 (4), 57–64.

SHOSTAK, A. B., & GOMBERG, W. (Eds.). *Blue-collar world: Studies of the American worker*. Englewood Cliffs, N.J.: Prentice-Hall, 1964.

SIMMONS, H., & SCHOGGEN, P. Mothers and fathers as sources of environmental pressure on children. In R. G. Barker (Ed.), *The stream of behavior*. New York: Meredith, 1963.

SKOLNICK, A. *The intimate environment*. Boston: Little, Brown, 1973.

Special Task Force of the Secretary of Health, Education and Welfare. *Work in America*. Cambridge, Mass.: MIT Press, 1973.

SPECK, R. V., & RUVENI, U. Network therapy: A developing concept. *Family Process*, 1969, 8, 182–190.

SPEER, D. C. Family systems: Morphostasis and morphogenesis, or "Is homeostasis enough?" *Family Process*, 1970, 9, 259–278.

SPIEGEL, J. P. *Transactions: The interplay between individual, family and society*. New York: Science House, 1971.

STAPLES, R. Towards a sociology of the black family: A theoretical and methodological assessment. *Journal of Marriage and the Family*, 1971, *33*, 119–138.

STIERLIN, H. The adaptation of the "stronger" person's reality: Some aspects of the symbiotic relationship of the schizophrenic. *Psychiatry*, 1959, 22, 143–152.

STOKE, S. M. An inquiry into the concept of identification. In W. E. Martin & C. B. Stendler (Eds.), *Readings in child development*. New York: Harcourt, Brace, 1954.

STRAUSS, A.; SHATZMAN, L.; BUCHER, R.; EHRLICH, D.; & SABSHIN, M. *Psychiatric ideologies and institutions*. New York: Free Press, 1964.

SULLIVAN, H. S. *The interpersonal theory of psychiatry*. New York: Norton, 1953.

SYMONDS, M. Emotional hazards of police work. *American Journal of Psychoanalysis*, 1970, 2, 155–160.

TALLMAN, I. Working-class wives in suburbia: Fulfillment or crisis? *Journal of Marriage and the Family*, 1969, *31*, 65–72.

TEN HOUTEN, W. D. The black family: Myth and reality. *Psychiatry*, 1970, *33*, 145–173.

TERKEL, S. *Working*. New York: Pantheon, 1974.

THOMPSON, E. P. *The making of the English working class*. New York: Vintage, 1966.

U.S. Bureau of the Census. *Statistical abstract of the United States: 1977*. Washington, D.C.: Government Printing Office, 1977.

VANEK, J. Time spent in housework. *Scientific American*, 1974, *231* (5), 116–120.

VEROFF, J., & FELD, S. *Marriage and work in America: A study of motives and roles*. New York: Van Nostrand Reinhold, 1970.

VIDICH, A. J. Methodological problems in the observation of husband-wife interaction. *Marriage and Family Living*, 1956, *18*, 234–239.

VINCENT, C. E. Familia spongia: The adaptive function. *Journal of Marriage and the Family*, 1966, *29*, 29–36.

WALKER, K. E., & WOODS, M. E. *Time use: A measure of household production of family goods and services*. Washington, D.C.: American Home Economics Assoc., 1976.

WELLER, L., & LUCHTERHAND, E. Comparing interviews and observations on family functioning. *Journal of Marriage and the Family*, 1969, *31*, 115–122.

WHITE, R. W. Competence and the psychosexual stages of development. In R. S. Lazarus & E. M. Opton Jr., (Eds.), *Personality*. Baltimore: Penguin, 1967.

WILLEMS, E. P. A rationale for naturalistic research. In H. L. Raush & E. P. Willems (Eds.), *Naturalistic viewpoints in psychological research*. New York: Holt, Rinehart & Winston, 1969.

WINNICOTT, D. W. Transitional objects and transitional phenomena. In D. W. Winnicott, *Collected papers*. New York: Basic Books, 1958.

Women's Work Study Group. Loom, broom and womb: Producers, maintainers and reproducers. *Radical America*, 1976, *10* (2), 29–45.

References

WYNNE, L. C.; RYCKOFF, I. M.; DAY, J.; & HIRSCH, S. I. Pseudo-mutuality in the family relations of schizophrenics. *Psychiatry*, 1958, *21*, 205–220.

YOUNG, M., & WILLMOTT, P. *The symmetrical family.* New York: Pantheon, 1973.

ZARETSKY, E. *Capitalism, the family and personal life.* New York: Harper & Row, 1976.

ZELDITCH, M., JR. Some methodological problems of field studies. *American Journal of Sociology*, 1962, *67*, 566–576. Reprinted in G. J. McCall & J. L. Simmons (Eds.), *Issues in participant observation: A text and reader* (Reading, Mass.: Addison-Wesley, 1969).

Index

Index

hold aides, 244–246; isomorphism, 253–254; personal depletion and energy deficit, 254–257; reducing distances, 252–257; spaces and things, 250–252; *tables*, 245, 247, 248, 256; time as structural variable, 247–250; "two different worlds," 252–253

Children and paid work, 108–120: identification concept, 113–117; learning about interfaces, 117–119; psychological interface, 109–111; structural interface, 111–113; *see also* Children and household work

Chilman, C. S., 243

Chinoy, E., 59, 94

Class, concept of, 19: assumptions about, 13–14, 283–284; and children, 116; and research families, 18–19, 292–293; and social policy, 284–285

Clinical assessment intervention, 281–283

Clinical research, 12–13, 278–281

Closed family system, 32n

Cobb, J., ix, 5, 54, 61, 85n, 92n, 94, 125n, 220

Coding categories (of observational data), 25–26; *see also* Research process

Compensation hypothesis, 9, 14: evaluating, 98–100

Compensatory leisure activities, 14n, 100

Collaboration, 26, 315–317

Crawford, M., 90

Culbert, S., 4, 66

Cumming, E., 90

D

Daily timing, 68–71

Danger, 96–97, 113, 203–211, 279

Day, J., 3

de Beauvoir, Simone, 240n, 265

Dean, J. P., 315

"Defiant neglect," 233

Denial and repression, 203–211

Dependent wives and dependent children, 81

Discontents, household work (Bernard family case study), 219–238: anger, managing, 232–234; being housebound, 225; boredom, managing, 230; "defiant neglect," 233; evaluations, 227–229; griping, 233–234; management of, 229–234; psychological disengagement, 232; public image, 224–225; research participants, 236–238; self-rewards and invisible work, 230–231; and threat to self, 221–224, 231–232; work overload and role ambiguity, 225–227

Disengagement process, 90–98, 179, 232, 274: active psychological, 90–92; question

of being successful, 94–98; and threat to self, 93–94

Dubin, R., 7, 14, 73, 87

Dyer, E. D., 220

Dyer, W. G., 11, 108

E

Ecological systems approach, 4n, 274–275

Educational level, participating research families, 21

Ehrenreich, B., 7

Ehrlich, D., 296

Eisenberg, T., 174n, 175, 176, 186n

Emotional availability: *see* Availability

Emotional life, concept of, 15

Endler, N. S., 107

Energy, concept of, 39; *see also* Carry-over, Energy deficit

Energy deficit, pattern of, 31, 50–57, 61, 200, 254–257

English, D., 7

Erikson, E., 116

F

Fairbairn, W. D., 92

Families, participating: *see* Research families

Family life, household and, 239–264: children, 243–257; home as a work setting, 213–214; interactions, 214–216; interlocking with paid work, 216–217; *see also* Bernard family (case study), Household and household work

Family system, 3–4, 32n

Family system, work and: alternative view, 9–12; background of the study, 1–27; Bernard family (case study), 121–268; clinical assessment and intervention, 281–283; clinical research, 12–13; directions for theory and research, 276–281; interviews and observations (of participating families), 17–27; myth of separate worlds, 6–8, 87–98; opening up the family system, 4–6; paid work and families, 29–120; social policy and social change, 283–286; social systems approach, 3–4; summary and conclusions, 271–286

Faunce, E. E., 5

Feld, S., 5, 61

Feldberg, R., 106n

Fenichel, O., 39n

Ferree, M. M., 9, 235, 313

Fredericksen, N., 63

French, J. R. P., Jr., 5, 61

Freud, S., 195, 291

Fried, M., 19

Index

Index